CT 4000 REV. 1-77   CONSOLIDATED RAIL CORPORATION

DEPARTURE			ARRIVAL			DEF. CODE	LAST 4 DIGITS WB NO.	HDL CODE	SYSTEM CLASS		INTERCHANGE			CONSIGNEE		DESTINATION		CONTENTS	NET TONS	GRADE	CHAR	KIND	L OR E	CAR		CARD NO.
TRAIN SYMBOL	HR.	DAY	TRAIN SYMBOL	HR.	DAY				INITIAL	FINAL	JCT OFF	ROAD TO		CITY	STATE	CITY	STATE							INITIAL	NUMBER	(6)

DEPARTURE			ARRIVAL			DEF. CODE	LAST 4 DIGITS WB NO.	HDL CODE	SYSTEM CLASS		INTERCHANGE		P N U M B E R	RAMP DESTINATION				TRAILER		NET TONS	GRADE	CHAR	KIND	L OR E	CAR		CARD NO.
TRAIN SYMBOL	HR.	DAY	TRAIN SYMBOL	HR.	DAY				INITIAL	FINAL	JCT OFF	ROAD TO		CITY	STATE	T-C L-E-M	NUMBER	INITIAL							INITIAL	NUMBER	(8)

DEPARTURE			ARRIVAL			DEF. CODE	LAST 4 DIGITS WB NO.	HDL CODE	TRUCKER MARINE INITIALS	P L M A B N E R	INTERCHANGE			CONSIGNEE		DESTINATION		CONTENTS	NET TONS	GRADE	CHAR	KIND	L OR E	TRAILER		CARD NO.
TRAIN SYMBOL	HR.	DAY	TRAIN SYMBOL	HR.	DAY						JCT OFF	ROAD TO		CITY	STATE	CITY	STATE							INITIAL	NUMBER	(5)

X FOR ALL SPECIAL EQUIPMENT

COMMODITY INSPECTED AT

LOCATION

DATE

CIRCLE ONE-GRADE A-B-C-D-E-F-G-H-U

	LENGTH	HEIGHT	DOOR		WET OR DRY
BOX					
GON	LENGTH	END	FLOOR		
HOP	CAPY		REFRG		

EMPTY CAR BILL
TYPE   DESTINATION

ROAD TO

SHIPPER/ORDER NO.

DATE

AUTHORITY

HOME ROUTE INFORMATION
CAR INITIAL NUMBER

DATE RECEIVED   ROAD FROM

JUNCTION

advanced 82246   PRINTED IN U.S.A.

MCRS MOVEMENT & HOME ROUTE CARD

RIGHT
from the Beginning

RIGHT
from the Beginning

by Patrick J. Buchanan

LITTLE, BROWN AND COMPANY
BOSTON   TORONTO

FIRST EDITION

The author is grateful for permission to include material from
the following copyrighted publications:

Excerpt from *The Desolate City* by Anne Roche Muggeridge.
Copyright © 1986 by Anne Roche. Reprinted by permission of
Harper and Row, Publishers, Inc.

Excerpt from *The Idea of a Christian Society* by T. S. Eliot.
Copyright 1939 by T. S. Eliot; renewed 1967 by Esme Valerie
Eliot. Reprinted by permission of Harcourt Brace Jovanovich,
Inc. and Faber and Faber, Ltd.

Library of Congress Cataloging-in-Publication Data

Buchanan, Patrick J.
  Right from the beginning.

  Includes index.
  1. Buchanan, Patrick J. 2. Politicians — United
States — Biography. 3. Journalists — United States —
Biography. 4. Conservatism — United States — History —
20th century. 5. United States — Politics and
government — 1981–   . I. Title
E840.8.B83A3 1988   973.927′092′4   87-35354
ISBN 0-316-11408-1

10 9 8 6 5 4 3 2 1

Designed by Jeanne Abboud

MV

*Published simultaneously in Canada
by Little, Brown & Company (Canada) Limited*

PRINTED IN THE UNITED STATES

For My Brother Bill

William B. Buchanan, Jr.
(August 25, 1936–September 21, 1985)

A Note of
Acknowledgment

WITHOUT the constant encouragement and assistance of four special women, *Right from the Beginning* would have gone wrong from the start: Helen Rees, my agent (also raised in Washington, D.C.), who steered me through the shoals of the publishing industry, and cheered me on through each draft; Agnes Waldron, Special Assistant to Presidents Nixon, Ford, and Reagan, who read and reviewed the first draft and directed me to return immediately to the Macintosh word processor; Fredrica S. Friedman, my editor at Little, Brown, who pursued me for two years to write this book, and whose ideas and specific editing suggestions (which numbered in the hundreds) were invaluable, and saved whatever has been salvaged herein; and my wife, Shelley, who read each sentence in each chapter in each draft, and lovingly criticized every single one.

Pat Buchanan
October 6, 1987

Contents

RIGHT
from the Beginning

Is That Churchill under the Bed?

"If you can't bear the cross . . ."

L ET the bloodbath begin!" came the voice from the back of the room.

John Lofton, the columnist, was casting his lot in favor of a Buchanan run for the Republican nomination in 1988. Along with two dozen other conservative leaders, John had been invited to my house that night of January 14, 1987, to discuss a presidential bid. The meeting in my living room was chaired by my sister Bay, the former Treasurer of the United States.

John was speaking for the majority present. Most of them — some of the most dedicated, selfless people in American politics, like my old friend and Nixon-era comrade, Howard Phillips of Conservative Caucus — nodded agreement. Jack Kemp had had his chance, they said, but he had failed to catch fire and he never would; Pat Robertson could not be nominated; the moderates were quietly recapturing the party, and we couldn't wait any longer. Only a Buchanan candidacy could galvanize the True Believers for an eighteen-month, barn-burning campaign to prevent the nomination from being yielded up, once again, to the Republican Establishment, represented by Vice-President George Bush and Senate Minority Leader Robert Dole.

The race for the nomination was open, and the title of conservative leader, held only by Barry Goldwater and Ronald Reagan in the modern era, would become vacant in 1988. Why not go for it?

Reaction to my defense of the President in early December, in a

Washington Post polemic that lionized Ollie North as a national hero and derided the silent Republicans ("a portrait in ingratitude") for having "headed for the tall grass," had been electric.

The Monday it appeared on the op-ed page, I was on the evening news on all four networks, was interviewed by Peter Jennings at halftime on ABC's "Monday Night Football," and addressed a Reagan rally of thousands of cheering Cubans at the Dade County Auditorium in Miami. Excerpts from that speech ran on the networks all week; by Friday, I was ABC's Person of the Week. The largest vacuum in American politics — the vacuum to the right of Ronald Reagan — seemed to be pulling me into the presidential race.

As that meeting in my living room was ending, Tom Ellis, the senior man present, whose Congressional Club had rescued Ronald Reagan from permanent political eclipse in the North Carolina primary of 1976, got up to speak. He did not know if we could win or not, Tom said; hell, he didn't know if America was going to make it or not, with the Soviets pouring a billion dollars in military hardware into Nicaragua, right on the mainland of North America, and nobody seeming to care. What he did know was that he had an obligation to his children and his grandchildren to do his damnedest to give it the best shot he could for his country — and, at this time and place, Pat Buchanan represented that best shot. Damn the torpedoes, full speed ahead.

Four days later, from the White House, I issued a statement, taking myself out of 1988.

As "the Old Man," Richard Nixon, had taught me twenty years before, I had taken out a yellow legal pad, and listed, side by side, the arguments for and the arguments against running for President. While the heart said yes, the head said no.

Despite the enthusiasm in that living room, virtually no one there believed I could be elected; only a few thought we had a remote chance at the nomination. Allan Ryskind, a personal friend for two decades, brought up a national poll showing that while my name recognition was higher than Jack Kemp's, I had a 4–3 negative rating *among Republicans and independents,* to Jack's 5–2 positive.

Allan's lead article that weekend in *Human Events,* while lauding me for all I had done for the movement ("what elevates Buchanan above the common politician is his extraordinary capacity to define life-and-death issues in a powerful rhetorical style that moves men to action"), pointedly noted that most conservatives felt the likely consequence of my candidacy would be "to kill off the man many regard as the most viable conservative candidate on the horizon, Jack Kemp."

Looking down the yellow pad, I reviewed the arguments in favor: (1) The movement would be galvanized. (2) "Our" issues would be elevated. (3) The GOP would be pulled in a conservative direction. (4) I would have entered a strong claim to succeed Ronald Reagan as leader of our movement. (5) It would be exhilarating and great fun. What did I have to lose?

Unfortunately, a great deal.

If a Buchanan candidacy could not capture the nomination but did succeed in mortally wounding the campaign of Jack Kemp, a friend, it could fairly be said that I had crippled the conservative cause by indulging myself in the worst kind of dog-in-the-manger politics. (A parade of Kemp's staffers and supporters had urged me to give Jack six months to prove himself.)

Already, a Buchanan–Kemp preliminary bout was shaping up as the "bloodbath" Brother Lofton relished. My old buddy from the Reagan White House, Ed Rollins, now Kemp's campaign manager, was trashing me; and Baby Sister was reciprocating. "Starting out at 7 percent in the polls, Jack Kemp has risen, after two years of campaigning — to 7 percent," Bay was quoted as telling an amused national press.

Tom Winter, publisher of *Human Events* and a friend to us both, had warned at my house that night that whatever my decision, Jack Kemp deserved better than what the militant New Right seemed to have in mind.

Indeed, he did — but there was another side to the Kemp question that troubled me.

While Jack and I were friends and allies and agreed on almost every issue, we came to our beliefs from different backgrounds and we champion our cause in different ways. A convert to the supply-side faith, Jack Kemp speaks with the zeal of the convert; but he is at his most passionate when preaching about tax rates, monetary reform, the gold standard, and the interrelationships between investment and saving and entrepreneurship and opportunity.

To me, economics is an inexact science; it is not a matter for moral certitude; and Mazzini was more right than Marx: "Ideas rule the world and its events. A revolution is a passage of an idea from theory to practice. *Whatever men say, material interests never have caused and never will cause a revolution.*"

Economics is *not* the science that sends men to the barricades. The Abraham Lincoln Battalion did not march into Franco's guns in the Jarama with the Labor Theory of Value in mind; and Pickett's division did not march up Little Round Top because they feared the economic consequences of abolition. Whether the choice of weapons is words or guns, men fight to preserve the most beautiful of the pictures in their minds. And the pictures in my mind were different from the ideas in Jack's, because of whence we came.

Ben Elliott, who headed President Reagan's speech-writing shop and left to join Kemp, and I had often discussed what I called Jack's "Big Rock Candy Mountain" school of conservatism, where happiness is attained through endless tax cuts and uninterrupted economic growth.

To me, America was a good country and a great country, long before she was a rich country; Cal Coolidge notwithstanding, the business of America is *not* business. Ronald Reagan's economic agenda was not the reason some of us, as far back as 1975, urged him to challenge Gerald Ford. (I recall one wit, writing in the *Wall Street Journal* in 1984 as a "traditionalist" for Reagan, saying that the reason he objected to George Bush calling the Reagan tax program "voodoo economics" was not because he thought the phrase unfair, "but because we thought it was redundant.")

And Jack and I have different styles. A positive, outgoing, upbeat, ebullient, optimistic man of the Congress, Jack's rhetoric is sprinkled with phrases like "my distinguished colleague" and "my good friend." While his convictions are conservative, his mindset is congressional. To me, the times required that we not only boldly enunciate our agenda for America, but expose and attack, with all the political weapons in our armory, those in Congress driving the United States toward disaster in Central America, southern Africa — and Geneva. "Football is not a contact sport," Vince Lombardi is said to have corrected a questioner, "it is a collision sport; dancing is a contact sport." Better than most, Jack Kemp knows that about football; but that is how I feel about politics.

In the early days of the French Revolution, the Abbé de Sieyès declared: Now is the time to get more, after which we will demand and get everything. That is the correct mindset for our conservative counterrevolution.

My good friend, the late Bryce Harlow, the tiny lobbyist from Oklahoma who was about five feet high and one hundred pounds of political integrity, and who served three Presidents, told me that Eisenhower had once taken him aside and exploded in exasperation over the endemic congressional disposition to compromise: "Bryce, don't get your Presidents off Capitol Hill! Because, while the truth might be here [and Ike stretched his left hand out to the far left] or here [and Ike stretched his right hand out to the far right], your Congressman will always come down here" — and Ike brought his hands together, midway between the two points.

Among the reasons I wanted to run, then, was not only to make the case *for* us — but *against* them. And even though I had never held elective office (which some said was a fatal defect), I had spent eight years in the White House as an assistant to three Presidents; I had been to three Soviet summits and on Nixon's visit to China; and I had more experience in communication — radio, television, and the written word — than all the other Republicans taken together (with the possible exception of Pat Robertson). And communication, as well as convictions, is what modern politics and the modern presidency are all about.

Some of the younger "backbenchers" in the White House press corps, whom I had come to know as friends, were encouraging me to run. ("Pat, get in; you've got to; it's so boring!" said one young lady from a national newspaper. "Pat, you can beat Kemp; I know it; just get in," another told me.) Even Sam Donaldson was heard to say that if Buchanan ran, he would take a leave of absence from the White House to cover the campaign. But personal considerations at last became paramount, and decisive.

The *Washington Post* is not only a sometimes savage antagonist of what I believe, it is my hometown paper. My eight brothers and sisters and I were raised in Washington; my mother and father, five of my brothers and sisters, and eighteen nieces and nephews still lived there. While a presidential campaign would be exciting for the extended Buchanan family, it would not be uniformly pleasant. Did I want to surrender my cherished privacy — to live in that fishbowl? Did I want to spend much of my campaign explaining the million words I had written in my controversial syndicated column of ten years? And the second million, written confidentially in earlier White House days, and secreted in the Nixon files, which the presidential archivist seemed so anxious to dump?

Did I want to go from cocktail party to cocktail party begging for contributions, something I had never been able to do, and to borrow the millions of dollars for "prospective mailings," that could leave me, like John Glenn and Gary Hart, in debt the rest of my life? Is the transport worth the pain? wrote Emily Dickinson.

The answer was yes, indeed; all this *was* worth it, provided there was a chance to win. Yet, while the hot-blooded on the Right said, "Go," the cool-headed responded, "You'll never make it; you'll go down to defeat and probably take your friends Jack Kemp and Pat Robertson right along with you."

On the Friday after the meeting, in my "windowless office," as *Newsweek* described it, in the West Wing of the White House, I was ruminating on my decision, when a special-delivery letter arrived, from Bill Schulz, Washington editor of *Reader's Digest*. Adding flattery to his admonition, my friend gave it to me, as Cactus Jack Garner used to say, "with the bark on":

> *I write as a friend and one who agrees with you on virtually every public policy issue. But I think you would be making a grave mistake to run for President.*
>
> *First and foremost, you can't win.*
>
> *To plunge into a campaign in which you have no realistic chance . . . you do more than make likely the nomination of an issueless candidate who is doomed to defeat in November. By appearing to be a spoiler, a gadfly, you jeopardize the reputation you have built ever since your virtuoso performance before the Watergate Committee. . . . You are the conscience of the conservative movement and should be for years to come. To risk that in a campaign that many will view as an ego trip is to permanently jeopardize a vast influence for the public good.*

An "ego trip," the man said.

After agonized appeals from Howard Phillips and Tom Ellis — men I had given every reason to believe I was running — I put out a statement, saying I feared a Buchanan campaign could be "the Pickett's Charge of the conservative movement," crippling the already prepared campaigns of fellow conservatives. I hadn't joined up with Richard Nixon twenty-one years ago to advance the conservative cause, only to become the instrument of its permanent injury in my middle age.

After work that evening, as I drove up the George Washington Parkway toward home in McLean, I felt an immense weight had been lifted off me, and I felt at peace with myself. My wife, Shelley, greeted me, smiling. "Now you won't be staring at the ceiling all night." Although she would have loved the campaign, she, too, was relieved. For Shelley is a realist. A veteran of Richard Nixon's staff, having traveled with him during the campaigns of 1960 (Kennedy–Nixon), 1964 (Goldwater–Johnson), and 1968 (Nixon–Humphrey), she had spent six years in the White House from Nixon's inauguration through Watergate and the final days. And she was right. For the first time in weeks, I slept soundly. Yet, in the back of my mind, I could hear the refrain of the old gospel song I used to listen to as a boy on WWVA: "If you can't bear the cross, then you can't wear the crown."

The tensions of that time, however, were not unrelieved by humor. At my home that night, Tom Ellis suggested I might be the "Churchill of our time"; the phrase had found its way into the press. When one angry and disappointed right-winger, who was trying energetically to change my mind, was asked by a reporter how he was making out, he retorted curtly, "We're still trying to get Churchill out from under the bed."

"You did the right thing," wrote Bill Gavin, an old friend from the Nixon comeback days of '68. Had I entered, "the Republican primaries would have looked like the outskirts of Basra." Chief of Staff Don Regan, who seemed intrigued by my running when we talked about it privately (and was reportedly intrigued by the idea of me out of the White House), brought word from the Oval Office that the Gipper agreed with my decision. As did my old mentor in Saddle River, Richard M. Nixon.

Some of the Democrats, however, had reportedly been "salivating" at what the presidential candidacy of Pat Buchanan might do for their fund-raising. "I think [Buchanan's] taking his motto from *Studs Lonigan*," sniffed liberal activist Ted Van Dyck, "'Live fast, die young and leave a good-looking corpse.'" Then, Ted dropped this little bon mot: "My only concern is that he'll make a fool out of himself and be out of it in short order." Mr. Van Dyck was then senior campaign adviser — to Gary Hart.

Now, a predictable press howl began, led by the eminently predictable John Chancellor. I was exploiting my position, Mr. Chancellor pouted in his nightly commentary on NBC, and should leave the White House forthwith. (That George Bush had his White House office twenty feet down the hall, and also seemed interested in running, did not bother John quite so much.) But my "friends" in the press corps were pushing against an open door. What most did not know was that I had already planned to leave.

In mid-October, before the 1986 congressional elections, I learned that Dave Abshire, U.S. Ambassador to NATO, would be leaving. NATO was a spot in which I had always had a secret interest, so I went to see Don Regan, and told him I would like to be the White House candidate. I thought perhaps I could get a recess appointment and be in Brussels by the New Year. The Chief of Staff agreed to support me.

After the Democrats recaptured the Senate, however, my chances fell to next to zero. As the weeks went by, I finally told "DTR" not to pursue it. Not only would the Democrats hold up my confirmation for months, leaving me in limbo for much of 1987, but Secretary of State George Shultz, with whom I had clashed on South Africa policy, was vehemently opposed.

"Tell George he's won this one," I told the Chief.

March 1 was my new departure date. By then, I would have been the White House Communications Director for two years; it was time to go. With Iran–*contra* crashing down upon him, the President needed a fresh team that would stay to the end of his term. And, as the White House had decided in November that its approach to the Iran–*contra* would be conciliation and cooperation with Congress, the President no longer needed his old pit bull.

Six weeks after standing down, I went into the Oval Office for the farewell handshake and final picture with the President, and introduced him to my brothers Hank and Crick and Jack and Tom, my sister Kathleen, and their spouses. Then we repaired to the Roosevelt Room where the President, after a gracious little talk, handed me a surprise going-away present — bronzed running shoes (for having captained "Reagan's V-Toes" and "Reagan's Re-Runs" — White House jogging teams in two Nike Capital Challenge three-mile races).

"We are with you in this embroglio; we are with you to the end of this administration, and we are with you to the end, because no one has done more for our cause, our country, and our movement than you have," I told the President before he walked back to his office.

I did not leave the White House, however, without a sense of sadness. Ronald Reagan was, and is, among the most decent and gracious human beings ever to serve in high office, a delight to work for and with, a genuinely lovable man; and now, I knew in my heart — and I don't think he really did — that he was going to have to endure some of the same hell we had known during Watergate.

If the President didn't notice, when he handed me those bronzed running shoes, my own eyes were glistening.

As I left that last day, I remembered what I had told a reporter back in 1973, after Richard Nixon had won the greatest political triumph of his embattled career, the forty-nine-state victory of 1972, and the full fury of Watergate was suddenly upon us. "We rolled the rock all the way up the hill, only to see it roll right back down on top of us."

Everything we had worked for the past two years was now at risk.

When I had accepted Don Regan's invitation to join President Reagan's second-term team in early February of 1985, the President was already being dismissed as a "lame duck." But, together, we had won battle after battle that "lame ducks" do not win.

We won funding for the MX missile; then, after a series of disheartening reversals, we won $100 million in military aid and support for the *contras,* the Nicaraguan democratic resistance, whose defunding had been the highest priority of Tip O'Neill. By taking his case to the country, the President had built immense public support for strategic defense; even if SDI funding was lagging, it was beginning.

After a bruising Senate collision, William Rehnquist had been elevated to Chief Justice; and Antonin Scalia, the first Italian-American nominee in history, had been confirmed to the Supreme Court. To elevate jurists of the quality, character, and philosophy of Rehnquist, Scalia, and Robert Bork was among the reasons some of us, ten years before, had broken with our own President, Gerald Ford, to enlist in the insurgency of Ronald Reagan. (That

Robert Bork was subsequently savaged — and rejected — by the Democrat-controlled Senate is only added testament to the man's character and credentials.)

In 1986, the President had seen a year of speeches and phone calls bear fruit with enactment of the most sweeping revision of the U.S. tax code in memory, reducing top rates in the Reagan years from 70 percent in 1981 to 28 percent in 1988 — truly landmark legislation.

In November of 1985, we had gone to Geneva for the President's first encounter with Secretary Gorbachev, with the press warning the summit would blow up if we refused to compromise on SDI. The President refused, and we came home in triumph.

In October of 1986, we had gone to Reykjavik, where the President played that wild Sunday afternoon poker game on nuclear weapons; and when the President angrily walked out of the first-floor room at Hofdi House, rather than yield up SDI to Mikhail Gorbachev, he escaped the Russian bear trap and returned home to another triumphant welcome — to the puzzlement, again, of a press corps that had already laid at Ronald Reagan's feet blame for the summit's collapse.

From an approval rating in the mid-50s in February of 1985, Ronald Reagan, by the fall of 1986, was in the mid-70s — an unprecedented register of national esteem for a second-term president.

Then, suddenly, came the shocking revelation the United States had been secretly selling weapons to Iran.

Like Mr. Nixon before him, Ronald Reagan had handed his enemies a sword. And, given the savagery of American politics in 1986, I knew the day the story broke they would drive that sword in, right up to the hilt. For Ronald Reagan, the fifth of November, 1986, was the day the music died.

In his own favorite short story (and one of mine), *The Snows of Kilimanjaro*, Ernest Hemingway opens by pointing to the highest mountain peak in Africa and noting an oddity: "Close to the western summit there is the dried and frozen carcass of a leopard. No one has explained what the leopard was seeking at that altitude."

What this book is about is what we were seeking at that altitude, "close to the western summit" of American politics, and about how I got there. It is about how a student of pious nuns and traditionalist Jesuits, an expellee from Georgetown University, and an antediluvian oddity at the Graduate School of Journalism at Columbia in New York wound up, at age twenty-seven, standing at the tomb where there commenced the Resurrection of Richard Nixon.

The late Herman Kahn, the famous futurist from Hudson Institute with whom I became friends years ago, used to coin his own aphorisms. For almost all men, Herman told me, there are only two times in life when one's ideas, attitudes, and convictions can be radically altered: when you go to college, and before you are six. I think he was right.

As the child is father to the man, I have written here of the times, places, and people — from boyhood through college and the beginning of my career — that shaped me and my view of the world. This book, then, is about another time in America, in many ways a better time.

As he approached a certain and painful death, the journalist Stu Alsop, whom I had come to know and admire, said that he felt himself passing away at a time when America's greatness lay behind her. He had been privileged, he said, to live through the glory years, but a day was coming to America he really did not care to see. To me, he, too, was right. I loved those years; nothing since has matched the singular sweetness of their memory.

We, my three closest brothers and I, were "raised Catholic" in the '40s and '50s in a militant and triumphant Church in the days of the Legion of Decency and Pius XII; we grew up when the Faith was unquestioned and patriotism unconstrained, in a time when flag-burning was unheard of, and Vatican II was only a gleam in the eye of Monsignor Roncalli.

Our hometown was the sleepy and segregated southern city of Washington, D.C., an unrebellious fiefdom of the federal government, a quiet, pleasant place that has since disappeared beneath the risen cosmopolitan capital of the West.

Our childhood encompassed an era, the tone and style of which were set by the returning veterans of World War II. In four years, these millions of young men had crushed the Japanese empire and overturned the Thousand Year Reich; and they gave to American society a toughness and maturity it has long since lost. They were the heroes of my childhood. To my mind, the quiet men and women of my parents' and uncles' generation, who survived the

Depression and carried our country through the Second World War, were the finest young generation we have ever produced. When I would hear that phrase routinely ascribed to the over-privileged campus protestors of the '6os, I thought it obsequious prattle.

Conservatism in 1988 is a house with "many mansions."

There are "economic conservatives," who believe the highest priority is reducing budget deficits, and supply-side conservatives, who predict deficits will fade away, if only we provide enough incentives for entrepreneurs to bring full employment. While both agree on the superiority of the free market, they have a theological quarrel over monetary policy and the gold standard.

There are foreign policy conservatives, for whom the overriding concern is the enormous military power and malevolent ambitions of the Soviet empire.

There are social conservatives, who believe with Burke that in order to love one's country, one's country ought to be lovely—and that an America that has destroyed more unborn children in the fifteen years since *Roe v. Wade* than Australia has people can no longer be called lovely. Among the social conservatives resides the Religious Right, to whom the expulsion of God from the classroom, the rise of the drug culture, and the "sexual revolution" are unmistakable symptoms of cultural decadence and national decline.

There is also a libertarian annex in our conservative house now; its occupants see as the ultimate enemy of freedom the inexorable growth of government, which taxes away one in every three dollars America earns, and spends two in five. Dining with the social conservatives and the Religious Right, our libertarian cousins often appear ill at ease.

Growing up, ours was the "street corner" conservatism of which William F. Gavin wrote, the conservatism that comes of absorbing the attitudes and values my mother learned in a German-Catholic family of eight children, which she left as a girl of seventeen in 1929 to become a nurse in southeast Washington. It is the conservatism that comes of being raised alongside eight brothers and sisters by a Scotch-Irish and Irish father, an Al Smith Democrat, whose trinity of political heroes consisted of Douglas MacArthur, General Franco, and the junior Senator from Wisconsin they called Tail Gunner Joe.

We did not learn our values and convictions from books or bull sessions with college professors (we didn't have bull sessions with college professors); our conservatism was learned at the dinner table, soaked up in parochial school, picked up on the street corner, and imbibed in a high school where the Jesuits emphasized, first and foremost, the "salvation of your immortal soul, Buchanan."

Not until my twenties did I learn to conscript the intellectual arguments of the sages to reinforce the embattled arguments of the heart. When a boy approaches manhood, he gives or denies assent to what he has learned in home and school and church. He affirms, or rejects, the traditions and beliefs and values of his childhood. In his heart, he respects and loves, or he writes off and ridicules, what he came from. To me, the lessons of those years, however uncomplicatedly they may have been taught, retain the ring of truth.

This, then, is a book about who we are, and whence we came, and why we believe as we do.

In its final chapters, this book is about the attitudes and ideas our movement, in its current midlife crisis, must, I believe, adopt, to restore this materially rich but morally confused country of ours, and to save the remnant of the West. This would have formed the heart of a Buchanan campaign.

Beneath our surface prosperity and seeming social peace, we Americans are a people who have lost our way. Behind our immense prosperity and military might stands a leadership class divided and paralyzed by its incapacity to distinguish flawed friend from mortal enemy. In the wilderness world we inhabit, that lost capacity can prove a fatal failing. Great empires and tiny minds go ill together, Burke wrote; the same holds true for great republics.

While more prosperous and affluent than ever we were in the 1950s, America today seems a flabbier society. Universal military service was accepted without protest by the Silent Generation; today, reimposition of the draft would bring a firestorm from Left and Right, and widespread civil disobedience.

The sense of national unity and purpose America had in the Eisenhower and Kennedy years is gone. We have become a more quarrelsome and disputatious people. Two decades ago, the great American foreign policy consensus forged at Pearl Harbor fractured on the reef of Vietnam; today our social consensus is breaking down, and our political strength is being sapped by our deepening divisions.

In the twenty-eight years between 1932 and 1960, America elected three Presidents; in the twenty-eight years since, we have had six. President Kennedy was murdered, President Johnson was run out of office, President Nixon resigned, President Ford was rejected, and President Carter was repudiated. President Reagan, after an extraordinarily successful six years, stumbled badly on his weapons sale to Iran; and, suddenly, the same forces that broke Lyndon Johnson and Richard Nixon fell upon Ronald Reagan with similar ferocity. We Americans are paying a price for this propensity for regicide.

The proposition that America was a beneficent force in human history was universally accepted in the 1950s; today, it is controversial. Denunciations of the United States at the United Nations, as an ally of reaction and exploiter of the poor, find echoes in our college classrooms, on our editorial pages, even in the pulpits of mainline Protestant denominations and the American Catholic Church.

America is becoming again a house divided against itself. In the savagery of our politics we imitate the Third Republic; in our social and cultural life, we begin to resemble Weimar.

"You can't turn back the clock" is a cliché thrown up constantly to conservatives; and there is truth to it. Neither the world nor the United States will ever again be what we were in the aftermath of the Second World War. The American high is over. But much of what has been lost in the intervening years can be retrieved — the ideas and ideals that made America a uniquely good country, and that sense of purpose and mission needed to confront and confound the enemies of the Republic. And, that, too, is why I wrote this book.

2
Brer Rabbit

"Keep your left up!"

L ET us begin at the beginning.
For most of our lives, the Buchanans have been taken for
pure Irish, and we never protested the honor. (That I was
given the Christian name Patrick and carry the initials P.J. is surely
among the reasons.) The truth, however, is more complex.

My father's people on his father's side are Scotch-Irish; they
came out of the Ulster "Plantation," and before that, the Scottish
Highlands where the Buchanans are a renowned clan with their
own ancestral tartan and lands near Loch Lomond. The Buchanans
formed part of the Scots contingent under Henry V at Agincourt.

From Northern Ireland, our branch of the family migrated to
North Carolina in the late 1700s, and, from there, moved on to the
hill country of northwest Mississippi, settling near the town of
Okolona. On the road north of Okolona toward Tupelo lies a
graveyard with a dozen tombstones clustered inside a large, single
square; the monument bears the name BUCHANAN. It was the family
burial ground.

Two of my great-great-grandfathers, Cyrus Baldwin — whose
family had settled in Virginia before the Revolution — and Thomas
J. Buchanan, were rabid secessionists. As the Buchanan plantation
in Chickasaw County was a slaveholding enterprise, the family
must have viewed with foreboding the election in 1860 of the radical Republican from Illinois.

(In May of 1977, when Shelley and I drove from Birmingham

northwest into Mississippi to try to locate some lost cousins, I mentioned to a lifelong resident of Okolona that I intended to visit the half-dozen Buchanans listed in the phone directory. "I don't think they'll be much help, Mr. Buchanan," the old lady said sweetly. "They're all Negroes — but they're very nice people.")

When the War Between the States broke out, Cyrus Baldwin — whose older brother, the gifted Joseph Glover Baldwin, had penned *The Flush Times of Alabama and Mississippi* — volunteered as a forty-two-year-old lieutenant. Cyrus Baldwin died on the road to Vicksburg. William M. Buchanan, eldest son of Thomas J., enlisted for the duration, and was captured outside Atlanta during the battle of Jonesboro that sealed the fate of the city. "Captured by forces under Maj. Gen. W. T. Sherman," his war record reads; he spent his remaining months in the Camp Douglas prison compound in Illinois, which enjoyed a thoroughly rotten reputation for brutality. In May of 1865, he was sent south to New Orleans in a POW exchange, and went home to Mississippi to wed Bessie Baldwin, daughter of his father's late friend.

My grandfather, Henry Martin Buchanan, born to Bessie Baldwin Buchanan on September 10, 1877, was raised in Mississippi with a cordial contempt for the Yankee who had invaded his father's country — and an abiding love for the Lost Cause. He harbored the native Southern distrust of Roman Catholics, a sentiment that abated only during a summer's stay in an army tent hospital in Florida in 1898. On the outbreak of war with Spain, he had gone to Jackson, Mississippi, and enlisted; but, on his way to Cuba, he came down with "yellow jack." The women who nursed him back to health in that muddy army camp were the Sisters of Charity. "I thought all Catholics had horns," he told my father. Six years after the war, he married one.

My grandmother, Mary Agnes Smith, was one of seventeen children of Irish immigrant parents, eight of whom were carried away in a diphtheria epidemic in Brooklyn in the 1880s. Her mother, Anna Kerrigan, and her father, Thomas Smith, were potato famine people; they had come over from County Cork in the wake of the great Irish disaster of 1845–49. It was the lifelong honor of his family that Thomas Smith had been among the skilled laborers who built — in 101 days at the Brooklyn Navy Yard — Mr. Lincoln's first ironclad, the *Monitor,* which arrived off Hampton Roads the evening of the day the *Merrimac* devastated a Union flotilla.

A spirited girl, Mary Smith had been given a medal as the only child to have come to school during the Blizzard of '88. While still a girl, she crossed Brooklyn Bridge to take a job in Manhattan as a milliner, and was turned down because of her age. She went home, dressed up in her mother's clothes, came back, and got the job.

In 1904, Mary Smith, a milliner in Baltimore, and Henry Buchanan, an investigator with the Treasury Department in Washington, were married in a church rectory. (A Church wedding was not then permitted for a "mixed marriage" between a Protestant and a Catholic.) The couple honeymooned at the St. Louis World's Fair, and came home to live in Alexandria.

On my mother's side, no Irish are to be found. Her maiden name was Catherine Elizabeth Crum; her mother's, Anna Blanche Crock. The Crums and Crocks were of German immigrant stock from Fulda, Ohio. (They are still there, in Wayne Hays's old congressional district.) John Edward Crum, one of ten children of Francis and Elizabeth Null Crum, moved with his wife, Anna, to Belle Vernon, Pennsylvania, and, soon, across the Monongahela River to the town of Charleroi, where he raised his six sons and two daughters. Until he lost his job during the Depression, Ed Crum was superintendent of the Charleroi streetcar company.

At seventeen, after graduating from Charleroi High, Catherine Elizabeth Crum moved to Washington to become a student nurse at the old Providence Hospital at 2nd and C St. Southeast, just below the Capitol. Among the little-known charitable features at Providence was a "dry tank," which serviced the Congress of the United States.

Of medium height, slim and pretty, with brown hair and brown eyes, Catherine Crum graduated in three years to become a visiting nurse. Even after she was married, had two children, and was living beside the tracks in Takoma Park, Maryland, Mom would take the midnight calls to go back into the inner city to minister to the sick, Negro and white. Washington was not an affluent city in those years, but neither was it the crime capital it has since become. And when the cabs brought my mother into some neglected neighborhood to help some black woman deliver her child, the black men would be waiting at the head of the alley to make sure she got into the tiny houses, and out again, safely. What the "visiting nurses" did in those Depression days was what our Church meant when it spoke of the corporal works of mercy.

Five years after arriving in Washington, on December 28, 1934, she married my father, whom she had met on a blind date.

Raised for twenty-one years in a home where the mother's side was German, and the father's Scotch-Irish (and Irish), I have come to appreciate the insight of my friend Tom Sowell, the famed black economist and social scientist who wrote in *Ethnic America*:

> The Germans were noted for their order, quietness, friendliness, steady work, frugality and their ability to get along with the Indians. The Scotch-Irish were just the opposite — quick-tempered, hard drinking . . . constantly involved in feuds among themselves or with the Indians. . . .
>
> The early German settlers were usually pious . . . avoided strong language and strong drink while the Scotch-Irish . . . were given to hard liquor and language that pious people considered blasphemous. After a century of sharing hundreds of miles of the great valleys of the Appalachian range, there was still little racial intermixture between the Germans and the Scotch-Irish.

We took care of that.

The village of Georgetown, where my father lived his early years, was a different place then, a mixed Catholic and Protestant community, heavily Irish and German, spreading out in "row houses" east and north for a dozen blocks from Georgetown University and Holy Trinity — the oldest parish in the city.

When my father was eight, his grandfather, William M. Buchanan, the Confederate veteran of Atlanta and the Yankee prison, died in Okolona; and my father made his only trip south to the ancestral home. What he remembered was the uncommon closeness of the Buchanan clan and the black servants who lived with them. All his life my father would insist that while there were brutal white Southerners who reveled in mistreating black people, there also existed, between the decent country peoples of the South, Negro and white, feudal bonds of friendship, affection, and mutual regard Northerners did not understand. They had, he said, a way of living together down there that made life, for both, less harsh than the callous and cold indifference both confronted in the segregated cities of the North.

Walker Percy, the great novelist, also a Southerner and a Catholic, is a man of similar view:

> One of life's little mysteries: an old-style Southern white and an old-style Southern black are more at ease talking to each other, even though one may be unjust to the other, than Teddy Kennedy talking to Jesse Jackson — who are overly cordial, nervous as cats in their cordiality, and glad to be rid of each other. . . . [T]he old-style white and the old-style black — each knows exactly where he stands with the other, the first because he is in control, the second because he uses his wits. They both know this and can even enjoy each other.

One of my father's convictions, inherited from his father (and later passed on to us), was a belief in the greatness of the Confederacy. Whenever movies about the Civil War played, the Washington theater would be in an uproar — with half the boys cheering the Yankees, the other half cheering the Confederates. After the silent films (among them *Birth of a Nation*) were over, the boys would take the battle out into the streets, where my father always fought on the same side as his grandfather.

When my father was eleven, his father sent him off to the Mount Washington boarding school in Baltimore for the fifth grade; and one fateful afternoon, an elderly nun came to the basement cafeteria to tell him his father had come to visit. Riding with the boy on the rickety wooden elevator, the old nun said, "My, but your father is a handsome man." My grandfather told the boy he wanted to talk. Together, they went out onto the hillside of Mount Washington, where my grandfather told his older son he was leaving his wife and leaving Washington, for good, moving to Milwaukee as a special agent for the Treasury Department. Rarely would my father see his father again.

The desertion was a scarring wound to the boy, who idolized his father. Seventy years later, Pop would speak wistfully of how he used to run down the halls at school and down the streets of Georgetown to catch up with any "red-headed man" in the hope it might be his father. It never was. From the searing experience of his own father's abandonment, my father determined to be there, every day, as his own children were growing up. We reaped the harvest of a father's love that grew out of the cold, hard ground of his own father's indifference.

Out in Milwaukee, my grandfather left the Treasury, set up his own one-man accounting firm (he was an expert on the new income tax law), and made tremendous piles of money on major tax cases, which, invariably, he squandered during long drinking binges.

Once, he came back to Washington on a major corporate case, won it, and took home $60,000 as his fee — a fortune in that era. "He shot it out of a cannon," Pop told me.

With sharp, handsome features, muscular and well proportioned at five feet, eleven inches, Henry M. Buchanan was a tough and volatile Scotch-Irish brawler whose lost weekends often ended in some barroom fight, and occasionally in a jail cell. Years later, my father found out what happened to the straw hat his father had worn that fateful day at Mount Washington. As soon as Special Agent Buchanan arrived by train in Milwaukee, he went to his hotel, washed up, and headed for a saloon to tie one on. There, a huge lumberjack named Dunc smashed his straw hat. Grandfather left, returned with his knife, stabbed Dunc in the back and sliced him up — getting himself arrested, at age forty. As Dunc was reputed to be among the meanest men in Milwaukee, it was a legendary brawl; and grandfather talked openly and proudly of how he exacted retribution for his straw hat.

In 1920, my grandmother won a final divorce decree charging Henry Martin Buchanan with having "willfully deserted and abandoned" her and her two sons. The desertion transformed the family's economic condition. What the Scotch-Irish warrior left behind was another poor and "broken" family. Not long after he left, the money stopped coming. Grandmother had to pawn her rings to buy herself and two sons a house, for $4,900, at 1411 30th in Georgetown.

In the eighth grade my father had suffered an infection on his ankle — a small cut from his skates was infected with the dye of his sock — that almost cost him his leg, if not his life. Coolidge's son, Calvin, Jr., would die from an almost identical ailment, blood poisoning from a blister he got playing tennis on the White House grounds.

The ankle infection, which had to be painfully "scraped" to the bone, drained and cleansed repeatedly, produced an osteomyelitis that plagued my father until he was nineteen, when, suddenly, it was gone. He bore the scars of the knife work all his life, and pieces of bone regularly came out of the ankle until he was forty.

At nineteen, he was able to take up tennis in a serious way, winning in the early 1930s both the D.C. Doubles Championship and the Middle Atlantic title. From Baltimore to Cumberland to Cleveland, he "traveled the circuit" with his partner, Dooley

Mitchell, former D.C. junior champion, and Bob Considine, later a famed columnist and the author of *Thirty Seconds over Tokyo*. The yellowed press clippings of the era show a handsome, self-confident, athletic man with black curly hair. Until his early forties, Pop played a good game of tennis; but then he was down to weekend tournaments at the Edgemoor Club, which he and Dooley and friends had converted into an all-tennis club that produced the finest players in the city.

On graduation from high school, my father had desperately wanted to go to Marquette University in Milwaukee. He traveled out by train, but discovered there was no place for him with his father — and his father's new lady, Miss Emma Carola Helms. So, he came back home and went to Georgetown.

After his first year in "pre-legal," he switched to law school, but discovered, after one semester, he would not be allowed to continue. His father had failed to send in the tuition. He had to drop out, and went to work as a bookkeeper, putting off forever his dream of becoming a trial attorney.

Not long after leaving Georgetown, my father joined Councilor & Buchanan, the most prominent accounting firm in the city. The Buchanan was William Gordon Buchanan (no relation), but, because of William Gordon's citywide reputation, my father had to identify himself to clients for decades as W. Baldwin Buchanan, emphasizing a middle name he could not stand. In 1937, James A. Councilor, Sr., broke up his partnership with William Gordon Buchanan to advance his son and namesake. It was a nasty split; when my father cast his lot with Councilor, it cost him his teaching job at Georgetown. Buchanan, who had gotten him the job, now got him fired.

While my father was made a junior partner in the new James A. Councilor & Co., Big Jim, as he was called, regularly used to boast, "Boys, I will never walk out of this office; they will have to carry me out." In January of 1945, that's what they did. A heart attack felled Big Jim, and he never came back. My father and Dooley Mitchell ousted the foremost claimant for the title of senior partner and formed a new partnership, with Little Jim's name leading the masthead. Councilor, Buchanan, Mitchell & Hayes, a partnership he and Dooley have run for forty-three years, came into existence.

At thirty-nine years of age, in 1945, my father, for the first time in the three decades since his own father had deserted him, had both feet planted firmly in the middle class. Now, there would be no need for second and third jobs teaching at night at Georgetown or Strayer College or Ben Franklin or Catholic University. His economic future secure, my father could now realize his and my mother's true life's ambition: to raise a large family of sons and daughters, and to enjoy, vicariously through his children, the good times of childhood his own father's desertion had denied him. He was off to a good start; there were already five of us.

William Baldwin Buchanan, Jr., was born on August 25, 1936.

He was followed on October 15, 1937, by Henry Martin (Hank), named after his grandfather; by Patrick Joseph, born All Souls Day, November 2, 1938; and by James Michael, whom we always called "Jimmy Cricket" (after Jiminy Cricket, the character in *Pinocchio*), on June 11, 1940. We were all delivered at the old Providence Hospital, where my mother had been a student nurse. Dr. Joe Mundell was the obstetrician in attendance. (His son, the Monsignor, runs Immaculate Conception parish in Washington's inner city.)

Because we were then living in a rented house on Brandywine Street in upper northwest in 1938, I was baptized in the old Saint Ann's Church off Tenley Circle, now the gym. But, soon after, my father moved us back to Georgetown, renting a tiny row house at 3618 Whitehaven Parkway. Both the house, and the little park at the end of the street, where my mother took us for walks, are still there.

Behind the house, an alley runs parallel to the street. In a garage on that alley occurred one of those unforgettable minor tragedies of childhood, that recur decades later in dreams. Neighborhood boys had filled the garage with newspapers, collected for the war effort. After smoking a few cigarettes, they closed the garage, locking their dog inside. The animal suffocated in the fire that brought what seemed like half the D.C. fire department into the alley. We watched the sad finale to the little tragedy from our back porch. It was the same August day they buried my grandfather at Arlington.

Baptized in infancy, we were all instructed on how to pray as soon as we could talk. Even in the crib, I caught on quickly. When my older brothers were still toddlers, on their knees stumbling through the Our Father, the Hail Mary, and the Glory Be, from the playpen would come an impatient, "Holy Mary, Mother of God, pray for us sinners now and at the hour of our death. Amen!" Elated with the early signs of precocity, my parents would show off the indolent little boy called "Paddy Joe," who "could talk before he could walk."

My older brothers were not amused. The four of us in those years slept in individual cribs, which were on stilts and rollers and could be maneuvered around the otherwise empty room. To start the crib rolling, all we had to do was stand, hold firmly onto one of the horizontal bars, and rock back and forth energetically in the direction we wanted to go. Nightly, the four of us made a tremendous racket, rolling from one side of the bedroom to the other and back again, in our tiny mobile homes. One night, after the older brothers had their prayers interrupted and corrected yet again from the playpen, my father heard horrible screams from our room. Rushing in, he found blood and milk all over Paddy Joe's head and face. There was a gaping wound in my forehead, and glass was strewn all over the crib and floor. The perpetrator was at hand. Hank had maneuvered his crib over next to mine, reached in, jerked the milk bottle out of my mouth, and smashed it over my head.

The lesson never took.

Growing up together, the four of us each a year apart, taught us much not found in books. There was only a brief period when the youngest was the favorite; before we were even aware of it, a new infant had arrived to be admired and attended to. If you had been spoiled in infancy, it didn't last.

And if, temporarily, one of us became the favorite of one or both parents, that brother paid a price. Showing off did not pay. The only way four boys can live happily sleeping in a single room for a dozen years as we did is by practicing deference and tolerance, learning diplomacy, and nurturing the bonds of affection. Early on, the four of us established a mutual truce and formed a sibling alliance against external dangers, especially the man with the strap.

Rarely did my father use an open hand to discipline his older boys. The "strap" was the preferred instrument. So regular a procedure did it become that, as we got older — if we had warning — we would stuff comic books into the seat of our pants, taking three or four of Pop's best wallops, and then start whimpering. As soon as the tears started, Pop would let up. So expert did Hank and I become by the time we were in grammar school, that, at times, it was hard to get to the top of the stairs without laughing.

Under this benevolent dictatorship, we learned there were clear and stated rules to be obeyed without question; and there was a ladder of punitive sanctions. The most severe of these was the black leather belt. While plea-bargaining might be entertained, there was no due process, and no court of appeal.

In those years on Whitehaven Parkway, my mother was still in her twenties, a thin and lovely woman with brown hair and eyes, in the bloom of life; you can see the pride in her face in the numerous pictures of her, holding up for the photographer one of the four little boys she had borne.

More bookish than my father, she had been an excellent student who came to Washington at seventeen to be a nurse, and had never gone to an academic college; so she transferred her own academic interests and ambitions to her children. Serene, calm, and reasonable in every family crisis — which usually involved a collision between father and son — she was the one who would intercede, privately, with Pop, to persuade him the discipline had gone far enough, that now was the time to wipe the slate clean and move ahead. In the family, she was the diplomat among warriors.

My father, then in his mid-thirties, and still playing regular tennis, was by now almost completely bald. The thick crop of curly black hair in the pictures of his tennis triumphs was almost entirely gone. The black "sidewalls" left behind made him look like a younger version of Daddy Warbucks. When I was a teenager, my friends, who gave nicknames to everyone, used to call him Grantland Rice, after the famous sports writer who had named the Four Horsemen.

Pop was broad in the shoulders and powerfully built. With huge forearms from the farm work he had done as a boy, the garden work he always did, and the tennis, he had a proletarian aspect. While almost all of us grew up smooth-skinned, his hands and arms were hairy. Unlike my mother, who was the essence of emotional self-control, my father was given to explosions — of laughter, applause, anger, and delight. His moods came and went quickly. Called "Wild Bill" as a young man, for his forensic encounters over religion, politics, and sports, he loved debating and had a distinctly Irish side, which enjoyed jokes (only clean ones), loved funny stories, and appreciated powerful rhetoric and good language.

Whenever you were in trouble with Pop, the way to plea bargain — other than to ask Mom to file your appeal — was to exhibit some wit. If you could get him to appreciate the humorous aspects of the episode, Pop would gradually cease to see himself in his necessary role as father, guide and disciplinarian, and begin to see himself as vicarious participant, someone who, after all, had gotten into similar scrapes as a boy.

When I went to St. Louis to write for a newspaper, he was elated with my chosen profession and relished the editorials I sent back home. He saw me one day writing my own syndicated and by-lined column and appearing in newspapers all over America. And when I first told him I was leaving journalism to work for Richard Nixon, as a political aide, I could sense he felt I was giving up an honorable career in writing for one in politics that was somehow not quite so.

The great event that occurred while we lived on Whitehaven Parkway was the Japanese attack on Pearl Harbor. My parents were at the Redskins–Eagles game, the last game of the season, as the shocking news came back from Oahu. Throughout the game, the voice on the loudspeaker kept calling out the names of navy and army officers, cryptically telling them to return to their units. When my father and mother left the stadium, "Extra" editions of the newspapers were on the street. Years later, I discovered in the bottom drawer of my parents' dresser the *Washington Daily News* edition with the terrible headline "JAPS BOMB PEARL HARBOR!"

The war was on. All the arguments about the wisdom of American involvement ended with Japan's treacherous attack and Hitler's insane decision to back his Axis partner and declare war on the United States. From the time I turned three until I was seven, the war served as background to my growing up.

One by one, my mother's younger brothers, the Crum boys from Charleroi, would come through Washington to say good-bye before they were shipped off to the European theater of operations. Regis, "Uncle Peachie" as we called him, was already in the army and went first, landing with every U.S. invasion force in the ETO, save Normandy. He was with the first U.S. troops to land in North

Africa and was at Kasserine Pass when the green Americans were hit head-on by the Desert Fox, and American troops got their first blooding from Erwin Rommel's veteran Afrika Korps. Peachie landed in Sicily with Patton's army, and was later pinned down with the American forces on the Anzio beachhead; in 1944, he went into southern France, and came home with a Silver Star.

When he came home, Peachie looked up the parents of the boy who had been killed only feet away when he took the full brunt of a German mortar shell intended for them both; he gave them his Silver Star.

In the Italian campaign Peachie had suffered from something called trench foot. It was an ailment, the gravity of which I never fully appreciated until, forty years later, I read about it in William Manchester's splendid war chapter in *The Glory and the Dream*: "Without a change of socks, GIs accumulated wet mud around their feet and, eventually, trench foot. The pain became excruciating, and when they crawled to the battalion aid station (nobody with trench foot has ever walked), and the medics cut off their shoes, their feet swelled to the size of footballs. Sometimes they had to be amputated."

Bill, the middleweight fighter we always called "Uncle Bull" — who had lived with us on Whitehaven Parkway while he attended the Knights of Columbus college on a boxing scholarship my father had helped to get — quickly made sergeant and was sent to Italy; Jim, who graduated from the Merchant Marine Academy, transported weapons and supplies to the Red Army on the North Atlantic "Run to Murmansk." At eighteen, my mother's youngest brother, Art, volunteered for combat so as not to miss the great event of his lifetime. To get Art into a battle zone in 1944 required a waiver of the O'Sullivan Rule, which said no more than three sons from one family could be in combat at one time. (The five O'Sullivan brothers had perished together when the light cruiser *Juneau*, on which all five served, was sunk by a Japanese torpedo off Guadalcanal. The U.S. government did not want another such family devastation.) Grandfather Ed Crum had insisted that Art go to war as soon as he came of age, saying, "There are no shirkers in the Crum family."

When they came home, none of them liked to talk about the war. "Pat, I never killed anybody," Peachie told me, when I pressed him as a boy. And I never heard them express any hatred of the enemy. It was a job, and they had done it; now it was over. Indeed,

Art described to me how he and his friends sat on a hillside watching a German Tiger tank knock out one American tank after another, like the "tin cans" the American tanks were. The Germans sat on the other hillside. When I asked Peachie what it was like at Kasserine, he said, "Scary, but exciting." The Germans they had encountered had been excellent soldiers, my uncles told me; and one of them said he was sure the German people would come back. He had seen women and children picking up the bricks of the bombed-out cities and chipping off the mortar, to use them again to rebuild their country.

They were all easygoing men, my uncles, and they had belonged to an American army that, by the end of the war, as Manchester wrote, Julius Caesar himself would have been proud to lead into battle.

To maintain morale and solidarity with the men overseas, we five-year-old chauvinists collected magazines and newspapers and delivered them in our wagons to the public schools. Scrap metal was left at the end of the street. Crushed tin cans were collected as well. During nights, there were blackouts in Washington and air-raid wardens would come by, halting all smoking in the house and demanding "Lights out!" lest we lead the German bombers to their targets in the capital of the United States. At night, we could see the sky above Washington being scraped by giant searchlights, looking for signs of the Luftwaffe. My father thought it all nonsense. "Hell's bells," he used to say, "if the German bombers come, they'll follow the railroad tracks by the light of the moon, right into the city." But, like everyone else, we complied.

Even though I was only three when World War II began for the United States, and about to turn seven when it ended in 1945, the war made an indelible impact upon me and upon, I believe, the children who grew up in those same years.

Those formative years are among the most impressionable of one's life. Stamped forever upon my imagination in those glory days was that, in Uncle Peachie, we had a genuine "war hero" in the family; and our uncles were fighting and defeating the Germans. Every report from Europe and Asia was of victory and triumph for the United States. The great captains of that era, MacArthur, Eisenhower, and Patton, were always names to conjure with.

The first idea, then, that formed in my mind about America was of a glorious and militarily invincible Republic that "had never lost a war," that could conquer the world, if it wished, which it did not. We had been treacherously attacked; our cause was just; and our enemies were paying the awful price of imposing war on the United States. Between 1941 and 1945, that idea of America was stamped upon us for life; and it helps explain why my generation, which grew to manhood in the 1950s, was so different from the generation that followed.

Patriotism, an innate love of country, is natural to all men; ours was powerfully and constantly reinforced by every outside image from the time we knew anything until we reached what the Sisters of the Holy Cross would call the "age of reason," seven years old, the age at which we could think for ourselves.

Americans who had grown up in the late 1920s and early 1930s had memories of a time when the United States was denounced at home and abroad as an unjust and failed society, a country that exploited the poor and sided with the exploiters. We had no such memories. The 1960s were thus more of a shock to us than to them.

Before Pearl Harbor, my father's sympathies had been with the isolationists, with Charles Lindbergh and the America First committee. "I was all for 'em," Pop told me.

Sending millions of American boys to fight and die in Europe a second time, to pull Britain's chestnuts out of the fire, was something he could not accept. A popular sentiment, "Let Hitler and Stalin fight it out," would have summed up his attitude in the late 1930s. After Pearl Harbor, however, and Hitler's insane declaration of war on the United States, isolationism ended, forever.

While my father had been an Al Smith Democrat and thought FDR a "great" president in his first term, like the Jim Farleys and Al Smiths and Ray Moleys, he was turning against FDR, even before Roosevelt made his 1937 attempt to pack the Supreme Court. When FDR went for a third term, my father was not a Republican; but, like millions of conservative Catholics, he had become a disaffected Democrat. He had also settled by then on who was the greatest columnist writing in America; and it was not Walter Lippmann. The ex–sports writer, Westbrook Pegler, blistered FDR and Eleanor with a venomous wit and acid pen my father cherished.

When I was nine or ten, he would take me downtown to his office on Saturdays during "tax season," which ended March 15, sit me down, and pull out of his desk the best offerings of Pegler and George Sokolsky, the one-two punch of Colonel McCormick and Cissy Patterson's *Washington Times-Herald*, and say, "Read these, and tell me what you think." Even at nine, one did not need to read Pegler twice to get the point.

Pegler could string words together in a brighter, wittier way than any American of his time, and, as pure writer, he had no peer. He had once written of the fur-clad Yale football partisans at an Ivy League game one afternoon that they "rose as one raccoon." He displayed a gift for invective few Americans have ever matched.

In Pegler's prose, FDR, with whom the columnist broke after 1938, was Old Moosejaw, and Eleanor was La Boca Grande — for all the speeches she delivered. The seedy deal by which Huey Long escaped federal justice in return for delivering his state was the "Second Louisiana Purchase." Of FDR's Interior Secretary, Harold Ickes, Pegler wrote, "That Ickes is for me and I can take him anytime." Having caught Ickes freeloading during the war at the new Bethesda Naval Medical Center, Pegler cut loose: "Hey, Ickes, you penny-ante moocher, tell us about the two times you put yourself up in the Naval Hospital in Washington for $3 a day, all contrary to law and you a rich guy able to pay your way at the regular hospitals as all the sick civilians have to do. . . . Why, you cheap sponger, you couldn't rent a hall-room in a pitcher-and-bowl flea bag for three bucks a day. You know who paid for the over-head for your hospital bargain, don't you? Well, I did. And George Spelvin did. We paid it."

One wonders how our Lords Temporal would today react to such as Mr. Westbrook Pegler.

When Harry Truman came into the presidency, Pegler welcomed him. "We grow good people in our small towns, with honesty, sincerity and dignity," he wrote; but earlier, Pegler had told his readers the man from Missouri was someone to watch out for. "This Truman," Pegler wrote, when Harry was nominated for vice president, "is thin-lipped, a hater, and not above offering you his hand to yank you off balance and work you over with a chair leg, a pool cue or something out of his pocket."

Peg did go overboard — on not a few occasions. When the ex–First Lady falsely suggested that Pegler was bitter with her late husband because he hadn't been given a plush Washington job in the New Deal, Pegler used snake venom to describe a visit to Hyde Park where he had witnessed Eleanor taking her daily turn in the pool: "She used to hop off that board up at her swimming pool, let out that nerve-wracking whoop, take off above the horizon and come down with the splash of that poor horse that goes off the thing at Atlantic City."

It was at Whitehaven Parkway in 1942 that my father's father came to visit for the last time. Near sixty-five, he was a different man from the handsome forty-year-old T-man who had cut up the lumberjack his first day in Milwaukee. He had suffered a stroke; his red hair had gone white; but the old ways had not changed. One day, he slipped away from the house and was found by Uncle Bull in one of the bars on Wisconsin Avenue. "Mrs. Helms," as my father called his father's second wife, blamed Mom for grandfather's escape. Several months later, my father went out to Milwaukee for his last visit. "He was out of his mind," my father told me later; "his head was rolling from side to side in the bed; he didn't even recognize me."

Henry Martin Buchanan died in the veterans hospital in Milwaukee and was buried in Arlington beside his comrades from the Spanish-American War. "He had everything," Pop told me; "he was an expert in the new tax law when no one else knew it; he was smart and handsome and tough; and he blew it all." Henry M. Buchanan died apparently never really knowing how much he was revered by — nor how deeply he had disappointed — his eldest son.

Early in 1943, my father and mother got another shock: The owner of the house on Whitehaven Parkway sold it out from under us. With no housing being built in Washington, and the existing housing occupied by the burgeoning wartime bureaucracy, my parents and their four sons, aged six, five, four, and two, were about to be put out on the street.

Hearing about a house in the far northwest section of the city being vacated by an army officer and his family, my father packed me, the talkative one, into his red Dodge; together, the two of us drove out Wisconsin Avenue, along the streetcar tracks past McLean Gardens, just then being built, to Western Avenue and over to Chevy Chase. I still vividly remember the trip. The house was on Chestnut, the last street off Western before entering Rock Creek Park. To the north was woods; to the west was Maryland farmland. Even the D.C. bus line did not extend as far as Chestnut, stopping at Pinehurst Circle, half a mile away. Listed at $16,000, the house was everything we had been looking for; we drove home full of excitement.

Borrowing $5,000 from James A. Councilor & Co., my father made a down payment; and the Buchanan family had the first home of our own.

During the years we lived at 3250 Chestnut Street, from 1943 to 1951, the next four children were born: Kathleen Theresa, or "Coo," on April 27, 1944; John Edward (Jack) on Christmas Eve, 1947; Angela Marie (Bay) on December 20, 1948; and Brian Damien (Buck) on July 8, 1950. (While Bill was named after my father, and Hank and Jack after our grandfathers, the names of canonized saints were used for the rest of us.)

It was an idyllic neighborhood in which to grow up; there were dozens of children ranging in ages from toddler to high school. While the Catholic families were large (the Beattys, who lived next door, had six children; and the Lillys, who lived behind us on Beech Street, eventually had ten), it was a Protestant (or non-Catholic) neighborhood, where most of the children went to Lafayette until the seventh grade, then to Alice Deal Junior High and Woodrow Wilson High School near Tenley Circle.

Today, the view of that house on Chestnut is blocked by the massive trunks of two giant maples; they were sticks when we helped my father plant them. Before the postwar building boom, the land behind Chestnut Street was woods and thicket and brush. Here, the older boys in the neighborhood set up a mock boot camp, with themselves as colonels and captains, and the smaller and younger among us as enlisted personnel. We would spend days clearing brush and digging and fortifying foxholes. For training exercises, the "officers" tied string between a series of pegs about eighteen inches high, and, as we younger recruits crawled beneath, the older boys threw stones and clay and dirt at us. When one of us was hit too hard and started crying, we were sharply reminded that all American soldiers were taught to crawl on their bellies in boot camp, while live machine-gun fire poured over their heads.

From our back porch, a hundred yards away, my father viewed the little encampment — with a score of shirtless kids in World War I helmets digging foxholes — and said it was indistinguishable from the real thing.

The Japanese were the preferred enemy. We hated "the Japs."

"Remember Pearl Harbor" was the battle cry to which we practiced our bayonet charges. We had all heard of the Bataan Death March; and our comic books depicted the Japanese as yellow, bucktoothed molesters of women who routinely bayoneted wounded American soldiers and Marines.

Once, during the war, my father drove us at night down to East Potomac Park, to look at captured war matériel. It was all Japanese: swords and bayonets and flags and rifles and canteens, and a Japanese Zero of the make and model used in the attack at Pearl Harbor.

Radio reports, newspapers, newsreels, stories of family, neighbors, and friends, all spoke of the heroism of American victories, the justice of America's cause, and the barbarity of America's enemies. That was the message drummed home; and it took.

Being young, we forgot our childish hatred after the war; but for many Americans — closer to the horrors than Chestnut Street — the savagery of the Greater East Asia Co-Prosperity Sphere would never be forgotten.

In 1973, my father-in-law, Dr. Herman Scarney, an ophthalmologist and retired admiral, was on his deathbed. Hospitalized with melanoma that had spread to his pancreas, he was rapidly wasting away. I tried to make conversation with him by telling him the great news: The American POWs were coming home from Hanoi to Clark Field. In great pain, he lifted himself up, looked at me, and said, "We bombed the hell out of Clark Field!"

A forty-three-year-old flight surgeon on the aircraft carrier *Cabot*, "The Iron Woman," whose exploits Ernie Pyle had witnessed and written about, Commander Scarney had watched the young pilots take off, many never to return, and had been awarded the Bronze Star for heroic service in tending the burned and wounded when the kamikazes struck the *Cabot* during operations off the Philippine Islands in November 1944. He never forgave the Japanese. When my wife took him to the special visitors section on the south lawn of the White House — to watch the Japanese Prime Minister be greeted by President Nixon — he was shocked into silence to see the blazing sun of the Japanese flag fluttering side by side with the Stars and Stripes. When the ceremony closed, he spoke of nothing else.

Not until the 1986 Economic Summit in Tokyo did I ever visit Japan. Each morning, however, at the magnificent Ohira Hotel,

when I came down for coffee and eggs in the nearly empty breakfast room, I was greeted by a pretty Japanese waitress of no more
than eighteen. Daily practicing her English on me while I dawdled
at the table reading my news summaries, she would suddenly appear and say in her singsong English something like, "Take your
time, prease." Then, she would put her hand over her mouth,
giggle, and disappear. The thought washed over me: On the night
of March 9, 1945, when I was a boy, hating the "Japs" and cheering the Americans on, 334 B-29s under the command of General
Curtis LeMay appeared low in the skies over this very place, unloaded their incendiary bombs, and burned to death eighty-three
thousand old men, women, and children just like this little girl. My
father and the Jesuits, who taught me about Saint Augustine's
requirements for conducting a "just war," and the proscription
against the direct and wanton killing of innocent civilians, were
right. No matter the barbarity, the savagery of the Japanese empire, no matter the justice of America's cause, we had no moral
right to kill like that.

Our encampment back of Chestnut Street was an allied effort;
we even had a Russian on maneuvers: Roland, whose father was an
American diplomat and whose family had gotten out on one of the
last trains to the East and Vladivostok before Moscow came within
range of Hitler's bombers. Half-American, Roland was open, engaging, and energetic, although he had a terrible time with the
English language; when stymied, he literally sprayed it in your
face. His mother and older half brother, George, however, bore the
emotional and psychological scars of having lived in Stalin's Russia
in the 1930s. In a neighborhood where doors were unlocked and
often open, where there were no fences, Roland's mother had a
chain-link fence erected around their property, and two huge dogs,
bearing the Russian names of Arturo and Kozbek, guarded the
house. Whenever we visited and Roland was out, we rang and rang
with no answer, until eventually Roland's mother would peer cautiously around the curtain in one of the first-floor windows. (Roland's father never lived there.) Inside, the dogs were always
sniffing a few feet away, and one had the impression that if Stalin's
NKVD came after Roland's mother and George, Arturo and Kozbek would give a fine account of themselves. It is inaccurate to say
George "walked" those dogs; when the threesome came down

Chestnut Street in the evenings, Arturo and Kozbek, straining mightily at their leashes, were walking George.

One mistake the dogs did make, however, was Kozbek's attempt on the life of Brer Cat, our family pet. When Kozbek broke away from George and charged into the bushes in front of our house after Brer Cat, he pulled back a slashed and bleeding snout. Neither before nor since have I known a smarter or tougher cat. Steel-gray and white, he would sit sleepily on the front porch in his sphinx position, until a patroling dog sighted him from the street. As the curious canine tiptoed into the yard and approached the porch, Brer Cat would wait motionless, eyes closed. Then, as the dog barked up its confidence and put its first paw on the front porch, Brer Cat proved himself alive and well . . . all over the dog's face.

Late one night, while reading, my father heard a prowler jiggling the lock on the front door. He moved quietly into the hall, poker in hand, ready to bring it down on the skull of the intruder. The jiggling continued. Yanking the door open and raising the iron poker over his head, he looked out and saw no one. Beneath him, Brer Cat walked in from his midnight prowl and headed up the stairs to rack for the night.

While the neighborhood dogs never caught up with Brer Cat, the pack did usually settle with the other cats we owned, including the family favorite, Fancy Dan. Friendly, responsive as a puppy, Fancy Dan got caught out in the yard by two roaming neighborhood dogs, who gave him a horrible mauling. When we found Fancy Dan, he had been left for dead, and his wounds were open to the bone. We put him in the furnace room, to give him a warm place to die. Then, my mother spotted on a basement shelf some of the same sulfa drug that had been poured into my father's ankle infection when he was a boy. Pop poured the sulfa directly into Fancy Dan's wounds. The cat never cried; and he came back full of life, only to fall victim to another pack of mutts.

Those years bred in me a lifelong affection for those friendly but tough and independent little beasts to whom nature was so red in tooth and claw. When D.C. and Maryland finally passed their leash laws, I applauded one of the truly progressive reforms government has lately managed.

While my mother was always the one to keep peace in the house, Pop encouraged sibling rivalry.

When Kathleen, his first daughter, arrived in 1944, she quickly displaced the four boys as the altarpiece of her father's attention. Pop had never had a sister; for eight years, he had wanted a daughter; now he had one. The four Buchanan boys were suddenly superseded by my sister Kathleen. Sensing our resentment, Pop would tease us constantly, saying, "When this little girl grows up, boys, she's going to marry a great big tackle from Notre Dame who will come around and beat the hell out of every one of you." This was a mistake.

Lying awake in our twin bunk beds in our single room, the four of us nursed our grievances against the Autocrat and his new Infanta. Kathleen had a room all her own.

One evening, when the parents went out, I had Cricket go into Kathleen's room and tell her that "Dr. O'Brien," the family physician, had called and would be dropping by — to give her a "booster shot." She was terrified. Removing my father's hat and overcoat from the closet and putting them on, I slipped outside, rang the doorbell, had Cricket admit me, and started stomping ominously up the stairs. With the hat almost covering my face, I suddenly appeared in her doorway, a large butcher knife held aloft.

I thought an air-raid siren had suddenly gone off. You could hear her a block away. Only by ditching the disguise, reassuring her, and raiding the big cookie jar in the kitchen, did we calm her down and bribe her not to turn state's evidence.

My father's favorite bedtime reading for us, besides Robert Louis Stevenson's *Treasure Island*, were Joel Chandler Harris's books featuring Uncle Remus's tales of Brer Rabbit, Brer Fox, and Brer Bar. Pop laughed at the tales of Uncle Remus louder than we did. And he designated me Brer Rabbit, the small and clever one who always outwitted the other two; Bill was Brer Fox, and Hank was Brer Bar, the dumb and explosive one forever warning Brer Fox, "I'm gonna take this club and knock yoah head clean off." My older brothers smoldered with resentment over the Brer Rabbit designation, and for years I padded around softly, an early detentist, trying to keep out of Hank's way.

While the bonds of affection between father and sons were growing, so were the natural tensions. On my father's fortieth birthday, which was not only the Feast of the Assumption, but V-J Day in 1945, we four boys got Pop our first joint birthday present, a huge shiny apple Mom had purchased at the Safeway with our earned pennies. When we handed the box to him, Pop opened it with anticipation, and broke out laughing. On the apple was a piece of adhesive tape holding the penned inscription: "Happy Birthday — to One Tough Apple."

Mom had had a hand in thinking it up; and Pop thought it a great gift.

Most nights in our room, we four boys would listen to the radio until 9:30 or 10 — to Mr. Keen, "Tracer of Lost Persons," "The Shadow," "The Aldrich Family," "The Great Gildersleeve," Fanny Brice as Baby Snooks, "This Is Your FBI," and "Mystery Theater." In the afternoons, it was Jack Armstrong, "the All-American Boy," and on Saturdays, "Let's Pretend." We were the last pretelevision generation.

When the programs ended, we invented our own games, like "Begin With," where one of us would think of a subject, give the first letter, and then answer yes or no to questions, until someone guessed what was in our mind. For hours, we played "Begin With," muttered against baby sister, and laughed into the night, until the final ultimatum, "Last warning, boys!" When that ultimatum was ignored, we could hear Pop storming up the stairs two at a time; within seconds, he would be in our bedroom, pulling his belt off, and flailing away as we hid tensely under the covers. Most of the time he went for the top bunks, where Bill and Hank slept. When he was through swinging the belt, he would yell, "Now dammit, keep it down!" and "Go to sleep!" Seconds after he departed, the laughter and low whispers would start up again. Had there been any casualties?

The only defensive system we developed was to balance a pile of books between the top of the doorframe and the open door. If my father didn't see the booby trap as he charged in, the books would fall on his head and slow him down. While it worked with him once or twice, that load of books dropped in their tracks more than one of the fourteen-year-old baby-sitters the parents would hire for twenty-five cents an hour when they went out to play bridge.

For a child to have a room of his own may be ideal, but I would not trade those eight years in that same room with my three brothers for the Lincoln Bedroom. They cemented bonds of affection that have lasted all our lives.

Only rarely did we see our sports heroes live in those years —

like Johnny Lujack of Notre Dame. We heard of their exploits, read about them, and saw photographs of them — but the rest was left to the imagination. And the imagination can improve on reality. When television came, it could never match the technicolor pictures each of us had dreamed up separately in his own mind. Never, for example, have I been so gripped and paralyzed with fear as when listening in dead silence one night to "Mystery Theater," where two young couples, lost in some Western cave, suddenly realized the creatures clawing at them had to be blind descendants of the Forty-niners, who had been sealed up in that same cave a century before, on their way to the California Gold Rush. When, after a half hour of terror, the couple dropped down a hole in that cave into a stream that carried them out into the sunlight, I was never so relieved in my life. For years, I had nightmares about that program; and never have I gone into a cave.

Only on occasions would the parents go out; their evening entertainment was reading the mysteries of Erle Stanley Gardner, and playing bridge. On Sundays, we would drive out to the Edgemoor Club in Bethesda, where Pop would play tennis, while Mom took us swimming. After Pop came off the court and showered, he and my mother would play bridge for hours, while we sat around, bored to distraction. Fed up with the waiting one Sunday afternoon, I walked behind Pop at a critical moment in his bridge game, looked into his hand, and said, "Say, Pop, isn't that Big Casino?" Pop threw down his hand with the ten of diamonds, stared into the distance for a few seconds, then got up; and we were on the way home.

While my mother and father took fistfights as part of growing up, both were intolerant of bad manners. Manners were the mark of a gentleman, a mark of good breeding; rudeness toward elders, and especially women, was unpardonable. Almost as soon as we could pray, we were instructed in the proper way to handle a knife and fork, and in how to answer our elders and superiors. It was always "Yes, ma'am" and "No, ma'am" to anything my mother said, or to what any woman said, and "Yes, sir," always, to our father. With the determination of a drill sergeant, he hammered the lesson home. And it took. While my parents might get complaints on their boys' behavior with other children, they would get only compliments on how polite we were to nuns, parents, priests. How deeply the habit was ingrained came home to me a quarter of a century later.

Hank, who had been the accountant for CREEP, Richard Nixon's now infamous 1972 Committee to Re-elect the President, was suing CBS and Walter Cronkite for malicious libel. Cronkite had led his "Evening News," during the thick of the Watergate revelations, with the charge that Henry Buchanan, brother to White House aide Patrick Buchanan, had been operating a "laundry" in Bethesda for cleaning dirty money. The charge was utterly baseless; CBS had been worse than sloppy; and Hank intended to prove it in court.

At the Radio-TV Correspondents Dinner that year, as I was chatting away, I turned to have a friend introduce me, face to face, to the Most Trusted Man in America, the man I believed had libeled my brother. Cronkite extended his hand, smiled, and said graciously, "Hello, Pat, how are you?" Instead of some witty and cutting riposte, I responded, "Fine, *Mr.* Cronkite; how are you, *sir?*"

The rest of the night, I was beside myself for giving the appearance of having truckled. Both the "Mr." and the "sir" had come out automatically, reflexively, because Walter Cronkite was an older man, and because of those years of indoctrination.

Most of our summer days on Chestnut Street were spent at Rollingwood, or Rock Creek Playground, as it was called. Because Chestnut Street was inside the District line, we were ineligible for the Maryland parks program; but the camp counselors looked the other way.

For years, Mom would pack us each a lunch, give us a nickel for a Coke, and we were on our way, walking or by bike, down to Rollingwood for the entire day. Every summer, we played on the Rock Creek softball and hardball teams, and in their Ping-Pong and tennis tournaments. In 1951, following in the Old Man's footsteps, Cricket and I won the Montgomery County twelve-and-under doubles' championship on the clay courts at Montgomery Blair in Silver Spring; and I won the twelve-and-under table tennis championship for the entire county.

Montgomery County had a splendid program in those years, run by one or two professionals, who hired half a dozen camp counselors to coach us in everything from archery and horseshoes and high jumping to arts and crafts. However, one thing we learned down there that they didn't teach was atrocious language. Most of the kids at Rollingwood were from Bethesda's public schools; some were farmboys who used a vocabulary we had never heard. We picked up on it quickly, not having the least idea what these strange terms meant. At the dinner table one night, my father and mother were shocked into silence to hear their nine-year-old son, Hank, lately confirmed in the Faith, ask his eight-year-old brother, Pat, who had recently made his First Holy Communion, to "pass the pie, you little [expletive deleted]."

Rock Creek was the site of another of those indelible tragedies of childhood. One day we watched Bobby Wheeler climb a tree with a couple of friends near the clubhouse, and then fall onto the high tension wires. Burned horribly, he was not brought down until the rescue squad arrived. We thought he was dead. When he came back from the hospital weeks later, his burns were being repaired with skin grafts, but he had lost an arm.

During the war, we had crossed over, once or twice, on the Chesapeake Bay ferry, to vacation in Ocean City, Maryland, 150 miles east of Washington. With the long ferry wait, however, the trip could take eight or ten hours.

Almost every summer, during my father's three-week vacations, he took the family to the bay, to Chesapeake Beach or Scientist's Cliff, only a two-hour drive from Washington. It was a quiet, delightful place. We would swim in the bay — and go crabbing with my father, who would wait with his net for hours, at the opening of some inlet, for the tide to start moving slowly out and the big "blue channel" crabs to make their run for the open sea. We would catch them by the dozens; Mom would throw them alive and scrambling into a huge crab pot and steam them; and we would have a family feast. Past midnight, we would be sitting at an old wooden table, gabbing, and cracking and consuming by the dozens the steamed crabs and coleslaw. Since we were in our own cottage, and going directly to bed, my father would let the older boys have a glass of beer or two with the crabs. They were memorable occasions.

All my father's memories of the bay were good ones — except one.

The first day we arrived at Scientist's Cliff one summer, Hank and I borrowed a boat and decided to row it all the way to

Chesapeake Beach, a dozen miles to the north. When Bill trashed our project and refused to help, we kicked him out of the boat. Starting around two in the afternoon, we reached the channel south of Chesapeake Beach around six, turned around, and started back. While the bay had been smooth as glass on the trip north, on the trip home it got rougher and rougher. By dark, we were only half-way; when we reached the cliffs, we could see the surf pounding against them, riding up the face of the rock. If we got too close to the shore, and into the surf, we were done for. Not until almost ten at night did my father discover us, half a mile from home.

"I came down to the bay," he told me later, "and looked in every direction, and could see nothing for miles. It was the sickest feeling of my life." He walked back up to the cottage and thought of how he would have to explain to Mom, still back in Washington, how two of her older boys had drowned the night before. Finally, he had gone over to see Ralph Dwan, a neighbor from Blessed Sacrament parish; Ralph put his motorboat in the bay, and began the hour-long search. When we got home that night, my father didn't punish us, so elated was he to see us alive. He just stood in the kitchen, sipping whiskey, giving thanks he did not have to deliver that terrible message to Mom.

What killed the Chesapeake Bay as a vacation haven for bathers was the jellyfish; earlier and earlier, they began moving up into the bay, until, by the late 1940s, they saturated the beach areas by June. Once the jellyfish came in, we could not swim ten yards without being stung. Stung bad enough, we got chills and fever. When the Bay Bridge was built in the early 1950s, cutting to three hours the travel time to Ocean City, the bay was forgotten.

As Chestnut was one of the few streets in the city that extended through Rock Creek Park, it was busier than most, and harassing cross-town commuters became a popular diversion. Hank and I invented a game, the success at which hinged as much on acting ability as athletic skill. Taking an old golf ball, we would bounce it off a square brick section between two windows on the second floor of the house. While we pretended to be playing catch, the goal was to have the golf ball fly over our heads and strike a vehicle passing behind us in the street at thirty miles an hour — no simple feat.

When we succeeded, the car would stop and the outraged driver would come after us in the yard. Which was when the real test came. Rather than run, we would take the verbal abuse, and then politely point out how freakish an accident this had been — our playing catch, the ball going over our heads, hitting a passing car. We would apologize and ask the driver how we might make amends. By this time, however, the driver, usually tired and headed home from work, could see what a fool he was making of himself, berating these well-mannered boys for an accident not their fault. The driver would then begin apologizing for his behavior, his rash judgment, his accusations. We were astonished at how often an assumed posture of injured innocence on the part of a 4-foot, 6-inch kid could send a grown man into an examination of his conscience. Because we did not look guilty or act guilty, and because we apologized for an "accident," the confused driver suddenly disbelieved the evidence of his own eyes. The only time we were caught was when one suspicious driver, whose vehicle had been struck, kept on going around the block. Not recognizing his car, we nailed him a second time.

The game was canceled indefinitely, though, when, after a long wait for another car, the golf ball sailed through the new storm window and on through the bathroom window beyond, a thirty-five-dollar foul-up. As Mom, who was not fooled by our game, predicted, this was an offense punishable by the strap. The Classic Comics were in place when Pop got home.

Hassling motorists, however, was asking for trouble we could not always handle. One summer evening, half a dozen of us were standing idly in front of our house, flipping pebbles. When a convertible roared by, I stupidly flipped one in the direction of the car; it harmlessly bounced off. Three minutes later, however, the car had circled the block; and the driver, a tough, five-foot, two-inch creature of about seventeen, had decided to administer a beating to whoever had done it. I was eleven at the time and the smallest kid in the crowd. When he jumped out of his car and started interrogating us, I made my second mistake. Instead of keeping my mouth shut, the little kid who could "talk before he could walk" started into a Socratic dialogue. "How do you know anyone threw anything?" I asked. "How do you know the car itself didn't kick up a piece of gravel? What, exactly, was thrown?"

Confused, he seemed to be taking the point, but his rouged-up sweetheart was a better detective. She had listened silently to the exchange, and deduced the truth: "The little one here seems to be doing all the talking," she said, "I think he did it."

With that, she walked over and hit Brer Rabbit across the face as hard as she could with her open hand. Nobody said a word. Her blockhead of a boyfriend seemed satisfied, and he and his girlfriend drove away. Humiliation was total: a girl had just smacked me so hard I was seeing stars; everyone had seen it; no one had said or done anything. Unfortunately, at that age, I was inexperienced at stonewalling; later, we would learn. You never have to explain what you never said.

As school and Church in the 1940s prepared us for the coming struggles of mind and soul, my father was preparing us for other battles.

To Pop, fighting was a concomitant of man's existence; it was not something we would be able to avoid in life; every one of his sons must thus know how to fight. Indeed, he felt there were many occasions when a man had to fight.

Often, he told us the story of how, when courting my mother, she had taken ill one evening at the Wardman Park Hotel; as he walked her back to his car to take her home, a carload of drunken loudmouths began making crude remarks. "I didn't say a word," Pop said, "I just kept walking her to the car; she was white as a sheet. But when I put her inside the car to take her home, I told her to wait. Then, I crept carefully down the sidewalk, and when I got to their car, I ordered them all out. Startled, they began to lock the doors, roll up the windows, and start the car; so, I grabbed the door handle and tried to get in at them. As they pulled away, I tore the handle off the car door."

"They could probably have beaten me, if all of them had gotten out," Pop told me, "but I was about twenty-seven, playing tennis every day, and in good shape." The impression he left with me was that they would not have beaten him.

While he had learned how to defend himself without his own father's help, he would not neglect his paternal duty with us. Thus, after we moved to Chestnut Street, Pop hung a punching bag in the basement; and "hitting the bag" was not optional. When each of us turned seven, we had to hit that bag for four sessions a week — one hundred times with the left hand, one hundred with the right, two hundred with the "one-two." When we missed, we were punished.

Skipping rope was encouraged, but not required. You didn't need to dance around if you could whip your opponent quickly. My father also kept two pair of fourteen-ounce gloves in the basement, to teach us how to box, and in the prayerful hope one of his sons would be challenged to a neighborhood fight.

"Keep your left up!" was his constant command, as we boxed each other in the basement under his supervision. Although Mom, by the time she was twenty, had seen more wounds and bloodshed and suffering and dying at that inner-city hospital than the rest of us put together, she could not stand the sight of someone she loved being beaten. She had watched in anguish at ringside as her younger brother, Bill, had fought his way through college on a boxing scholarship, taking on the best that great boxing schools like Catholic University, Tennessee, and Villanova could put in the ring. But, while she had made my father promise never to make prizefighters out of her sons, she understood the need to know how to fight.

So, there was no dissent in the household, and week after week, month after month, we hit that bag, until we were proficient. Hank, however, was more than proficient. When he was nine years old, he could make that bag dance on its swivel like a professional fighter. To me, at eight, hitting the bag was an exercise in monotony.

My father's determination that we learn how to use our fists is evident from an episode he cherishes. He had come home from teaching accounting at Catholic University one night, and called each of us out into the hall. "How many times did you hit the bag this week?" he asked politely.

Having neglected our duty, each of us fibbed, suggesting that it may have been two or three times — "I can't exactly recall." One by one, we fell into the trap.

"None of you hit the bag this entire week!" he retorted, triumphantly whipping the bag out from behind his back. "Because I took it Monday morning to the sport shop and had it repaired!" It was entrapment, pure and simple, but 1947 was pre-Miranda, and lying was a worse offense than not punching the bag. We all got the belt that night.

But that training would pay off; and for my father and Hank, the jackpot came early. One summer's day, my father looked out the window and saw what he had been praying for: A kid two years older and twenty pounds heavier was chasing Hank up from Beech Street. Five minutes had not elapsed before my father had Hank and his pursuer in the basement, laced up in boxing gloves, circling each other and flailing away, while he acted as referee, calling out to Hank, "Keep your left up!"

The big kid had the height and weight and reach and was getting the better of it, until Hank hit him with an overhand right and snapped his head into the exposed iron girder in the middle of the basement. The kid's guard dropped, his knees sagged, and Hank was all over him. We went wild, cheering him on. With the kid almost out on his feet, the referee stepped in to stop the fight and declare the TKO.

Lesson learned. Even though Hank was naturally tougher and more aggressive than the rest of us, that training, that hitting the bag nightly, had enabled him to hammer and humiliate to tears a neighborhood pain-in-the-posterior, and become a young Jack Dempsey in his father's eyes. "Hammering Hank," my father called him.

Hank was Pop's golden boy. With blond hair, pale blue eyes, and fair skin, Hank was a naturally gifted athlete and student, who worked hard at both. The only one of us who wasn't "small for his age" growing up, Hank was Honor Roll, pious and devout in the Faith, an altar boy, popular with his teachers. When he made CYO quarterback in the seventh grade, he weighed less than one hundred pounds in a 130-pound league. Like the grandfather after whom he had been named, he took to fighting like a cat to cream; and he started as soon as he was out of the crib. Even on Whitehaven Parkway, Hank would never back down.

One afternoon, an angry woman from across the alley came to our back door with her battered son, demanding that my father punish the brute that had done it. "Would you like to see the brute?" Pop said politely; and proudly produced his five-year-old Viking. The lady looked down at Hank, who was half the size of her son, turned to her own son, and said, "You mean you let that little boy beat you up!" She then slapped her son across the head and chased him back across the alley.

Bill, my oldest brother, spent his childhood in Hank's shadow. (As did we all.) While my father worked with him constantly, to make a baseball pitcher out of him, Bill could never exceed Pop's expectations the way Hank routinely did in sports and I could always do in school. Small for his age until he reached college, Bill, whom we called Buchs (rhymes with dukes), was less aggressive as a boy, and more introspective. He made and kept only a few close friends. In one sad little episode, Bill sent valentines to every single girl in his classroom at Blessed Sacrament; he got not one back in return. Sometimes he was picked on by schoolyard bullies, who didn't want to mix it up with Hank. Once, when I was in sixth grade, I remember a crowd of eighth-graders marching up Quesada Street (cordoned off as a school playground), singing some mocking song they had made up about "Billy Boo," and the "toe plate" he wore on the right shoe of the baseball spikes my father had bought for him. While Bill would never "chicken out," he didn't pick fights.

Sometimes I felt sorry for my oldest brother, when he was having such a tough time growing up; but there wasn't much I could do about it. When he got into high school, he ran with our crowd, most of whom were a year or two younger than he, and he had a better time with us than he ever did with his contemporaries.

Eventually, he became the most disputatious brother in the family. Fully grown, Buchs could bring an argument to the shouting stage faster than any man I ever met. Because of his instant recoil to any wisecrack, I introduced him to my sister-in-law Carole Betterley's family in Springfield, Massachusetts, as "Chevy Chase's answer to the Springfield rifle."

Jim, or Cricket, as we always called the brother who followed me in age, and I got on famously. As children, we looked alike and, in a way, complemented each other. We were both lazy, but in different ways. While I enjoyed schoolwork and ducked yardwork, Crick earned plenty of money doing yardwork, but had almost a physical reaction to schoolwork. I read dozens of books as a boy, including twenty-six Hardy Boy adventures one summer, and enjoyed the world of the imagination; Crick dozed off so often during homework, we thought he had been bitten by a tsetse fly. He stammered and stuttered so badly we used to have to take him to Mom, who was the only one who could translate for him. Even after the war, "Jimmy Cricket" was still denouncing our enemies, "the Wermans and the Waps." While the rest of us brought home A's, Crick cruised along for years on a full tank of C's and D's.

Small and spindly like all the older brothers (except Hank) in boyhood, Cricket was the most relaxed. During infancy, he never cried; he just lay in his crib smiling. No problem at all. As with me, my mother finally had to pick him out of the playpen, put him on the floor, and give him a push on the diapers, or he, too, would never have learned to walk. A trusting soul, I used him like the Aberdeen Proving Ground, once feeding him some atropine I got out of our trash can (it had been for my eyes); after he drank it with no effect, I swallowed the rest. Mom had to dump coffee down the two of us half the night, lest the poison put us to sleep permanently. Crick rarely got into school or neighborhood fights, and seemed to get along with everybody.

While I would feel constricted by the demands of the Book-of-the-Month Club, Crick was a "joiner." He and his friend, Mike Boyd, formed the Thunder Riders in the neighborhood; he signed up for Boy Scouts at school; he formed "the Hawks," his gang in high school; he was president of his fraternity at Saint Francis of Loretto, in Pennsylvania.

Generous to a fault, one summer he spent every nickel he earned buying Good Humors — for both of us. (When I was making excellent money working for Richard M. Nixon, Esquire, in New York in 1966 and 1967, $12,000, then $15,000 a year, and Crick was living at home, going to dental school, and still, at twenty-five, getting date money out of Mom's purse, I was able to reciprocate for the Good Humors.)

Aside from that boyhood aversion to books, Crick was the most balanced and well adjusted of the older boys. The girls he dated (and the woman he married) were knockouts. Love the world, and the world loves you back.

If Hank was the athlete on whom Pop bragged, I was his scholar. One summer night, Pop was sitting out on the screened-in back porch of Chestnut Street with Dave Keppel, a friend who coached basketball at Roosevelt High, explaining how clever Pat was. When Mr. Keppel bet Pop he could immediately stump me in a simple spelling quiz, Pop put down his beer, hustled upstairs, woke me up, and brought me down in my bathrobe onto the porch.

"Pat, Mr. Keppel is going to give you some words to spell," Pop said; "now, I want you to take your time."

Mr. Keppel started reeling them off — *bat, cat, hat, rat,* etc.

I knew what was coming. When he used the word for flea that rhymed with cat, I ripped off without hesitation, "g-n-a-t." Keppel was astonished; even my father, who didn't know how to spell *gnat,* was surprised. "No one has ever gotten that right at Roosevelt," Mr. Keppel said. Reaching into his pocket, he handed me a fifty-cent piece, which is like five dollars today, and I walked out and went back to bed. Pop was beaming.

Two months before, *gnat* had sunk me in a school spelling bee.

But Pop was right about the Hobbesian world in which we were growing up. Driven the mile and a half to Blessed Sacrament school each weekday by my father, who would give the car to Mom and catch the L-4 bus at Chevy Chase Circle to his office downtown, we had to walk home. Unless Hank, who loved to hand me his books and fight, was along, Western Avenue could be a Via Dolorosa. Many of the kids had grown up cocky and mean while their fathers had been off fighting World War II; and even some of our patrol boys were bullies.

One of them, three years older than I, once stopped me three days in a row, to knock all my books out of my arms, before I got across Rittenhouse Street. I started to dread walking home. Not knowing how long this pastime was going to continue, I went to one of the best and toughest kids in the school, Jimmy Fegan, who had befriended the Buchanan boys, even though he was five or six years older than I. Quietly, I explained what was being done to me; Fegan walked me down to Rittenhouse Street, found my tormentor, dragged him by his patrol boy belt around the street for a minute, and told him if he didn't leave me alone, the next get-together would not be friendly.

Early in life, I learned the importance of good friends and the difference between being tough and being mean. That patrol boy was mean, and Jimmy Fegan was truly tough. In politics, the same distinction exists.

In grammar school, I did not enjoy fighting. I had had four surgeries before I was seven; I wore glasses for weak eyesight; I was small for my age, and while well coordinated and a good athlete, I knew I was never going to be a great one.

But Pop was right. Sometimes you have to fight, even if all you want is to be left alone. Once, in the first grade, when I had been bullied repeatedly on the playground by a fat, bespectacled kid, I turned and hit him in the face with everything I had, bloodying his nose, smashing his glasses on the asphalt, and leaving him crying. The nun who had seen the encounter was appalled (she had not seen what went before) and said she was going to call my parents. Which didn't bother me in the least; I knew Pop would be elated, which he was, and Mom would have no complaints. Brer Rabbit was taking after Brer Bar.

From before the war until 1947, the only car the family owned was an old red Dodge. No new cars were built during the war. Even had they been, we could not have afforded one, with the $5,000 my father owed his firm for the down payment on the Chestnut Street house, the $11,000 mortgage, and the five children. But we needed that Dodge, not only for shopping and doctor's appointments for the kids, but for Pop to get out to Catholic University in far northeast Washington, where he taught during the summer, and back over to Georgetown, where he was still working on his B.A. degree.

Gasoline was strictly rationed during the war; and the only way we managed to keep a full tank was to trade the excess meat rations we got for the five children for other families' excess gasoline stamps.

With the war's end, however, and the Mitchell-Buchanan takeover of James A. Councilor & Co., economic pressure eased. By 1947, my father was in the market for a new Oldsmobile that could take the family up the hills of Western Pennsylvania to my grandparents' home in Charleroi.

When he went to Capitol Cadillac-Oldsmobile, a client and friend, the manager Ken Moore, counseled my father not to buy the six-cylinder Olds, but the new eight-cylinder job; with all his luggage and kids, Pop would need the extra power. How much, Pop asked, for the eight-cylinder Olds? Twenty-four hundred, came the reply. And how much is that Cadillac over there? Twenty-eight hundred.

The new, blue, four-door Cadillac sedan my father wheeled home that night was the sensation of the neighborhood. No one else on Chestnut Street had ever owned one. One neighbor came up to the door to ask, "Say, Bill, isn't that a Cadillac?"

We had arrived. Even though we had a garage off Chestnut Street, every night we left that magnificent machine out in front of the house.

With its mighty V-eight engine and "hydromatic drive," the Cadillac was the sleekest, fastest, most powerful car on the road.

When we roared up the Pennsylvania Turnpike to Charleroi, even with five or six kids in the car, we swept past trucks, cars, everything on the road — with us looking out the window, waving at the poor folks my father sped past at eighty miles an hour.

For seven years, we kept that car; by the time Pop turned it in, Hank and Bill and I had learned to drive on it. It should have been retired by the parish, so many miles did my father and mother log on it, with the trunk open, loaded up with a Blessed Sacrament baseball or football team.

As there were soon four, then five, of us in school, requiring breakfast each morning and a lunch packed before 8:30 — plus two, then three, smaller children at home, Pop hired Anna Rose, a black maid, who lived with us for years in a curtained-off section of the unfinished basement.

To say Anna Rose was a hot-tempered and militant lady would be understatement. Had she been young in the early 1960s instead of the 1930s, Anna Rose would have been in the forefront of the civil-rights movement. She was fearless, black, and proud; and she brooked nonsense from no one. The first inkling I ever had that a race "issue" even existed, I got from Anna Rose, when I saw her grab the black rag doll my sister Kathleen had been given and which we innocently called "The Pickaninny." She hurled it across the room against a wall, yelling, "Get that damn thing out of here!"

A hard worker who took good care of the Buchanan children and infants, Anna Rose had little use for the neighborhood kids, and they were frightened to death of her, especially Roland, whom she had chased across three yards with a broom. One afternoon, when we went upstairs to change, and Roland nervously agreed to wait for us in the den, we suggested he hide in the closet, as Anna Rose was in a particularly foul mood that day — and the sight of our Russian friend might just set her off. Unfortunately, we forgot Roland, who remained closeted for more than an hour, while we were down on Beech Street and my mother and a neighbor chatted in the den. Finally, when Roland could stand it no longer, he wordlessly emerged from the closet. My mother pressed him on exactly what he had been doing, hiding there eavesdropping, while she had been conversing with friends. Roland was certain we left him in there deliberately.

As at our "boot camp," a neighborhood hierarchy existed, based on age and ability. Charles, four or five years older than I, was the natural leader. He invented countless versions of "war," and assigned us all to opposing armies.

One war involved our carving pistols and rifles out of wood, and attaching a clothespin to the handle — with tape or rubber bands — to shoot stretched pieces of inner tube at one another. Another utilized bows and arrows — saplings in the park for the bow, waxing a length of cord for the string, with whittled willow branches for arrows.

Before bubble gum and the famous baseball cards, everybody collected playing cards — dogs and ships and "scenes" being the quality cards — and traded them at daily bazaars in the schoolyard and the neighborhood. Sports pictures were also collected, especially the color paintings and photos of baseball greats like Bob Feller that accompanied articles in *Sport* magazine. Three or four full-page color photos usually came with each issue, which cost a quarter, a considerable sum. To build up our collections, we used to hitchhike downtown to the old Loudermilk Bookstore and buy, for nickels, scores of back issues of *Sport*.

Roland, who had a regular allowance from his absent father, had a collection to rival the National Portrait Gallery. Unfortunately, all his color photos were kept in a manila envelope, which — their having gotten damp — Roland placed inside his mother's oven. The priceless collection was destroyed in the conflagration. Roland was reduced to begging for replacement pictures from those of us who had been beneficiaries of his philanthropy.

Besides the sedentary entertainments, there were more active ones. During summer nights we would roam in packs, not unlike the neighborhood dogs in those days; and thanks to Roland's resources, we had a variation on the children's game of ringing doorbells.

Either Roland had purchased or his father had sent him a remarkable weapon after the war. It was a toy cannon. With a barrel some three inches in diameter and two feet in length, however, it looked less like a toy than like a giant sawed-off shotgun, or a tiny bazooka. While the cannon did not fire a projectile, it did emit — when packed with gunpowder — a tremendous roar, and a flame would leap three feet out of the muzzle. The heavy steel weapon was fired by cradling it in your left arm, holding it against your stomach, and, with the right fist, hammering down a little plunger on top of the cannon, which struck the flint and ignited the gunpowder. With Roland's Russian artillery and our American derring-do, the alliance was launched.

We would travel out of our own neighborhood, across the creek, and up into the neighborhood where "Albert's Gang" ruled, or across Western into the new housing rising from the Maryland farmland. Then, we would station Roland with his cannon at the end of a walk — it took a cautious ten minutes to load the artillery piece — and ring the doorbell.

When the door opened, the man of the house would see a tiny platoon assembled at the end of his walk and would start shouting at us for ringing his doorbell. At which point, Roland would bring his fist down smartly on the plunger, and the cannon would fire — with an explosive roar that could be heard a quarter mile away. It was a simulated bazooka attack; only the man at the door had no idea it was all fireworks, that there was nothing behind the flames leaping out of the barrel pointed directly at him from forty feet away. When the cannon misfired, we would take off, while resolute Roland stood there, hammering his fist frenetically on the little plunger, until our heroic Russian ally himself broke and ran.

Once, when we had it loaded and ready, and Roland was hauling the artillery between houses, "Evil Eye," a man on Winnett Street who always seemed to spot us as we passed through his neighborhood, suddenly threw open his window. "What the hell are you kids doing out there at this time of night?"

With a single sweeping motion, like a gunfighter drawing his six-shooter, spinning, and firing, Roland wheeled his cannon toward the open window five feet above him, and hit the plunger. The explosion was tremendous. Evil Eye disappeared; we didn't stop running for half a mile.

Unfortunately, one of the neighbors recognized us and called my mother, who called my father, who was visiting Grandmother downtown. When he got home, there was hell to pay. The great Roland cannon was decommissioned.

Unlike most of his sons, save perhaps Crick and Buck, my father was good with his hands.

Soon after we had moved to Chestnut Street, the entire attic was given over to his Lionel trains; they were his hobby, his diversion, his relaxation during the winter months, while Mom read the mysteries and novels, worked the crossword puzzles, and helped us with our homework. The Lionel passenger cars were steel and had been bought, but the freight cars were all of wood, and Pop had carved, built, and painted most of them himself, and put on all the decals. The carpentry was professional, as was all the electrical work; and the elaborate system of twin transformers, switches, decoupling areas, and side tracks enabled us, after several months of supervised training, to run two and sometimes three trains at once over a hundred feet of track. We even had an operating drawbridge.

Often, when he answered want ads from folks selling their trains, Pop would take me along. One day, as we were inspecting yet another new engine (we already had four of them), the head of the household looked down indulgently at me, and said, "Little boy, would you like me to show you how to work these switches?"

I looked up at Pop and he looked at me, and we both broke out laughing. Here we were, operating Union Station in our attic, and this guy wanted to show me how to throw a switch!

But the pride of Pop's railroad empire — most of the engines and track had been purchased early in the war for $60 — was the big fourteen-wheeler known to Lionel devotees as the Hudson Engine. The Hudson was at the heart of a story my brothers yet contend was most revelatory of my developing character.

A magnificent piece of machinery, the engine and its coal car must have been almost two feet long and weighed ten pounds; once, we harnessed it to every car my father had bought or built, freight and passenger, coal car and caboose. The mighty Hudson strained and strained, and slowly the procession began to move. Around and around that track the length and width of our house, the mighty Hudson pulled that train.

When he was reconfiguring the tracks in the attic, my father would keep his prized engine deep in the hat shelf in the closet in the den. Along with Cricket, I decided to take down the great Hudson engine for a personal inspection. We marveled at it, carefully put it back in its distinctive Lionel box, and, standing on a chair, I hoisted it onto the hat shelf. Suddenly, the heavy engine fell back, through the box, and crashed onto the floor — snapping off the iron "cow-catcher." My heart sank. To have broken Pop's

Hudson engine, while illicitly inspecting it, was close to a killing offense. Cricket, too, knew the gravity of the crime; so, we swore a pact of silence.

Weeks elapsed before my father went to get his precious engine. When he opened the box and the cow-catcher fell out, he was stunned, and determined to find out who did it. Hank and Bill had not gone near it; so he confronted me, and — like Saint Peter in the courtyard of Caiphas the High Priest — I thrice denied having played with the Hudson engine.

However, to be helpful, I suggested that I *might* have seen Cricket handling the Hudson one day in the den. With this excellent lead, my father confronted Cricket, who started stuttering at his most incoherent. He never got beyond, "Ay-ay-ay-ay-ay-ay-ay." His panic betraying his guilt, he took a terrific beating.

For years, I felt rotten about it.

On August 15, 1986, at my father's eighty-first birthday party, the family presented Pop, in its original Lionel box, a fifty-year-old Hudson engine. A collector's item in mint condition, it had cost $1,200 and the whole family had chipped in. Retired now, the mighty Hudson sits displayed in a glass case on a shelf in my parents' den.

As a boy during the summers, Pop had worked on the Arlington Experimental Farms, and every year, while Mom hung out the wash, he would spend Saturday afternoon working on his tomato plants, with the voice of Arch McDonald broadcasting the Senators' baseball game from the radio on the screened-in back porch. At summer's end, Mom would boil Mason jars and we would help her can the tomatoes in airtight containers, and shelve them in the basement. We ate from those jars all fall and winter. And therein lies a story.

Like us, Roland was chauvinistic; not only about his homeland, but about his family. After we explained to him that my father was unexcelled at growing tomatoes, Roland said his older half brother, George, would challenge my father to compete as to who could produce the tallest plants and biggest tomatoes. For George, a novice at gardening, it was a foolish wager. Even then, Russian agriculture was no match for American. By late winter, my father had already planted his Burpee seeds, and was nurturing dozens of tiny plants in his bedroom.

The night before he put his two plants in the ground, however, I noticed Pop digging a four-foot hole in his garden. First, he dumped in scores of corn cobs; then, he covered them with a fertilizer-compost mix he had prepared; then, he covered this up with a crust of dirt. A thirty-inch length of narrow pipe had been left in the hole, and protruded just above the ground.

"What are you doing?" I asked him.

Pop let me in on his "sting." The corn cobs are buried there, he said, to soak up and hold water during June and July. As the thirsty tomato plants drive their roots down to reach that water, they will be feeding themselves the finest tomato plant food he and the Burpee boys knew how to produce. I began to understand the pipe. The key to success, Pop explained, was for me to pour four quarts of water through a funnel into that pipe every other day — to make sure the corn cobs stayed saturated.

Pop didn't need the edge, but we were taking it anyhow.

The next day, our Russian pigeon came by and watched my father put his two tomato plants into the ground — and the bet was on. Within weeks, those two plants showed a robustness and growth that seemed almost unnatural. No other plants, even in my father's garden, remotely matched them. George, who came to visit regularly, was astonished and puzzled.

"They're really coming along, George," Pop would say, "How are yours doing?"

Meanwhile, I was faithfully pouring the quarts of water into the pipe after dark; and, by late June, the plants were beginning to look like Jack's beanstalk. My father had to tie a five-foot pole to each of them to keep them standing; then, a second pole had to be tied on top of the first, as the plants by late summer were reaching the second story of the house. By late August, we had tomatoes the size of grapefruits, and George had lost interest.

When we pulled them out of the ground at summer's end, those tomato plants had roots like trees.

But Roland never lost his competitive spirit. George was now a rising star on the Catholic University tennis team, he told us, and my father was getting along in years (he was about forty-four), so George wanted to challenge him to a tennis match at Rollingwood. Whether this was George's idea, I yet do not know. But, that Saturday morning, my father got his whites out and drove us down to Rollingwood, where George and Roland confidently awaited.

Pop and George hit the ball back and forth a few times, and my father then invited George to serve. Which George did. While his first serve seemed unimpressive and hit the net, his second serve had us howling before it arrived: it was delivered underhand.

It was the worst mismatch I ever witnessed.

My father, who had gotten into the local "Believe It or Not" with the longest tennis match on record, three days at Montrose Park, was now playing the shortest. Priding himself on his "big serve" followed by a "Western twist," he would call out, "Ready, George!" and rocket the ball at ninety miles an hour right at the immobile Russian. It was six-love, six-love; and we laughed all the way home.

George was a good sport, however, and more than a good sport; like his Americanized younger half brother, he was a genuinely nice guy. But, a Russian who longed for his own country, he seemed out of place in the America of the 1940s. He tried and tried but never quite mastered the language, as Roland did. Half a world away from the land where he had been raised, and from the people whom he remembered fondly, George would visit our home to talk privately with my father in the den about taking his mother and going home to Russia.

My father told him that Stalin was the greatest butcher on earth; that he had even murdered the Russian prisoners sent back after the war; that to go home to Moscow was to put George and his mother, who had married an American diplomat, at the mercy of one of the most ruthless tyrants in history. George took the advice, until one day, a couple of years after we had moved out of the neighborhood, he came by to tell Pop he was thinking of taking a chance and going home. We never heard from George or his mother again.

3

Blessed Sacrament

Catholicism is not just a religion: it is a country of the heart and
of the mind. No matter how resolutely they turn their backs on
it, people born within it never quite shed their accents. And there
are a great many who cannot emigrate, no matter how uninviting
living conditions become. We may freeze within it; we would die
outside it.

— Anne Roche Muggeridge, *The Desolate City*

WHAT parish are you from?"
When one Catholic asked another whence he or she
came, that is how the question was framed in the 1940s
and '50s.

The answer might be "Blessed Sacrament," or "We're out in
Saint Michael's," or "We belong to Lourdes." The first would
mean what is today the Chevy Chase area of D.C. and Maryland,
the second, Silver Spring, the third, Bethesda. And that is how we
identified each other. "Hogan's from Nativity" meant he had
grown up in or lived now in the north Georgia Avenue area of
northwest Washington before the Maryland line. "Holy Trinity" is
what we called Georgetown. Jerry O'Leary, the veteran reporter
who was raised in the city, remembers a day when you were even
more precise; you lived in "lower Nativity."

The Buchanans "belonged" to Blessed Sacrament, as did the
Flynns and Lillys and McCalebs and O'Neills and Warners and
Keegans. Even during the war years, when the public schools were
experiencing the birth dearth of the Depression, Blessed Sacrament was a booming parish. Carved out of St. Ann's, the school
and church — built in the late 1920s — sat on the District line, a
block east of Chevy Chase Circle. When I entered Blessed Sacrament in September of 1944, one hundred children were divided into
two classrooms that comprised the first grade.

Those were the halcyon years of American Catholicism.

Between 1941 and 1961, the Catholic population of the United States virtually doubled, from 22 million to 42 million; and between 1955 and 1960, 56 percent of the population growth in the United States was among Catholics.

While still a minority and subjects of suspicion to our Protestant neighbors (we were forbidden, under pain of sin, from entering their churches, and their children were told not to enter ours), Catholics manifested a self-confidence in those years that was extraordinary. By conscious choice, we inhabited a separate world of our own creation; we built and occupied our own ghettos. And not only were we content to live within, the outside world was powerfully attracted to what we had.

Six houses down Chestnut Street toward Western Avenue lived the McCord twins, Doug and Carol. Doug was my best friend in the neighborhood, and Carol, attractive and a tomboy, was the best female athlete I ever saw. One afternoon, she asked me to take her inside Blessed Sacrament Church, where she had been forbidden to go. Getting on our bikes, we rode up, and I spent half an hour proudly walking her through, while she marveled at the confessionals, the stained glass, the statues, the votive candles, the magnificent main altar, the side altars, the Stations of the Cross, and the semidarkness in which it was all enveloped.

There was an awe-inspiring solemnity, power, and beauty within the old Church, which attracted people who were seeking the permanent things of life — after having tasted of the unfulfilling affluence of the postwar. There was something within that Church that said to the open heart and mind, "What you have been searching for may be found here."

Not only did we proclaim ours to be the "one, holy Catholic and apostolic Church," under the watchful eye of the Holy Ghost — with all others heretical — we were gaining converts by the scores of thousands, yearly. On Sunday mornings at Blessed Sacrament, there were six masses — at seven, eight, nine, ten, eleven, and noon — to accommodate the parish faithful; and daily masses were at 6:30, 7:30 and 8:30 A.M. The Presbyterian church, across from the school on Patterson Street, had services on Sunday — and that was it. Ecumenism was not what we were about; we were on the road to victory. Why compromise when you have the true Faith?

Conversions were the order of the day. Regularly, non-Catholic mothers and fathers of Blessed Sacrament children were taken into the Church.

"The parish" was the hub of our existence. All the newborns — Kathleen, Jack, Bay, Buck, and Tom — were baptized there; all the older boys were enrolled there. (Bill had spent the first grade at Holy Trinity.) Blessed Sacrament was where we went for Saturday confession and Sunday mass, for daily "visits" and evening benediction, for First Fridays and First Saturdays, for the Holy Days of Obligation and Holy Week, for the Blessing of the Throats on St. Blaise's Day, for ashes on Ash Wednesday, for palms on Palm Sunday, for baptisms, confirmations, marriages, and funerals, for evening retreats and the Stations of the Cross. Blessed Sacrament was where the Knights of Columbus and the Holy Name Society and the Confraternity of Christian Doctrine and the Women's Sodality met. And that was where all CYO (Catholic Youth Organization) activities were centered. From the day in 1943 when we moved to Chestnut Street, my parents never left the parish.

While Blessed Sacrament was considered a "rich parish" and Holy Trinity relatively "poor" (Georgetown at that time had a large white working class and black population), it was actually a middle-class enclave. The tone and style were set by energetic young professionals: lawyers, doctors, dentists, accountants, and government workers with large families. (The parish had a Seven and Up Club, restricted to families with seven or more children.) Tuition at Blessed Sacrament School was free (paid for out of collections at Sunday mass), and milk at recess cost a nickel a day. With four boys in school, that would have been a dollar a week, so we skipped the milk. The true "rich" lived in Kenwood on the far side of Wisconsin Avenue, or aspired to move there.

For eight years, all my teachers were nuns, the Sisters of the Holy Cross; they lived in a cloistered convent that separated church from school. The remarkable success of Blessed Sacrament, and the other parochial schools in the city — with fifty children in a classroom taught from nine to three by the same nun — persuades me that much of modern educationist theory is self-serving hokum.

In the D.C. public schools today, the cost per pupil is almost $5,000 per year. Yet, in many, children are reading at levels three and four years below the national average. At Blessed Sacrament in the 1940s, tuition was free; we were taught in "overcrowded" (by today's standards) classrooms by women, some of them girls barely out of their teens, who were paid almost nothing. They had given up boyfriends, families, home, and the prospect of marriage and children to live in a convent and instruct these children in basic education and our common Catholic faith. The elements indispensable to the success of these parish schools were teachers who cared deeply, parents who cared deeply, and strictly disciplined children, upon whom constant demands were made. No nonsense was tolerated. Money had nothing to do with it, dedication not being a function of dollars.

While there were nuns whose sweetness of disposition precluded their raising their voice, one or two would grab you by the hair and drag you around the room. I watched one third-grade classmate, a future priest, have his head slammed repeatedly against the blackboard for clowning in class. In an incident in the boys' cafeteria, Sister Sara Ann, a stout and explosive woman who had been my third-grade teacher, walloped one unruly seventh-grader with her umbrella, until I thought they were going to have to call the rectory and have Father Gorman come over to administer Extreme Unction. (The miscreant survived and went on to become a D.C. detective.)

Although the parochial schools preached and promoted excellence — Hank and I were on the giant honor roll posted in the school entrance hall every semester — they were also egalitarian institutions. All the girls were required to wear identical white blouses and blue jumpers, so that the daughters of the wealthy could not outdress and outshine the poorer girls in school, as they could and did in the D.C. and suburban public schools.

Even then I had a great respect for those nuns; and affection has deepened with remembrance. And they reciprocated. Only sickness kept us home. Often, however, when we came down (as eventually we all did) with scarlet fever, mumps, measles, chicken pox, or whooping cough, the authorities "quarantined" the house on Chestnut Street. Bulletins in red lettering were posted on the door to alert visitors to the disease spreading through the family, and no one went to school. But Mom, who nursed us all back to health, who took us on our trips to Dr. O'Brien for "shots," took these diseases in stride. Pneumonia and polio were the dreaded killers; whenever it was mentioned that someone's child had "come down with polio," there was a sudden lowering of adult voices in the room.

Paddy Joe had other medical problems. While other children were "cross-eyed," I was born "wall-eyed." Both eyes stared outward, disconcertingly, at the opposite walls of the room when I was looking straight ahead. Taken to Dr. Frank Costenbader, a pioneer in healing children with eye disorders, each eye was operated on, separately. Costenbader did a magnificent job, although I remember him telling me, "Pat, you will never be a pilot." Eleven years later, a total lack of depth perception, and the fact that, when tired, I saw double, as a result of those operations, cost me a Naval ROTC scholarship to Notre Dame. The navy wanted pilots in the '50s, but, as they told me in 1956, you couldn't be a pilot if you couldn't judge how far away from the carrier you were — or if you saw two carriers where there was only one.

Those eye operations, coupled with surgeries in the same years to remove tonsils and an inflamed appendix, left me with a lifelong visceral reaction to ether, that awful gas they held to the face until the thrashing stopped and you went under. That unmistakable smell permeated Children's Hospital, where I had already spent too much time, and would spend more.

Once the ABC's were mastered at Blessed Sacrament, we were drilled in catechism, spelling, reading, and arithmetic — and art, history, poetry, and geography.

The reading, poetry, and art courses were saturated with Catholicism. While there were Whittier and Whitman, there were also Joyce Kilmer and Father Leonard Feeney, poet laureate of the parochial schools. Father Feeney's work was better known to Catholic schoolchildren than Longfellow's.

One year, however, the poems of Father Feeney suddenly disappeared from our poetry books. Father Leonard Feeney became a nonperson. The nuns who had praised his genius the year before now never mentioned him. Not until later did we learn the good pastor had been excommunicated from the Church for preaching a strict construction of the doctrine *extra ecclessiam nulla salus,* outside the Church there is no salvation. Father Feeney taught that all non-Catholics were destined for hell; the orthodox position was that non-Catholics could attain salvation through a "baptism of desire." (We reassured Protestant playmates on this count.) Not even the famous Father Feeney could defy the orthodox church of Eugenio Pacelli, the serene autocrat who ruled the world of Roman Catholicism through the 1940s and '50s as His Holiness Pope Pius XII.

Those parish schools were enclaves of Americanism as well as Catholicism. America was God's country; there was no conflict then between nation and church. The United States, after all, had been consecrated to the Blessed Virgin Mary. Every noon, after lunch hour, the whole school assembled — each grade and class in its designated position and line — and, following several minutes of prescribed prayers, turned on signal, faced the flag, and made, hand over heart, the Pledge of Allegiance to the United States. Then, we were marched back into school.

When the older brother of a classmate was killed at the war's end, a special ceremony was conducted by the principal, Sister Frances Rose, and the flag was lowered to half staff. Priests and parishioners alike spoke proudly of how well-represented Catholics were in the armed forces, especially in such glorious fighting units as the U.S. Marine Corps. Although when I mentioned this to one of the more intellectual priests, Father Charles Gorman, as he drove me over to serve mass for him in the basement church of the unfinished Shrine of the Immaculate Conception, he cautioned me that Marines were not individuals on whom to model one's behavior.

As early as 1884, at the famous Third Plenary Council of Baltimore that mandated the parochial school system and created Catholic University, the U.S. bishops dealt head-on with the nativist slander against the loyalty of American Catholics: "We believe that our country's heroes were the instruments of the God of Nations in establishing this home of freedom; . . . should it ever — which God forbid — be imperiled, our Catholic citizens will be found to stand forward as one man to pledge anew 'their lives, their fortunes and their sacred honor.'"

The patriotic fervor of the faithful was shared by the clergy. More than three thousand Catholic priests had served as chaplains during World War II, and of the 11,887 conscientious objectors, only 135 were Roman Catholic.

While patriotic, Blessed Sacrament was apolitical. Even though we lived in the nation's capital, I cannot recall a single "field trip" in eight years to visit the monuments or institutions of government.

While we were all proud to be Americans, running the country was somebody else's job. The only political manifestation I ever remember at Blessed Sacrament was the Wednesday in November of 1948 after Harry Truman upset Tom Dewey; the playground was alive with argument and enthusiasm. Some of the girls in my class, whose fathers worked for the government, were the most exultant and militant; they were as elated that Dewey and the Republicans had been humiliated as they were that the Democrats had won. Not in my wildest dreams had I imagined there were that many people who preferred Truman. (Neither had Dewey.)

Our indispensable textbook was the Baltimore Catechism. Containing hundreds of questions and answers — all of which had to be learned by rote — the catechism instructed us on the central tenets of the Faith contained in the Apostles Creed, on each of the Ten Commandments (what they required and what they forbade), and on the Seven Sacraments (their precise purpose, and the spiritual conditions required for their worthy reception). For a grounding in Catholicism, it was unsurpassed.

The Church of the 1940s also copied heavily from the secular society. If they had "The Whiz Kids" on radio, we had a weekend radio program, during which children from competing parishes were quizzed on the catechism. Chosen to represent Blessed Sacrament, a great honor, I was drilled until hundreds of answers were letter perfect.

"What does the Eighth Commandment forbid?"

"The Eighth Commandment forbids lies, rash judgment, detraction, calumny, and the telling of secrets we are bound to keep." Correct.

"When does a person commit the sin of detraction?"

"A person commits the sin of detraction when, without a good reason, he makes known the hidden faults of another."

To miss a phrase, or a single word, was like missing a letter in a spelling bee. You were out.

In May of the second grade, we made our First Confession and First Holy Communion, having reached the "age of reason" at which point we could be held accountable for our sins. In the fourth grade, we were Confirmed in the Faith by the newly installed Archbishop of Washington, Patrick A. O'Boyle, and given a new confirmation name we carried all our lives.

Bill had taken Aloysius, for Aloysius of Gonzaga, the boy Jesuit, and Hank had taken the name of the great founder of the order, Ignatius of Loyola. Keeping with family tradition, I had chosen Francis Xavier, a contemporary of Ignatius and perhaps the greatest missionary the Church had produced since Saint Paul.

But, when Sister Thomasina told me I could not have two names and pressed me as to whether I wanted Francis or Xavier, I panicked. "Francis," I said.

When I got home, Pop let me know I had blown it. "Why didn't you take Xavier?" he demanded. Francis could as well mean the pacifist with the pigeons as the great missionary. "Well, don't worry about it," Pop said finally, "Francis is a great name, too." (Later, I was relieved to learn the sainted Francis of Assisi had accompanied, and not condemned, the fifth Crusade.)

Twenty-five years after I went through that preparation for Penance, Holy Communion, and Confirmation, I was heading a delegation of young political leaders in the Soviet Union, in one of the final "exchanges" before formalization of Mr. Nixon's "detente." In Kiev, the capital of the Ukraine, we were taken to a Young Pioneer Palace, to watch dozens of six- and seven-year-olds inducted into the Young Octoberists. Having spent six to ten hours a week being indoctrinated in the Communist faith, they were now making their formal profession of faith — in the gospel according to Lenin. Watching those fresh faces, full of anticipation and delight, took me back a quarter century. With all the formality, if not the solemnity and beauty, attendant to my own First Holy Communion, these children were being formally received into the Church of Marxism-Leninism.

My friend Rick Stearns, who would put together McGovern's delegate victory at the Democratic convention in 1972, described the experience at that Pioneer Palace as "chilling." It confirmed for me what I had already come to believe: The war between West and East is not between the economic systems of capitalism and Marxism; it is a religious war for control of the soul and destiny of mankind, the outcome of which cannot be arbitrated or negotiated.

Supplementing the catechism were the lives of the saints, as embellished by the piety and enthusiasm of the Sisters of the Holy Cross. (Virtually every day of the calendar year was a feast day of some particular saint.) The North American martyrs, especially

Saint René Goupil and Saint Isaac Jogues, the French Jesuit, beloved of the Queen of France, who was tortured by the Iroquois and tomahawked, were among the favorites, as was Saint Lawrence, who said when being roasted on a spit for his Catholic faith, "Turn me over, I'm done on this side," and Blessed Maria Goretti, the twelve-year-old Italian schoolgirl stabbed to death in 1902, when she resisted the advances of Alexander Serenelli, son of her father's partner. She was canonized by Pius XII in 1950, in the presence of her murderer, who had completely reformed his life after having a vision of Maria.

I never understood what harm was supposed to have been done by the telling, and occasional embellishing, of these stories of martyrdom and virtue. Every one of us grew soon to an age when we knew what was true and what was mythical, and what was on a par with the Easter bunny. Yet, the same trendy Catholics most exercised over "superstitious" myths and "outright falsehoods," from which children had to be protected, turned out to have their own little hagiographies.

In recent years, politicians and the secular clerisy of the national press, who succeeded the routed Christian clergy as our Lords Spiritual, have not hesitated to use the power of law to insist that all Americans, including us "heretics," set aside as a day of reflection and remembrance the birthday of the late Dr. Martin Luther King, a secular saint whose interests appear to have been somewhat broader than peace and civil rights. The Church of yesterday never insisted that nonbelievers observe our feast days or Holy Days of Obligation; yet, the triumphant humanists have no reservations about imposing their household gods upon us.

But we did not need stories to know that, even then, there were men and women being martyred in Catholic countries like Poland and Hungary that had been deeded over to Stalin at Yalta.

When the Communist regime in Budapest announced in 1948 the coming trial for treason of Joszef Cardinal Mindszenty, the Primate of Hungary who had resisted both the Nazis and the Communists, there was enormous anguish. Cardinal Mindszenty was constantly in the prayers of the nuns and the schoolchildren, and when the newspapers displayed, months later, the shocking picture of the drugged and broken prelate as he "confessed" at one of Stalin's ugliest "show trials," the Catholic world was stunned. We did not need any classroom discussion about Marxism to recognize the evil of Communism; it was written all over the tortured face of that Catholic priest.

The Church of that era — the Church of Cardinals Wyszynski, Stepinac, and Mindszenty, and of Pope Pius XII — did not believe in "coexistence" with Communist regimes persecuting and murdering the faithful in Czechoslovakia, Poland, Hungary, the Ukraine, and the Baltic republics. At the end of every mass we said the "prayers at the foot of the altar"; among them was the Prayer for the Conversion of Russia, which ended: "Blessed Michael the Archangel! Defend us in the day of battle! Be our safeguard against the wickedness and snares of the enemy. Rebuke him, O God, we humbly pray! And do thou, O Prince of the Heavenly Host, thrust back into Hell Satan and all other evil spirits who wander through the world seeking the ruin of souls."

That is not the rhetoric of detente.

For those of us raised in the old Church, today's calls for "Marxist-Christian dialogue" will always sound ludicrous. Either men are, or they are not, children of God, with immortal souls, destined for eternity and possessed of God-given rights no government can take away. If they are, Communism is rooted in a lie; and every regime built upon that lie is inherently illegitimate. We were taught that, and we believed that, then — and we still do.

While the nuns had cut themselves off from the life of the world (they were not permitted to go to movies at the Avalon, three blocks away; and they shopped only rarely on Connecticut Avenue, and then always in pairs), they knew what they were about. They were preparing their charges for a Catholic life in that secular world. Anti-Catholic works were forbidden reading, but they were out there, and the nuns knew it. Once, in the fourth grade — when I had done well in catechism and religion — Sister Thomasina asked me to remain after school. Calling me up to her desk, she pulled out a pamphlet from a side drawer.

"Patrick," she said, "do you know who Paul Blanshard is?"

I had only the vaguest notion of the writings of the premier Catholic-baiter of the era; and told her so.

"Well," she said, "Mr. Blanshard is constantly attacking Mother Church; he is a cunning, skillful enemy, and I want you to sit down and read this pamphlet by Mr. Blanshard, and write an answer to it."

I carried out my assignment.

She knew — and we were taught — there were enemies of Catholicism out there; and the more intellectual of the sisters were constantly on the lookout for future Defenders of the Faith.

When we reached the sixth grade, the better students had the opportunity to become altar boys, whose instruction was under the supervision of Sister Marie de Carmel. Weeks of after-school preparation went into learning the Latin responses of the Tridentine mass, and the precisely specified movements of the two altar boys who served.

"Book" and "bells" were the assigned roles, the former carrying the book from one side of the altar to the other several times during mass, the latter handling the bells that were rung at precise intervals. The senior of the altar boys always took "book," as it involved frequent movement, while "bells" spent almost the entire mass on his knees.

Each assignment consisted of a series of three daily masses, say 6:30 in the morning Monday, Tuesday, and Wednesday. Sunday masses were assigned separately. For daily mass, we arrived fifteen to twenty minutes early, put on our black cassock and white surplice in the basement, went upstairs to the sacristy, helped the priest put on his vestments in the approved order — amice, alb, cincture, stole, chasuble, maniple, beretta — prepared the cruets (with water and wine), bowed together before the crucifix in the rectory exactly at 6:30, and led the priest out onto the altar. Altar girls were unheard of.

After learning to serve at mass, we learned to serve at Benediction, the 7:30 Monday-night worship of the Blessed Sacrament, the large consecrated host contained inside a vessel called the monstrance. Benediction required five altar boys, two relative juniors who knelt beside the priest and — in descending order of rank — the Master, Thurifer, and Boat, who knelt farther back. Boat carried a small vessel that held the incense. Thurifer carried the censer, which contained a smoldering lump of charcoal, into which the incense was spooned from the boat. Master presided. With High Mass and Solemn High, the complexity of the ceremonies increased, the most impressive being services like Tenebrae during Easter Week. During major Holy Week services (except Good Friday), our cassocks were a bright red; and with the lace surplices and sashes and collars and bows, the senior altar boys were as brilliantly attired as the priests.

In those years, the Catholic Church was indeed *Mater et Magis-*

ter, Mother and Teacher. While, as children, we took for granted what we had, and often chafed under the discipline and demands, we never doubted that not only did we live in the capital of the greatest nation in history, we belonged to the One True Church.

We were taught, and believed, that we were the fortunate ones. And that Church was indeed a loving mother. When one had sinned, the confessional was there, waiting, to restore one to God's grace. When we had personal problems or, more often, personal desires, we drove up on our bicycles and prayed for them.

A sense of relief and comfort and security was always there, inside that empty church. It was like coming home.

In the solitude, you could explain things silently and work things out. When Catholics drove past the front of the church, they made the Sign of the Cross inside their cars, as a mark of respect, because they were passing before the Blessed Sacrament. And there are no few pangs of personal regret that when much of this was being thrown out like so much old furniture during the 1960s, some of us, who should have been there, were AWOL at the time.

Among the nastier slanders of the modern era is that in the old Church we children were taught by the nuns and priests that Jews were "Christ-killers." Not until I was in politics did I ever even hear the phrase; and the notion that these pious women, whose heads bowed when the name of Christ was mentioned, would either preach hatred or deploy so ugly a term is preposterous.

When the Communists celebrated the once and future revolution on May Day, Catholics celebrated the month of the Virgin Mary, with a vast procession involving every child in the school. The altar boys led the long march out onto Patterson Street, west to Chevy Chase Circle, around to Western Avenue, up Western to Quesada Street, and down Quesada into the front yard of the rectory, where the May Queen, an eighth-grade girl chosen for grades and beauty and presumed virtue, crowned the statue of the Virgin Mary. The boys wore their best suits, preferably dark, and every girl was dressed in white and wore a veil. The competition for May Queen among the daughters of the leading families of the parish was intense. The runners-up were maids of honor to the May Queen. As the May procession wended its way for a quarter mile, thousands of parents, aunts, uncles, and family friends lined the sidewalks to photograph their favorites.

While the nuns managed the first five grades handily, by the sixth, seventh, and eighth grades, the boys especially were becoming too unruly. The smoking in the alley, the clowning in the classroom, the fistfights on the playground, and the behavior of the athletes — some of whom had citywide CYO reputations at age thirteen — were too much to handle. The boys had to be gotten quickly into the hands of the Jesuits or the Christian brothers; or they were lost. As for the girls, the brightest would usually go on to Georgetown Visitation Convent, most of the rest to Holy Cross, two miles down Connecticut Avenue.

The idea of education that pervaded at Blessed Sacrament, four decades ago, is utterly antithetical to the view that dominates public education today.

Modern theory holds that children should be presented with facts, shown a menu of values and beliefs, and be permitted to make up their minds, at maturity, as to what is right and wrong, and what they wish to believe. We held to the opposite view.

We already had the truth. For two millennia Catholics had lived it; and the best of them had died for it. Now it was being handed down to us from the ages; the Church was there to impart it; and we were there to receive it, and to be its custodians and defenders for the next generation. The notion that children should decide for themselves what they should believe would have been considered scandalous, if not laughable. Indeed, instruction in the truths of the Catholic faith was considered infinitely more important at Blessed Sacrament than learning the facts of mathematics and spelling and geography. After all, that is why the Catholic schools existed; that is why parents, priests, and nuns were making such immense personal sacrifices.

All ideas were not equal at Blessed Sacrament; and heresy had no rights. Parents did not send their children to Blessed Sacrament to have them come home spouting heretical nonsense. We began our education with the answers. Even before we knew what the great questions were — how men should live, what they should believe, what they should value most highly — we knew how to respond. Nor was there any apology on the part of the Church as to what she was about. As a nation does not send its soldiers into battle before arming them and teaching them how to fight, so the Catholic Church would not send its sons and daughters out to do battle with the world, the flesh, and the devil without arming and equipping them in the Faith.

Because saving one's soul was more important than saving one's life, the nuns did not wait until the upper grades to begin teaching right and wrong. If the child became a scientist or composer or scholar, that was ancillary to the central task of the parochial school, the making of good Catholics. If, however, the child turned out at twenty-one to be a brilliant student, but lost the Faith and left the Church, then the nuns had not succeeded; they had failed in the mission to which, after all, they had dedicated their lives.

Those nuns and priests were in no more doubt as to what they were about then, than the secularists, who control public education today, are in doubt as to what they are about. "Indoctrination" is the derisory term secular critics use to disparage the Catholic education of four decades ago. Yet, even by secular standards, those Catholic schools "worked." If, today, however, parents asked that their own children receive a like education in the public schools, they would be told by the Supreme Court that this is unconstitutional, and by the education industry that this is outrageous. But, Catholic or Protestant or Jewish or Moslem, it is parents' rights that are paramount in early education, not the ideology of bureaucrats, judges, or Supreme Court justices. And there is nothing wrong with parents' demanding that schools — attended by their children and paid for by their tax dollars — turn their children into good men and good women, by *their* standards of morality . . . even if those standards are the ones written down in the Old and New Testaments. Nor is there anything wrong with the government insisting that the literature and history taught in public schools be tailored to inculcate in children a reverence for their national past, a respect for their democratic institutions, and an unabashed love of country.

If the current Supreme Court says such ideas are not constitutional, it is not the ideas that need changing.

School and Church imparted lessons that are yet carried in the subconscious even of those who subsequently rejected their Catholic faith.

Hate the sin and love the sinner, we were taught. When Cardinal O'Connor said the Archdiocese of New York would give up municipal funds rather than endorse homosexuality, and then poured millions of Catholic dollars into hospices for dying AIDS patients, the secular world may have called this hypocrisy; to us, it is a precise rendering of the catechismal injunction.

Your life on this earth, we were taught, was a time of testing. While God loved you and His Only Son had died on the Cross for your sins, faith alone was insufficient for salvation. You had been baptized and confirmed in the True Faith; you had been given a guardian angel to watch over you; you had Penance and the Holy Eucharist to keep you in a state of grace; you had indulgences to be won, and prescribed ways to win them, to wash away the consequences of past sin. But whether you went to Purgatory and eventually Heaven, or to "Hell for all eternity," was up to you. To die in a state of mortal sin meant eternal damnation; there was no appeal from a death sentence of the soul, and there would be no one to blame but yourself.

To impress upon us what the loss of the soul through mortal sin meant, my father would light a match, grab our hands, and hold them briefly over the flame, saying: "See how that feels; now imagine that for all eternity."

We lived in a world of clarity and absolutes. Unlike neighborhood friends, few of whom seemed to have any religious convictions, we exuded a sense of certitude. While they would readily admit they were ignorant, we spoke and behaved as though we alone had the truth. And we did not doubt it. We were raised to believe that they were the underprivileged; our neighborhood friends were, in a sense, to be pitied. Unlike us, they had not been given the Gift of Faith. In the 1940s and early '50s, most of the non-Catholic kids seemed to be question marks; we Catholics were exclamation points. While there was resentment at our sometimes smug self-confidence, there was also a magnetism about our certitude. None of us wished to be like them; some of them, secretly — and some openly — wanted to be like us. And we both knew it.

Men seek certitude. That is what the Catholic Church of the midcentury offered — and the modern Church in America does not seem to understand. We had the Way, the Truth, and the Light. Other ways were not equally valid; they were false.

While Catholicism made hard demands, it offered to those who kept the Commandments of God and the Commandments of the Church an ironclad guarantee: eternal life. Agnostics, atheists, and Protestants of the war generation accepted the offer by the tens of thousands, and signed on. But the legacy was squandered by those to whom it was entrusted. The coffeehouse clerics of the 1960s and '70s who sought to make Catholicism "relevant" to a hedonistic age found themselves irrelevant to youngsters searching for meaning in life. After you've "witnessed" for civil rights and peace, and the Voting Rights Act has been extended and "peace" has been brought to Cambodia and South Vietnam, what do you do next?

What people seek in religion today is what people sought then: answers to the questions that keep one awake at night. They want to believe that this life has meaning beyond the day-to-day, that there is life after death; and they want to be told what they have to do to attain that eternal life. They have neither the desire nor the time to sit down and "rap" like college students in an all-night bull session about whether God exists; nor are they going to be satisfied with a "social gospel" some trendy Catholic cleric seems to have picked up in the vestibule of the First Church of Christ, Socialist.

While one hears endlessly from Catholic pulpits today of the need to give food to the poor, in America's suburbs and inner cities, the true hunger that needs feeding is not physical at all. Fundamentalist and Evangelical Protestant denominations, whose preachers speak with conviction and authority of sin and salvation and Heaven and Hell, today gather the converts that in the 1950s were fighting their way into the Catholic Church. At some Catholic parishes today, not in a month of Sundays can you hear the subject of Hell even mentioned; the sermons are all about being considerate and kind and nice. The Church Militant has been superseded by the Church Milquetoast.

While teenagers give themselves up to drugs and despair, leading to appalling crime and violence in the inner cities and to indiscriminate sex, suicide pacts, and even satanic cults in the suburbs, the National Conference of Catholic Bishops labors away on pastoral letters to manifest the American Church's impatience with the most successful economy in human history. Remarkable. Today's clergy seem to be casting about blindly for economic and political solutions to problems of the human heart — to which they once had the answer. The moral capital of the Catholic Church in the United States, piled high over two centuries, has been squandered in two decades, invested in such fly-by-night secular stocks as boycotting lettuce and saving the Sandinistas.

What a distance we have traveled since the Maryknoll missionary, Bishop James Edmund Walsh of Cumberland, Maryland, was imprisoned and tortured by Chinese Communists for preaching the

Faith. Today, some Maryknollers seem permanently enraged that
the United States would interfere with the sovereign right of the
Brothers Ortega to impose the same evil system that persecuted
Bishop Walsh upon the Catholic people of Nicaragua. From American pulpits, priests tell us Marxism should be accepted as a useful
"tool of analysis." One wonders what these modern clerics most
appreciate about the old devil's doctrine: his preaching of class
hatred or his virulent anti-Semitism? The Catholic Church of the
1940s and '50s, that assertive, self-confident institution which un-
apologetically preached the truth to its own, as well as a hostile and
disbelieving world, no longer exists.

Whenever, today, I read of some political acquaintance described as a "devout Catholic," it is usually cause for chuckles.
That phrase had a meaning for Catholics then that can be applied to
few of us now.

For eight years at Blessed Sacrament, we went to 8:30 mass
every day. In our home, the family nightly prayed the Rosary
together before homework began. When friends dropped by to pick
me up for the evening's festivities, they were invited, Catholic or
not, to join in. When Father Patrick Peyton's Rosary Crusade
came to the Monument grounds, the Buchanan family was there
with fifty thousand others. There was no vote in the household
about whether we would attend. Dissent was not something I heard
a great deal about, until I left home for Columbia University.

In CYO games, players on both sides wore either the miraculous
medals of the Virgin Mary or the scapulars of the Sacred Heart. We
prayed before CYO and high-school games — and made the Sign of
the Cross before foul shots. At the top of my test papers, I automatically wrote the letters A.M.D.G. — *Ad Majorem Dei Gloriam*
(For the Greater Glory of God), the motto of the Jesuits.

One night, my father woke me up and took me along, for conversation and company, as he drove over to do his duty with the
Nocturnal Adoration Society. The men of the parish who belonged
(their names were kept confidential) would take turns driving to
Sacred Heart Church off 16th Street, after midnight, and praying
before the exposed Blessed Sacrament during the early morning
hours, because, as the parish bulletin explained, "so many of the
sins of the world are committed at night." Remembering him
kneeling there, broad shoulders squared, bald head bent in prayer,

in that darkened church, where the only light came from the distant tabernacle beyond the altar rail, I am reminded of what the Centurion had said to Christ: "For I too am a man under authority."

The impact of the Catholic Church upon my parents' outlook on life, and upon our family, is almost impossible to overestimate.

My father's religious beliefs permeated everything. Abandoned at eleven years old by a father whom he idolized, my father transferred his total loyalty to the Church, to the nuns and Jesuit priests who had instructed him in the Faith. They had shown him affection, loyalty, and love; and he returned it, tenfold. Whatever the Pope taught, *ex-cathedra,* that was it; there was no more debate, discussion, or dissent. My brother Bill once suggested, only half in jest, that Pop's great regret in life would be that he wasn't martyred for the Faith.

Among Pop's favorite expressions was "Offer it up," an all-purpose phrase that meant "stop whining and offer up your pain for the suffering souls in Purgatory." Whenever we were hurt or injured or scraped, and we complained or cried, we would hear a loud and impatient "Offer it up!"

Years later, I read where the coach Vince Lombardi, one of Fordham's Seven Mules and a man of my father's generation, had stopped one of his Green Bay Packer linemen, who was grimacing as he limped off the field, and yelled at him, "What the hell's the matter with you?"

"I think I've broken a couple of ribs, coach," the Packer lineman said, grimacing with pain.

"Shake it off!" Lombardi said, and turned his attention back to the field. The phrase had a familiar ring.

To show emotion and feeling was considered an unmanly thing to do; we were to be stoic about pain. Take your punishment, don't let anyone see you cry. Whenever I read in today's press about some individual, especially some man, "revealing himself" (e.g., bleating and bleeding in print about his "feelings" and his "hurt"), I always feel a sense of profound embarrassment.

On Sundays, my father and mother guaranteed we never missed mass. We were all awakened at eight o'clock, and all four of the older boys were outfitted in matching brown slacks, brown caps, and camel's-hair coats, and so presented at nine-o'clock mass. Mom would stay home, fix breakfast for us when we got back at ten, and then hurry to make the eleven o'clock herself.

Every Christmas Day, my father was up knocking at the door of the convent; his hat would come off as soon as the door opened, and he would hand over, as a Christmas gift, a grocery bag with four bottles of the finest wine we could afford.

"Why are you giving the nuns booze, Pop?" I once asked him. "Do they drink?"

"No," he said, "but they sometimes might enjoy a little wine with their Christmas dinner."

And my father and mother lived the Faith.

When I was twenty, my mother got from Dr. John O'Brien, the family physician for two decades, about the worst news a parent can receive: Angela Marie, my ten-year-old sister, whom we called Bay, he said, was dying; she had only months to live. The news came as a complete shock.

A healthy, dark-haired girl, Bay, with her Prince Valiant haircut, had been taken in for an emergency appendectomy in May. During the summer, she failed to regain her energy. She was lethargic, and for months failed to improve. Worried, my mother had taken her to Children's Hospital around Halloween, for X-rays. When the X-rays returned, they showed her liver swollen to three times normal size with hepatitis, and one kidney was shot through with sarcoma. Before telling my mother, Dr. O'Brien had gone to a fellow doctor, who confirmed the diagnosis. The radiologist agreed. All three gave her only months to live.

Shattered, my mother called my father at the office with the shocking news. Though shaken, "he was like a rock," Mom told me. "We must look at it this way, Catherine; God was good enough to give us this child for ten years, and now he has decided to take her home."

But, for my mother and father, acceptance of God's will did not rule out a final appeal to God's mercy. The nuns and priests at Blessed Sacrament were asked to make Novenas, as were the Jesuits at Gonzaga. My mother's friend Betty Beatty went to a group promoting the canonization of American-born Cornelia Connelly, founder of the Sisters of the Society of the Holy Child Jesus. They began an around-the-clock vigil for Bay's recovery.

Weeks passed; Mom went to the hospital every day; and Bay's condition worsened. Bone marrow was taken constantly.

Around Christmas and her eleventh birthday, Bay was "going downhill fast," and the doctors wanted to operate, though one surgeon suggested it was pointless. What is the sense, he asked, of making this little girl suffer, by removing her kidney, when she has only months to live? My father agreed. "I was resigned to the thing," he said.

Nevertheless, the decision was made to go ahead and operate. But, when the final X-rays were taken, the surgeon could not even see the cancer; and the liver was dramatically reduced in size. Dr. O'Brien called to say he had a belated "Christmas present" for the Buchanan family.

"The best news I ever heard," my father said.

While my mother, who was in the consultations every day and knew as much as the doctors from her years of nursing, believes Bay was the victim of a dirty needle during the appendectomy, and developed hepatitis, my father yet believes otherwise: "There is no other plausible explanation for it," he told me more than once, "except a miracle."

A decade later, Bay went to Rosemont, to be taught by the Sisters of the Society of the Holy Child Jesus, the order founded by Cornelia Connelly; two decades later, in 1981, my parents were standing nearby when she was sworn in as the youngest Treasurer in the history of the United States.

Several years ago, when I stopped briefly in a small Catholic bookstore in Bethesda, the lady at the counter recognized me. "Mr. Buchanan, your father was in here, several weeks ago," she said. Then, she volunteered the exchange she had had: "I said, 'Isn't it terrible what's going on in the Church today, Mr. Buchanan?' And he answered, 'No, there is nothing to fear. We have it on the authority of Christ Himself — the Rock shall not break.'"

We could always argue with Pop about almost anything, and we did; but if one of his sons or daughters questioned the Faith, he would say, "If you think that, you can leave my house." Faith, for him, came ahead even of family bonds.

Raised in the Catholic environment that he and my mother made of our home, their two oldest sons believed they had vocations — and entered the Jesuits and Maryknolls to test them.

While believing in that Catholic faith was no guarantee of superior behavior (as preceding and subsequent chapters demonstrate), it did provide us with what our non-Catholic friends did not have: a code of morality, a code of conduct, a sure knowledge of right and wrong, a way of acknowledging personal guilt and of seeking out and attaining forgiveness and absolution. We had a hierarchy of values; we knew where we were going and how to get there; even in childhood, we were not confused. We had certitude.

To the Catholic youth of my generation, the death of Pius XII in 1958 was as great a jolt as the death of FDR was to Americans who had known no other president. With the coming of John XXIII and Vatican II came the "reformers." With Pius XII dead and buried, it was their time now; and, brimming with new ideas, they were going to "throw open the windows," to modernize the Church, to make it "relevant" to the outside world. Lord, what a mess they made of it.

The Catholic Church of the 1950s was not taken from without; it was surrendered from within. Pope Paul VI was right when he said, "The smoke of hell has entered the vestibule of the Church." In the last quarter-century, the Roman Catholic Church in the United States has been utterly demystified — as prelude to establishment of an American Catholic Church. The Holy Sacrifice of the Mass as prescribed by the Council of Trent has been replaced by a communal meal celebrated in the vernacular. The Latin is gone; the sacred liturgy has been transformed; a banal English is the *lingua franca* of the new American Church; many of the new churches look on the inside like assembly halls, college classrooms, or off-Broadway theaters. The Douay-Rheims version of the Old and New Testaments, a rival to the King James Bible in the majesty of its prose, has been rewritten again and again by tin-eared clerics who never learned that language is the music of thought, that tone-deaf people ought not to rewrite Mozart.

Recently at Sunday mass, I watched as a priest, perhaps a decade younger than I, having improvised on half the prayers at mass, decided to give the "Sign of Peace" to half the congregation. As he went on and on, shaking hands, hugging people, smiling up a storm, it was all I could do to contain myself from shouting, "Get back up on that altar!"

Mass attendance is down, vocations are down, Catholic school enrollment is down, conversions are down from the 1950s. Many of the nuns who remain — having been told their earlier sacrifices were unnecessary — are in acrimonious rebellion against the "patriarchal" Church. Priests and theologians from "Catholic" campuses can be heard pontificating on the nation's airwaves in contemptuous condescension of the orthodox pronouncements of the Holy Father in Rome. A quarter century after Vatican II, we need another Council of Trent.

The old Church, which was always there, unchanged and unchanging, seems to have disappeared. Visiting the modern churches today is like coming back to the town where you grew up and finding that the oldest landmark, the great mansion on the hill, has been gutted and rebuilt to fit in architecturally and devotionally with the bustling suburban scene. Outside a sign reads UNDER NEW MANAGEMENT.

"Things reveal themselves passing away," Yeats was fond of saying. It was a magnificent institution in a splendid era; but that old Catholic Church, militant and triumphant, lives only in the recesses of memory. And yet, as Peter responded when asked, "And will you, too, leave?" "Where else shall we go, Lord? Thou hast the words of eternal life."

4

As We Remember Joe

"Olson won the fight, Father."

T HE Catholic world of the postwar era was not an us-versus-them world, but it was us-and-them. We were different, and we considered ourselves different; we were raised apart.

While they followed the Big Ten or the Big Eight ("Oklahoma and the Seven Dwarfs") in big-time college football, most of us had only one team: Notre Dame. Like the United States and the Catholic Church, it, too, was superior to all the rest. Names like Leon Hart and Johnny Lujack and Red Sitko and Frank Leahy were known to virtually every Catholic boy. Notre Dame was almost always undefeated; and, on Saturdays, those were the games we listened to. Long before the famous 0–0 tie in 1946 — the year of Glenn Davis and Felix (Doc) Blanchard — my father was predicting that when all the veterans had returned, even mighty Army would not stand up to the Fighting Irish. He was right.

It was in the immediate postwar years that the CYO was expanded to create a separate social world for the burgeoning population of Catholic youth. By the late 1940s, we had our own teams, our own leagues, our own city play-offs, our own Middle Atlantic tournaments. Not only were non-Catholics not permitted to play CYO sports ("Don't forget to bring your baptismal certificate to practice tomorrow!"), they were carefully screened out, and kept out, of CYO dances. Catholic girls were to meet, date, and eventually marry Catholic boys. Once, when we tried to sneak a non-Catholic friend into the Blessed Sacrament CYO dance, the alert priest at the door headed off the suspected heretic by demanding on the spot that he recite the Apostles Creed. The kid didn't even take a cut at the ball; he just turned around silently, walked up the stairs and out into the parking lot, where he spent the rest of the dance sitting in the car. From time to time, we went out and visited him.

The central CYO social activity, however, was sports.

By the time I reached fifth grade, Blessed Sacrament — under the guiding hand of the Reverend E. Carl Lyon, who somehow managed to buy us the finest equipment and uniforms in the city and hire the best coaches — had become a football powerhouse, losing to Saint Anthony's in a city championship game at Griffifth Stadium in that fall of 1948 that half the parish attended. When I reached sixth grade, family interest peaked. The starting quarterback, and the only starting seventh-grader, was brother Hank.

This was the fall of 1949, and all our regular CYO games were played on the Ellipse, just south of the White House, on Saturday mornings. The fathers of team members would load up the family cars with players and cheerleaders and kids from Blessed Sacrament, and drive down Connecticut Avenue, past what I thought was the ugliest building in the world — the monstrous Old State, War and Navy Department complex now known as the Executive Office Building, or EOB. (Two decades later, I spent a six-year tour of duty in that magnificent edifice, working for Richard M. Nixon.) Occasionally, the games on the Ellipse would be interrupted by cheerleaders rushing off to get the autograph of Harry S Truman, taking his morning walk across the Ellipse in the company of three secret servicemen.

While Saint Anthony's in far northeast and Saint Joseph's Home (the orphanage school) were the class of the other league, the archrival of Blessed Sacrament was Saint Michael's in Silver Spring, Maryland. Caryl Rivers, a Saint Michael's girl, wrote in her book of reminiscence, *Occasional Sins*, of the intensity of feeling between the parishes:

> *"Blessed Sacrament" is the name of the sacred body and blood of Christ in the Eucharist; but to me the words bring to mind only one image — a group of tall, willowy girls in gym suits the shade of a glass of burgundy. Blessed Sacrament parish was near ours in suburban Maryland. They were like*

*us, only richer. A Blessed Sacrament forward's father was
likely to be a doctor; our fathers were somewhere in the middle
range of the G.S. [federal government] scale.*

*With us, and Blessed Sacrament, there was none of the
"It's-not-whether-you-win-or-lose-it's-how-you-play-the-game"
nonsense. We were out to kill them and they were out to kill
us. Our coaches eyed each other across the width of the
court like a pair of mountain lions after the same hare.*

After Blessed Sacrament defeated Saint Michael's for the second
year in a row, the embittered Saint Michael's coaching staff demanded a forfeit on the grounds that the Blessed Sacrament center,
John Carmody, was obviously overweight. (There was a 130-pound
limit, but during the season, a player could go up to 135.)

The abashed Carmody was marched over in full uniform to the
water fountain at the White House end of the Ellipse, stripped to
his underpants, and weighed, while angry fathers from Saint
Michael's and Blessed Sacrament glowered at one another. Carmody came in right at 135; and we were on our way to Griffith
Stadium to face a Saint Anthony's team that had not only been
undefeated and untied — but unscored upon since 1947.

Almost forty years later, I can yet remember the raw tension and
spirit surrounding that game; it was unlike any other I have ever
awaited, or played. Everyone in the school was caught up in it;
China might be falling to the Communist armies of Mao Tse-tung,
but we talked of nothing else but the great game. I was writing
"Beat Saint Anthony's" in chalk the width of Chestnut Street. The
coaches' final letter to the Blessed Sacrament players the Friday
before the Sunday game caught the mood and excitement of the
moment. Titled "Beat St. Anthony's: The Bigger They Are The
Harder They Fall," the exhortation by Coach Frank Gilmore
reflected our anticipation and hope:

*Fellows: We have at last reached the goal that we have been
looking forward to. . . . It has been a long year since we played
St. Anthony's in the Stadium. We have hoped and prayed that
you would get another crack at them. Our chance has now
come. . . .*

*St. Anthony's has been unscored on for two years. We have
been practicing all week to score on* this *particular team. We*

will score *if you will block thoroughly. St. Joseph's got down to their 3-yard-line. Let's show them we can go at least 3 yards farther than St. Joseph's. . . .*

Now let's hit them right from the start. If we jolt them in the first three minutes, they are so proud of their record, that they won't know what to do. . . . Now let's see you hit Bernie Divver and McAleer hard enough to make them fumble.

We expect all of you to go, together as a team, to 8 o'clock mass and to Communion and to sit up in the right hand side in the first three pews. . . . We want you at the stadium in the dressing room at 11:50, all dressed and raring to go. . . .

Your parish is all with you, your coaches, your teachers and your parents will be rooting for you. Let's see you take them into camp. We know you can do it.
BEAT ST. ANTHONY'S.

In that CYO championship game in Griffith Stadium, December 2, 1949, the miraculous transpired. Blessed Sacrament did score in the first three minutes, after a Saint Anthony's fumble on their first play from scrimmage; and the dramatic three-column photograph of fullback Jimmy Hayden going over for the first crucial touchdown showed the Saint Anthony star, Bernie Divver, lying on his stomach looking on in helpless desperation — with brother Hank lying on top of him. Hank was chosen to appear with six other Blessed Sacrament stars on Jim Gibbons's television show, and at the banquet celebrating the triumph at the Shoreham Hotel, which a thousand parishioners attended, the main speaker, who handed Hank the trophy for "best blocker" in the CYO, was the legendary Frank Leahy himself. My father thought he had died and gone to Heaven.

Hank was going to be a tough act to follow.

Sports held a far greater meaning for us in those years than they do today.

First, they welded together the family — and our parish — in a common enthusiasm. While we would practice and play, my father would coach, and my mother would be out at all the games. They were always interested in how well we were doing at practice, how well the teams were doing. Our sports teams were things we talked about, agreed about, laughed about, and cheered about, together.

At their best, competitive sports manifest in action some of the finer values of democracy. On the playing field, title, lineage, wealth, suddenly count for nothing. The sons and daughters of the working and middle class are given, for two hours, that equal chance at the starting line America is supposed to promise. On the playing field, or on the basketball court, suddenly the rest of us have the same opportunity, to succeed and fail, as the scions of the well-to-do.

Competitive sports are a nonviolent (or at least nonlethal) way of manifesting the equality, or even the superiority, of one's own. When a group is on the rise, in the ascendancy — as Catholics were in the 1940s and '50s — victory and defeat at sports become metaphors for victory and defeat for one's cause. It was in those years of self-assertiveness, when Catholics were still less than full participants in American society, that an *undefeated* season for Notre Dame became so damned important, and a defeat for Notre Dame became a cause of embarrassment and anguish. Notre Dame, after all, represented us Catholics: With the aftermath of JFK's election (with 80 percent of the Catholic vote), and the emergence of the ecumenical movement in the 1960s after Vatican II, whether Notre Dame won or lost suddenly became less central to one's existence.

While much of the Establishment press is endlessly attitudinizing that we must put an end to this chauvinistic business of national flags and national anthems and national teams at the Olympics, this would be the quickest way to kill the Olympics. It is patriotism, a healthy spirit of nationalism, the sense by millions that America's prestige is on the line, that makes tens of millions of us stay up late at night to watch a televised game of women's volleyball, in which we would otherwise have not the least interest. Men and nations do need moral equivalents of war; and, until a better comes along, the Olympics will have to do. The legendary victory of the American hockey team at Lake Placid in 1980 ("Boys," the coach told his young players before they skated out onto the ice, "you were born to play this game tonight") brought America to her feet not only because the American kids were young and green — but because they had triumphed over the great Red Army team itself! It was a national triumph at the moment America was undergoing a national humiliation in Iran.

And, it was not only a triumph for two individuals, but for America, when Joe Louis hammered Max Schmeling senseless in the opening minute of the first round of their second fight, and when Jesse Owens came home with four gold medals — when pitted on equal terms! — from a 1936 Olympics that were supposed to be dominated by the Master Race. Black Americans of the humblest origins had proved that, given an equal opportunity, they were more than the equal of the finest athletes of the Third Reich. That was the message the world received. Those two triumphs probably did more for American patriotism, black pride, and race relations in the United States than any other two events in our history.

What brought thousands of parents down to Griffith Stadium, and hundreds every Saturday down to the Ellipse, was not only the opportunity to watch thirteen-year-old kids play football. CYO sports gave the fathers and mothers and sons and daughters of the parish a shared and common interest; sports welded the families together; then they welded the parish together, and, finally, the archdiocese of Catholics together. Then (and even today), they are the stuff of my fondest memories. Forty years later, I can still hear the Lourdes's coach yelling to his left end, who was missing our fullback Jimmy Hayden on every play, to "Box 'em in, Kelly!" Forever after, he was known as "Box 'Em In Kelly."

The next fall, 1950, when I made second-string halfback, the team was not the giant killer of '49. And the week before the Saint Peter's game, my football career came to a temporary end. In a one-on-one drill, the running backs were lined up, given the ball, and told to run over an opposing lineman. After a couple of hits in this mindless drill, I felt a tingling sensation in my left thigh; but, when my turn came again, I ran the ball straight into a large, immobile fifth-grader named Ed Lilly. The next thing I remember is lying on the ground in agony, with the assembled coaches looking down at me. After twenty minutes, the famous Bethesda–Chevy Chase Rescue Squad was hovering over me. Turning on the sirens, they delivered me back to Children's Hospital on 13th Street, where X-rays revealed a fractured left femur. Not only had the bone snapped in half, the lower part had slipped over the upper, shortening my leg. My thigh was twisted and bloated, though the bone had not quite broken through the skin. While four interns held me down, a doctor pulled the broken leg back into its proper position, "resetting" the bone. You could have heard me half a mile away. (We beat Saint Peter's 12–0; and Hank, the hero of the day, brought me the game ball signed by every player on the team.)

Put immediately into traction, I lay on my back, immobile for three and a half weeks, while a system of weights and pulleys, attached to my left foot, maintained enough pull pressure on the broken leg to prevent the lower severed part of the bone from riding up again over the upper. Night after night I was sleepless from the pain.

When taken out of traction, I was encased in a body cast beginning at my armpits and extending down the left leg to the toes, then down the right leg to the knee. To turn me over, my parents had to lift the heavy plaster container and turn *it* over.

Wednesday, November 1, 1950 — the eve of my twelfth birthday — was an easy day for me to remember.

Early that afternoon, a White House policeman, Leslie Coffelt, gave his life defending Harry Truman from Puerto Rican terrorists. Twenty-seven shots were fired outside Blair House; and a Secret Serviceman had to yell to the President, "Get back, get back!" from the window where a curious Chief Executive was trying to observe. When my parents and brothers came by the hospital that afternoon, they were full of news about the attempted assassination.

Those four months spent on my back made a permanent impression. I came to appreciate what it meant to be utterly dependent; from October almost to February, I was on a bed pan, and could not turn over onto my stomach, even to sleep. The sense of helplessness was always present, the moments of embarrassment many and acute. When I was taken home in my body cast, my mother made a bedroom for me on the first floor in the den; and three times a day, she brought me all my meals on a tray. With nothing to do but read, I began consuming newspapers, magazines, and books.

Those months coincided with some of the most crucial events in American history. The Korean War had begun with the North Korean invasion of June 25, and I had followed closely, as the daily newspaper maps depicted the shrinking "Pusan Perimeter" into which the American and South Korean forces had retreated. Then, MacArthur, at age seventy, delivered the master stroke of his military career: the landing at Inchon on September 15, one hundred miles behind the front lines. With the disintegration of the North Korean army, and with American forces rolling north toward the

Yalu River and victory, I was reading the *Times-Herald*, the *Evening Star*, and the *Daily News* every day. It was exhilarating: the Americans, led by the invincible MacArthur, were winning again! Then came unnerving reports of Chinese "volunteers" showing up among enemy POWs, and, suddenly, massive Chinese intervention. "We face an entirely new war," MacArthur was saying by the end of November.

What's going on? I wondered. Soon, I was reading horrible reports of American trucks driving over the bodies of wounded American troops in the flight south back across the thirty-eighth parallel, and of U.S. Marines fighting their way out of the Chosin reservoir toward Hungnam and the sea. Every foot of the way out of North Korea, I followed Chesty Puller's First Marines — and can still recall the film of the docks of Hungnam being blown up by the departing Americans, who took with them a hundred thousand North Korean civilians. Why doesn't Truman drop the atomic bomb on the attacking Chinese armies who are killing thousands of Americans? I recall asking myself. Five years before, he had dropped it on two defenseless Japanese cities. With U.S. forces in headlong retreat, I picked up the paper to read that Harry Truman had just penned a stupid letter to the music critic of the *Washington Post*, for criticizing daughter Margaret's singing. Maybe Pop is right about Truman, I concluded.

Reading those newspapers every day engendered a lifelong interest in the events and issues and personalities of that dramatic moment in America's national history — the nadir of the Cold War. For one whose vague memories of Americans in battle, reinforced by the wartime and postwar films, was of glistening and glorious victories, what was happening in Korea was profoundly unsettling. Americans, who had never lost a war, were being defeated; and Douglas MacArthur was himself retreating!

Uncle Peachie, who had won the Silver Star, came to visit me in the hospital and brought me a magnificent rosary blessed by Pius XII himself, the crucifix of which was hollow and contained dirt from the catacombs. But I could never get Peachie to tell me about the war; he always changed the subject.

Not until February did I return to school, and then it was on crutches. In that seventh grade, I lost eighty-six days of school, but, thanks to a caring and scholarly nun named Sister Aquin, who would come by the house and give me assignments and tests, catching up was no strain. After leaving that parish school in 1952, I never saw her again, but when Richard M. Nixon named me a Special Assistant in 1969, I received a beautiful letter. Her penmanship was magnificent, and she was immensely proud of me, she wrote. A couple of years later, I was shocked to hear that she had died. I never had the chance to see her and personally thank her.

(There was one consolation from the months of convalescence. For a year or more thereafter, at the Saturday movies, I could watch myself — in the short promotion film for the BCC Rescue Squad — being carried in agony on a stretcher off the Chevy Chase playground, and shoved into the back of an ambulance.)

By April, I was off the crutches and trying out for pitcher on the baseball team, successfully. The one memorable event of that season for me came when, following the sustained shelling of our starting pitcher ("Captain Ears," as he was dubbed by Richie McCaleb, our catcher) by the best team in either league, Saint Gabriel's, I was sent out to the hill in relief.

To rollicking laughter from both benches, I took the mound, at eighty-five pounds, against the league's leading hitter, Bill Russell. With the bases loaded, I struck Russell out swinging on three pitches. For a minute or so, I stood on the mound, gazing at the outfield and savoring the moment. It did not last long. The next batter, Charlie May, had figured me out. My control was excellent — my father, trying to make pitchers out of Bill and me, used to catch for us every evening in the backyard of Chestnut Street — and everything I threw up was in the strike zone. But May had observed that his friend Russell had gone around swinging before the ball reached the plate. Digging in, Charlie May waited, and drove the first pitch deep into the trees above our center-fielder, Mike Loh, who waited beneath the branches as the bases emptied. The Lord giveth; the Lord taketh away.

An excellent athlete, Charlie May was in the first graduating class at John Carroll High School in 1955, and the first graduating class at the U.S. Air Force Academy in 1959. I never knew what became of him, until, early in 1987, while in the Reagan White House, I watched a taped briefing on the MX, by the ranking officer in the strategic missile program, a Brigadier General Charles A. May.

But the strikeout of Bill Russell was not the signal event of the spring of 1951 in the Buchanan household; not remotely. The great event that spring was the firing of five-star General Douglas

MacArthur, followed by the General's magnificent farewell address to the Congress of the United States. My father was not given to vulgar language. Although "damns" and "hells" were sprinkled throughout his vocabulary, they were about as strong as he, a member of the Holy Name Society, usually mustered. A hundred times, however, I heard him denounce "that little Son-of-a-Buck who fired the greatest general since Julius Caesar." To him, MacArthur was the greatest military genius the country had produced since Stonewall Jackson and the greatest man since Robert E. Lee.

He had admired immensely MacArthur's Pacific campaign; where, instead of losing whole divisions in heroic beachhead assaults, the general had bypassed the Japanese island strongholds and starved the enemy out. Meanwhile, in the Central Pacific, Americans were dying by the thousands in heroic frontal assaults against fortified Japanese positions. For almost fifty years, MacArthur had served his country with courage, imagination, brilliance, and panache; his triumphant return to the Philippines, his magnanimous treatment of the defeated Japanese, were the stuff of legend. And here was National Guard Captain Harry Truman, firing the American Caesar for speaking the truth about what needed to be done to win the war against the Chinese Communists in Korea!

Pop thought Harry Truman was a little man in an office that was too big for him; and the country was beginning to feel the same way. Truman's approval rating that spring of 1951 was in a free fall toward 25 percent, a depth even Mr. Nixon, in the nadir of Watergate, and Mr. Carter in the summer of 1979, never quite tested.

MacArthur's address to the Joint Session was a portent of things to come in the fall of '52. As my friend Pat Hillings, then a twenty-eight-year-old Congressman representing Richard Nixon's old district, told me years later, "When MacArthur finished his address with that line from 'Old Soldiers Never Die,' there wasn't a dry eye on the Republican side of the aisle — or a dry pair of pants on the Democratic side."

Douglas MacArthur did as he predicted, and began gradually to "just fade away." But a new comet was already coursing across the heavens of my father's political firmament, the fighting junior Senator from Wisconsin who called himself Tail Gunner Joe.

About Joseph R. McCarthy, it is impermissible today to speak kindly. Men who would smilingly pardon Harry Truman for the faux pas of calling Stalin "Good old Joe" would not be so forgiving of an American President who referred to the late Wisconsin Senator as "Good old Joe."

Dead now these thirty years, Senator McCarthy is probably the most loathed political figure in America's twentieth century. In the demonology of liberalism, no man is more reviled. Joe McCarthy, it is said, ran rampant through our civil liberties, imputed treason to some of the greatest patriots America ever produced, and created a climate of suspicion and fear that poisoned American politics, long after his deserved political demise. *Anathema sit.*

And yet, today's near universal fear and loathing leaves much unexplained. If McCarthy was so great a menace, if this was a time of national "hysteria," why does not a single Gallup Poll of that era show even 1 percent of Americans viewing McCarthyism or witch-hunting or anti-Communist extremism as a significant national problem? If Joe McCarthy was a genuinely evil and malevolent force, why did the first family of American politics so warmly embrace him? Old Joe Kennedy was a friend, admirer, and supporter; the Kennedy girls dated Joe; Bobby worked for him; Teddy played touch football with him at Hyannis Port; JFK walked out of a Harvard dinner in 1954, when a speaker expressed approval that the college had produced neither a Joe McCarthy nor an Alger Hiss. "How dare you couple the name of a great American patriot with that of a traitor!" roared Jack Kennedy, storming out into the night.

If Joe was so horrific, why, after years of charges and counter-charges, of hearings and headlines, of incessant warfare with the American establishment, Republican and Democrat, did he yet enjoy such public support? There was truth in the song title of the period, "Nobody Loves Joe, but the People." In January of 1954, four years after the famous speech in Wheeling, West Virginia, Joe McCarthy had a Gallup approval rating of 50 percent positive and only 29 percent negative, numbers any presidential candidate today might envy.

The loyalty Joe McCarthy attracted and held for four years had little to do, I am persuaded, with whether Owen Lattimore was a gullible fool, or a sympathizer of Stalin — or "the top Russian agent" in the United States, as Joe once foolishly charged. It had nothing to do with whether Annie Lee Moss was a Communist (which she was); or whether there were 205 or 57 "card-carrying

Communists" in the State Department, or whether Joe had said, or had meant to say, "security risks." There is a simplicity that exists on the far side of complexity; and there is a communication of sentiment and attitude not to be discovered by careful exegesis of a text. That half of a nation to which McCarthy appealed as late as 1954 supported him, I believe, not because of precisely what he said, but because of what they *understood* him to be saying. To the Americans who sustained Joe McCarthy for four years, he was saying that the governing American Establishment, our political elite, was no longer fit to determine the destiny of the United States; it had disqualified itself by having poured down a sewer everything for which twelve million Americans had fought and bled and died at Bataan and Corregidor and Midway, at Anzio and Normandy and Bastogne — and by having delivered up half the world to Joseph Stalin. "The reason we find ourselves in a position of impotency," Joe had charged at Wheeling, "is not because the enemy has sent men to invade our shores, but rather because of the traitorous actions of those . . . who have had all the benefits that the wealthiest nation on earth has to offer — the finest homes, the finest college educations, and the finest jobs in Government we can give."

Strike the explosive word *traitorous,* and you have the gravamen of Joe's case; this (not the numbers) was the sweeping indictment with which America roared agreement. That is why Joe's stock was soaring as Harry Truman's was plummeting. That is why Joe was loved by men who did not know Owen Lattimore from Millard Fillmore, and why Joe was, and is, hated by men who could not today name a single individual whose life or career he ruined.

When Joe flew to Wheeling, I had just turned eleven. Yet, re-reading the history of that era (Professor David Oshinsky's *A Conspiracy So Immense* is the finest book on the period I have read), I am persuaded the "Tail Gunner" did not launch a crusade; a crusade, desperately casting about for its Richard the Lion-Hearted, launched Joe. Joe McCarthy flipped a match into the woods, and, suddenly, the forest was ablaze.

Why did Americans, by almost two to one, side with Joe McCarthy against an academic, political, and press elite that urged all decent Americans to revile him? Why was America ready for Joe McCarthy's boisterous, bellowing call for the overthrow of its reigning Establishment?

The answer, I think, lies in the sobering and disillusioning events that followed hard upon the American triumph, and the national euphoria, of 1945. Review, again, the shocks, the jolting events, of that postwar era:

• On Roosevelt's death, Americans learned he had been feeble, sick, and dying when he sat down with the Man of Steel at Yalta and signed away Eastern Europe and Catholic Poland — Poland! — the nation on whose behalf the British and French declared war on Hitler. Moreover, Roosevelt's people *knew* at the time he was sick and dying.

• Even before the war's end, OSS agents had broken into the offices of the pro-Communist publication *Amerasia* and discovered thousands of classified documents. Two State Department officers, John Stewart Service and Emmanuel Larson, were arrested and implicated.

• In Canada, Igor Gouzenko, a code clerk at the Soviet embassy, defected, and named twenty-two people in a spy ring passing secret documents to Stalin. The new proximity fuse had been compromised.

• In 1948, a Soviet coup took over Czechoslovakia; the Berlin Blockade was imposed; and Alger Hiss, a man of immense privilege and exalted position, was exposed as a traitor, operating on Stalin's behalf at the highest levels of the government of the United States.

• The names of other alleged traitors and spies — Harry Dexter White, the number-two man at Treasury, Lauchlin Curie of FDR's personal staff, William W. Remington, the foreign trade expert at Commerce — come spilling forth in the sworn testimony of confessed Soviet courier Elizabeth Bentley.

• In 1949, the greatest shocks of all: The Soviets explode an atomic bomb; and China, the most populous nation on earth, falls to Communism, 600 million people on whose behalf we had challenged the Japanese empire. Chiang Kai-shek, our only major Asian ally in World War II, is driven off the mainland.

• In 1950, Judith Coplon, a Justice Department employee, is arrested during a New York rendezvous with a Soviet official; since 1946, she had been turning secret FBI files over to the Soviets.

• In June of 1950, North Korea attacks and MacArthur's brilliant Inchon landing is canceled out when the hordes of Mao Tse-tung —

the "agrarian reformer" of State Department prose — come hurtling south, killing thousands of American boys and threatening to drive the U.S. army and Marines into the sea.

• One month after the North Koreans attack, Julius Rosenberg is arrested, and his wife, Ethel, follows him to jail in August. The charge: wartime treason, the betrayal of the secret of the atomic bomb to Joseph Stalin.

• In 1951, MacArthur is fired for insisting that America seek victory over Asian Communism, and, upon the conviction of Alger Hiss for perjury, in denying he was a Soviet spy, Secretary of State Dean Acheson magnanimously intones, "I do not intend to turn my back on Alger Hiss."

These events "loosed within American life a vast impatience, a turbulent bitterness, a rancor akin to revolt," according to historian Eric Goldman.

Precisely.

And it was not illegitimate to ask who was responsible. Who the hell had been in charge?

Five years after V-E Day and V-J Day, after twelve million soldiers, sailors, Marines, and airmen had come home and turned the affairs of the nation back over to the politicians and diplomats of the Establishment, we were reeling in retreat. Hitler's East European empire had been annexed by the Communist empire of Joseph Stalin, and, now, China, too, had gone over to the Communists. Moreover, Stalin had been shamelessly appeased by elements of the U.S. government, while home-grown traitors had stolen our vital secrets, including the secret of the atomic bomb. Even McCarthy's Senate nemesis, Republican Ralph Flanders of Vermont, conceded Joe would have had no influence at all, "had it not been for the fact that our late, departed saint, Franklin Delano Roosevelt, was soft as taffy on the subject of Communism."

McCarthy was cheered because for four years he was daily kicking the living hell out of people most Americans concluded ought to have the living hell kicked out of them. And if he kneed Drew Pearson in the groin at the Sulgrave Club, well, what was that compared with frittering half the world away to the bloodiest tyranny on the face of the earth?

The war of legitimacy that Joe launched had undertones as well of class warfare. Senator Saltonstall of Massachusetts said of the McCarthy censure motion in 1954: "The issue was poison. One day I'd campaign in Pittsfield and the factory workers would plead with me to support McCarthy. The next day I'd drive down to Smith College and the audience would boo every mention of his name." Those factory workers of Pittsfield were the brothers, sons, and fathers of veterans, and veterans themselves. Reading the history of that era, the conventional mythology seems to me awry. The country that stood by him during four years of astonishing abuse would never have abandoned Joe McCarthy simply because some weepy Boston lawyer cried, "Your forgiveness will have to come from someone other than me." No, Joe McCarthy committed political suicide when he took on the Army of the United States.

The Americans who loathed the Ivy League–dominated Department of State that presided over the postwar disasters, loved the U.S. Army, which had brought America her wartime victories. After all, the army was MacArthur and Eisenhower and Patton and Bradley; it was Audie Murphy and Willie and Joe. Why was Joe going after it? When Roy Cohn and David Schine maneuvered Joe into his battle with the army (with Cohn accused of trying to get the wealthy Schine pampered army treatment other American kids had never got), they put him on the wrong side of the right institutions and symbols; they put him on a collision course with his own constituency.

No matter how army bureaucrats had blundered in promoting the Red dentist Peres at the vital Fort Monmouth installation, General Ralph W. Zwicker, the commander, was not some desk officer; he was a decorated combat veteran of the European theater, cited by Eisenhower himself for defending the "north shoulder" during the Battle of the Bulge. A young lieutenant of the time told me his officers' club was 100 percent solid for McCarthy, until McCarthy went after the army, then, loyal to their own, to a man they turned against him.

That half a nation, which supported Joe in January of 1954, fell steadily to a third in May; and his negative rating rose from 29 to 49. By the time of his censure in December of '54, Joe's army of loyalists was mustering out. Why, then, the necessity, thirty years later, to unearth and desecrate the political remains of Joe McCarthy, again and again? The answer lies — I believe — not in any outrageous charge Joe made or tactic Joe used. (His enemies, after all, had resorted to planting spies on McCarthy's staff and blackening his reputation with whispered allegations of homosexuality.) The need to drive the stake through the heart of Joe McCarthy again and again proceeds from an awareness by the American establishment that what Joe was charging them with was something next door to treason — and, for four years, half the nation agreed with the Senator from Wisconsin.

The Senate censure of Joseph McCarthy, as a political struggle, had much in common with the impeachment of Richard Nixon. The passions were identical; the coalitions for and against both men were roughly the same; and both men were despised antagonists of Establishment liberalism and the American Left.

Just as you cannot explain the virulence of the hatred of Joe McCarthy by proving he violated Senate traditions or abused Senate witnesses, you cannot explain the hatred of Richard Nixon by proving he authorized Bob Haldeman to tell Pat Gray to impede the Watergate investigation. (The use of federal agents to conduct break-ins and do wiretaps was an honored tradition of Democratic Presidents from FDR to LBJ.)

No, what was behind both flaming controversies were warring concepts of morality, of legitimacy, of patriotism. Who is the legitimate moral authority in America? Who, by conviction, background, character, and belief, should rightly determine the destiny of the Republic, and which is the illegitimate usurper, incompetent to identify and protect America's true interests from her real enemies?

Joe McCarthy's memory is spat upon today, not because of what he did to Owen Lattimore or Annie Lee Moss — but because he did to the American Establishment precisely what the New Deal Democrats had done to corporate America and Wall Street. He shattered, forever, the nation's confidence in their capacity to govern. Indiana's Bill Jenner said it succinctly in his own way: "Joe was the kid who came to the party and peed in the lemonade." Never again, after Tail Gunner Joe, would liberalism be entrusted with governance of the United States. Stevenson, Humphrey, McGovern, and Mondale were all ultimately rejected for the reason Joe McCarthy had given: Liberals, of the ADA variety, were too naïve, too incompetent, too "soft on Communism," to manage the portfolio of the Republic in a world where the enemy was the Soviet Union.

The wounds inflicted upon America's ruling class in the years 1950–1954 were permanent wounds. Academia carries the scars to this day. Growing up in the 1940s, I was aware of an immense esteem in which certain intellectuals, like my father's friend Paul Doolin, the great Harvard historian who taught at Georgetown during the war — when my father was still trying to get his degree at age thirty-nine — were held. These professors were men apart; if they visited our home, they were honoring the house. By the middle '50s, the intellectuals who had been the "Brain Trust" of the New Deal were the "eggheads" of the Stevenson campaign, academic fops not to be entrusted with serious matters like national security. By the time I reached college, the running joke was that a B.S. degree meant "bullshit" and Ph.D. meant "piled high and deep." By 1972, George Wallace was the leading vote-getter in the party that had twice nominated Adlai Stevenson, bringing audiences of *Democrats* cheering to their feet by mocking "pseudo-intellectuals" and "pointy-headed professors who can't park a bicycle straight." All part of Joe's legacy.

Rereading Oshinky's book, one comes to understand why so many working-class people loved Joe.

Tail Gunner Joe was a populist, showing up at the posh Madison Club in a soiled Marine shirt open at the collar, to tell "Boss Tom" Coleman that, whatever his disposition, he, Joe, was running for the Republican nomination for the U.S. Senate, and he, Joe, was going to win it. If loyalty to his "boys," Cohn and Schine, got him into the final, unwinnable fight of his career, loyalty, even if misplaced, is not an unattractive quality. Many of the reporters who disagreed with Joe profoundly liked him personally.

Whatever his failings, in a rough and turbulent and more honest era than our own, Joe McCarthy did not lack for guts. Politically fearless, he took on Senators of both parties, challenged Ike as well as Acheson, Marshall, and Truman, took on the army as well as the State Department; and gave back as much as a vindictive national press could dish out. He even warned the mighty Henry Luce to get off his case; and the Luce empire backed down. America in 1950 was a Rocky Graziano–Tony Zale kind of country; and Joe instinctively knew it. Asked once about his tactics, the Tail Gunner responded, "I will have to blame some of the roughness in fighting the enemy to my training in the Marine Corps. We weren't taught to wear lace panties and fight with lace hankies." At the end, when

Ev Dirksen came to tell him a simple letter of apology to Senator Hendrickson might save him from censure, Joe balked: "Ev, I don't crawl; I learned to fight in an alley; that's all I know."

Others might desert Joe McCarthy; others might conveniently forget they had cheered him on. Pop never ran out on him. Thirty years after Joe's censure by the Senate and his death in 1957, my father would wonder aloud why some dictionaries had devoted so much space to "McCarthyism," so little to "Stalinism." Nor did my father give a damn who knew about his regard for Tail Gunner Joe.

In February of 1985, when I was named Director of Communications at the White House, Don Regan's announcement produced thirty minutes of angry and nasty questioning from Lou Cannon of the *Washington Post* and Sam Donaldson, who, on hearing of the appointment, almost leapt the length of his chain.

Several weeks later, as I was driving my father to dinner up I-270 in Maryland, he volunteered that two "lovely girls" — from *Newsweek* and the *Washington Post* — had been around to interview him.

"What did you tell them?" I asked.

"Well, that you were all interested in athletics, and that, while you got into some boyhood fights, you were all fine boys."

"How long were they there?" I pressed.

The *Washington Post* girl was there about ninety minutes, he said, and the "lovely young lady" from *Newsweek*, "about three hours."

I almost drove into the median strip.

"Pop," I said nervously, "you didn't by any chance get into General Franco, or Joe McCarthy?"

"I most certainly did," he said. "I explained to those young ladies that General Franco was a great man who had saved Spain, and all Senator McCarthy was ever guilty of was of having fought the Communists. We talked about it quite a while."

I could see the lead: "The father of Pat Buchanan, a devout Francoist and supporter of the late Senator Joseph R. McCarthy, said today. . . ." But they *were* "nice girls," and they simply stored the quotes for future reference.

To understand why so many in my father's generation sided with General Franco and against Madrid, with Joe McCarthy and against Acheson and Marshall, with General MacArthur and against Truman, is to begin to understand not only his generation but ours.

We have a different sense of what is truly morally evil. What, after all, is McCarthy's bullying of witnesses compared with Harry Truman's coercive "repatriation" of two million Russian POWs to the tender mercy of Joseph Stalin in Operation Keelhaul — one of the bloodiest and greatest crimes with which this country has ever been associated? We have a different sense as well of what truly threatens what we cherish most: family, faith, and country. It is not Botha or Marcos or Pinochet; it is the Soviet Union and its genuinely evil ideology.

Unlike the fascist movements, Communism could not be diverted or halted by a single rifle bullet. Despite its determination to "last a thousand years," the Third Reich collapsed in twelve. Once Hitler was dead, Hitlerism was dead. Communism, however, did not die with Lenin or Stalin. Wherever it has triumphed, churches have been gutted, priests massacred, and children indoctrinated in Communist lies; the family has been subordinated to the state, and the betrayal of friends has become a matter of duty. The Catholic Church of Pius XI and Pius XII, in which we were raised, never lost sight of the truth that the permanent, irreconcilable, and decisive conflict for the destiny of mankind was between a West, built upon Judeo-Christian values, and the Communist East.

To my father's generation, General Franco had driven the Communists off the Iberian Peninsula. While American liberals embraced the Republic, and American Communists fought with the Abraham Lincoln Brigade, American Catholics did not see the war that way at all. In 1935 and '36, reports poured in of the burning of churches and monasteries and the murder of priests and nuns for practicing the faith in which my parents believed. What had happened to Orthodox Russia, twenty years before, was happening to Catholic Spain. When Franco and his nationalist troops landed and marched on Madrid, they became the armed champions of millions of American Catholics.

If the Left had Guernica as its rallying cry, the Catholic Right had the Alcazar, the old Moorish castle near Toledo that housed Spain's West Point. Besieged by loyalist troops, Colonel José Moscardo was informed by telephone that his son, captured by the Communists, would be executed if he did not surrender. When the boy was put on the line, the colonel said to him, "Commend your soul to God, my son. . . . The Alcazar does not surrender."

The boy was shot.

While the divisions in the 1930s were less bloody than Vietnam, they were no less deep. My father sided with his own. In Franco, McCarthy, and MacArthur he saw men who were fighters, men who waged war relentlessly against the true enemy. Any blunders they made were, in his eyes, mistakes of the head not of the heart. After all, what was MacArthur's "insubordination" — i.e., writing a letter to the Minority Leader saying what he believed about the war in Korea — compared to State Department complicity in the loss of China? And whatever Joe McCarthy's sins, he did not deliver up whole countries and peoples in Eastern Europe to a Communist system that is the most successful variant of fascism the world has ever seen; nor did he forcibly "repatriate" those two million Russian and Ukrainian POWs — to be executed at the railhead, on their return to the "embrace of the Motherland."

Modern liberals who today talk of the early 1950s as a time of "national hysteria" tell us more about themselves than about the era; they no more understood my parents' generation, which gave the Democratic Party five successive presidential victories, than they understand us.

Like the Third Republic from the Dreyfus affair to the fall of France in 1940, the United States in the second half of the twentieth century remains, deep in its soul, a house divided against itself.

Even the Era of Good Feeling presided over by Mr. Reagan proved evanescent, disappearing with startling suddenness when the President stumbled in the Iran affair. Suddenly, we saw again the same old coalition forming up, to expose, humiliate, and bring low the latest of its antagonists. As the Soviet bloc rolls up Central America, the envenomed political battlegrounds of the 1930s, of the McCarthy era and of the Vietnam era, are going to be revisited again. Because nothing has been settled; the chasm has never been closed; and the fundamental issue has not been resolved. Joe's lasting contribution was to have ripped the bandages off the underlying wound in America's body politic: Them or us.

With the tremendous popularity of the CYO, parishes began to extend it into high-school years. Soon, there were Intermediate basketball and baseball teams (sixteen and under) and Senior teams (eighteen and under). You have to have grown up Catholic to appreciate Mark Russell's crack, "I was eighteen, before I knew Protestants played basketball."

By the start of the 1950s, Pop had taken over coaching the Intermediate baseball and basketball teams. Now that he was his own boss, he took his afternoons off. With both Mom and Pop, family was their avocation as well as vocation.

By his third year of coaching, Pop's basketball teams were not only in the CYO playoffs every year at Catholic University, we were representing the city in the Middle Atlantic tournament that rotated between Washington, Wilmington, Philadelphia, and Baltimore. In 1954, with Richie McCaleb, Hank, "Rabbit" Sinclair, Tommy McCloskey, and Denny Flynn, all of Gonzaga, starting, we swept past the CYO competition, and headed for Philadelphia. It was the greatest sports year in parish history. Of the six CYO championships in the Washington area — Junior, Intermediate, and Senior girls and boys — Blessed Sacrament had won five. All three Blessed Sacrament girls teams were traveling on the same train to Philadelphia, which is where the problems started.

When we arrived on Saturday afternoon, the senior boys disappeared into the downtown bars of Philly; and some of our ball club trailed along. After they returned, we went visiting the Intermediate girls. Socializing was still going on at two in the morning, when Father Lyon deputized the girls' coach, Dave Ritter, and together they formed a posse to round up the missing athletes and get their five teams into their respective rooms, so the parish and archdiocese would not be disgraced — either on or off the court.

Hank and I were visiting two girls in their room when Father Lyon suddenly pounded on the door. Terrified, we slipped into the closet. The girls shouted their denials through the door that anyone was in there, but Father Lyon demanded the room be opened for inspection by him — and Deputy Ritter. Politely, Father Lyon came in and inspected the bathroom, while Ritter looked under the bed; then they apologized for the intrusion. As he was about to depart, however, Padre noticed the crack in the closet door, and pulled it open.

Paralyzed, we stared silently at Father Lyon, and he stared silently back at the two of us. Usually, I would be quick with the words, but I had never been caught in *this* compromising a situation before; and a priest had caught me. As though I were staring at a firing squad I kept my eyes locked on Father Lyon. Nobody moved and nothing was said, until Hank broke the silence with, "Olson won the fight, Father."

It was the greatest irrelevancy and non sequitur I had ever heard; but it flummoxed Father Lyon and bought us enough time to walk stiffly to the door, and out of the girls' room. That was the night of the title fight between Carl (Bobo) Olson and Kid Gavilan, about which all America was talking.

The next morning, we were down 10–1 in the first quarter, and were almost disgraced by a Wilmington team. But, when the beer was sweated out, it was all over for the boys from Wilmington. We headed for the hotel to rest up for the afternoon final game against Philadelphia, whose leading scorer was a tough, hard-driving Italian center. My father assigned Richie to dog him every minute he was on the court, until Richie ran him into the ground, or collapsed. Our scouting report also revealed the Italian kid, who was left-handed, drove only to his left, and shot comfortably only from the left side of the basket. So, at each foul, my father had Tony Carroll run up court (McCloskey had "mono" and didn't make the trip) to capture the left position under the basket (which was permitted in those days). Pop's strategy worked brilliantly; the Italian kid was frustrated and griping aloud during much of the game; and we were Middle Atlantic Champions. The Senior girls won as well. The three other Blessed Sacrament teams went down to defeat, with the Intermediate girls' coaches publicly ascribing their failure to our prowling the halls and their rooms the previous night.

For Pop, and for the whole family, it was the greatest sports triumph since the Saint Anthony's game five years before. Not only did Pop have two sons on the team, he himself was coach. Basketball in 1954 was as new to him as it was to us; we were learning together; and we had pulled it off together. "Those were great years," Pop says of those days; and I am sure the memory he cherishes most is that first triumph in Philadelphia, when he put together a victory strategy that would have won the admiration of the great Red Auerbach of the Boston Celtics, whose book Pop studied with the zeal of the convert.

Father Lyon, who loved sports and had worked for years to provide the Blessed Sacrament kids with the best in uniforms and coaches, now presided over a triumph. He was coming home to

Washington as the Branch Rickey of a parish franchise that had just won five city championships and two Middle Atlantics in the same year! When he got on the train, for the ride home to Washington, Father Lyon had General Absolution written all over him — for what might or might not have transpired the previous night. He was himself now telling and retelling the "Olson-won-the-fight-Father" story to anybody who would listen; and he and my parents celebrated all the way down the east coast to Union Station, where the winning teams were photographed for posterity. For the whole family, it was one of the proudest and most pleasant memories of growing up.

5

The Pope's Marines

"All right, boys! Pair off in threes!"

I T WAS on a Sunday afternoon in September of 1919 that there arrived at the door of my grandmother's house on 30th Street a man in black. He was Father Edwin McGrath, S.J., assistant pastor at Holy Trinity, and he had come to demand to know why young Bill was not going to Gonzaga, the premier Catholic high school in the city. (My father, on graduation from Holy Trinity, had been enrolled in McKinley Tech, a scandal for a Catholic family.)

"Because, Father," my grandmother answered, "we don't have the money."

"We don't want your money, Mrs. Buchanan, we want your son," the Jesuit replied.

Seven decades of Buchanan family association with that splendid institution began the next morning. My father was graduated in 1923; his seven sons were graduated between 1954 and 1972; his two eldest grandsons are enrolled today. Across the street from Gonzaga is Buchanan Family Field. When my brother died in 1985, the Gonzaga boys' choir rode out in buses to the Shrine of the Blessed Sacrament to sing "Amazing Grace" at his requiem mass.

My father's virtual adoption by these tough, devout, and caring men, the scholastics and priests of the Society of Jesus, helps to explain his lifelong allegiance to Gonzaga and fidelity to the Church. To him, they were the Defenders of the Faith, *non pareil*. Because the Jesuits taught my father that a "liberal education," heavy on Latin, Greek, philosophy, and theology, was indispensable to the development of the "whole man," that is how he had his own children educated.

Thirty-three years after my father's introduction to the city's oldest high school in 1919, my own introduction was different.

"I want everyone in this auditorium to look, first, to his left, and then to his right. [pause] Because, gentlemen, one of you three will not be here for graduation."

That was our introduction to Gonzaga, Washington's foremost Catholic high school, by the new headmaster, Father William Troy, S.J. Father Headmaster did not speak in jest; of more than 180 freshmen seated with me in that auditorium that cool September morning in 1952, only 120 graduated in 1956.

Gonzaga was a meritocracy. At the end of freshman year, and midway through sophomore year, dozens of students were "flunked out." From the contingent sent down to Gonzaga in 1952 from Blessed Sacrament parish, a third never finished. They were all expelled on academic grounds, even though the fathers and brothers of several were famous Gonzaga alumni. No other Catholic high school, not even Jesuit Georgetown Prep, flunked out students like that. The Jesuits at Gonzaga were implanting in the remnant that survived the idea that we were an elite.

Following Father Troy's words of welcome, we were marched in silence through the school to the "upper church" at Saint Aloysius for a three-day spiritual retreat conducted by a veteran retreat master of the Society of Jesus. So that there would be no communication among us, we were spread out, two to a pew, in the vast upper church; then, the doors of Saint Al's were shut and sealed, so that Catholics stopping by for a "visit" would not break the spell the retreat master was weaving. First, he walked us through the "facts of life," and then he walked us back again, enumerating in rich and graphic detail the "proximate occasions of sin" we must avoid, and all the conceivable sins we might commit, from the lesser, venial ones of temporarily indulging an "impure thought," up through the mortal sins, which merited damnation for all eternity. While some of my new classmates affected a sophisticated boredom, a helluva lot of it was new to me. I was thirteen at the time.

"Souls today are falling into Hell like leaves off of trees because of sins of impurity," the Jesuit thundered, echoing the Virgin Mary at Fatima. Where the sisters at Blessed Sacrament had emphasized God's love and mercy, this veteran custodian of souls was talking about God's justice, hanging us out over the fires of hell, suspending us there, and bringing us back again. For two days, I was riveted to my pew; childhood was obviously over.

That freshman year, we started classes at nine in the morning with religion, followed by an hour of Latin at ten; in the afternoon at one o'clock, it was Latin again for another hour. Every day in our freshman year, we also had algebra, English, and history; there were no "electives." The only academic choices during our high school career were whether to take Greek or science, and whether to take French or German as a foreign language. The Jesuits knew what we ought to learn, so our inconsequential opinions on the curriculum were not sought. The top students were pressured into Greek. Eight times a year, we were graded, with four "marking periods" each semester. Midyear and final exam scores were factored in to give the semester and year averages. Grades were given in numbers; 70 was passing.

There was an exact system of honors and awards. For the top student in all subjects in each of the five freshman classes there was a General Excellence Gold Medal. A "Premium" (usually an inscribed book) was given to the top student in each of three subjects: Greek, math, and apologetics (religion). The student with the highest overall average over thirty-two marking periods won a full scholarship to Jesuit-run Georgetown University; and every student who maintained an average of 80 or above won a half-scholarship. The Jesuits were determined not to lose to the secular colleges the best and brightest of the Catholic young. For some at Gonzaga, that half-scholarship meant the difference between a college education and entering the labor market for life — at age seventeen. They sweated and worked, night and day, in the knowledge that it did.

At the close of each monthly marking period, a school assembly was held. At the lectern, Father Headmaster would read out the names and Father Rector — Alfred F. Kienle, S.J. — would hand out honor cards, beginning with the seniors in 4A down to the freshmen in 1E. First honors was 90 or above in every subject. At the assembly's close, Father Kienle would deliver his homily, congratulate the winners, and admonish the majority of the 600 students at Gonzaga that they, too, if they would work harder, could one day be up on stage. Then, we all filed out.

Students came by streetcar, bus, and hitchhiking to Gonzaga from all over the Washington metropolitan area, some from as far away as Poolesville, Maryland, an hour's ride by train. The librarian alone excepted (a middle-aged lady), there were no girls or women permitted at Gonzaga, either as teachers or students; our all-male enclave would not comport well with the zeitgeist of 1988.

While I had won a half-scholarship to Gonzaga in the competitive examination given all Catholic eighth-graders in the Washington Archdiocese (which then encompassed the city, northern Virginia, southern Maryland, and suburban Prince Georges and Montgomery counties), I was listed eighth, out of nine winners, in the *Washington Post*. Three students, including Mike Cavanaugh, the son of my parents' friends from Holy Trinity days, had won full scholarships; and one of the three, Stanley Fiore, a tall, dark, spindly, intense, hyperkinetic Italian kid from beyond Silver Spring, was sitting across from me in 1A. Stanley had read the *Post* as closely as I, had memorized the nine names, and noted where they had stood in the citywide exam. On the first day of class, he appeared at my desk, smiled, introduced himself, informed me he had a genius IQ, and let me know he saw me as his academic competitor. He was trying to "psych me out" as we used to say.

My first months at Gonzaga, I had more enthusiasm than sense. I joined Sodality, *The Aquilian* (Gonzaga's newspaper), the debating society, played freshman basketball, and was elected president of 1A. After several weeks, I dropped off the newspaper. I had to: the academic competition in 1A was tougher than anything I had known at Blessed Sacrament; we were being tested in every subject every week, with "spot quizzes" on our homework dropped in, whenever the fancy took the teacher. I was studying three hours a night and still not putting daylight between myself and my competitors in 1A, let alone the rest of the freshman class. While I had always felt a healthy tension before taking tests and exams, the Jesuits were putting us under a constant pressure I had not known. All the competitive instincts my father and mother had sought to instill in me were now channeled toward academic excellence, and, more important to me then, academic honors. If the pressure was on me, it was on Brother Fiore as well.

At Gonzaga, discipline was strict, and punishment could be severe. To be late for class meant automatic "jug," or detention after school until five o'clock, sitting in silence while writing some monotonous assignment beneath the watchful eye of the Prefect of Discipline. Coats and ties were required. Anyone arriving at school without a coat and tie was sent home; when he returned, he was jugged. Anyone caught removing his tie within a block of school was jugged. One day, Father Headmaster sent around word that a home-bound commuter had phoned to say he had been heckled by Gonzaga students at Michigan Avenue and North Capitol Street, two miles north of the school. How was he sure they were from Gonzaga? They all wore coats and ties, he said.

"Gonzaga men are always gentlemen" was a school slogan.

During the semifinal game in the W & L High School tournament in 1956, I glanced up into the stands and observed a Washington and Lee fan giving me the middle-finger salute. We were winning. Every time I looked up, he hadn't moved an inch; he was still staring at me, his middle finger extended in front of his nose. He was what my father called a "hair tree," with the "duck's" and grease on his head and a face that looked like maybe he could use a couple of tubes of Clearasil, but he could sense he had gotten to me. Finally, I used some sign language of my own to convey to him that, postgame, if he didn't come down, I was coming up. Joe Kozik, Gonzaga's athletic director, sitting beside me on the bench, saw all this, and, following the game, hustled me into the locker room.

"Don't take yourself down to that clown's level," he said.

To be caught smoking within a block of school (except in the "senior lounge") meant three days of jug; the second time meant "suspension" — i.e., indefinite jug and 9 points off every grade for that marking period. For a mediocre student, suspension could mean academic expulsion at the end of the year. In my junior year, I was caught smoking in the locker room with Clarence Mitchell III, a sophomore and son of the future famed civil rights leader. Father Donahoe, who had stormed into the lockers on smelling smoke, was elated. It was 1954, the year of *Brown v. Board of Education*, and Father Donahoe happily announced to the students gathered outside that, "at long last, integration is coming to the jug." Mitchell and I did separate but equal time. (Mitchell went on to become a Maryland State Senator; but in late 1987 he was caught up in the Wedtech scandal that brought a bipartisan slew of indict-ments — to politicians, lobbyists, Congressmen and even my old White House friend from Nixon days, Lyn Nofziger.)

To be caught with "dirty pictures" was about the most serious offense at Gonzaga. Punishment was immediate expulsion. Four of Crick's freshman classmates were summarily expelled in 1954 — for passing around dirty playing cards.

Late in senior year, I, too, almost got netted, through no fault of my own. My classmate and chum John was wholly responsible. With a small body, a large head, and thinning hair (he resembled the "Smile" buttons worn today), John looked older than the rest of us, was quite bright, but rarely studied; and he was given to penning scatalogical verse and passing it around class to make his friends laugh. John was the school's primary source of the porno-graphic little cartoon strips we used to call "eight-page bibles." One morning before class, when I was a senior no less, John strolled over, his big head split horizontally by his lewd smile, and handed me a thick folded note. Then, he silently walked back across the hall, still smiling. Puzzled, I started opening the note. It unfolded and unfolded, until I found myself in Gonzaga's central hall, arms spread apart, staring at a *Playboy* centerfold. With the new headmaster, Father Anthony McHale, moving up the hall, nodding to students right and left, I almost had a coronary occlu-sion. Bringing my hands together in a lightning clasp, I crushed the centerfold into a ball, and dropped it into the large trash barrel in the hall, as nonchalantly as a sixteen-year-old can with a heartbeat of 200.

John was insane; and I told him so. Had Father McHale spotted the centerfold, I would have had the alternative of stonewalling, and jeopardizing my academic career, or telling Father McHale the truth about who pulled the stunt (i.e., "squealing"), which would have been the end of John's academic career.

Filthy language was almost as severely punished as dirty pic-tures. In my junior year, someone wrote on a lavatory wall in Kohlman Hall a commonplace obscenity about our math teacher, Mr. Hohman. When word got back to the headmaster's office, he broke off from his work, went over to the lavatory, inspected the wall personally — and called an emergency assembly of the entire school. "A disgusting phrase has been written about a Jesuit brother who has given his life to Christ," Father Troy said, his mouth grim, his eyes staring coldly out into the silent auditorium through the wire-rimmed glasses he always wore. He wanted to know who did it, so that the student's immediate expulsion would set an example for the school. No one said a word. The auditorium was like a tomb.

"What would decent people think of Gonzaga," Father Troy asked, "if they knew such things happened here?" He paused for effect. What would become of Gonzaga's reputation, if the gentleman from Formal Wear, who had just come through school measuring the juniors for their tuxedos for prom night, had chanced upon this disgusting phrase? At that, the entire auditorium literally exploded — in laughter. It was not in disrespect of "Billy" Troy, but in derision of the lascivious reprobate from Formal Wear, whose ribald comments to every junior being measured for a summer tuxedo were a standing joke throughout the school.

While disciplinarians, the Jesuits believed in exact justice.

Once, in my junior year, I was jugged by my French teacher, a Jesuit scholastic. Unlike most of the younger Jesuits, he was effeminate, spoke with a lisp, and was mocked behind his back — and he did not much like me. While the friend caught with me was sent down to jug, the French teacher held me back after school and coyly suggested he was considering taking nine points off my French grade that month. "How would you like that, Mr. Buchanan?"

If he had wanted to get my attention, he had. This would have meant an academic disaster that might put in peril everything for which I had been working for three years. Shaken, I requested an audience with the Prefect of Discipline. Almost choked up with apprehension, I told Father James H. (Jiggs) Donahoe that to cut my French grade nine points was to single me out, unjustly, and wipe out three years of academic sweat. Father Donahoe reflected on it, called in the scholastic, and gave him a scorching sermon on the matter of justice; then, he came out and told me solemnly I would do my jug like everyone else, but there would be no drop in grades.

I had heard the reaming of the French teacher being carried out; so I waited around, and when the scholastic came out of Father Donahoe's woodshed, red-faced, silent, and sullen, I gazed steadily at him now with what Mark Twain once described as "the calm confidence of a Christian, with four aces.'' I made sure, however, never to cross him again.

By the consistency and honor with which they kept to their declared code of justice, the Jesuits not only generated respect for themselves — but respect for the code. It was an excellent system, grounded in the realism that boys will be boys, that they will break rules, that they should know, beforehand, exactly what punishment to expect. No one got away with anything, but no one was punished more severely than the code dictated. Nor was there any school psychologist or psychiatrist around to discuss what it was deep inside that may have motivated you to want to look at the pornographic pictures in the first place. There was right and there was wrong, and you knew it! Punishment was swift and sure. But, when you had done your time in jug, you were restored to the student body; and the incident was over, forgotten and not thrown back up in your face. With sometimes thirty or forty kids a day (6 percent of the school) serving time, the system operated with extraordinary efficiency. New kids were coming into jug every day, taking the place of veterans who had done their time. Father Prefect sat at the front of the room, reading impassively, sometimes for two hours without ever looking up. Would that America's system of justice worked as well.

In a sense, the precise balancing of offense and punishment in the scales of justice at Gonzaga reflected the mathematics of salvation we were being taught in class. Just as venial sins brought Purgatory, temporary punishment, so minor offenses at Gonzaga brought temporary punishment. Just as mortal sins, unconfessed, meant permanent expulsion from Paradise, so major offenses at Gonzaga meant permanent expulsion. (In later years at Gonzaga, the letters *j-u-g* would come to stand for Judgment Under God.)

During a break in a television interview, a quarter-century after I left Gonzaga, a penologist told me that not only had he come to believe that all men have an innate sense of justice — i.e., a sense that punishment should precisely fit the gravity of the crime — but that, among men in prison, that sense of justice seemed even more acute. He was right, I think; men are born with an inherent idea of justice; and the rules and regulations at Gonzaga conformed precisely with that idea and ideal. Which is why no one ever protested the system, even as they chafed under its sanctions. Among the many deficiencies of our present system of criminal justice is its perceived unfairness. Some men walk, because they have found a lawyer or a team of psychiatrists to prove they were "temporarily insane," while others go to prison. Had we offered as an excuse at Gonzaga our disturbed "state of mind" at the time of the offense, Father Donahoe would have laughed aloud at the brazenness of the explanation, and then sent us on to jug.

At the desk closest to the door of each classroom sat "Beedle," the student designated to keep track of late arrivals, absences, and jug assignments. At day's end, Beedle's "sheet" was signed by the home-room teacher, and sent down to the Prefect of Discipline, who awaited your arrival. If, however, you were jugged, but your name did not appear on Beedle's list when it arrived at the Prefect's, he would not be expecting you. Beedle was a man to befriend.

While many of our teachers were Jesuit priests, most were "scholastics" or "misters" as we called them. In that era, it required thirteen years of study after entering the seminary before a young man was ordained, eleven and a half years of study if a college graduate entered the Jesuit novitiate. There were virtually no Jesuit priests under thirty. (Even the brilliant John Courtney Murray, who had entered the Society at sixteen, in 1920, was not ordained until 1933.) Most of the scholastics were men in their middle twenties who had finished part or all of college, and had already had three years of postgraduate study — primarily in theology at the Jesuit seminary at Wernersville, Pennsylvania. (Washington, Baltimore, and Philadelphia belonged to what was called "the Maryland Province" of the Society of Jesus.) Trained to be educators, they were approaching or passing midpoint in the curriculum of study prescribed four hundred years before by Ignatius of Loyola.

Most of them I remember as serious, self-confident men who tolerated neither nonsense nor disobedience. There was not much playfulness about them. Like the Sisters of the Holy Cross at Blessed Sacrament, these Jesuit scholastics had walked away from friends, family, and home, had given up all dreams of career and marriage and children. Unlike many modern clergy and religious, they did not seem caught up with politics or issues or the things of this world. Even though we were in the very shadow of the Capitol and the Supreme Court, I cannot recall having visited either building in those years. There were no courses in government or politics or social studies at Gonzaga, no "field trips" to Congress, the Pentagon, or the White House.

They were now on this earth to pray, study, teach, and serve God the rest of their natural lives in the vocation to which He had called them. Living in cloister at Gonzaga, the scholastics had taken temporary vows of poverty, chastity, and obedience, and the Jesuits' special "fourth vow" of special obedience to the Pope, His Holiness Pius XII. Final vows would come at ordination, half a decade or more away. Dedicated, disciplined, tough-minded, they were considered to be the intellectual vanguard of Roman Catholicism; the Jesuits were the Pope's Marines. (Lenin himself is said to have considered the Society of Jesus as a model for his revolutionary vanguard.

Between these self-confident young men who taught us in the early 1950s, and the befuddled professoriat routed from its perches in the 1960s, by the children of the counterculture, there was, literally, a world of difference. The Jesuits were in no doubt as to who they were and what their mission was; and they were unconcerned with our fourteen- and fifteen-year-old opinions as to how we should be educated. We had been sent there to be taught, not to teach; and, from centuries of experience, the Jesuits knew how to educate. To them, the purpose of an open mind was to close on something — and that something was the truth; and faith and tradition taught us what was.

While my friend, the octogenarian philosopher Dr. Sidney Hook, might profoundly disagree with the old Jesuit approach to education, he would have respected these men; because they were able to stand their ground and defend their right to teach precisely as they were teaching. In the 1960s, however, on campus after campus, professors, some with great names, proved unable to defend the "relevance" of subjects they had taught all their lives; they proved unable to stand up, intellectually, to student barbarians trampling all over the cherished concept of academic freedom and demanding to be told why they were wrong.

There is a crucial distinction between the education we received, and that offered now (even in many Catholic schools). We were sent to Blessed Sacrament and Gonzaga to study and learn the truth — the truth about God and man of which the Catholic Church had been mankind's custodian since the death of Christ. Today, children are sent to school to participate in some joint "search" for a truth they are told is either unknowable or has no greater claim to belief than someone else's "truth." Education becomes a moral scavenger hunt, with teachers and students participating together; and we ought not be surprised, when the hunt is over, at what some of the children have brought in.

Men who believe in something (even if wrong or evil) will always prevail over men who believe in nothing; the twentieth century has taught us that. And because these Jesuits lived the truth they taught, and because that truth had immense magnetism, millions in the moral confusion of the postwar world turned in their direction and sought that truth. Today, even some Jesuits exhibit the "What's it all about, Alfie?" attitude of the secular world they were once sent to teach and convert.

From the time we first heard of Gonzaga, we knew we were going there. It was my father's school; it would be his sons' school. As early as seven, I was taken along to Gonzaga–Saint John's football games at Griffith Stadium; it was the oldest rivalry in the city. In the late 1940s, the teams were famous, featuring the Hogan brothers from Nativity Parish and Billy DeChard; in 1946, Gonzaga traveled by train to New Orleans to play the famous Boys' Town team of Father Flanagan; and, in 1948, lost to Central and the great Jimmy Pantos in the city championship. We were there.

The Gonzaga coach in those years was Joe Kozik. Short, tough, bald, all neck, chest, and arms, sometimes profane. Polish-American, Joe Kozik was a bull of a man, who personified to critics what was wrong with Gonzaga, and personified to us the manly virtues that set Gonzaga apart from, say, Saint Alban's and "Prep." Our distinctive spirit, as well as our flaws, were writ large in this one man; which is why we all relished the stories about Joe Kozik, and which is why he became a legend to forty-five graduating classes. At a famous night game at W & L (a largely Protestant school then) over in Virginia, I watched, transfixed at ten years old, while a giant brawl erupted on the field, with players, coaches, referees, and fans all caught up. The riot occurred after a winning Gonzaga touchdown was called back in the final minute. From somewhere near where an enraged Coach Kozik was standing with his players had come the cry, "Okay, boys, let's go get 'em!"

The following year Joe was moved up to athletic director.

I first personally encountered the already legendary Joe Kozik when, in eighth grade, I was playing in a CYO basketball game at Gonzaga, and Kozik was referee. Our coach, an explosive Irishman named Tracy Mehr, who had played at Holy Cross, blew up over one of Joe's calls, and the next thing I knew coach and referee were in the middle of the floor shouting in each other's face, about to trade blows.

My father, acting as assistant coach for Blessed Sacrament, started out onto the floor to keep them apart; but Father Patrick McSorley, the then Prefect of Discipline at Gonzaga known as Black Pat, who was miffed at Kozik at the time, put a restraining hand on my father's arm. "Bill," the priest said coolly, "let 'em fight it out." Disregarding this clerical counsel, my father ran onto the court, and grabbed and held Kozik, trying to keep the two apart. That night he told me he thought he had taken hold of a piece of iron.

Joe taught freshman history, and — while he had a thing about the cocky kids from Chevy Chase — was an easy marker. As I said at his testimonial, thirty years later, as long as you wrote down that this great event, be it Xenophon's Anabasis or the death of Alexander the Great, "took place in Asia Minor," you got half credit. Given to Yogi Berra-isms ("All right, boys! Pair off in threes!" "Okay, line up in alphabetical order — according to height!"), Joe was a volcanic character. One day in the gym — where we took physical training, mainly for the benefit of the kids who were nonathletic — Joe called me out. I had been talking with Clagett, a classmate from southeast with a D.A. and about seven pounds of white petroleum jelly encasing his head, when I heard a terrific noise. Joe's five pounds of keys had hit the far wall of the gym. "Buchanan, where the hell do you think you are," Joe yelled, "out in Montgomery County somewhere? I'll put your head against that Goddamn wall!"

But Joe loved the boys. After he watched a freshman classmate of mine enter and leave school on the coldest winter days without an overcoat, Joe called him in and asked him why the hell he didn't wear his coat.

"Because I don't have one," the kid responded.

Joe got out of inventory one of the heavy Gonzaga jackets — modeled on World War II Navy pea jackets — and handed it to him. "Now, you have a coat and now you wear it," he ordered.

Twenty-five years later, the head of his own cable TV company,

Dick Loftus walked into Kozik's office in the new Carmody Athletic Center and said, "Joe, I've come to pay for that coat." He handed over a $20,000 check made out to Gonzaga.

Every school rally held in that auditorium would end with the same chant, "We want Kozik! We want Kozik!"

Letting the frenzy build, Coach Kozik would suddenly appear, smiling his "aw shucks" smile, swaggering down the right side aisle; and the auditorium would explode. The speeches that followed were not memorable; the man surely was.

In my freshman year, we discovered how progressive our capital city was. There were only four black students in school, three sophomores and a junior named Gabe Smith. As a sophomore in the fall of 1951, Gabe had played junior varsity football; so, Gonzaga informed all its opponents that we expected Gabe to try out for, and, almost certainly, to make, the varsity, the following season, 1952. And, if he did, we put the opposition on notice, Gabe Smith was going to be on the Gonzaga bench.

Every public high school in the District of Columbia, Maryland, and the Virginia suburbs immediately canceled its 1952 game with Gonzaga.

To find teams, other than Catholic rivals and Episcopal High over in Virginia, Joe Kozik, Frank Gilmore, the new coach who had come down from Blessed Sacrament, and the Jesuits scouted out schools in distant Pennsylvania, where we would travel for five hours on a chartered bus to play, and, late that night, travel back to D.C. to arrive at Gonzaga around 3 A.M. Go back over the 1953 yearbook, and you will find Gonzaga versus Salesianum, Gonzaga versus Hershey, Gonzaga versus Conshohocken, Gonzaga versus Harrisburg Catholic. The entire school supported Gabe Smith. Not because we were great progressives on civil rights, but because Gabe was one of us; Gabe was a Gonzaga man.

In the late 1960s, Patrick A. O'Boyle, Cardinal Archbishop of Washington, was derided in the secular press as a reactionary prelate, because he had stood with Paul VI against the dissident priests on *Humanae Vitae*, the papal encyclical on birth control. But two decades earlier, this same Irish priest, Washington's new archbishop, had decided — more than half a decade before *Brown v. Board of Education* — that all Catholic schools in the city would be immediately desegregated and that the black community of Wash-

ington D.C. needed a new Catholic high school. We had Archbishop John Carroll built, opened, fully integrated, and operating
— four years before the Supreme Court decided the public schools
of America's capital city should be desegregated.

In the summer of 1987, I was in attendance at Saint Matthew's
Cathedral for the nearly three-hour requiem mass and funeral for
the ninety-one-year-old Cardinal Patrick A. O'Boyle, who had
confirmed me in 1948 and whose lifelong credo had been *State in
Fide*, Stand firm in the Faith.

Early my freshman year, we freshmen learned the meaning of
school solidarity.

Following a game at Wilson in upper Northwest, a carload of
Gonzaga students — some of the toughest seniors in the school —
was attacked by a mob at Nebraska Avenue and Reno Road.
Dragged out of their car, they were beaten and stomped; and when
they arrived at Gonzaga the next morning in horrible shape, the
school was in an uproar, with the Jesuits trying to prevent carloads
of juniors and seniors from heading out to Wilson to do some
stomping of their own.

But the greatest disgust was not over the Wilson students; it was
over the lone Gonzaga student who, frozen in the back seat of that
car, had not gotten out to help. Word swept through the school
about the student who remained in the car. The disgust was universal. Forever after, that student was known as "Stick-in-car." (In
writing this chapter, I had to go back to the yearbooks to learn
what his real name had been.) Message received: Anyone who
didn't stand with his classmates or buddies in a brawl, and take his
medicine alongside them, was anathema.

By the early 1950s, Swampoodle, the neighborhood where Gonzaga was located, had long since ceased to be Irish, and was almost
entirely black. The row houses across from Gonzaga were half a
century old; only the poor lived there, and one of the houses, at 48
Eye Street, was an openly operating whorehouse. The cops ignored it. When drunks used to trudge up Eye Street in the morning
from North Capitol, carrying a little white slip, trying to read the
address they had been given, the white boys would yell out the
windows of the school, "Keep going, keep going; it's number

forty-eight." The men would smile and laugh and mosey on up to 48.

When I was a senior, and we were gathered in the senior lounge after lunch, one of the ladies from 48 was spotted on our side of Eye Street, leaning into a car, making her deal. We made some comments to her, and she gestured back; and turned back to the car. I got an apple from a classmate's lunch bag, cleared the area round the window, and, using that pitching control my father had taught me in the backyard at Chestnut Street, but with a lot more speed now at seventeen, fired the apple forty yards, hitting her square in the fanny. She let out a howl, at which point, the bell rang, and we headed back to classes on the first floor.

Outside, a crowd of "girls" and their boyfriends had gathered, hurling the most abusive invective in the direction of the school. I was terrified one of them would have the sense to walk calmly up to the school, explain to the Jesuits what had happened, and demand a formal apology from the student responsible. I knew the Jesuits; there would have been an investigation. Fortunately, they just kept cussing and hollering and making a stink, and the old priest in class, who had no idea what provoked this outburst, kept turning around and gazing out the window in puzzlement, mumbling something like, "I will never, never, understand these people."

To get to Gonzaga, in the center of the city, we hitchhiked every day. Around eight in the morning, my brothers and I would get out on Utah Avenue, get picked up almost immediately and carried across Rock Creek Park to Missouri Avenue and Fifth Street. From there, we hitched a second ride — usually from one of the government workers coming in from Silver Spring — down Fifth Street (one-way south), around Soldier's Home, then over to First Street (one-way) and down to Gonzaga. The vast Washington Hospital Center didn't exist.

After the Supreme Court decision of 1954, Washington's racial composition began to change with startling speed. As we rode down Fifth Street, "For Sale" signs appeared and began marching in the opposite direction. Monthly, we watched them move north, block by block by block, until, by the time I graduated, there were "For Sale" signs north of Missouri Avenue. The white residents of the nation's capital were running away from integration.

In the 1952–53 academic year, our freshman basketball team played junior highs like Taft and "Horrible Hine," which were 100 percent white. By the time we were seniors, the high schools fed by those junior highs, like McKinley Tech and Eastern and Anacostia and Roosevelt and even Coolidge, were all desegregated, and on the way to becoming 100 percent black. Within a decade, the *de jure* segregation of '54 was replaced by a *de facto* segregation that endures to this day.

A few blocks north of Gonzaga, on First Street, was the most famous black high school in America. We passed Dunbar every day. Like Gonzaga, Dunbar was a magnet school, an elite high school that drew the best and the brightest from the black families from all over the city and the Maryland and Virginia suburbs. What Gonzaga was to the Catholic middle class, Dunbar was to the black middle class: a center of academic excellence to rival the wealthiest Protestant prep schools in the city. With an all-black faculty, many of whom had Ph.D.s, Dunbar had a rigorous academic curriculum, a crack cadet corps, and a nationwide reputation. Unable to conform to the leveling ideology of the 1960s, however, Dunbar was sacrificed on the Altar of Progress, and converted into another neighborhood school. The D.C. public high that once boasted the highest percentage of college entrants in the city, some 80 percent of the graduating class, now led the city in broken windows. Like a lot that was thrown over in the '60s, Dunbar did not belong to the people who discarded it; and it was not they who felt the loss.

Once we had gotten past sophomore year, there was a reversal of attitude. The Jesuits were now determined that this select body of students would graduate. When Whitey, our junior quarterback, was arrested for stealing cars in Northeast ("joyriding" is the more accurate description), Father Troy himself went down to the station house.

"How many cars, Whitey?" he repeatedly asked.

One, Whitey responded; then, two; then, three; then "seventeen, Father." Whitey went to "indefinite jug," but he graduated.

Embellished or not, the story made the rounds as gospel, and made of "Billy" Troy, who left Gonzaga in 1955 to become founding father of Wheeling College in West Virginia, a hero to the student body. On my graduation night, he suddenly appeared in his wire-rimmed glasses and black cassock in the central hall; and the seniors broke into spontaneous applause. A rare tribute for a rare man. A few years later, Father Troy, still a young man, collapsed and died of a stroke.

In his book about his father, *The Chief*, Lance Morrow of *Time*, a '58 graduate, writes of how astonished he was on returning to Gonzaga, a quarter-century later, to see students jostling their Jesuit teachers, slapping them on the back in the halls. We never dared touch a Jesuit, he remembered; nor did they ever use corporal punishment on us. They didn't need to.

One violent exception proves the rule. In our senior year, the new Prefect of Discipline, a moody, black-Irish priest by the name of Aloysius McGonigol, S.J., exploded over some forgotten incident and ordered the entire senior class held after school. It was unprecedented; seniors were thought beyond such discipline. But an enraged Father McGonigol patroled the aisles, using his fist and open hand to punish imagined offenders against his command of look-straight-ahead silence. His temper building, the short but powerfully built Jesuit slammed Joe Kelliher, who was sitting frozen at his desk, in the head, driving him to the floor, and later to the hospital, with a concussion. Yet, no one moved. Finally, the new headmaster, Father McHale, arrived; and Father McGonigol disappeared, sent, we were told, "down to southern Maryland," where Jesuits with "problems" were confined and cared for.

Not for a dozen years did I hear anything more of the angry and explosive Jesuit priest. Then, from a Columbia classmate who had covered Vietnam during Tet, I heard about a wild priest who, apparently, AWOL from the army unit he served as chaplain, had charged the citadel at Hue in a company of Marines, and been shot through the head by the VC. On the black wall of the Vietnam Veterans Memorial on the Mall there is listed the name of Aloysius P. McGonigol, S.J. *In pace requiescat.*

(Father McGonigol was not the only Gonzaga man to give his life in Vietnam. My classmate, Paul Bayliss, was killed flying out of Thailand; Dougie O'Donnell, who alternated sixth man with Cricket on Gonzaga's outstanding 1958 basketball team, was a Marine forward observer killed in action. And on September 27, 1965, while a journalist in St. Louis, I noted coming across the wires a story about the latest Communist atrocity. The enemy, having held for almost two years a U.S. Army sergeant and captain, had marched them out, shot them, and proclaimed their heroic act of retribution to the world. As I read the copy closely, the captain's name was unmistakable: Humbert Versace. The VC had put Hank's classmate Rocky Versace in front of a firing squad, and executed him.)

At Gonzaga, athletics were considered vital to rounding out the "whole man." There was as great an emphasis upon competition in sports as in academics. Jim Conner, the scholastic who would go on to head the Maryland Province, used to require the athletes in class to read the front page every day, and the scholars to read the sports pages; and we were tested on both.

And every Gonzaga student was expected to be loyal to his school. When I was a sophomore in Greek class, and the game with Episcopal was coming up, "Mister" Conner produced a cheer in Homeric verse that we memorized, and held for the game. (Since Gonzaga had no football field then, the game was always played across the river at Episcopal in northern Virginia.) When the immensely spirited Episcopal student body went into their patented and rehearsed Ivy League–style chants and cheers, we waited, and then from the other side of the field came:

> Τρέχετε, τρέχετε εἰς νικμυ.
> *(Run, run to victory)*
>
> Σιαγετε, τφέπετε εἰς φυγμυ.
> *(Carry [it] over [the goal]; turn [them] to flight)*
>
> Πμρὸς, γλαμκός
> *(Crimson, gray [the school colors])*
>
> Τρέχετε, τρέχετε
> *(Run, run)*
>
> *Team, team, team!*

Then we went into it again. The Episcopal cheering section was dumbfounded by these cadenced cheers in some strange tongue coming from the Catholics' side of the field. They didn't know if we were cheering our team or insulting theirs.

In the mid-1950s, Gonzaga and archrival Saint John's were the class of the Catholic League, and the class of the city. The annual game was the last of the season, played in Griffith Stadium, where the Redskins entertained their NFL adversaries on Sundays.

In my senior year, Gonzaga was first in the Catholic League, and first in the city, in both football and basketball. The football team lost only to Easton High in Pennsylvania, and battled all-black Cardozo to a 6–6 tie in the first city championship game held after the *Brown* decision. The basketball team compiled a 19–3 record, losing only to Saint John's in the W & L tournament (we had beaten the Johnnies twice in league play), to the Georgetown University freshmen (on which Hank played), and to mighty Saint Francis of New York, with the famous Stith brothers, Sam and Tom, who beat us in the finals of the Washington Catholic Invitational Tournament at Maryland's Ritchie Coliseum, to which the best Catholic teams in the East were invited.

There were three reasons why that 1956 basketball team — which had no "height" by today's standards — was first in the city. The first was my friend Tommy McCloskey, who, although only 6 foot 1 inch, was voted best player in the metropolitan area two years after the honor had gone to a black kid from Spingarn named Elgin Baylor. The second was Coach Tommy Nolan, who drilled us harder than any other coach in the city, and whose two years at Gonzaga won him the coaching position at Georgetown. The third was our gym — a converted swimming pool. The walls of that gym (the sides of the old pool) were only three inches from the out-of-bounds lines. In the corner, we had to get our jump shots off quick, or be bumped into the wall. When we drove the basket too hard, we landed on the concrete steps of the pool, just beyond; thus, we were good outside shooters. Inside that gym, we could have beaten Cousy, Sharman, and the Boston Celtics.

Along with the Catholic League and city titles came other honors to the class of '56. Gabe Kajeckas was one of four finalists in the American Legion oratorical contest — nationwide. With the faculty immensely proud of the class, Father Kienle came to the auditorium one day, and declared a "McCloskey-Kajeckas" holiday for the entire school.

When graduation day came, the class of '56 had garnered more scholarships than any other in school history. Ranked first, with a

98 average over four years, I won the President's Scholarship to
Georgetown. (Stanley Fiore finished second.) With the graduating
class behind me, and a packed auditorium in front, including Pop,
Mom, and most of my brothers and sisters, I opened graduation
proceedings with a fifteen-minute oration on how at Gonzaga, we
had been trained to be "Christian gentlemen with a sense of responsibility," forged like "trains that can travel on any track" in
life, I said. A satisfying ovation attended the close of my remarks.

Two steps forward, one step back.
Two days after I addressed the parents and graduating class on
how we had been prepared to be "Christian gentlemen with a sense
of responsibility," Billy Barnes, our quarterback and starting
pitcher, and I were hauled into the Ocean City jail 150 miles away,
after a ninety-mile-an-hour race up Ocean Highway. Taken to the
cell block to await our friends with the $50 in fine money for speed-
ing, we observed fellow classmate Michael Keating sleeping in a
nearby cell. Mortified, I hoped word would not get back to Father
McHale that the class of '56 was off to an uneven start.

As with a first love, almost all my memories of Gonzaga are fond
ones. The spirit was contagious. I can still see that 1955 assembly
pouring out into the streets of that startled black neighborhood to
attempt the two-mile march through the city to Vermont Avenue to
raise the chant "Beat Saint John's!" (In 1986, when Iranscam fell
upon the Reagan White House, and I denounced the "whole damn
pack" of Republicans for having deserted Dutch and "headed for
the tall grass," one administration ally walked into my West Wing
office, held his fist up, and said, "Beat Saint John's!" It was Education Secretary Bill Bennett, Gonzaga '61.)
Three years ago, a *Washington Post* reporter, doing a long take-
out on Gonzaga, came over to the White House and asked, "What
did Gonzaga teach you?"
The truth is that Gonzaga not only taught lessons, in Latin and
Greek and math; Gonzaga imparted values. By their own lives, the
Jesuits, who received a tiny allowance from the Jesuit community
for personal effects and were permitted to own nothing — even the
watches sent them by their families were on "loan" from the Jesuit
community — were teaching us, in a way no book can, the inconsequentiality of the things of this world. They lived a communitarian

existence ("From each according to his ability, to each according to his need"), but it was a voluntary one. That material wealth was near the bottom of the rung of values was a lesson, the personification of which stood at the front of the class. These men had their priorities in order.

Religion was not simply an academic matter. Every Thursday, each class was marched down to Saint Al's, where the Jesuit priests heard confessions. I can still recall standing in a line outside a confessional, observing an identical line across the "lower church," when a voice from within the confessional bellowed loudly, "You did what!" Smiles broke out all over the church, as we watched the line outside that confessional melt away, and waited for the hapless victim to emerge.

While the expulsion of the four freshmen, for having the dirty playing cards, seemed, and indeed was, harsh and perhaps excessive punishment (one father left the Church over it), the point was driven home: The food that enters the mind must be watched as closely as the food that enters the body.

To the Jesuits, pornography was degrading to women, addictive, self-indulgent, corrupt, sinful, and poisonous to the development of healthy and positive attitudes about sex, attitudes crucial to building and maintaining strong families. While the public schools today affect a blasé indifference to pornography on the playground or in the classroom, these men took with deadly seriousness what was contained in books. They knew what the modern world has forgotten. Far greater harm has come, not only to souls but to nations, from polluted books and evil ideas — racism, militarism, Nazism, Communism — than has ever come from polluted streams or rotten food. With the Bible they taught that it is not what goes into the stomach that "defiles a man, but what comes out of his mouth."

If the salvation of the soul was the most important business of life, excellence was the temporal value most esteemed. The number of examinations, tests, quizzes, and "spot quizzes" over four years must have exceeded a thousand. The Jesuits enjoyed putting us under constant pressure and sudden tension. If we failed to do the required three hours of homework, we were humiliated in class. If a mediocre student neglected his homework, he would be called on a few times, then ignored, because everyone knew he wasn't going to be around after the midyear. When the newly formed John Carroll basketball team, all five sophomores, defeated Gonzaga in 1953, Joe Kozik sauntered into our freshman history class, held up his open hand with the fingers spread wide, and said with a sardonic smile, "Five soph-o-mores, boys!" and repeated "Five soph-o-mores!" Joe did not sugarcoat it; this should be considered a collective humiliation.

Counterbalancing pressure from the Jesuits to excel, however, was peer pressure in another direction.

Students who remained after school, who fraternized with the scholastics, who did outside reading and wrote unrequired reports, were "brown-nosers." When word leaked out that Mike Loh had gone bike-riding, at the invitation of "Moose" Bourbon, our freshman home-room teacher, he was not permitted to forget it. (And some of the scholastics had it rough; they became victims of the "pack instinct" among six hundred boys, aged thirteen to eighteen. PeeWee Davie, a year ahead of me from Saint Michael's, had given the appellation "Moose" to Mr. Bourbon in his freshman year; and for the entire three years Frank Bourbon was a Jesuit at Gonzaga he could not cross a crowded lunch room or assembly hall without the entire student body taking up the muffled call, "Mooooooooo!" Even an enraged Father Troy could not bring a halt to it.) And when Richie McCaleb spotted Mike carrying home more books than normal, he called him out, inspected the pile skeptically, looked quizzically at his old buddy, and said, "Now, Mike, I don't believe all these books are in the curriculum."

When my parents, at Christmas of freshman year, gave me a handsome leather briefcase, I was deeply embarrassed, and used it only until it was no longer impolite to leave it in the closet. Only wimps carried briefcases; we tied our books together with a strap.

While some of us wondered about the "relevance" of the Latin we were taught every day for four years, most of us would one day learn that it had been training the mind in logical processes even as it opened the door to our Western civilization, heritage, language, and culture. As did the three years of Greek. (By the time I reached the second year of college, I could read Horace and Virgil as well as I could French.) In the history courses, no one suggested that "Custer had it coming" or that Squanto, who helped the Pilgrims, was a traitor who sold out the Native Americans, as would be the case in some schools in the 1960s. We studied *American* history. We were the descendants and heirs of heroes, living in a nation built by great men; and nothing could be found within those history books to cause us to question the justice of America's wars or the greatness of America's past. Nor do I recall the young Jesuits of that era attempting to introduce their political opinions. (Indeed, I cannot recall them ever talking politics.) But I received the distinct impression that, unlike my father, the young intellectuals of the Society of Jesus in the 1950s were not all that enamored of the Roman Catholic Senator from Appleton, Wisconsin. Stylistically, Joe McCarthy was not of their breed.

For me, the most difficult subject at Gonzaga was always English. Writing was tough, hard work, and the grading was always rigorous. Each weekend in sophomore year, an original 500-word composition had to be produced, written in longhand and turned in Monday morning, with five points off for every single mistake in spelling, punctuation, or grammar. One Tuesday morning, having graded the essays, the taciturn Jesuit scholastic came into class, called out, "Buchanan!" then threw my composition book across the room to me. My heart sank; I had sweated blood over that composition. Then, he said loudly for all to hear, "There's a man who's really working!" One of the finer compliments I ever received. Any writing ability I brought to the Graduate School of Journalism at Columbia in 1961 can be traced back to that composition class of Mr. W. F. Lamm, S.J.

Debating, however, turned out to be a personal disaster. That year's national topic was: Resolved, the United States should get out of the United Nations. Following my father's inclination and direction, I took the affirmative. Kick the U.N. out of the U.S., I said; let's turn the U.N. Secretariat building into a New York general hospital.

After my original speech — which argued that the U.N. couldn't succeed, since it didn't open with a prayer — had won few debates, I wrote a second, livelier speech. Committing it to memory, I rode off to deliver it to the Holy Name Society of some northeast parish whose entertainment that evening was the brilliant junior debaters from Gonzaga. Brimming with self-confidence, I launched into my speech, but midway through my memorized remarks, I drew a blank and forgot the rest. As my sweating hands gripped the lectern, I stared, paralyzed, for what seemed an eternity into the impassive faces in that audience of two hundred men.

Finally, Frank Bourbon, S.J., who had escorted us there, ended the agony. "Tell us, Mr. Buchanan, in your own words, exactly what is wrong with the United Nations?"

Groping feebly for some argument I had heard in a previous debate, I answered, "The United Nations could easily lead to world government."

"And what exactly, Mr. Buchanan, is wrong with world government?" came the return volley.

I mumbled something inane and was permitted to move away and sit down. Each of the other three debaters got at least some audience votes as "best speaker." Not a hand was raised for me. Humiliation was total. I decided then that there were some things that came naturally for some people, and public speaking did not come naturally to me. So, for years, I avoided it. When I had to address the parents and graduating class of 1956, I memorized my speech, but the lectern was put on the right side of the stage, and a Jesuit was planted not four feet away, behind the curtain, with a full text. Neither he nor I was taking any chance on my icing up again — especially at that altitude.

Even today, my stomach churns more when I have to address a hundred people than when I have to appear on television before a million. Among the capacities of Ronald Reagan I came most to admire and envy was that extraordinary self-confidence that enabled him to stand and swap jokes with us right up to the moment he rose to speak to a live audience of tens of thousands.

Had I to do it over again, the activity I would have taken at Gonzaga would have been dramatics. Growing up in Chevy Chase, we considered dramatics to be something in which only sissies took part, but when I saw my classmates up on stage, in the one-act play contests where Gonzaga excelled, playing, persuasively, dramatic roles assigned to them, I knew it not only required talent, but nerve. Compared with acting on a stage, debating seems to me a single dimensional exercise. If you can entertain people by assuming a role, however, you can probably also persuade them.

The world of the 1950s is gone forever; and Gonzaga itself, the oldest high school in the city, barely survived.

In the early '70s, the squalor and crime that enveloped the neighborhood around 19 Eye Street meant fewer and fewer parents willing to risk their children's safety for the education offered in that inner-city school. Enrollment fell to 450; there was talk of closing.

Then came Father Bernard Dooley, S.J., the current president; his arrival was providential. Through his devotion, dedication, and hard work, he not only saved the school, he led Gonzaga into her Silver Age.

As Father Dooley was contacting alumni for financial support and bringing in new teachers, the slum housing was cleared, Buchanan Family Field was being built, and the Carmody Athletic Center began to rise where the concrete playground had been. With the new (subsidized) D.C. subway system, the trip to Gonzaga became as safe and swift for suburban students in the 1980s as it was when we hitchhiked there in the early 50s. Today, enrollment is higher than ever; school spirit is as high as 1956; waiting lists are longer. The Washington elite is now sending its sons there. Arguably the finest high school in Washington, it is well on its way to becoming one of the most famous in America.

There was a night when I knew for certain the school was coming back, and coming back somewhat as we remembered her. It was in the early part of this decade; my brother Tom and I had gone out to the Saint John's football game, played out in Maryland at Bishop O'Connell High. It was a cold night, with the temperature below freezing, as we stood, shifting our weight from foot to foot to keep our toes from freezing on that barren hillside. Standing with us were about a thousand alumni of Gonzaga, praying for the kind of victory we had known, but that had eluded Gonzaga for a decade.

As I was standing there, chilled, someone tapped me on the shoulder and wordlessly handed me an ice-cold beer; it was a guy I had not seen in a quarter-century. We laughed and sipped the chilled beer on that frozen hillside, as Gonzaga started running up the score on a scoreless Saint John's. Then a Gonzaga halfback, a speedster with college potential, swept around right end, and headed for the end zone. As he did, though, he slowed down enough to let the Saint John's defender get close, and then he held the ball out in his left hand in the Johnny's face, taunting him, as he trotted laughing into the end zone. Whistles blew all over the field over the unsportsmanlike act; and the touchdown (if you can believe it) was called back. But that did not matter; that hillside was roaring and bellowing and howling like a pack of Sioux the night after they finished off Custer at the Little Big Horn. Gonzaga was back.

Laughing at our outrageous behavior on that hillside, sipping that cold beer on that icy night, I thought to myself: These are the people whence I came. This is the camp to which I belong: middle-aged men with middle-class values, who entered the 1950s from their parochial schools and passed through high schools run strictly and sometimes severely by self-confident Christian brothers and Jesuit scholastics and Catholic priests. That was our time.

Gonzaga was back. But, as Lance Morrow found on his walk-through, it is not exactly the same place we knew.

6

Then and Now:
A Tale of Two Cities

"Where have you gone, Joe DiMaggio?"

W ASHINGTON, D.C., is today a cosmopolitan capital, the
beauty of whose monuments, buildings, boulevards, and
parks rivals that of Paris. Though 70 percent black, it
boasts a per capita income higher than almost every state in the
Union. More lawyers, lobbyists, politicians, diplomats, journalists,
bureaucrats per capita work in Washington than in any other city in
the world. We have all the features of a great metropolis in the
post-Christian era: fancy French restaurants, five-star hotels, styl-
ish boutiques, trendy singles bars for Yuppies and Buppies, and a
militant gay community, to which the city's black power structure
pays political tribute.

Though a city of only 600,000, the D.C. government employs
42,000 police, firemen, social workers, teachers, politicians, and
civil servants, the highest ratio of government employees to private
citizens in America. The leading "industry" is a federal government whose ranking civil servants earn in the top 2 percent of all
Americans in annual income. Yet, Washington is another city, a
city where more than half of all pregnancies end in abortions, more
than half of all live births are out of wedlock — a city where the
"welfare culture" has consolidated its beachhead, and narcotics
and crime are always with us. From Chevy Chase to Anacostia,
from Turkey Thicket to Cleveland Park, everyone preaches "civil
rights." Yet, most live separate lives; white folks rarely visit the
black sections of town, and white commuters rarely drive around

the black neighborhoods. To the friendly, law-abiding, churchgoing men and women of the black community, life is more comfortable than ever it was in the 1940s or '50s; it is also more dangerous. Murder is now the leading cause of death among young black males; and the probability is one out of two for a Washington resident to become the victim of a major crime in the next five years.

If TV sets and cars, freezers and garbage disposals, washers and dryers, air conditioning and stereos are the indices of the good life, Washingtonians, black and white, are far better off than we were in 1958, or 1948. The economic and social progress is real and visible. And, certainly, the opportunities, for black as well as white, to rise above our parents' station and reach the heights of professions closed in previous decades are present today. But, today, the nightly news and daily press are saturated with stories of drug busts, serial murders, multiple rapes, allegations of corruption, and charges of "racism" rarely heard thirty years ago. An incivility has entered the public discourse, and a coarseness has entered our politics that never existed in the Washington we once knew.

Pearl Bailey once told me that Washington was a wonderful place to have grown up in before the war, with the black community centered culturally and socially around the black churches where she sang. She preferred those days to these, she said, because now the "drugs" are awful. One wonders what a secret ballot would show, if the older people in the black community were asked: Are you better off now than you were thirty years ago?

Any resemblance between this cosmopolitan capital and the sleepy Southern city where we grew up is coincidental. Segregation was a way of life in postwar Washington, but, unlike parts of the Eastern Shore of Maryland, which were little slices of Mississippi, Washington never belonged to the "mean South." The only genuine "racist" I ever knew was the father of a grammar-school classmate, a red-faced, black-haired Irishman who kept a rack of rifles and shotguns in his dining room, and talked incessantly of "the niggers." His wife and kids, however, were the nicest of people, polar opposites.

Over the years, I have come to agree with a friend that "racism is an obsessive preoccupation with the subject of race. The racist sees everything in life, education and politics, from the standpoint of race. His viewpoint on everything is pervaded by this obsession." By that definition, racism is as prevalent in black America today as in white America. In the late 1940s and early '50s, however, race was never a preoccupation with us; we rarely thought about it.

There were no politics to polarize us then, to magnify every slight. The "Negroes" of Washington had their public schools, restaurants, bars, movie houses, playgrounds, and churches; and we had ours. Neither community could have been called rich.

We had no right to vote, when I was growing up, no elections. We were governed by three "commissioners," appointed by the President, and governed well. One of them, Walter Tobriner, was my father's good friend; he didn't need a limousine, but drove to work in his own car. The white public schools were run by one appointed commissioner, the black schools by another. And the schools ran well; the best of them were the equal of the Catholic schools.

Not until the Twenty-third Amendment was ratified, in time for the Johnson–Goldwater election, did my father cast a ballot. He was almost sixty, and my mother was in her fifties, when the two of them first went to the polls. Perhaps we did grow up in "The Last Colony," but I don't recall ever feeling "deprived." We had been raised in that school of conservatism which holds that, "When it is not necessary to change, it is necessary not to change." Believing ours to be a beneficent government, we accepted the traditions handed down to us; we never challenged their legitimacy or authority.

When Archbishop O'Boyle in 1948 had ordered immediate integration of all Catholic schools, a dramatic step in this still Southern city, the archdiocesan schools complied without question or protest. We Catholics were (and largely remain) a politically docile people. (Which is why we have failed to win on tuition tax credits and abortion, even as the black community has won enormous concessions from the federal government, and the Jewish community has won $3 billion in annual aid for Israel.)

Before me, the only member of the Buchanan or Crum families to have been politically active was Uncle Francis, my mother's oldest brother. A powerful local politician in Monessen, Pennsylvania, he was indicted for "voting the blind." Uncle Francis had apparently gone into the voting booth with the blind people from the county hospital to "assist" them in picking the correct candidates. In my teens, I came across, in my mother's dresser drawer, a Monessen newspaper with the delicious headline: ELEVEN CONVICTED; CRUM ACQUITTED!

Uncle Francis was a Democrat.

In the 1950s, there were no food stamps or Medicaid payments or rent supplements. The relief agencies were the churches. But no one starved; no "homeless" froze to death, and no shake-down artist extorted millions out of the White House by threatening to starve himself to death; and everyone worked. Black teenage unemployment was 9 percent in 1948, today, it runs between 35 and 50 percent.

In 1950, the same bus that was jammed with white-collar workers in their snap-brim hats coming south from Kensington to Chevy Chase Circle, to catch the L-4 downtown, carried the "maids," the black cleaning ladies, back out to Kensington to work all day in the houses the white men had left an hour before. When it snowed, the kids at Blessed Sacrament would gather at the circle and barrage the "Boston Blackie" with snow balls as it rolled by, heading north out the two-lane road that was Connecticut Avenue. The white driver was always more outraged than his passengers, who laughed at the diversion from the day's drudgery provided by the little white boys.

Now the cleaning ladies in the affluent suburbs of Washington are Korean and Mexican and Salvadorean, and tens of thousands of Washington's black women and their children are second- and third-generation welfare clients. Supposedly, they are better off.

By 1951, the house on Chestnut Street, with only three bedrooms, could no longer contain the family. With my parents, eight children, Anna Rose, and grandmother, the twelve of us were spilling out into the street.

In the postwar inflation, Chestnut Street had doubled in cash value; so, my father put our home on the market for $32,000, and bought a magnificent Spanish-style house on Utah Avenue for $44,500. Set back sixty yards from the road, the house was the largest in the neighborhood, with almost an acre of land.

While there were four upstairs bedrooms at Utah Avenue, they had to be divided among eleven people. (Anna Rose had gone; her explosions had brought a parting of the ways.) So, Uncle Peachie began, and some professional carpenters finished, two tiny bed-rooms at either end of the attic. Cricket and Buck moved into one, Jack and I into the other. Hank and Bill each got his own room on the second floor; and the girls, Coo and Bay, shared another. Thomas Matthew, my youngest brother, whom we called "Thompson," did not arrive until December 28, 1953 — seventeen and a half years after Bill.

While large, the Utah Avenue house did not have central air conditioning. Sleeping in those attic rooms during the steamy Washington summers was an advance taste of Purgatory. To cool the house, Pop invested in an attic fan so powerful it could pull hot air from all four floors and expel it through my bedroom window. Encased in a screen cage with a heavy, noisy motor, the fan was immense; it took two men to carry it to the attic. For six summers, I slept three feet away from the propeller of a B-29. Whenever the door to the attic was closed, however, and Cricket's window was opened, our tiny attic quarters became a wind tunnel; and my parents' bedroom would become a furnace. That giant fan would suck the air into Cricket's room, and drag it through the top of the house with tremendous force, before expelling it out my window. To be in Norway, all we had to do was shut the door to the attic. Half an hour after we did, we would be awakened with the shouted call, "How many times do I have to tell you — keep this damn door open!"

Utah Avenue was different. There were fewer houses in the neighborhood, and fewer children, until the Catholic families, the Keegans and the Aburrows, started moving in. But their children were as young as we had been in 1943. Within a year of arriving, Bill, Hank, and I were in Gonzaga; our interests were high school, CYO sports and dances, playgrounds a mile and a half away, and girls not to be found in the neighborhood.

When we moved from Chestnut Street, we hired a new maid, Laura. A huge black woman and a devout Christian, Laura sang all day long the gospel songs she sang at night in her inner-city Church of God. Each evening, my father would have one of us drive her across Rock Creek Park to the bus depot on 14th Street, to cut in half the time it would take her to get back home. On the ride over, I would ask Laura why she gave half her meager income to a "bishop" who was a transparent charlatan, taking these good black folk for all they were worth. Laura just laughed. "Oh, Paddy

Joe, come on,'' she would say. One day, it occurred to me: Why try to unsettle Laura in her faith, if that faith made her such a good woman, and so happy she sang to the Lord all day long?

Laura was a delight. One afternoon, when we asked her to come outside for a second, we turned the hose on her for three minutes; she joined right in, laughing, running around the yard, grabbing the hose, and turning it on us. Twenty years later, she was still laughing about how "Paddy Joe done cut the hose loose on me." Lord only knows what Anna Rose would have done to us, had we tried a stunt like that.

The differences that can exist within families are considerable. Bill, Hank, Crick, and I were born during the late Depression and reared during World War II — by my mother, who was still in her twenties when we were born, and a father who was a junior accountant in his thirties, a tough, athletic man who held down two jobs, while attending Georgetown at night to get his college degree at thirty-eight. We grew to manhood "When the Going Was Good" in the title of columnist Jeff Hart's fine book. Jack, Bay, and Buck were Baby Boomers; they grew up in the 1960s, a time of doubt and dissolution in the Church, of rebellion against authority, of drugs and "sexual revolution" — a time when it seemed the center would not hold. When they raised Jack, Bay, Buck, and Tom, my father was senior partner in the largest accounting firm in the city, and my mother was well known in the parish, the Gonzaga Mothers Club, and northwest Washington.

To Mom, Bill and Tom, her oldest and youngest, were "the bookends," and the younger children were "the second family." (One Christmas, Bill gave my mother Tom Braden's autobiographical book, *Eight Is Enough*, about *his* eight children. On the flyleaf Bill had inscribed, "This is dedicated to Tom!") Sister Kathleen, pretty, brown-haired, intelligent, studious, who in her early twenties looked very much like Mom, bridged the two sets of four children. She was four years younger than Cricket, and four years older than Jack; "I was an only child," she explains.

Where Bill, Hank, and I went to college in the 1950s, Tom went to college and law school in the '70s. We had been raised by a young man, who taught us how to box, who could spot Hank five games and thirty points and still blow him off the tennis court, when Hank was fifteen; Tom's father turned sixty before he turned twelve.

On Utah Avenue, the "commuters" franchise passed on to the younger brothers; but one operation, perfected on Chestnut Street, was brought over.

As our house was on the curve where 27th Street became Utah, it was not unusual that speeding cars — having crossed Rock Creek Park at forty miles an hour — would start up 27th at the same speed, accelerate as they started down the hill toward our house, miss the dogleg to the left, and wind up in our front yard. One morning, we discovered a sixteen-wheeler halfway up the hill to our house, its radiator smashed against the tree in the middle of the yard.

To bedevil the speeders and drunks, the four of us at night would split up, go to opposite sides of Utah Avenue, and station ourselves just beyond the turn. There, the driver would be coming at maximum speed; and, there, we stretched our "wire" across the road — an arresting cable, to catch the vehicles speeding down 27th Street. Only the wire was imaginary. As the car sped around the turn, all the driver saw was four boys, two on each side of the street, crouched, grimacing and straining — holding a "wire" stretched across his path in an insane effort to stop his speeding Buick Roadmaster. The instant he saw us, the driver would hit the brakes. You could see the fear in his face. As his car crossed the invisible wire, we would tumble all over the street. If we had him hooked, the driver would get out, swearing softly to himself, to see who was still alive among the bodies writhing in the roadway.

When we moved to Utah Avenue, Grandmother Buchanan had come with us.

Fond of the older boys, she had taken us on our first visit to the Glen Echo amusement park, out the trolley line from Georgetown; though she did use part of the "ride money" Pop had given us on the slot machines. When she retired from the Treasury, my father would take us downtown to visit her on Sundays in her rented apartment, and she would make us presents of dimes and quarters out of her meager pension.

One day in 1948, however, Grandmother had come home from

Atlantic City with what my father thought was sunstroke. He had had to pick her up at the bus station; and she never recovered. Maybe it was a minor stroke, maybe it was Alzheimer's disease, but she was no longer able to care for herself. When Pop brought her home, she quickly became too much for Mom to handle, with her constant demands, added to those of Mom's eight children. Grandmother was one of the few matters about which I heard my parents argue.

Clearly senile now, she had flashbacks to an earlier time when my father and his brother, Buck, were young. "Where's Buck?" she would repeatedly ask my father; then, she would ask us. After hearing "Where's Buck" for the fiftieth time — and telling her he was in New York working as a commercial artist — Cricket and I, bored one afternoon, decided to play a practical joke.

In Grandmother's bedroom was her favorite piece of furniture, a large old radio, almost chest high. Slipping inside the hollow rear of that old radio, I had Cricket fetch Grandmother and tell her to hurry and hear an alarming report. When she came rushing into her bedroom, Cricket pretended to cut on the radio; and I started broadcasting from inside: *"Good Afternoon. This is a late news bulletin. Henry (Buck) Buchanan, known as "Uncle Buck," was arrested this morning following an armed robbery at the Riggs Bank. "Uncle Buck," as he is known, is being held without bond and faces a prison sentence of up to ten years. . . ."*

The joke worked — too well. Before I got out from behind the radio, Grandmother, in hysteria, was tearing out of her bedroom to call my father at his office, to tell him that he had to get home, that Buck was in terrible trouble. My father calmed her down, but — even though Cricket and I fessed up — Grandmother's credibility never recovered. Not long after, in a wrenching decision for my father, who was intensely loyal to the mother who had raised him alone, she was on her way to the nursing home.

The big radio was brought upstairs to my attic room, where it was permanently tuned to the great country music station, WWVA, in Wheeling, West Virginia.

Griffith Stadium, on 7th Street (Georgia Avenue) just north of Florida Avenue, was "our" Center for the Performing Arts. All Redskins and Senators ("Nats") home games were played there, as well as important college and high school games. In the early

1950s, my brothers and I would take the bus across the park, and the streetcar down Georgia Avenue, to spend the afternoon and early evening watching double-headers with the New York Yankees or the Boston Red Sox or the Detroit Tigers. We were never bothered; and there was constant banter between the white kids and the black men who had taken the afternoon off to sit in the bleachers and sip whiskey from the bottles inside their brown bags. We were their audience; and they entertained us with their running commentaries about the starting nine on our eighth-place ball club. Griffith Stadium was where genuine integration began — and virtually ended — in Washington. Even in the late '50s, when we drove to the stadium for night games, we never felt any physical danger; though the ten-year-old black kids used to ask, pointedly but politely, for "a quarter, mister, to watch your car?"

Hank and I would arrive in the bleachers long before the game. While he and Bill remained loyal to the teams of Mickey Vernon and Bob Porterfield and Eddie Yost, and suffered with each loss, I was a Yankee fan as soon as I read about Ruth and Gehrig, "Murderers Row," and Joe DiMaggio. As the Yankee Clipper glided through his laps in the outfield and passed beneath us, I knew I was watching a legend, and I would talk him up from the bleachers. "Looking good, Joe," and, "Put one up here today, Joe."

Before he would turn to run back toward the Yankee dugout, I would ask DiMaggio — and later other Yankees like Whitey Ford — to flip a practice ball over his head into the bleachers. DiMaggio, or one of the pitchers who worked out in the outfield, would flip the ball; I would run for it; and Hank would go for the guy closest to me. The CYO's "best blocker" would crash into my competition, knocking him on his fanny, and I would grab the ball. As the issue had been decided ("Possession is nine-tenths of the law," we used to say), why fight? We used the same technique whenever Mantle or DiMaggio drove one into the left-field bleachers during the game — me going for the ball, Hank going for the competition. We took home half a dozen official American League balls that way. After the game, we would wait under the stands either with the ball, or our autograph books or programs, to get the Yankee autographs — Berra, Mantle, Rizzuto, Reynolds, Raschi, Lopat, Keller, Henrich, Bauer, Ford. From 1947 through 1964, the Yankees won fifteen pennants and eleven World Series, including five successive pennants and World Series under Casey Stengel from 1949 to 1954.

When they stopped winning pennants, I stopped watching baseball.

My father and brothers, however, were devoted to a Washington ball club that invariably had a death grip on the cellar by July 4th. (My father had memories of the great Walter Johnson throwing both ends of a double-header, and winning thirty-five games. So splendid was the memory of the Big Train that, in suburban Maryland, they named a school after him in the 1950s, a rare tribute to a ballplayer.)

"How can you fall in love with U.S. Steel" was the jibe against us Yankee fans in that era. But, to me, it seemed almost unpatriotic to root against the pin-striped Bronx Bombers. When the Yankees went down to defeat, even to the Brooklyn Dodgers in the World Series, I was sick about it; it seemed like a defeat for America's Team.

Hank did not share my adulation of the Yankees or of Joe Di-Maggio. And not without reason. One afternoon, when the great center-fielder emerged from the locker room under the stands, and Hank approached and asked for his autograph, the Yankee Clipper brushed him aside and headed for the team bus where DiMaggio sat moodily staring ahead, while patient Yogi Berra and the other Yankees signed every program thrust up at them. To Hank, it was an unforgivable affront; he never forgot it and enjoyed seeing DiMaggio strike out. When DiMaggio wed Marilyn Monroe in 1954 — a blow to my father, who shared my admiration for the Yankee Clipper and believed divorce and remarriage impermissible for Catholics — Hank waited for a lull in the dinner conversation, and jammed the needle in: "Well, Pop, what do you think of the old Yankee Clipper now?"

To me, Joltin' Joe was a mythic figure. Even though Mickey Mantle, "The Natural" of the '50s, remained a favorite until he retired, the Yankee Clipper inhabited a higher sphere. At the close of his career, I knew I was watching a legend out there. I can still remember standing, frozen, as a DiMaggio double hit the tiny screen, above the left-field wall, directly in front of me, 402 feet from home plate. Two feet higher and it would have knocked me cold; I didn't have my glove that day.

That Hemingway made "the great DiMaggio" a centerpiece of his *Old Man and the Sea* — a book the Jesuits had given me for the Math Premium in 1954 — only added to his extraordinary stature.

Battling the pain of the bone spur, sitting separate on the Yankee bench, gliding alone across that outfield at the close of his career, never taking the field during the absurd dust-ups when the benches cleared, always coming through "in the clutch" — Joe DiMaggio was the greatest "class act" in American sports. I thought so then, and still do. When I had heard — and later learned the reason why — that, rather than shake hands with Senate candidate Bobby Kennedy at an old-timers game in 1964, he stepped back out of line, he only rose in my regard. That he regularly put roses on his lady's grave was, again, the mark of a gentleman. Simon and Garfunkel penned the best lines in America's rock music of a turbulent decade, when they produced the melancholy couplet in "Mrs. Robinson":

> *Where have you gone, Joe DiMaggio?*
> *Our nation turns its lonely eyes to you.*

Our neighborhood theater was the Avalon on Connecticut Avenue two blocks south of Chevy Chase Circle; it is still operating (though now part of a chain) while many of the other neighborhood theaters — the Calvert in Georgetown, the Apex between Ward and Westmoreland circles, the Hiser in Bethesda — have been torn down. Admission was twenty-five cents in the 1940s, and rose during the next decade only to fifty cents. We were addicted to the flicks. We were there almost every Saturday morning in the summer when they ran the double features, and the serials with Superman. They were, even in retrospect, quality popular entertainment, though heavy on war films like *Thirty Seconds over Tokyo*, *Back to Bataan*, *Battle Cry*, and *The Sands of Iwo Jima*.

The impact of these war films on children of my age and era is easy to underestimate. Other than grainy newsreel, they were all we saw of World War II, the glorious enterprise that permeated our early childhood; and they were the best of what we saw. When a British cynic ridiculed Americans for the outpouring of popular grief over the death of the "celluloid hero," John Wayne, who had never gone near combat in World War II, the Brit revealed his ignorance about what America was mourning. There is nothing in the imagination that is not first in the senses. What films like *The Sands of Iwo Jima* — about Sergeant Stryker training and leading his Marines into battle, dying of a sniper's bullet in the back just before the flag-raising scene on Mount Surabachi — did was introduce into the imagination of the generation growing up during and after World War II a riveting "moving picture" of the courage and grit of the men who had fought World War II. We were being "shown" in "living color" what we revered, from the most glorious chapter in America's twentieth century. On that glistening screen, Wayne was surrogate for the soldiers, sailors, airmen, and Marines; he was showing us we were the sons and daughters, nieces and nephews of heroes. Wayne's films may have glorified war; they also served as a bond of memory between the generation that served and the generation that grew up during World War II. That's what we lost, and what we missed.

When we didn't have the money for a movie, or wanted to save our movie money for a Coke and custard pie at Peoples Drug Store, we used to sneak into the Avalon, in crowds of three and four. One of us would buy a ticket, walk far down the right side of the theater, and open the fire exit — as if to throw out an empty candy box. In the alley, several of us waited on hands and knees, and, when the door opened, crawled, lickety-split, into the seating area. From the back, the usher could see only the door opening and closing.

Those were the years of the Legion of Decency; and the Catholic Church was a feared and powerful force in Hollywood. Shows treating of Catholic institutions and themes — *Going My Way*, *The Bells of St. Mary's*, *The Song of Bernadette* — portrayed the Faith, the clergy, and the nuns in attractive and positive lights. *Agnes of God* and *Hail Mary* were light-years into the future.

The Avalon simply did not show "condemned" films. If Howard Hughes's *The Outlaw*, starring Jane Russell, played there — the most famous condemned film of the '40s — I cannot recall it; surely we did not see it. But, when the Avalon was about to show *The Moon Is Blue* with William Holden, a film that used words like *virgin* and *virginity*, and treated the latter lightly, the priests denounced the threat to faith and morals at Sunday mass; a picket line went up outside the theater; and a permanent boycott by Blessed Sacrament parishioners was threatened. With the moral authority of Catholicism invoked, the Avalon beat a hasty retreat; the manager pulled the film.

What a difference a decade makes.

While today, such "Catholic action" by the bishops would

be denounced as censorship (and the bishops would probably back down), there is nothing wrong with a minority uniting and using its economic power to protect values it cherishes. The priests at Blessed Sacrament believed they were protecting something far more precious than the daily take at the Avalon box office. With the federal courts having opened the floodgates for the rawest of sewage, the economic boycott — the weapon of the labor and civil rights movements — may be the most effective social sanction left — against truly "bad" films and "bad" ideas.

"Hanging out" was done at the corner of McKinley Street and Connecticut Avenue, outside Peoples Drug Store. We shot hoops at the Chevy Chase Community Center across the street, or played football or softball a block away at Chevy Chase Playground, and then repaired to Peoples' soda fountain — sweaty and shirtless in the summer — for half an hour of sipping a cherry Coke, produced with the syrup and soda water on the spot.

We were not popular there. Sweaty, laughing, loud-talking kids took up time and space and tended to drive away lunch and dinner customers who would be buying more than a nickel Coke. Besides, Fitz (Tommy Fitzgerald), a friend from grammar-school days, had a big, randy Irish setter, who used to pick up the ten-cent Mounds Bars in his mouth, right off the candy counter, and deliver them to us, whenever we let him in the store.

Eventually, we moved across the street to the Piccolo, which became the famous Chevy Chase Lounge, but not before Mr. Adams, the sour manager of Peoples, and Balderson, his two-legged mastiff and deputy, had called the Eighth Precinct and had my friends, the Kadow twins, arrested and fined for "incommoding the sidewalk," a violation we did not even know existed. Some of the police from the Eighth Precinct ("Number Eight"), who worked Connecticut and McKinley, were decent types; they walked the beat, took the free coffee and doughnuts handed out at the Piccolo bar, got along with everyone, and saw themselves as neighborhood peacemakers. They preferred not to arrest anyone, if things could be talked out and worked out. Other cops were forever on their muscle, looking for ways to throw their weight around. We bumped up against them constantly. One night, Kevin Kadow was handed a traffic ticket for "jaywalking," when he failed to wait for the light to change before walking across a deserted Connecticut Avenue — at one in the morning. Some of the cops were into that sort of thing.

By the mid-'50s, Friday and Saturday nights usually ended at the Connecticut Avenue Hot Shoppe. The Hot Shoppe was Mecca; pilgrims from the four corners of Chevy Chase arrived. The food was inexpensive, tasty, and filling; the double-decker "Mighty Mo's" Mr. Marriott sold by the millions (some kind of mixed Russian and Thousand Island dressing was used in the sauce) was the greatest hamburger ever invented; and the Hot Shoppe was where the action was.

Around eleven, the athletes would come riding in with their dates after the games; the dateless would come looking for girls or action; the girls came in carloads; and the auto nuts came in to compare cars. One Friday evening, "Bear" O'Neill and I were sitting in his car, waiting for curb-service Mighty Mo's and milk shakes, when a souped-up Chevy, its engine barking like a kennel of unfed dogs, pulled in, halted, then roared in reverse into the parking slot beside us. Both doors flew open simultaneously, as though the interior of the vehicle were on fire. While the driver strode purposefully toward the front of the Chevy and threw up the hood, his giant companion sauntered to the trunk, threw it open with enough force to tear it off, and began rummaging inside. The driver's head was bent over the motor, inches away from the blasting engine — vibrations from which were shaking our car. Like a family doctor, listening carefully for detectable signs of a heart murmur, the driver listened to the heartbeat of his Chevy. He had clearly heard something amiss.

"Uncle Huge!" bellowed the family doctor.

"Yo!" came the voice from the trunk.

"Number nine wrench, Uncle Huge!" said the doctor.

"Yo!" said the voice from the trunk.

Uncle Huge brought the wrench to the front of the car, handed it to the doctor, who reached in, tuned or twisted something, cocked his ear, listened, shook his head, reached in, turned or twisted again, cocked his head again, and smiled. The Steinway was tuned; the dogs were again barking in rhythm. As he came back to get into his car, wiping his paws and squinting into the middle distance as though the sun were shining here at midnight, Uncle Huge saw we had been observing. Extending a greasy paw toward the car window, he said something like, "Jimbo, from Rockville!" and asked where we "hung out."

"The Piccolo, mainly," Bear said, "but tonight, we were over at the Zephyr."

Uncle Huge recoiled as though he had been struck in the chest. "The Zephyr! Man, that place is scheduled to be scuttled!"

I had to turn away to keep Uncle Huge from seeing me smile. The language these people used was priceless, but what on earth did it mean to say a neighborhood bar was "scheduled to be scuttled"?

Like an endless Indian rain dance around a bonfire, cars circled the Hot Shoppe for hours on Friday and Saturday night, moving around the building, out onto Connecticut Avenue, and back in and around the Hot Shoppe, again and again. If a carload of girls drove around three times and then parked, it was a signal they would be amenable to a visiting delegation. The cheerleader types, Catholic girls from Holy Cross, Protestant and Jewish girls from Wilson, in their size-too-small cashmere sweaters, would stride across that large parking lot, feigning ignorance of and indifference to whoever was observing from inside the cars, and swivel their way into the Hot Shoppe — to buy a pack of cigarettes. "That brave vibration each way free," wrote the poet Herrick, "O how that glittering taketh me!"

Washington's finest from the Eighth Precinct would slip into the parade of circling cars, then, after one or two trips around to see if trouble were brewing, the "guns" would slip back out again. Occasionally, one of the cars would peel off from the great circle route, tear up Connecticut Avenue, leaving as its "Ave atque Vale" in the night a screaming patch of rubber as it hit second gear.

In a few of the cars that made the rounds, the driver, jacket collar up, would sit sideways, with his back to his window, left arm draped over the steering column, right hand using a "gunner's knob" to direct the vehicle. As he rumbled through, mufflers barking, the only way he could look out of his own side window was to glance down and to the left, like Bob Feller glancing toward first base, to check the runner. If five or six males were in a single car, circling, they were probably open to trouble. When fistfights would break out, negotiations would be held and sometimes quick agreement reached to "go up to Hearst," the darkened school playground half a mile away. The winner usually returned.

One evening, Smitty, a brawny and thuggish type who had moved to Chevy Chase from Northeast, tried to block our entrance into an open parking slot. "This spot's reserved!" Smitty said, defiantly, blue eyes blazing, heavy arms folded, feet apart.

"Smitty, get out of the way," Hank said, as he revved his '49 Merc.

Smitty didn't budge. So, Hank pulled it into first gear, drove right at Smitty, and over his foot, as he scrambled to safety. As Smitty hopped around, cursing, Hank looked up from the open window and said, "Little problem there with the corns, Smitty."

A bully, not quite as tough as he looked, Smitty hobbled off; next week he would be back, looking for smaller game.

For twenty years, the Connecticut Avenue Hot Shoppe was the Friday night oasis of northwest Washington, landmark to a generation. More than one date on Friday was arranged by hastily talking into a car window the previous Saturday. When we began drinking in taverns and bars, the Hot Shoppe was left behind, for the next generation. When I went to work in Mr. Nixon's White House in 1969, my mother called me one Saturday at my Connecticut Avenue apartment and asked me to come by and take my fifteen-year-old brother, Tom, over to Sibley Hospital to have his face stitched up. Keeping with tradition, Tom had been stomped at the Connecticut Avenue Hot Shoppe.

Even though the real estate became much too valuable for a fast-food restaurant, I was sorry to see Mr. Marriott let it go.

Many times, my father would relate to us his personal parable of the "game rooster." When the game chickens are young, he said, the game rooster chases them all over the barnyard; they scatter when they see him coming. But there comes a time when the game chickens, because of their breeding, will stand and fight; and the game rooster will go through that barnyard and kill every one of them. It was at the dinner table on Utah Avenue that the game chickens began to challenge the game rooster.

The Autocrat sat at the head of the table and carved; and he instructed us, *ex cathedra*, on history, politics, sports, faith, and morals. Hank sat to his immediate right, Bill to his left; I sat next to Hank, and Crick sat next to Bill; Kathleen sat next to me, and, so on down the line in chronological order. My mother, who sat at the far end, opposite Pop, put leaves in the table to accommodate us all.

The problem with the Buchanan Dinner Table Debating Forum was endemic. Every one of us was opinionated; and we were all taught not to back down. Whatever our positions lost in logic might be recovered with invective. If you never quit an argument, presumably you never lost. To make oneself heard as the argument got intense, we got louder and louder. The only one who could halt the uproar was my father.

Arguably the most opinionated of us all, he would invoke the authority of *pater familias*, shifting from the role of embattled disputant to that of moderator, timekeeper, and judge. After stating his views and impatiently tolerating several contrary opinions, he would silence the table, restate his view, and announce it as the final decision. The dinner conversation was a cross between a papal audience and "The McLaughlin Group."

On manners, my parents were uncompromising. Manners were the mark of a gentleman; and, dammit, Pop would make gentlemen (and ladies) of us all. Glancing far down the table once and seeing Tom out of order, Pop roared, "Get your damned elbows off the table!"

Only it wasn't Tom. It was Tom's little neighborhood chum, invited over to dinner. In the heated discussion, my father had failed to recognize the tyke, who sat paralyzed as if he had just been stunned by a Bull-Buster cattle prod. My father hastened to reassure the kid it was a mistake, that he was certainly welcome; and, please, enjoy your dinner. The rest of us took these blasts in stride.

One subject Pop brought up constantly was his conviction that lying British propaganda about the "bayoneting of Belgian babies" had gotten tens of thousands of American boys killed in a war with the Kaiser's Germany we had no business fighting. "The Kaiser begged his cousin, the Czar, to demobilize," he would tell us, again and again, at the dinner table. "Before the war broke out, the Kaiser wrote the Czar and pleaded, 'For God's sake, Nicky, demobilize!' " The *Lusitania had* been hauling contraband to the

British, he argued; and the Germans had given repeated warnings it would be torpedoed if it sailed. All our lives he taught us that World War I was a bloody and senseless slaughter, in which millions of young men died for interests that could not remotely justify so horrendous a sacrifice of human life — and he was right.

When "Black Jack" Pershing had led the bronzed heroes of the Argonne and Belleau Wood up Pennsylvania Avenue in the great victory parade of 1919, my father had a ringside seat on the steps of the Treasury, where his mother worked. Yet, even though his father's brother, Uncle Charlie, had fought in France as a captain with the AEF, too many of those heroes had died, "pulling Britain's chestnuts out of the fire."

Sex as a topic was taboo. Not once in my life did I have a conversation with Pop about sex. The morality of birth control, abortion, and so on, fine — but sex, *per se*, was simply not for discussion in the household or at the dinner table of a Catholic family.

Unfortunately, friends were unaware of the unwritten commandment. One Sunday night, Danny Boland, who was an eighth Buchanan brother in his run of the house, was sitting at the long table, when the subject turned to movies and Ingmar Bergman came up. Excited about the film he had just seen, Boland brought up *The Virgin Spring*. All the older brothers snapped to attention; we tried every head and eye signal we knew — to warn Boland he had just crossed into the family mine field. Oblivious to the anticipatory silence falling on the table, Boland plunged ahead, telling the story of how the vagrants had encountered the daughter of the knight. He was building toward the rape scene and the knight's revenge, when the hammer fell.

"Danny, we don't discuss things like rape at our dinner table, and we certainly do not discuss them in the presence of Mrs. Buchanan," Pop said in a cold, low monotone. For sixty seconds, the silence remained unbroken, as Boland desperately searched the impassive faces of the Buchanan brothers for some sign of recognition, sympathy, or reprieve. Having started dinner around 6 feet 1 inch, Danny finished his dessert unable to see over his plate. As we drove off to the movies later that night, he kept saying, "Why didn't you bastards warn me; why didn't you stop me; why did you let me go on like that?"

Monday morning Danny arrived at my father's office, penitent and contrite. Fifteen years later, I cannot see him on the streets of Washington without us breaking out laughing at the memory.

Even when I was working at the White House, the arguments continued, and on one occasion, which lives in family lore as "The Easter Massacre," degenerated into a fistfight between the youngest of the older brothers and the oldest of the younger.

"Captain Crick" of the 101st Airborne had just come home from Vietnam. At Easter dinner of 1969, he was venting his opinions on Jack and Bay and Buck. When the subject turned to marijuana, and Bay and the younger boys suggested that "everyone" in college today had tried marijuana, that it was "no big deal," Cricket had some pertinent thoughts.

"One morning, we found our perimeter man stoned in his foxhole from marijuana," Crick said; "we told him that if the VC had got through and killed one of us, we would have shot him. And if we caught him stoned again, that's what he could expect. People are getting killed all over Vietnam because of that crap."

At that point, Jack replied, "Tell you what. Why don't you take those Vietnam medals and ribbons and shove 'em?"

The bell sounded for round one, the '50s against the '60s, the "big boys," as we were called, against the "second family." Within seconds, I had hold of Jack, and Pop was coping unsuccessfully with Captain Crick, who was shaking his father off his back, like a dog shaking off water, to close and settle with little brother who had landed the first blow.

Buck, who had been upstairs in the bathroom, heard the commotion. Hitching up his pants, he came storming down, ran into the dining room, spotted Danny Boland trying to hold back Jack, and planted a right fist beside Boland's right eye. Buck had mistakenly assumed Boland, a peacemaker, had taken sides with the older brothers.

My father and I finally separated the fighters. Then, I noticed Mom heading into the kitchen near tears at how her sumptuous Easter dinner, which had taken days to prepare, had ended in ruin and rancor. Pop followed her, and I could hear him saying, "Catherine, don't worry about it; these things always happen when you raise strong boys." He felt it a natural manifestation of healthy competitive family spirit.

A year later, I had co-authored the Nixon speech announcing the U.S. incursion into Cambodia. Brother Buck, at Xavier in Ohio, had served as "marshal" for the march following the killing of the four Kent State students. That summer at the beach, we were at it again.

"That invasion saved American lives," I told Buck at dinner, voice rising. "After it was over, weekly casualty lists were cut in half. The Communists have no damn right to hide in Cambodia and attack from a 'privileged sanctuary.' Nixon should have done it the day we came into office. We never even heard of Kent State."

Buck, however, was enraged at the shootings. "Instead of calling out the incompetent National Guard," Buck demanded, "why didn't they call in some firemen and douse the demonstrators?"

Generational tension was building. Littlest brother Tom, a roaring reactionary at fifteen, retorted, his voice dripping with sarcasm, "Because, Buck, we don't pay firemen to hose down hippies!" For a second, we were almost in it again; but Tom was half Buck's size; he had broken the tension and everybody laughed.

Running the Buchanan Boarding House & Diner was Mom's job.

Each weekday, she would get up around 6 A.M., prepare and package (in brown bags) lunches for nine children, fix hot breakfast for us plus Pop, feed Ace and Deuce, the family cats, and Shultz or The Baron, the family boxers, and have us all out before nine.

After the house emptied, Mom would take her cup of coffee, read the paper, clean the dishes, and start on the household chores with Laura's help. Then, she would do the grocery shopping, usually at the Safeway on Connecticut Avenue, although, in the 1950s, Broad Branch Market delivered; as did my father's friends at Circle Liquor. ("Hey, Pop, your afternoon shipment just came in from Circle Liquor," we would needle the Old Man about the beer and booze.) By the time we started pouring back into the house after 3 P.M., Mom would have on the kitchen counter a cake, a pan of brownies (to this day Shelley's favorite), or one of the pies in which she specialized: butterscotch, lemon meringue, pumpkin, pecan, or apple. In the ice box would be half gallons of milk; and for the skinnier kids, a bottle of Poundex.

Being on time for dinner was not optional. If grace had been said in your absence, you heard about it. Following dinner, the Rosary was recited. There was no television until homework was complete. On birthdays, Mom would take the celebrant aside and ask what menu he or she wanted for dinner that night (for me, it was fried chicken, corn on the cob, french fries, and pumpkin pie with whipped cream), and she would spend the day preparing it for the family.

Mom ran the best restaurant in northwest Washington. Sundays, we were fed in two shifts. The younger children would go to 9 A.M. mass; and the older boys, after a late night "tanking" (as brother Tom would say), would go to the 11:15. When we got home, platters of sausages, scrambled eggs, scrapple, and toast, bowls of hominy or "grits," and pot after pot of coffee were waiting. Sunday breakfast was the best meal of the week; there was a delightful informality. The older brothers usually had some wild story to relate from the weekend; and we talked rather than argued. Sometimes we were sitting there at that dining room table sipping the coffee my mother would keep brewing until the middle of the afternoon.

Mom's nurse's training was sometimes lifesaving. When I came home at fourteen with a bee sting on the nose, and chills, she had me over to Doc Keegan's in Georgetown for an adrenaline shot, recognizing that the hives breaking out all over my body were a reaction that could have been fatal. When Tom woke up one morning, choking with the "croup," she had him in the bathroom, his head held over a tub of steaming water, to break up the mucus, until my father got the car ready so Tom could be rushed to Children's Hospital for an emergency tracheotomy.

The real liberators of American women were not feminist noisemakers; they were the automobile, the supermarket, the shopping center, the dishwasher, the washer-dryer, the freezer, the garbage disposal, and frozen food. As soon as the remarkable conveniences of the Affluent Society were introduced, Mom could spend more of her time reading books, teaching public school kids their Catholic faith at CCD, organizing the Gonzaga Mothers Club, and, when the children started leaving home, operating Meals on Wheels in Chevy Chase. Until the feds nationalized that, too.

When the women's movement declared that women deserved equal opportunity, and equal pay for equal work, it was pushing against an open door in our household. When it started disparaging the role of wife and mother, and promoting "abortion rights," the feminists lost every family like ours.

In conflicts between father and sons, which were becoming more frequent before the older boys left home, she prevented the breaches from becoming irreparable. One evening, after I had been brought home from the Eighth Precinct — Hank and I had put on masks and threatened a neighborhood busybody who had called the police to hassle us for no reason — my father walked out into the backyard. Mom brought me a couple of hamburgers, sat down, and said, "Patrick, you boys had better not force me to choose between you and your father; because I will choose him."

Mom alone could intervene and get car privileges restored. When we were "grounded," she could win us a reprieve. While we were too proud to ask Pop for money, we could always ask Mom for a buck in high school for an evening out, or for ten bucks for a date when we were in college; and she never reminded us of the generosity later.

She didn't like to argue; she preferred to talk and listen and discuss. She felt these dinnertime "debates" — so often traversing the same plowed ground — to be insignificant squabbles in which too much pride was invested, and too many hours were wasted. Who really cared whether the older athletes were superior or inferior to the modern ones? "For heaven's sake, calm down," she would say when arguments began to heat up; she would wait until coffee and dessert to hold her conversations with daughters and sons.

If dinner was Pop's Hour, Christmas was Mom's Day. Every year, she began shopping in July; by Christmas Eve, each of her nine sons and daughters had a separate pile of gifts. The tradition continues, with daughters-in-law and sons-in-law and twenty-four grandchildren now included, each with his or her own separate pile. In those turbulent years — when the game chickens began to challenge the game rooster — she kept the family together.

For Christmas, the nine children pooled resources and bought a single gift for the parents. While the younger children were not required to pony up much, they were required to pay something — or their name did not go on the card. If they had no money, they would take on any chore for a quarter or fifty cents, to insure their names were on the card.

That family experience persuades me that removing all demands from America's poor is the worst thing we have done to them. If seven-year-olds are willing to rake up half an acre of leaves to get their name on a Christmas card, to contribute "something" to a present for their parents, what must it be like for grown men and women to know that they are not only contributing nothing to the society to which they belong, but their contributions are not even wanted?

While marijuana and cocaine were unheard of, many of us were smoking regularly by fourteen. Pop was forever admonishing us to "get rid of the damn things" (he promised each of us $500 when we were twenty-one, if we didn't smoke), but he did not expressly forbid it. (The connection between cancer and smoking was only asserted then, not established.) Besides, both Mom and Pop were then as addicted as I was. So, they were tolerant; and Crick and I were smoking a pack a day early in high school, with Mom secretly providing us the cigarette money.

By the time I was fifteen, we also imbibed almost every Friday and Saturday night. For the normal-sized among us, a six-pack was usually adequate for the evening: Gunther, Old German, Iron City, Lebanon Valley, and Hals. A six-pack of Gunther was only one dollar. (At one time Hals was ten for a dollar; the next morning you paid a second time for your bargain.) We tried to buy it by the case (rather, have it bought for us) at "Pat's" Chevy Chase Liquors on Connecticut Avenue just down from Peoples. On really big weekends, we bought Schlitz. Consumption was a function of size. The Kadow twins, who were on the far side of 250 pounds from the time they were sixteen, could consume eighteen beers a night and, on principle, would not start an evening with fewer than twelve on board. Some Saturdays in the summer, they would start in the early afternoon and have made their way through an entire case by midnight. Fortunately, the more they drank, the mellower they became. At parties, we would match them up in "chugging contests." Two guys, the best in each crowd, would crack a beer in the garage, hold it to his mouth, and, on a signal, consume it as fast as he could. Three to five seconds was as fast as the beer could be sucked out of the can and swallowed.

Getting sloppy drunk was another matter; and we suspected something was wrong with the few who drank constantly, or drank alone, or drank until they were stupid. We were out to have a good time, and beer, in those days, was an indispensable element. Coming home, we would concede to the parents that we "may have had a beer or two.'' In excellent physical condition, we "held" the beer well. And sipping beer, while riding around and laughing and trading witty remarks with your friends, was, I must confess, great fun. Today, they would call it "male bonding."

The first introduction of the Buchanan brothers to high society came with a surprise invitation to attend, at ultra-exclusive Chevy Chase Country Club, the debutante party of the eldest daughter of my father's friend and client Page Hufty, of Washington and Palm Beach. A nationally famous schoolboy golfer, Page Hufty had grown up in Georgetown, established himself as a successful businessman in his twenties, and married an heiress of Standard Oil. As friend and accountant, Pop handled his books — and Page Hufty was reciprocating by inviting Bill, Hank, and me to the coming-out party for the lovely Alexandra.

It was the first time I had ever worn a tuxedo. After we moved through the receiving line, I made two observations: first, I was among the youngest at the party; second, I didn't know anybody. I stayed close to my brothers. With regularity, however, the waiters at the posh club moved through with glasses of champagne, which my brothers and I had never tasted. No one asked my age, and we picked them off the trays and downed them like the little ginger ales we took them to be.

Two hours into the party, I was talking loudly to everybody, asking the older girls to dance, when the room began to spin. Time to call Ralph on the porcelain telephone. This was no laughing matter. Throwing up on the floor of the debutante party of the eldest daughter of my father's most important client at the Chevy Chase Club would not only be a social disaster, it could be a financial reversal at Councilor, Buchanan, Mitchell & Hayes. Desperate, I asked Hank to accompany me to the pool, so I could walk it off. While he sat in a poolside chair, out of sorts with little brother's incapacity to handle champagne, I walked around the pool for half an hour. Finally, my head began to clear. So, I walked over to Hank, and said, "Thanks, now let's head back to the party."

Hank didn't respond. In fact, Hank didn't move. He was out cold in the chair; I thought for a second he was comatose. Now, *he* was the problem; and I had to get him out of there, before *he* disgraced the family. To haul Hank back through the debutante party, and the lobby of the Chevy Chase Club, in a fireman's carry seemed out of the question; I didn't know Mr. and Mrs. Hufty quite that well. So, I decided to carry Hank through the woods north of the club, and down Connecticut Avenue to the car. When I picked him up and threw him over my back, however, I could only stumble a few feet before collapsing beneath him. He was thirty pounds heavier than I, and dead weight. So, I dragged the tuxedoed corpse back across the pool patio, sat it in its poolchair; and went back into the party to brief Buchs on the family crisis.

When we got back out to the pool, Hank hadn't moved a centimeter. Together, we picked up his lifeless body and dragged it through the woods north of the main building toward the parking lot. But, in the woods, we ran into a barbed-wire fence as high as we were — to keep out the riffraff. Together, we hoisted Hank and threw him over, and Buchs thoughtfully tossed some leaves on top of him for camouflage. Then, we traversed the party, went out the front door of the club, retrieved the body in the woods, transferred it to the back seat of the family car, and returned. There was nothing more we could do for him. Hank was through for the night.

The party got better and better. Falling back on my eighth-grade training at Mrs. Murphy's Dancing School, where I had excelled, I even squired a couple of the older girls around the floor. Early in the morning, the party moved upstairs for a huge buffet breakfast of ham and eggs and bacon and sausage and potatoes and juices and toast; it was the most bountiful spread I had ever seen at that hour of the morning. Then came trays of coffee. This sure had the Toddle House beat. We made it home around 3 A.M., the family reputation for courtliness fully intact.

Several years later, in 1958, when Hank and I were staying with Uncle Jim, his wife, Mary, and their eight kids in Fort Lauderdale at Easter break, we were invited to represent the family at Alexandra's wedding. Picking up my girlfriend, Beth, who was staying at the Marlin Beach Hotel, and Hank's new girl, Colette, who was from Chicago, we borrowed Uncle Jim's old station wagon, with the kiddie seats and toys in the back, and headed up A1A, along the ocean and through the sparsely built communities of Pompano, Boca Raton, and Delray Beach. It was the first time I had ever seen this slice of America. When we entered the southern outskirts of Palm Beach, we were astounded at the size and beauty of the mansions, with their iron gates and manicured lawns, all painted in either white or the softest of pastels. We couldn't find the church; but when that beat-up station wagon rolled up to the Hufty home (the first time I had ever heard of valet parking), we must have looked like Flem and I.O. Snopes coming for a visit.

The wedding reception at that house on the inland waterway proved as splendid as the debutante party. Behind the house was a lawn with soft grass in the style of a golfing green; beyond the lawn was a seawall at which the cabin cruisers moored. Midway through the reception, we noticed a commotion. In strolled, smiling and nodding, the junior Senator from Massachusetts.

Tanned, handsome, charming, left hand jammed in his jacket pocket, smile flashing like a strobe light toward anyone glancing toward him, Jack Kennedy introduced himself all around, had himself photographed on the lawn with the bride and groom, and moved out as smoothly and confidently as he had moved in. I had recognized him from pictures and film of the hearings of his Senate labor committee; even then, I knew he was a leading candidate for the Democratic nomination. In the judgment of a nineteen-year-old college sophomore, who noticed his eighteen-year-old girlfriend observing Kennedy equally intently, the Senator from Massachusetts was indeed impressive. I did not know how to describe what Kennedy had that made the ladies' heads turn, and the men nod and lift a glass from a distance; later, they would call it charisma.

Besides the Piccolo at Connecticut Avenue and McKinley Street, we spent idle evenings in the Zephyr, the Friendship, and Maggie's, all on Wisconsin Avenue near Tenley Circle, and, occasionally, "The Den," across the street from the zoo on Connecticut.

In Maryland, one had to be twenty-one to drink; but in the District we could buy or drink beer in any bar at eighteen. In your own neighborhood bar, like the Piccolo, they would serve you younger, so long as you behaved yourself. Which you usually did in your own place. Not until we were in college did we drink much hard liquor (except for prom nights). Except for a few girls, and guys with serious drinking problems, nobody drank wine.

We knew of no "nightclubs" in downtown Washington, except the Casino Royale, which was too expensive. The "singles bars" were Benny's on 14th Street, where the rock-and-roll band of my friend Walter Smith from Gonzaga performed nightly, and the Hayloft, around the corner. When we took a date out on the town, we went to the 823, on 15th Street, and drank beer by the pitcher, or to Fogarty's on Calvert Street. (Following a late, late night at Fogarty's one summer, Brother Hank and I almost started out with our respective girlfriends for Elkton, Maryland, marriage capital of the East.) On M Street in Georgetown, the only bar I remember was Mac's Pipe & Drum; Georgetown was dead in those days.

It was one night in Georgetown, while wandering with Hank and Chick Leasure and the Kadows along M Street, that we were startled to come across racks and racks of genuinely raunchy publications. (In Washington porn was not to be found — not in nice neighborhoods.) The stuff was inside a street corner book stall. While today, they would be considered "girlie" magazines, for those times it was pornography, and fairly hard core. Noting the presence of this material, right in the shadow of the university, the rest of us moved on deeper into the shop, looking for *Street & Smith* or the *Collier's* All-American issue. Hank did not.

Though he didn't smoke, Hank had borrowed some matches, and after several minutes, we saw why. Flames were shooting up from dirty magazines, toward the roof of the little shop. The porn was ablaze, and we were being cut off from the exit. Hastily, we put our magazines back on the racks and started filing silently past the smoke and flame, out onto the street. Then, we started running; Hank had a head start.

Suddenly, the proprietor saw his inventory of filthy magazines going up in smoke. "Jesus H. Christ, Frank," he yelled to his partner, "the sons of bitches have lit fire to my books! Look to the books, Frank, I'm going after 'em." He came running through Georgetown after us, yelling, "I know the fathers up at the university; you'll pay for this, you sons of bitches. I know Father Bunn!" (Father Bunn was president of Georgetown.) It was probably best he never caught us. For Hank, quite devout, leaving a pornographer unconscious in the street would have meant time off in Purgatory.

An aversion to pornography was natural, ingrained, instinctive. The only "porn" theaters in town were sleazy "art" houses far downtown. If you were seen entering one of those, people would have thought you were some kind of pervert. We didn't need a presidential commission to tell us something was wrong with it. Everybody knew that — then. Even Tommy, the retarded kid who has wandered Chevy Chase all his life and is known to one and all, understood that. Finally getting a job as substitute mailman at the Chevy Chase Post Office, Tommy, then in training to be a church usher, was given the copies of *Playboy* to distribute along his route. Silently picking up his designated pile of *Playboys*, Tommy went out and dumped the consignment down a sewer. Several days later, calls were pouring into the post office from area Yuppies demanding to know where their *Playboy* was. To Tommy, this was "Catholic action," as the nuns had taught him. Our family thought the story hilarious; I never heard a word of reproach for Tommy or of sympathy for the subscribers.

In 1956, we sold the blue '47 Cadillac, and for half a decade, all the new family cars were Oldsmobile 88s. First, my father would buy new ones; then, as they were racked up, one after another, he would buy what Capitol Cadillac called "cream puffs," second-hand cars with a few thousand miles on them. While I was only in one inconsequential collision my entire life — at sixteen — my brothers crippled and totaled half a dozen Oldsmobiles between 1955 and 1962.

After a while, my father's return appearances on the "cream puff" lot became a subject of amusement for the mechanics at Capitol Cadillac. One of my father's two Oldsmobiles would be towed in in the morning, and, in the afternoon, he would be prowling the "cream puff" lot for its replacement. "Boys rack up another one, Mr. B.?" they would chuckle. (He was then on the board of Capitol Cadillac and got special deals.) Smoldering with rage, "Mr. B." came home one night, and silenced the dinner table as he went into his monologue.

"I have had it," he roared. "The mechanics at Capitol Cadillac are *laughing* at *me*; my friends on the board at Capitol Cadillac are *laughing* at *me*; worst of all, the insurance company has notified me they are cutting off my insurance. No more insurance! Do you understand that? I am fifty-four years old, the head of a respected accounting firm, and I can't even buy auto insurance!"

No one said a word until I looked up to the end of the table and said, consolingly, "Pop, none of this would have happened if you didn't drive like a damn fool."

The worst of the family accidents took place at the corner of River and Falls roads, in the heart of what is now the wealthy community of Potomac, Maryland. Then, it was rural and farm country. Cricket had been given my mother's green-and-black Olds for the night; he and Jimmy "Jiggs" Donahue had gone to a picnic in some farmer's field, partied, and then Cricket turned the keys over to Jiggs, who headed east on Falls Road at eighty miles an hour. Where Falls reaches River Road, there was a stop sign, with a slight veer to the left. Jiggs swept through the intersection at seventy, missed a telephone pole by a few feet, demolished the phone booth in the gas station, and totaled the car in a ditch.

When I got home around midnight, my father and mother were shaken. Cricket was unconscious in Suburban Hospital, having smashed his head on the windshield. The three of us drove up McKinley Street in the surviving Oldsmobile, my father at the wheel, and we stopped at the light at Connecticut. Just as it turned green, we started across, only to have a car — filled with blacks — run the red light directly in front of us. A few more feet; and they could have killed all of us.

My father let loose a blast through the open window; where-upon, some familiar vocabulary emerged from inside the jammed car. All of them were plowed. Hearing them use this kind of language on the parents, I got out, determined to clock the first ine-briate out of their car. But, they were having the devil's time trying to figure out how to open the car door. Red-eyed, one of them finally started out, yelling obscenely, when my father yelled, "Pat, get back in the car!" Which I did.

When we got to Suburban Hospital on Old Georgetown Road in Bethesda, we found Jiggs, uninjured but penitent and alarmed at what he might have done to his best friend. Cricket was still uncon-scious; but, after a while, he started to come around. The doctors concluded there was no permanent damage; we could go home. Immensely relieved, the parents forgave Jiggs on the spot, and we started up Old Georgetown Road, stopping at the light at Wiscon-sin. A Montgomery County police car pulled up alongside.

The cop looked over at us; we looked over at him; and, then, we looked into his back seat. There was Hank. He had been ap-prehended following yet another scrape and was en route to the station house for the obligatory $27.50 fine for disorderly conduct. The cop driving the county car had heard the accident report; he knew Crick was in unknown condition at Suburban; so, he asked us to pull over. "Take this one home with you, Mr. Buchanan," he said, letting Hank go. "You've had enough trouble for one night."

Like many of the working-class cops in the Eighth Precinct and Montgomery County, he was a decent human being.

At seventeen, Hank had bought a '47 Chevy convertible with a "vacuum shift" (we had two flat tires on that lemon before we got it home from the lot), and, at eighteen, he bought a '49 Mercury, an exact replica of the car driven by the late James Dean in *Rebel Without a Cause*. Hank wore his red windbreaker as we motored around in that "lowered" Merc, with its dual exhausts.

While Hank's '49 Merc gave us a measure of freedom, it was not a inexpensive proposition. On one occasion, we thought his Mercury was dying. It had lost its pickup and power, and conked out every few blocks. We thought he might have a cracked engine block. Taking it to Call Carl's at Nebraska and Connecticut, Hank had $30 worth of repairs done. As soon as we picked it up, however, the thing died again right in the middle of Connecticut Avenue; we had to push it back into the station. Puzzled, the mechanics told us they would spend another day on it, free of charge. When we arrived back at Call Carl's to pick it up, the mechanic was still wiping the grease off his hands; he gave us a quizzical look and pulled us aside.

"Whose girlfriend are you guys messing around with?"

"What are you talking about?" I said.

"Well," he said, "last night, when we couldn't find a thing wrong with your engine, we decided, on a chance, to take off your gas tank; and this is what we found."

He showed us his pan full of rocks.

"We got these out of your gas tank; somebody doesn't like you fellas," he said.

On closer inspection, the rocks seemed familiar; indeed, they were familiar. They were stones from our own driveway! Beside the stones was the smoking gun, a tiny plastic car of the very kind with which five-year-old Tom had lately been seen playing. Hank silently paid his bill, and we headed directly home for reimbursement. Tom had no alibi, and there were no other suspects. Little brother's pants were pulled down, and Hank used his belt on Tom's fanny as it had rarely been used on us. Pop was not pleased; Hank "had no right to do that," he said. If Tom needed discipline, that was his prerogative.

One of the books Hank and I read avidly was *Somebody up There Likes Me*, the fictionalized account of the life of Rocky Graziano. Paul Newman had played "Rocky" Barbella in the film; and we thought him tremendous. We imitated his manner, plagiarized his lines, and howled at the wild anecdotes of Rocky in the book. That summer, when Hank and I had been invited to stay with Dave Woll, whose father, a Teamsters' lawyer, was using one of the union hideaways in Easthampton, Long Island, we had what we thought then was a memorable encounter.

As we walked along the boardwalk, we were stunned to see walking toward us, not fifty yards away, Paul Newman himself, in bathing trunks and a pullover. "It's him," I said, "It's Rocky Barbella." We steered toward Newman to make sure, and Hank said, "Hi, Rocky," as though we were passing an acquaintance from the neighborhood. Newman said, "Hi, how are you?" as though he knew us as well, and kept on walking.

Since that summer, Newman has been a lifelong favorite (as actor, not political theorist), starring in more quality films (and fewer donkeys) than any other actor of his generation — from *Hud* to *Cool Hand Luke*, from *The Hustler* and *The Sting* and *Hombre* to *Butch Cassidy and the Sundance Kid*, from *Absence of Malice* to *The Verdict*. (The train scene in *The Sting*, where Newman as Henry Gondorf, the confidence man, relieves Robert Shaw, the Scotch-American crime king, of a bundle in that fixed poker game, is among the funniest scenes in modern film.)

In today's popular culture, from plays and films like *Grease* with John Travolta, there is a notion that the '50s were all about tough guys who wore leather jackets and boots, combed their greasy hair into duck tails, drove motorcycles, and fought one another with snapped-off automobile aerials and baseball bats.

While such people were around, they were rare in northwest Washington and Chevy Chase. The only ones I recall hanging around Peoples in that kind of costume were a pair of twins we called the Wildroot Brothers. "Barnacle Bill," older and tattooed, who used to buy beer for us at Chevy Chase Liquor, might have qualified. But hardly anyone else.

In a way, I felt sorry for the guys we occasionally ran into, with their tattoos, and leather jackets and boots; few of them were athletes; almost none were students; they were subject to constant ridicule and mocking imitation. I had a sense their tough-guy get-ups and their swaggering demeanor covered up for a felt inade-quacy deep down inside. Several of them I knew had come from broken homes; their fathers had walked out on them. While often personally brave, only a few really knew how to use their fists.

We imitated their walk and talk, and mocked them constantly. One night, we were walking out of a redneck bar, across the street from the Ebbitt Hotel, when we spied one sitting drinking at a table. Besides the de rigueur boots and hair, however, this one had on a white coat and white pants, made out of the same material as the Levi's we wore when working outdoors.

"Aren't you cute?" we said as we went by, laughing.

"Hello there, Snow White," Hank said.

Snow White rose to do battle, and followed us outside. Now, whenever Henry was about to go into action, there was a telltale signal. While still talking, he would take his handkerchief out of his back pocket, and nonchalantly start wrapping it tightly around his right hand — an improvised handwrap of the kind we used when boxing. When the handkerchief was wrapped tight, Hank would close his fist on it; and the main event was about to begin.

As Snow White got up to follow us outside, I noticed Hank reaching for his handkerchief. And he didn't have a cold. Snow White, however, was reaching for something in *his* pocket. But Snow White's hand was still in his pocket and his feet had not quite touched the pavement when Hank spun around and sucker-punched him; when Snow White tried to get his knife, Hank dropped him. The last we saw of poor Snow White he was holding a bleeding mouth and clomping away in those ridiculous heavy boots in the direction of 11th Street.

Everyone we hung around with wore khaki pants, sports shirts or sweaters, "gunboats" from Flagg Brothers in early high school and, later, cordovans. Almost all of us had crew cuts, and later a "flattop" — given by the most famous barber in northwest Washington, Milton Pitts, who had invented the flattop and operated Cathedral Barbers on Connecticut Avenue across from the zoo and right next to "The Den." Milt's shop was neutral ground; and customers for his famous flattops came from as far away as Anacostia and Rockville. For thirty-five cents, Milt would sell you a tin of Even Up, to guarantee the flattop didn't collapse.

The next time I saw him, Milt wasn't doing flattops anymore; he was barber to the President with his own "shop" in our White House basement, scheduling interviews with Hugh Sidey of *Time* and the national press. As Jesse Jackson would say, Milt, too, was "movin' on up."

During those years, summer jobs — especially good-paying jobs like construction work — were not easy to come by. We would travel from one construction site to another; no one would hire us, unless our parents "knew someone." Nor were my parents insistent we go to work. Pop had had to work as a boy; and he wanted his sons to remember the summers of their youth. "You'll be working soon enough and working your whole life," he said. "Now is the time to enjoy yourself." He only wished, he said, he could have spent his summers on a baseball diamond.

The first part-time jobs I had were working the booths at the Saint John's Carnival, delivering the *Washington Post* — as too many subscribers were deadbeats, pay was uneven — and acting as Latin tutor to Sheila, a junior at Holy Cross, not doing at all well, academically. Because Sheila thought well of me, she had her mother hire me, at $5 for each two-hour session; but, no progress was made; Latin was not what Sheila was interested in.

One summer, Millard Crouch and I toured the country clubs of Montgomery County, applying for work as caddies; and, at Burning Tree, President Eisenhower's own club, we connected. The work was simple, but boring; sometimes we had to sit and wait on the caddy log for four hours, and then carry two golf bags around in the hot sun for eighteen holes, for which we were paid $2.50 a bag, plus perhaps a fifty-cent tip. Some days, we never even went out.

Several times, I was sitting on the caddie log, when the President of the United States arrived and teed off, his Secret Servicemen moving smartly down opposite sides of the fairway, looking earnestly toward the woods, their phony golf bags shouldered, containing, we were told, automatic rifles.

With the exception of Crouch and Pete Cook, a friend from Rollingwood, all the caddies were black. Most were several years older than we, and caddying was their full-time job. As we were given bags based on seniority, the black caddies would go out twice some days, make $10 or $15 with tips, and we would go out not at all. Our best bet was to wait for a late-afternoon tee-off, when "John Doe," the most popular of the caddies with members, and other veterans already had their morning and afternoon carries.

One afternoon, when Pete Cook and I were the last two on the log — everyone had gone out for the afternoon — and were about to head home, we saw Max Elbin, the pro at Burning Tree, bring out of the clubhouse the plaid golf bag we all knew belonged to the Vice President of the United States. Soon, a car drove up, and out stepped Richard M. Nixon, himself. Elbin and Don Sailor, the assistant pro, called Cook and me up to carry the bags for the Vice President's party, which included a retired army general.

While only fifteen, I was fully aware of Nixon's role in the Hiss Case, of the "fund" scandal and the "Checkers" speech. In fact, Nixon was a hero of mine; he was a famous anti-Communist, the second youngest Vice President in history — and Nixon was known as a fighter. So, the whole time out, I stayed close to the Vice President. When he relieved himself in the bushes (it was, and still is, an all-men's club), I stepped up alongside and did the same, even though we caddies were supposed to go off separately or wait until we got back to the bench area.

What I recall most vividly was the language these great men used — language my father never used — and how sycophantic some were. You did not need to be Ben Hogan to see that the Vice President of the United States was uncoordinated. His swing was not smooth and natural like an athlete's, but stiff and jerky. Yet, from the comments his fellow players made, you would have thought we had the young Palmer out here.

"Great shot, Dick, a real beauty," one said, watching at the tee, as the Vice President popped a drive 150 yards down the fairway. "Your game is really improving, Dick," the general interjected smoothly at another point — which made me wonder what it had been like a year ago. When the ball would go dribbling down the fairway like a grounder at Griffith Stadium, or shank off into the woods, you could see the shared pain etched in the faces of the Vice President's partners. "Tough break, Dick," they would say with a grimace. When he lost the ball and we found it deep in the forest, three strokes from civilization, they would call out, "Take one, Dick, and put it on the fairway!"

Even though his language was rough (this was, after all, the Vice President of the United States!), I liked Nixon immensely, and even jabbered with him a bit myself. And he was obviously enjoying himself hugely in that exclusive fraternity. Banging the ball around in that summer sun, he seemed genuinely happy, laughing heartily at the men's jokes and wisecracks. But mainly I stayed close and listened to him.

At one point on a tee, he turned around and blurted out, "Those [expletive deleted] Democrats cut our [expletive deleted] every chance they get." Great, I thought. Wait'll they hear that one up at Peoples tonight!

Spying someone he knew two fairways away, Nixon called out, "Hey, Stu, they're voting up on the Hill; why aren't you there?"

"Tell 'em to shove it," "Stu" hollered back from a block away — and strode purposefully up the sixteenth fairway. Damn!, I thought, that is *him*; that is "Sanctimonious Stu" Symington — of Joe McCarthy's derisive depiction! That was all I knew of the Missouri Senator whose endorsement by the *St. Louis Globe-Democrat* I would write a decade later.

Clearly, there was a camaraderie among America's power elite of which I had been unaware; and now I was right in the thick of it. This was terrific.

Eleven years later, in December of 1965, when I had my fateful interview, in his New York law office, with the former Vice President of the United States, I casually recalled having caddied for him, and mentioned the old plaid golf bag he remembered so well. I didn't mention the language.

For two summers after that, I went without work. My first summer in college, I finally landed a position. But when I came home, and told Pop I was going to be the Good Humor Man for most of Chevy Chase, he was appalled, and went right to the point. "Where are you going to park the truck?"

"Right out front, Pop," I said; "no use my taking a bus over to Southeast every morning to pick it up."

"There's not going to be any damned Good Humor truck parked in front of my house," he said. What would the neighbors think? That he couldn't afford to feed his own family, that's what they'd think.

Mom's intercession did not help. "I don't give a damn, Catherine; he's not parking a Good Humor truck in front of *my* house."

"But, Pop," I said, "you told us that all work had 'dignity' to it."

"Maybe you didn't hear me. No damn Good Humor truck is going to be sitting in front of my house every night — for the neighbors to laugh at. Is that clear?"

Thus ended my career as the Good Humor Man.

The job I did get later that summer, from a want ad, was at an animal hospital on M Street in Georgetown. When I first visited the facility with my résumé, the veterinarian indicated that, while my academic credentials were indeed impressive, a working knowledge of Virgil and Cicero was not central to what he had in mind.

My job entailed arriving at the cat-and-dog hospital at six each morning, cleaning out the cages, walking the dogs in an enclosed, paved area out back, shoveling up the deposits they left, and then hosing the place down. Instead of a noble calling like selling Good Humor bars to delighted children, I started shoveling crap for a living. Long before Don Regan brought me back to the White House, I ran my own shovel brigade.

The next summer I went to an employment service; and they came up with a genuine "job" — running the mimeograph, addressograph, folding, posting, and mailing machines at a small business service company in Bethesda, a tiny husband-and-wife operation. The proprietor's wife would type up on stencils the monthly mailing pieces, for the Bethesda Lions or the Rotary, and I would attach the stencils to my mimeograph — and run off several hundred copies.

The tiny firm was precursor to the giant computerized mailing houses that would one day dominate political fund-raising; and I learned the business on the ground floor. More important, it was a real job; I was getting genuine work experience; I had a boss, a timeclock, and duties; and I was starting to learn how to pay for the things I wanted. Now, when I took my girlfriend, Beth, out, I paid myself, and felt better about it than when I had had to "borrow" the money from Mom.

That sense of independence and responsibility, more than any amount of money earned, was crucial. Today, when poor kids, black and white, are denied that opportunity because some proprietor can't (or won't) pay the minimum wage for the kind of work he wants done, the kids are the real losers. And their loss is much greater than the dollars they didn't earn.

The proprietor at the business service was an irascible old gentleman, impatient with my lack of facility with his machines. Whenever one malfunctioned, he would shove me aside to get it working — muttering about the incompetence of the kind of help you could hire these days. But, the $40 a week I made for eight hours a day — to go to $50 a week after the first month — was excellent money. And I loved the work.

I soon discovered the cause of my employer's moodiness. When the wife wasn't looking, he used to swig from a hidden bottle; and, while sometimes he would come to work choleric and impatient, by afternoon, he might compliment me on how fast I was learning.

After the third week, I got a shock. Mom had given me cash in exchange for my first two paychecks, which she had signed over for groceries at Broad Branch Market. Family friends, the boys at Broad Branch quietly informed my mother, before word got out that her son was into hanging bad paper, that the checks had bounced.

Taking back the checks stamped "Insufficient Funds," I picked a moment when the proprietor's wife was outside the building, wordlessly handed them to him, and waited for his reaction. I could sense the panic.

"Listen," he said, "we'll work this out; just don't let my wife know you and I discussed this."

Now, I had the whip hand; and I was magnanimous. Right, I said, I am sure it was an oversight; and there would be no need to mention anything to his wife or anybody — so long as the money was forthcoming, real soon. "And, by the way, sir, when does my salary rise to fifty dollars?"

After that, we hit it off tremendously. By summer's end, I could run the machines better than he, and was busy training his friendly and bubbly niece, Mary, who had come to work for the summer.

It was while working at the business service company that I first became politically "active."

This was the summer of '58, and, following the overthrow of the pro-American King of Iraq, when his body and that of his pro-American Prime Minister Nuri-a-Said were dragged through the streets of the capital, it appeared Secretary Dulles's Baghdad Pact was collapsing, and revolution might sweep through pro-Western Lebanon and Jordan. Ike was unhesitant. Early on the morning of

July 15, the Sixth Fleet appeared on the horizon, and the first of ten thousand Marines — on the "invitation" of the Lebanese government — came ashore. They were met by cheering girls in bikinis.

Impotent to interfere, Khrushchev resorted to threats and bombast; and the Politburo sent a mob to attack the U.S. embassy, showering it with rocks, eggs, and ink bottles, while the Moscow militia stood by. I was irate, and decided to respond in kind, on behalf of the United States. After work, I got in touch with T. Gaffney, an all-Catholic graduate of Saint John's, just home from Parris Island, who was equally enthusiastic about doing something to the Russians, and John Keaveny, who had fought Golden Gloves and was known as Hatchet.

Gaffney brought along a rope he had learned to tie into a hangman's noose at Parris Island, and we headed for Maggie's on Wisconsin Avenue to enlist recruits. There, we hooked up with Denny Forster, who had the family car (and an empty house) while his father, a famed neurosurgeon who had treated Eisenhower, was in conference in Tokyo. We impressed a few others into the service, talked and drank our nerve up, and, around ten, left for the Soviet embassy — without the foggiest notion what we were going to do.

As we left Maggie's, we were waving the hangman's noose; and a friend yelled, "Hey, Pat, what are you gonna do — hang the Ambassador in effigy?"

"Effigy, hell," I yelled back, "we gonna hang Smilin' Mike for real."

Smilin' Mike was Mikhail Menshikov, immediate predecessor to Anatoly Dobrynin, with whom I would share the President's cabin on *Air Force One*, on the flight from Moscow to Yalta in 1974, when the President rode in Brezhnev's plane. (On that long flight down to the Black Sea, I thought of telling Ambassador Dobrynin of my first visit to his embassy, but then thought better of it; he was busy photographing his wife, and having me photograph him, sitting in the President's chair.)

When we reached the cars, however, nobody seemed to know where the Soviet embassy was. We reconnoitered; someone in the other car yelled, "Sixteenth Street!", so we let them have the lead, while we puzzled over what action to take when we got there. The lead car solved the problem by taking a sharp left turn in the middle of the block on 16th Street, straight through the open gates, and up to the door of a darkened building. We followed right behind. The plate on the wall read: EMBASSY OF THE U.S.S.R.. Realizing we had just violated the territorial sovereignty of the Soviet Union, I started yelling to Forster from the back seat to get out of the driveway and back onto 16th Street, where we could decide what to do. Too late.

We had taken the beefed-up U.S. security force by total surprise. (They must have thought terrorists were about to take out the building.) As we drove back out onto 16th Street, plainclothesmen blocked both cars, demanding to know what we thought we were doing. We made a wrong turn, we explained.

"Don't you know what's going on in the Middle East?" an agent demanded of me in the back seat. Well, yes, I told him; we heard about the Lebanon thing, but what did that have to do with us losing directions to the Hayloft?

He didn't know whether to believe us or not, but reinforcements were on the way, and he ordered us not to move. Which was ridiculous. I told Forster to ignore him and drive off.

"No," Forster insisted, "they've got my license number, and this is my father's car."

"We'll split the fine, Denny," I told him; "just get moving back toward Maryland."

Forster didn't budge; neither did the other driver. We all stupidly sat there in our cars, and waited for the D.C. patrol wagon to pick us up. Meanwhile, the press had been alerted, and photographers were all over the street, snapping away as the police marched us into the wagon. Since we hadn't actually done anything but go in and out of the embassy driveway, I waved to the photographers as I was getting into the paddy wagon. Forster and a couple of the others did the classic hands-over-face routine, as they would later be pictured in the international press. The only smart thing we did was stuff the hangman's noose under the front seat. It was never found.

Taken to one of the downtown precincts, we were lined up for booking at the long desk, opposite the revolving door where you entered. Then and there, I decided I wasn't going to drop $50 or $100 (two weeks' gross pay) in a D.C. fine for a political action that had never come off. As there was nothing more I could do for my buddies, I decided to take a gamble — to prevent yet another "arrest" on a record already embarrassingly long. Slowly and unobtrusively, I worked my way down to the end of the line of suspects, near the revolving entrance door, where cops were coming in and going out. As running for it would have brought a dozen cops out the door after me and produced an added charge of resisting arrest, I tried a less risky maneuver. After the cops who arrested us were replaced in the station by cops to watch us, while booking took place, I moved toward the revolving door; and from there walked loudly over to the desk where the sergeant was writing, with his head down.

Pounding the desk with my open hand, I hollered, "Why are you holding these guys?" gesturing toward my astonished buddies back in the lineup. The sergeant looked at me, surprised and puzzled, then he looked at the line, then he looked at the door.

"Why are you holding these guys?" I yelled again.

"Where did you come from?" he said. "Weren't you just standing in that line?" Ignoring his question, I told him I had heard about the arrest of friends of mine at a bar on Wisconsin Avenue and had rushed downtown to get them out; but that was not important. "Why, exactly, are they here?" I demanded again.

"Tell you what, buddy," the sergeant said, "if you don't want to be standing there in that line with your friends, you had best turn around and get the hell out of this station house the same way you came in — because your buddies are going to be here a long, long time."

I nodded in defeat, turned around, and walked through the revolving door out into the summer night, giving a final salute of farewell to my incredulous friends Keaveny and Forster, still waiting to be booked. As Paul Newman's Luke the convict reminds us, "Sometimes, *nothing* can beat a real, cool hand."

For fast cash, there were no better jobs than in the post office at Christmas, where we worked twelve and thirteen hours a day as "temporaries," and were paid in the big green checks of the government of the United States. This was how we earned enough to buy our girlfriends and parents Christmas gifts — and there was plenty of party cash left over. The Chevy Chase post office would hire students by the dozen; the regular mailman would sort and pigeonhole, and we would do their deliveries over postal zone 15, now zip code 20015. Twice a day, we made the rounds, walking miles.

As anyone who has been a mailman knows, the hereditary enemy is the canine. Either Maryland did not have, or did not enforce, a leash law, because, north of Western Avenue, the beasts had the run of the neighborhood. For two years, I had the same delivery zone, an area in Maryland west of Connecticut Avenue and just south of East-West Highway and Columbia Country Club. The area was dog heaven. They got to know you; and every day they were waiting for you. Those dogs loved Christmas more than we did. They would spot you at the top of the street, and start barking signals to one another, all the way down to the end of the street, working themselves up for the confrontation, when you were three doors away. Sometimes, cowardly, I would skip half a dozen houses, rather than mix it up with them — and, when the protests came to the post office, I would get on the phone and yell, "Get the damn dog inside the house; or come get your Christmas mail at the post office."

Even when they were kept inside, they growled their hatred through the door when you came up the front steps. So, a few of us decided to make the residents pay for their ill-humored animals. One way was to push the mail through the slot, piece by piece, teasing the Doberman on the other side until he became frenzied. Then, push the folded-up *Life* magazine through the slot, until the now-insane Doberman grabbed it firmly in its teeth — then ram it home. The next day, the stupid dog would be back for more.

Another way to make the dog's life as miserable as he was making yours was to put the mail through the slot, slowly, piece by piece, until the dog was frenetic. Then, having held back the most important piece of correspondence — say, a Social Security check — gently push this letter through the slot and take it back, again and again, while the crazed dog snapped at it and tore it to bits. After this vital piece of family correspondence had been torn and chewed beyond salvaging, push it through the slot — and let the dog explain to the master of the house that night why he had ripped up the family's monthly check.

Once, when I was working this procedure — pushing and pulling a government check through the mail slot at the very bottom of the front door, working the dog beautifully — suddenly the door jerked open, and the head of the household looked down at this mailman on his hands and knees, his head inches from his front door, and yelled, "What in the hell do you think you're doing?"

What he was doing home at that hour of the morning I don't know.

Some of the stories of those beasts, however, were terrifying.

Over on the appropriately named Shepherd Street, one huge animal of German descent reportedly scaled an eight-foot fence to get his mailman. Even my father agreed we had a problem, and he had a solution. Water, mixed with ammonia and squirted into its eyes, will immobilize any dog, no matter how vicious, he insisted. So, he and I mixed the solution; I filled up a water pistol, and headed up Connecticut Avenue on my route. Soon, I came upon an ideal proving ground. One large black dog of no discernible ancestry was sitting silently atop the steps, faithfully guarding the family domicile. As I started up the long flight, with a passel of Christmas cards, a low growl emanated from deep in its throat. I had no need of a translator; his message was clear: If you want real action this morning, Mr. Mailman, just keep walking up those steps.

I put down the bag, pulled out the watergun, and let him have it from about a dozen feet. Nothing. Again and again, I squirted him. He sat there, his snout wetting up, his eyes getting redder, not making a sound, just staring at me. I squirted him a few more times. Nothing. So, I put the water pistol back into the bag and went off down the street. If that dog had not been determined to kill me when I first started up those stairs, he was now. Either somebody had sabotaged the solution, or his eyes were stinging and, as soon as I was on that top step, he was going to close the books. Victory was his; the rest of that Christmas season, however, his owner picked up his mail from the family down the street.

Some of us took to carrying baseball bats, to fend off a pack attack. Hitchhiking back to the post office one morning, I was picked up by a black delivery man, who, noticing the Louisville Slugger sticking out of the mail sack, said, "I guess you carry that so you can be prepared in case a game comes up, right?"

We both laughed, and all the way up Connecticut Avenue swapped "dog stories." That delivery man not only understood; he deeply empathized.

We were the last pre-television generation; we entered and left adolescence before drugs and the sexual revolution, but we were in on the golden era of rock 'n' roll — from Bill Haley and the Comets to Elvis, from "Fats" Domino to Chuck Berry, from the Coasters to the Platters to Sam Cooke. In Alexander Solzhenitsyn's luminous address to the graduating class of Harvard in 1976, the only point where I dissented was when he deplored America's "intolerable music."

Thirty years ago, rock 'n' roll was not acid rock or hard rock or satanic rock; it was a manifestation of the energy and exuberance of the generation that grew up under Ike, in the peacetime years of the Cold War. The melancholy simpering of Johnny Ray and his "Little White Cloud That Cried" that opened the decade was utterly unsuited to so robust an era.

While the 1950s passed before America's sexual revolution arrived, it was hardly a Victorian era. There was a sea change, however, between how girls dressed and behaved then, and how they dressed and behaved ten years later. At the junior and senior proms in high school, and bashes like the Fall Festival at Georgetown, or the Military Ball for ROTC cadets, the girls dressed with the sophistication and attractiveness of grown women. They wore high heels, low-cut gowns, modeled their hairstyles on Hollywood stars and starlets, spent hours beautifying themselves for the big night. That cosmetics were a form of consumer fraud, that one's hair should simply be washed and worn naturally, that high heels were sexist and bad for the calves, that jeans and sweatshirts were adequate attire, these attitudes were — *Deo Gratias* — far into the future.

Sex was too serious a matter, in the '50s, for the casual attitude that developed in the next decade. (Though, not until I became a syndicated columnist and discussed with my colleagues how many newspapers their columns were carried in, have I known a subject about which there was so much prodigious male lying.)

Whenever someone "moved in" on your girl at a party, it was a direct challenge to your manhood — and everybody watched to see how it would come out. Outsiders who had innocently taken a girl out on a date often found themselves mano-a-mano in the front yard at midnight with her ex-boyfriend. Many of the bloodiest fights in those years were rooted in someone's attempt to "move in" on someone else's girl.

Not until I reached the spring of freshman year in college, when I met Beth, then a graduating senior at Bethesda–Chevy Chase High School, did I acquire a steady girl. Perfectly proportioned and handsomely packaged at 5 feet 4 inches, dark-haired, dark-eyed, pretty, saucy, and sexy, with a tiny waist and small hourglass figure, Miss Beth had been a junior-high pom-pom girl in Bluefield, West Virginia, before moving to Bethesda. Because she had the spirit and charm of Miss Scarlet in *Gone with the Wind*, I always called her Miss Beth. She was the great love of my youth.

The antithesis of a tomboy, she could easily pass for twenty-four when she dressed up at eighteen. When I was still being asked by waitresses and bartenders, "Lemme see your draft card," she, six months younger than I, never had any trouble being served.

When she was still eighteen, Joe, the barkeep who ran the Piccolo and was twice her age, invited her to be his official "date" for the big opening after the Piccolo had been remodeled. I let Joe know he was out of bounds.

For more than two years, Miss Beth and I went together, and had a thousand laughs; but she was mature as well as fun-loving. Right out of high school, she had gone to the Washington School for Secretaries, from there to work at the National Bank of Washington. She wanted to marry and start a family, but found herself attached to a college boy of no discernible ambition, who hadn't the vaguest notion what he wanted to do when he "grew up," which, from his social behavior, seemed decades away. She put up with more than she should have, and, finally, had enough.

Once when the loyal Miss Beth had come by to visit when I was bedridden, Mom told me, "Patrick, that girl is in love with you; if you're not going to marry her, you ought to let her go." I thought about it many times, but simply wasn't ready; my horizons didn't stretch beyond college; had I been two years older, or she, two years younger, life might have been different.

Enamored in high school of a blonde from Wilson who lived on McKinley Street, about whom my friend Chick Leasure observed, "I just danced with her, Pat, and you're exactly right; there's not a hard spot in that girl's body," there was inconsequential reciprocity. What was the problem? I asked a buddy. "The problem, Pat," he said, "is that Peggy Shaw is A work; and you're only a C student."

It was a good line. As she was Presbyterian, and her parents suspicious of "RCs," as we Catholics were called, I gave it out that the problem was rooted in "religious differences." No one picked up the line, however.

As usual, Hank was more intense about this matter of girls than I. In December of 1954, when I had just gotten my driver's license and was amenable to driving anyone anywhere, he asked me to chauffeur him over to Silver Spring, to deliver his girlfriend, Yola, her Christmas present. I volunteered, and we headed across Rock Creek Park, up Kalmia Road for her apartment, on the first floor of a four-unit complex.

Hank had quarreled with Yola, and I thought this a gesture to patch it up. It may have started that way, but if so, Hank must have changed his mind en route, for when we got there, he said curtly, "I won't be long."

So, I waited in the car for him to deliver the Christmas present to his girlfriend. True to his word, Hank was not long. Taking several steps up the walk toward her apartment, he paused, then, like Campanella picking off a runner at first base, he fired that wrapped-up box of perfume straight through the front window of Yola's apartment and walked serenely back to the car. Through the smashed window, I could see Yola's old man, trying to discern the make and license of my father's car.

All I could think of on the way home was, "Why me?" and what I was going to do for the next six months without the car.

Whenever Hank's relationship with his girl was in a bear market, he was not averse to seeing to it that yours ended up there as well.

Around that same time, my father had given me the car for the evening; and I had filled it up with Buchs and Hank, a couple of others, and a couple of six-packs. Fortified, we drove over to Rittenhouse Street, where Peggy Shaw was visiting her friend Susan. Susan's family was of German extraction; and the father, Dr. Richwine, was known to be no one to trifle with. As I approached the door, leading the pack, an empty beer bottle arched over my head and slammed into the front door, smashing on the porch. Another followed, landing on the steps. Hank was giving notice of our arrival.

For a split second, I was frozen with panic. Either I could do the honorable thing and continue to the front door, face an enraged Dr. Richwine, apologize for the smashed glass and the dent in his door, and take my medicine, or I could do the cowardly thing and run and hope he didn't get the make of the car.

By the time I got into the driver's seat, everybody had piled in; and the swiftness of the departure of the black-and-white Olds made me think we had gotten away. I was wrong. When I got home, Pop was waiting up. Dr. Richwine had called, said his home had been struck with several empty bottles, and a car, matching the description of the family Oldsmobile, had been spotted speeding away — with its lights out.

"You had the car, Pat, what do you have to say for yourself?"

"Well, it *was* our car, Pop," I admitted.

"Okay, Pat," the Old Man said, "now, I want the truth. Did you throw that bottle up on Dr. Richwine's porch?"

"No, sir."

"Who did?"

Unwilling to rat on my brother, I said, "I can't say."

"Okay," he said, "no car for one month!"

Buchs was brought in for the same interrogation.

"Bill, did you throw that bottle at Dr. Richwine's house?"

"No, sir."

"Who did?"

"I can't say," Buchs answered, covering for his brother.

"Okay, no car for *you* for a month!"

Exasperated with Buchs and the Black Sheep, my father turned to his Pride and Joy, and said sorrowfully, "Hank, who could have done such a thing?"

I could not believe it.

Hank could do no wrong in his father's eyes. But we took our medicine. At least giving Hank exclusive use of the car for the next month meant we might have a ride.

7

The Adventures of Schuyler Colfax

"When I was a child, I thought as a child, I spake as a child, and I acted as a child. Now that I have become a man, I have put off childish things."

— *Saint Paul*

BY THE mid-1950s, a group of us in Chevy Chase, known as the Homers, had begun to gather, on weekends and virtually every evening during the summer, for cultural and social activities. In this loose fraternity of perhaps two dozen, the Buchanans and the Kadow brothers were regulars.

Jan, the eldest of the Kadows, was of normal size. His twin brothers, Brian and Kevin, however, called by their mother "my Bobbas," had glided past the 200-pound mark at around fourteen years of age; by seventeen, they were both about 6 feet 3 inches, approaching their collegiate football weights of 265 and 275. For that time, they were enormous. Of Polish and Irish extraction, they were perpetually smiling, laughing constantly, and seemed to live for the good times. Academically, the Kadows did not excel. Though Jan was almost two years older than I, he graduated from high school the same year I did, 1956; and though Brian and Kevin were half a year older than I, they graduated a year behind me. Jan matriculated at so many area colleges and junior colleges that it was said he had developed blisters behind his ears — from wearing so many freshman beanies.

One night, when the twins were still working their way through John Carroll High School, and I was already at Georgetown, they interrupted my calculus studies with a hellish mathematics conundrum that had confounded them. I picked up the phone to hear an exasperated Brian Kadow saying: "Blade [my nickname], if one man can mow a lawn in four hours, and another man can mow the same lawn in two hours, how the hell long would it take the two of them to mow it together?"

Identical twins, the brothers could most easily be distinguished by the fact that one had a chipped front tooth. By their final year in high school, 1957, the Kadows were already famous throughout the Washington area. An incident involving Brian had been recorded in the city's athletic lore. At the Gonzaga–Carroll game in 1956 — to decide the Catholic League title — Brian was kicking off for Carroll. As tension built in the crowd, Brian approached the ball, put his foot into it with tremendous force, and missed it completely. As though he had kicked it sixty yards, he charged upfield with his Carroll teammates, while the football sat immobile on the tee now far behind him. Seeing what had happened, one of his alert teammates circled around and completed the kickoff, while the other ten Carroll players were halfway down the field — and thus offside. Griffith Stadium was rocking with laughter.

Among the Homers, it had become a subject of amusement how often Mr. Buchanan and Mrs. Kadow would meet at Number Eight to collect one or more of their sons.

Each set of parents soon began to blame their sons' social retardation, and recidivism, on their having fallen in among "bad companions." My father would pull me aside, "Pat, I like the Kadows; they're terrific guys; they've got a wonderful sense of humor — but they're headed for trouble; and if you continue hanging around with them, you're going to wind up in the same place."

Stanley and Helena Kadow were even more alarmed. They admonished Brian and Kevin and Jan that "the Buchanans are all crazy," that Hank was certifiable, a "psycho," and that Pat was "nothing but a gay blade," whose sole interest in life was having a good time. If they continued associating with us, they would end up as we were going to end up, in trouble, and possibly in jail.

So, the Kadows renamed Hank "Psycho," and me "Blade"; and we roamed Chevy Chase and Bethesda piled inside the new "Hi-Drive" Plymouth Mrs. Kadow had purchased for Jan and the Bobbas, which we had christened the Mo-Par.

Everyone we ran with had one or more names. Among the Homers and the BMF (most of whom had gone to Wilson) with whom we merged after high school (the derivation of BMF need not concern us here), there was not only Blade and Psycho, but Doder, Roller, Roach, Rabbit, Ox, King, Beef, Bear, Ace, Dart, Gator, Flinter, Ram, KAK, BAK, Dumb-Dick, Dum-Dum, Homo (a parody, I assure you), Shack, Wappy, Squeaks, Hatchet, Greek, Gort, Wine, Good Times, Fat Back, Red Dog, The Commissioner, The Tolbuck Corporation, and Jerome Filthy McNasty. Like settlers discovering a new world, we not only gave new names to individuals, but to places. Kitty O'Day, for example, a friend of Yola's, who had taken a fancy to me, lived "beyond Jones Mill Road in Sunny Dell Acres (which we named after B. O. Plenty's place of residence in Dick Tracy) across the Bridge of the Partially Painted Dog." (Someone had painted the private parts of the large bronze dogs that guarded the tiny bridge a flaming red.)

Because of the constant scrapes, where we would be identified and reported, one night at the Piccolo we decided each of us needed a permanent "alias" — a name to be automatically invoked in time of crisis. I had two I favored. The first was Skyresh Bolgolam, the malevolent minister of Lilliput in Swift's *Gulliver's Travels*. (But no cop in the city would buy a name like that.) So, I picked the name Charlie Leasure had come across in his government class, that had a magnificent ring to it: Schuyler Colfax, Vice President of the United States under Ulysses Grant, who, unfortunately, had been badly tarred in the Credit Mobilier scandal.

Regularly, I would extend my hand and introduce myself to people I didn't know as "Schuyler Colfax." Not a single person picked up on the late Vice President. Until, one day, it caught up with me. Lying in bed with my recurring arthritis, my father came upstairs to visit; only he wasn't solicitous; he was, as we used to say, "ticked off." Looking at me grimly, he said, "Pat, do you know someone by the name of Colfax?"

Startled, I parried. "You mean Schuyler?"

"That's exactly right, 'Schuyler Colfax,' " he said angrily. "Do you know him?"

"Well, uh, yeah, I know him," I said, cautiously. "What about him?"

"What about him! He's been using my gasoline credit card! That's what about him! Now, who the hell is he?"

I explained to Pop that Schuyler was basically not a bad sort, but that he had no sense of responsibility; however, not only would I take the matter of his using our gasoline card up with Schuyler, I would personally guarantee he never pulled a stunt like this again. Pop seemed impressed with my determination, and let the incident pass.

Given the reputation of the Homers, all of us were deliberately not informed whenever private parties were being held. Yet, they were held all the time — by girls from Wilson and BCC and Visitation and Holy Cross. And, like the other gangs in northwest Washington and Maryland, we regularly crashed them. After we had imbibed a bit driving around in the Mo-Par, and party security had become lax, I would present myself at the front door, neatly groomed in a coat and tie, introduce myself to the parents, suggesting I was from Landon or Saint Alban's, the elite prep schools, or maybe "pre-med at Princeton," and ask if this were not Mary So-and-So's party to which I had been invited by one of Mary's friends. The parents would observe my appearance and demeanor, stare past me into the darkness, and, reassured, would say, "Come on in, young fellow; they're all downstairs." Which we already knew.

By the time I got downstairs, my cover was blown. By then, however, it was too late. Before the locals could say, "Who invited *him?*" I had the basement door unlocked and opened — with the opening filled up by the smiling Kadow brothers, leading an unfriendly looking pack of eight or ten into the basement, carrying several cases of beer on their shoulders.

On occasions, however, others at these basement parties were less impressed with who the Homers were — than with who *they* were. When that obtained, you could feel the tension building. One by one, the girls would make their way up the stairs, and the cellar emptied, except for the cobelligerents. Then, the action began.

But parties were not the only social activity.

There were marathon poker games in the Kadows' and Fitzes' basements, where the games were not only stud and draw poker, but Pass the Trash, Baseball, and Night Baseball, the rules for which were deuces wild, one-eyed jacks, and the man with the ax and a pair of natural sevens takes all. The unstated purpose of these all-night poker sessions was not to make money; it was to sip and talk and laugh and, while shuffling the pasteboards, to make more permanent the bonds of friendship. There is a correlation between what we sought there, not even knowing it, and what most men seek when they go into politics. It is not "power": it is a sense of camaraderie, of being part of a team, part of a cause larger than, and beyond, the self. The more enduring of the rewards of politics are not the spoils of victory, but the "stories" you carry with you all your life. Even the worst occasions in politics can contain, when you look back, a harvest of humor.

There were also "Mud Bowls" — tackle football games played without equipment at Chevy Chase Playground on Saturdays following thundershowers or several days of rain, when the field was so sloppy it was impossible to get traction. There was the annual Homer Ball at the Ebbit Hotel, which evolved into the Homer-BMF Ball, on which the statute of limitations, unfortunately, has yet to run. And there was the "Christmas Game."

During the holidays, when we were in college, several of the crowd would bring to our parties some new lovely the rest of us had never seen. When that happened, we would gather at the door to greet the sweetie, saying, "Merry Christmas, Sue; it's a pleasure to meet you; and we're delighted to have you here," note the mistletoe, and give her an extended kiss on the lips, a nice hug and a squeeze, and, then, hand her over to one of the Kadows, with, "Kevin, have you met Sue here; she's in town for the holidays, and Jack Toland brought her to the party; say hello to Sue." Kevin would start the routine again.

"Good Lord, your friends are friendly!" one girl exclaimed to "Whitey" Toland, after she experienced the Christmas Game for the first ten minutes after she got into the house.

Soon, we were playing the Christmas Game all year around, and the girls didn't have to be all that lovely. Somebody would call out, "Christmas Game," and we would all head for the front door. After a while, the guys who brought these ladies to the party would announce — at the front door — that, if the Christmas Game started with this particular date, somebody was going to answer in the front yard.

Then, there were the "keg parties," usually held on Saturday morning in the spring and summer. For fourteen dollars you could buy a half keg of beer, and with another fourteen-dollar deposit, rent the tap and coils. We would make arrangements with Chevy Chase Liquor on Friday, and on Saturday, someone eighteen or older would pick the contraption up. Only fourteen individuals were permitted at each keg party, to drink all one wanted for a dollar each, until the keg was tapped out. If we were two or three short, invitations were extended to Cricket and his fourteen-year-old friends like Jack Mitchell. Same price: one dollar admission, so long as Cricket's friends understood, as the Roach pointedly reminded Jack Mitchell during one keg party, "You are guests here, and you are to conduct yourselves as such."

We would pick up the keg, drive across Military Road on 27th Street, and drop down into the park. There, we would leave the cars, and haul the full, heavy keg through the deep woods, back up the hill, and out into an open space on Aerlie Playground. We would then tap the keg, and, to catch the rays of the June sun, some of us would strip down to our Fruit of the Looms, or Polio Pants as they were called, since that is all the little male polio victims wore in the March of Dimes posters. With woods to our back and a hundred yards to the road in every direction, we could be dressed and running, before some cop, in full uniform, had sweated his way across that immense pasture to apprehend us. We felt secure.

While Aerlie Playground was normally deserted on Saturdays, on one day several families were picnicking about a hundred yards away. Observing from that distance, the parents decided to cut short the family outing — unsure exactly what to anticipate from fourteen male adolescents, drinking and laughing in their underpants. Occasionally, a police car could be seen in the distance, cruising slowly, but, soon, it would go on its way. Then, two hours into the party, we saw the mirage. Coming swiftly across the field from Oregon Avenue were several park policemen. Only they weren't walking; they were galloping. The park police had sent several of their mounties up the horse trails; and, having emerged from the woods, they were now thundering down upon us. The panic was directly proportional to the previous security we had all felt.

"They've got [expletive] horses!" guys were shouting; and, suddenly, hopping around, yelling, "That's my shirt; where's my pants?" Others grabbed pants, shirt, and socks in their hands, and raced into the forest in their underpants as the cavalry descended upon us. From the woods around me, I could hear the howls and curses of those who had taken off barefoot.

The Kadows were conscripted to lift the heavy and cumbersome keg, still attached to the coils and tap, and haul it into the woods, avoiding the horse trails where they could be ridden down. Were we not minors ourselves, we would have been more concerned about being charged with contributing to the delinquency of Cricket's fourteen-year-old friends, who were blotto. But those boys did not need a book of instructions to tell them what to do in this kind of situation. Cricket, Mitchell, and Tommy Alder were gone. Not until that night did we learn everyone had made it; the keg had been returned, and the deposit refunded.

The Kadows had a first cousin named George, several years their junior. Raised down on the Chesapeake, George, as a boy, idolized his famous city cousins. Some summers, George would come up from the bay to stay with the Kadows on Grafton Street; he would sit merrily in the back of the Mo-Par as we made our appointed rounds. Eventually, George moved to the suburbs; but, by now, the relationship was competitive.

Almost as large as his cousins, George made up his mind he would become bigger than the Kadows — and, therefore, a more imposing figure. George always seemed to equate size with power and prestige. Daily, one summer, he tanked up on beer and burgers until he hit 295 pounds. Henceforth, he was known as Roller.

One Saturday evening around ten, as the Mo-Par was heading east on Layhill Road beyond Silver Spring — farm country — Brian, Kevin, George, and I were almost run off the road into a ditch. We caught up with the two characters in the Pontiac — and invited them out. They took off, with us in hot pursuit. When they reached Wheaton, however, they suddenly turned into a side street, parked, got out, and came striding toward our car. They were the size of the Kadows, huge. Their driver had a monkey wrench in his hand and he hammered Kevin's forearm, which was hanging out the window — breaking it, I thought at the time.

We piled out, but, as we did, I noticed people pouring out of the houses. We appeared to have stumbled into a nest of trolls. All the men looked like factory workers or farmhands; the women were yelling and cheering them on. But the Kadows were doing our fighting, and doing well. When one of the trolls walked up to me and said, "You stay out of this!" I looked down to see Brian hammering his opponent's head into the pavement, while Kevin had just driven another into a telephone pole with a blow to his head. Some woman started screaming at Kevin, "He's got a plate in his head! He's got a plate in his head!" If he does, I thought, that plate is broke. With our side prevailing, there was no need to enlarge the theater of operations, so, I turned to the wide-bodied troll and yelled, "I'll stay out of this — *if you stay out!*"

By now, the whole neighborhood seemed to be in the street. I was getting nervous, as this was not at all a disinterested or friendly crowd, when, suddenly, some short, beefy character yelled, "Get the hell out of here!" and jammed a long, single-barreled shotgun into my stomach.

"Take it easy!" I said, trying to calm the enraged troll. "Take it easy; we're all leaving now."

"Get the hell out of here!" he yelled a second time.

Putting my hands up, I turned around; and he rammed the shotgun into my back and began marching me toward the Mo-Par like a POW. I broke out into a sweat. When I reached the car, however, George materialized. Seeing his buddy in the classic hands-up posture of surrender, George starting yelling, "Don't let him bluff you, Blade, that thing's rusty; it'll never fire!"

"Get out of the way, George," I said calmly but firmly.

"He's bluffing you, Blade, that gun is rusty as hell; I'm telling you that thing'll never fire."

"George, get out of the way," I said in more explicit terms.

Expecting the single-barreled cannon to go off, ending my life, I desperately pushed by George, dove into the back seat of the Mo-Par, while the Kadows quickly climbed into the front. George finally got into the car, but, as we drove off, he was still bristling, yelling out the window at the lunatic with the shotgun. Head down I waited for the twelve-gauge blast through our back window. The only sound, though, was George yelling, "I can't believe you guys let him bluff you like that; I tell you that shotgun was rusty; it would never have fired!"

I lost track of George, until, almost two decades later, a veteran of Mr. Nixon's historic opening to China, I was speaking at a symposium in Knoxville on Sino-American relations. At one point,

I gazed out into the audience to see, occupying several chairs and smiling broadly, my old friend Roller. Happily married, George was now a respected professor of urban planning at the University of Tennessee.

Today, Ocean City, Maryland, resembles Miami Beach, with its miles of high-rise condos and hotels stretching north to Fenwick Island, Delaware, ten miles away. In 1953, it was a quiet vacation resort of several thousand, which swelled dramatically in the summer. The hotels — five stories was tall — ended with the Commander at 14th Street. Beyond were a few cottages and then, for miles, deserted dunes. Except for the small town of Bethany Beach, north of the observation towers for the shore guns to keep German ships away from the Atlantic Coast, the twenty-eight-mile stretch between Ocean City and Rehobeth was virtually deserted. For ten days in June after the D.C., suburban Virginia, and Maryland high schools and colleges let out, Ocean City was an occupied city, all its rental housing taken over by sororities and fraternities and anyone else searching for the good times to be had.

The girls all stayed in cottages, but some guys slept on the beach or in their cars. We usually stayed two to a room in tiny alcoves in a remodeled truck terminal called the Safe Garage. Rent was fifty cents a night. From 1953 to 1962, I rode down Maryland's Route 50 to Delaware's 404 half a dozen times every summer.

It was in Ocean City, in the summer of '57, that there took place what became known as "The Auto Show" at Eighth and the Bay. Hank and I and almost a dozen others shared a cottage on the bay side of Ocean City — opposite the beach side of a town only half a mile wide. We lived on hot dogs, purchased or liberated, and beer around the clock. It was a great time to be alive. We would get up late, boil some dogs, crack a couple of beers, recount and embroider what happened the night before, and head for the beach where there must have been twenty thousand girls. School was out; the summer job was weeks ahead; we had not a care in the world. When the sun started down, we started for our cottage, showered, picked up our dates, and headed out to the dunes for a beach party at 68th or 69th Street, and then came back and walked the boardwalk. While some of the girls had twelve-o'clock curfews, the girls from Wakefield used to sneak out for "late dates" to go swimming in the ocean at midnight. The same rock music was on every portable radio, and in every cottage. "Searchin' " by the Coasters was the song of the summer.

As Miss Beth was staying over on Baltimore Avenue, six blocks away, with her graduating girlfriends from BCC, I was more tied up than Forster and Red Dog and Hank and the others, who were unattached. One night, Miss Beth and I were strolling along the boardwalk, when my friends got into an altercation with a kid from Anacostia, and Forster knocked the kid's huge bucket of french fries all over the boardwalk. I was blameless in the incident, but the kid recognized me and started cussing and yelling. As he was younger and smaller than we, everybody laughed at him. He took off running, to find his friends.

My buddies headed home, and I walked Miss Beth back to her cottage on North Baltimore. As we were sitting on her front porch, talking, I noticed a crowd forming across the street, a crowd taking on the aspect of a mob. They were whipping themselves into a frenzy. I sat and listened, and what I heard concentrated the mind wonderfully. The little kid was in their midst, distorting and magnifying the atrocity on the boardwalk. Some of the others said they had had it with the cockiness and arrogance of the "Chevy Chase crowd"; it was time, a voice yelled, to go over to Eighth and the Bay and "kick the shit out of Hank and Pat Buchanan and the rest of those Chevy Chase bastards."

To hear oneself discussed in the third person in so forthright a fashion is a riveting experience. As the mob debated the merits of stomping me and my friends — and seemed to be leaning toward an affirmative vote — I took off running for the cottage.

"We're gonna have visitors," I told them, as soon as I arrived. "You boys better shape up." They were all drinking, and few took me seriously. "No joke," I said.

Still they laughed. "We'll clean their clocks, if they show up."

Suddenly, we heard a commotion outside, and as I looked out the window, somebody asked nervously what was going on.

"It looks like the auto show," I said. A dozen cars were pulling up, and the Anacostia crowd was disembarking for action. Leading the pack was a pair of brothers, Max and PeeWee. At that point, a group that seemed somewhat smaller than our full contingent inside the cottage walked out to meet them in the street, and Hank and Max were fighting within seconds.

The battle was running about even, when I almost collapsed to the pavement, from a sucker punch to the head. PeeWee wanted in on the action. Conditioned reflexes took over. Almost out cold on my feet, I started throwing lefts and rights at the head of the shadow that had clobbered me. Within seconds, I could feel them connecting and collecting a toll, because the blows coming back in my direction felt less and less heavy when they hit. For a fistfight, which often can last less than a minute, this brawl lasted what seemed like ten rounds. Other fights were breaking out; and, then, we heard the sirens and saw the police cars. Because I felt myself getting the upper hand, maybe on the way to a TKO if not a knock-out, I didn't want to break it off, so I kept hitting PeeWee; but he wouldn't go down. As the cops pulled up, PeeWee took off running, with me calling him names for quitting first. He had more sense; he wasn't about to spend his beach money in the Ocean City jail.

Now, the cops were out of their cars, some of them with guns drawn, and I still hadn't cooled down from getting sucker-punched. So, with PeeWee AWOL, I picked one of the Anacostia spectators, a guy about my size, and gave him as much notice as PeeWee had given me. In the moonlight, he never saw it coming.

With other fights still breaking out, one of the boneheaded cops — farm boys from the Eastern Shore who needed a job during the summer — started shooting. I never saw him; I just heard the gun go off and saw everybody scatter.

I headed for the bay, and crawled under an overturned rowboat; Larry Sullivan was already hiding beneath it. Together, we waited fifteen minutes for the area to clear, and then slipped over behind our cottage, where I discovered Brother Hank. He was sitting on top of some guy, with one hand on the guy's throat, the other pounding him into the ground. Even at that age, Hank enjoyed his work.

We slipped back into the cottage. Those of us who had been in the brawl showed it, with cuts and contusions all over our faces. Hank was so tired he could barely lift his arms. But we also discovered that a couple of those who had been loudest about what they were going to kick, if Anacostia arrived, had "been asleep." How they wished they had been there!

All through the night we laughed with the telling and retelling of "the auto show" story; and were fortunate to have, in the house as well as the street, "Red Dog" Folliard, who could recount a story better than anyone we knew. The next morning, Red Dog, Denny, Hank, and I went over to have our wounds tended by Miss Beth, Diane K., and the girls at 5th and Baltimore. Then, we bought a pair of six-packs and headed home.

Route 50 was still an undivided country road, and as we rolled eastward in Hank's '49 Merc toward the Bay Bridge, sipping our beer and laughing still, I saw coming toward us what looked like my father's newest Olds. As the vehicle approached, I saw it *was* my father's new Olds. Pop swept past us, staring grimly ahead — but in the back seat I could see my nine-year-old brother Jack, gesticulating wildly toward us, as the Oldsmobile roared by. When we got home to Utah Avenue, Mom informed us that Pop had to drive the 150 miles to pick up Cricket at the juvenile detention center at Snow Hill, where he and his friends had been taken for activities at the Safe Garage the night before.

With Red Dog and Forster relating in the bars of Northwest the story of the "auto show" at Eighth and the Bay, the tale took on mythic dimension. Weeks later, a friend told me his brother had heard an incredible story of how the Buchanans and half a dozen friends "had fought sixty guys from Anacostia down in Ocean City — and came out even."(Visit Dumoors in Bethesda, look up the stout red-haired gentleman sipping in the corner; and you, too, can yet hear it told.)

For one participant, it had not been much fun. We learned later that the cop who fired his weapon to end a street brawl had shot a kid in the groin.

That someone stood by friends in trouble, the way the Kadows and my brothers always did, was, in those days, about the highest compliment you could pay; and virtually the worst term that could be used about anyone was that he was "chicken," someone who, when fighting started, ran out on his friends.

During Watergate, when reporters would ask me how I could continue to defend Nixon now that it was clear the President had deceived everybody, including his own, I wondered where, exactly, *they* had come from. How, in that ultimate crisis of Mr. Nixon's life, could his own people *not* defend him? No one I grew up with ever faulted me for staying with Nixon to the end. Indeed, one day, when I was feeling sorry for myself, after another bombshell had detonated beneath us, I picked up the phone at the White House to hear my father say, "Pat, why aren't you fighting?"

That was the right question. Whether Nixon was wrong was not the relevant issue. Even if he had booted it, he had a right to be defended; and his friends had a duty to be there.

While we did not go looking for trouble in those years, it seemed to be looking for us. On many occasions, as my father had warned us, the only way to avoid fighting would have been to play the coward. A single tale, the story of "The Sunoco Massacre," should suffice.

In the fall of "that memorable year, 1957," following a party at Billy LaFond's (his father, the ex-fighter Eddie LaFond, had taught Hank and me boxing during our high-school days), I was sitting with Miss Beth in the back seat of "Slugger" Pekin's car. Hank was "riding point," and Hank's Belgian friend Paul was sitting beside him in front, when we stalled in the middle of East-West Highway. (Paul, a graduate of Prep, was known as "Gator," because he had a smile that spread so wide it revealed at least twenty-eight of his thirty-two teeth.)

Two characters, loitering in the Sunoco Station on the corner, sauntered into East-West Highway. We thought they had walked out to offer a hand with our stalled car. Instead, one of them, without warning, started throwing right hands through the open window at Hank's head. While Hank ducked, we sat there, stymied. Finally, I reached over into the front seat and pulled the handle opening the front door.

Hank rolled out backwards holding his head to avoid being kicked, and I dove forward from the back seat into the street. James Dean could not have done it better. By the time I was standing, Hank was belting the one guy soundly, so I went after his friend, a red-coated coward who ran as soon as he was hit. Instead of chasing him, I went back out into East-West Highway to lend Hank a hand. Together, we gave the guy who started that brawl a beating he must remember to this day, at the end of which we had to hold him up. Leaving him lying in East-West Highway beside Pekin's car, we went to settle with the coward. We had pretty much decided to go into the station after him, when two Montgomery County squad cars came screaming into the Sunoco lot. Hank and I ran around the station with the police running after us, and we came to a fence, below which was a ten-foot drop. There was no way back.

Hank went over the fence and dropped into the alley below, and I followed. We looked back up to see Gator, hands frozen on the fence, daunted by the prospect of leaping into the darkness.

"Jump, Gator, you can make it," we yelled.

"I can't, I can't," he said, and he stood there until a police arm dropped over his shoulder. As there was nothing we could do for him, we took off on foot back to LaFond's. Besides, Paul, whose father was a senior counselor at the Belgian embassy, had diplomatic immunity.

Feeling myself home free, I suddenly remembered I had left Beth in the back seat, surrounded by Montgomery County police. While her father might relish my right-wing opinions, he would not relish his eldest daughter's spending the night in the Greybar Hotel, thanks to me. I had to get her out.

We did not know it at the time, but the clown we had left lying in the street was en route to Suburban Hospital. The Montgomery County police, fearing serious injury and not knowing who had started the brawl, had an APB (all points bulletin) out to intercept the Buchanan brothers — who had, they assumed, perpetrated an unprovoked criminal assault and were making a run for the District line. Actually, we were headed in the other direction.

At LaFond's, we picked up Hank's Mercury and phoned the station to learn Miss Beth was indeed being held. I decided to walk directly into the station house and talk them into releasing my girlfriend. Since my shirt was torn, I borrowed Hank's raincoat, while he waited outside, engine running. Politely, I approached the desk.

"Good evening, officer," I said, adding that I had heard of the nasty altercation at the Sunoco station and had been sent around by the young lady's parents to pick her up and take her home. Would he please release her, if she wasn't being charged, and we'd be on our way?

The sergeant wasn't buying it. He stared at me a second, then said, "Tell me, how did you happen to get that blood all over you?'' As we had washed up at LaFond's, I was dumbfounded, until I looked down at the bloody sleeves of Hank's raincoat, sleeves I had put right up on the counter. Fumbling for an explanation, I heard Beth's voice from the next room, ''It's no use; it's no use; I've told them everything.''

Suddenly, cops were all over me, while a couple of others were taking the stairs two by two to apprehend my driver. It took two hours to roust Buchs out of bed and over to Bethesda with $53 for the standard $27.50 fines for ''Disorderly Conduct.''

During the night, the guy who started it all was brought back from Suburban. His appearance almost made it worthwhile. His face was almost unrecognizable and he had a thick bandage covering a wound in the back of his head, which had, we were told, been opened up by some sharp instrument, perhaps a beer can. Which explained the blood on Henry's sleeves.

There was one other surprise. Gator, sitting morosely in the police station waiting for his father, the diplomat, had a huge bulbous nose; he had apparently stopped cold the first right hand through the car window. His father arrived an hour later to collect Paul. Later, we informed Gator that insofar as he had received punches and thrown none, we were ranking him seventh among the Sunoco fighters — right behind Miss Beth. Gator later became a Trappist.

Gator was not the only one who had ''diplomatic immunity.''

Georgetown Prep had dozens of students who were the sons of diplomats; and the most famous was Dave, the son of the Irish Ambassador, a good friend and perhaps the greatest hellion I ever encountered. ''Let the good times roll!'' was written all over him.

One night, after Dave and I had been out on the town until three in the morning with a pair of lovelies whom we had driven home to far Southeast, they invited us in and brewed a pot of coffee, for fear the forty-five-minute drive back to far Northwest, with the famous son of the Irish Ambassador at the wheel, would end in headlines. Around 5 A.M., Dave and I said our goodnights and steered north through the city. Dave had brought along a six-pack as ''travelers,'' and, as we were enjoying the dawn ride up a deserted 16th Street toward Military Road, Dave suddenly took a sharp left turn — toward Snake Hill. Which was not too unusual. Then, however, he suddenly steered the old car up over the curb onto the vast and vacant Kennedy Playground, and, at 5:30 A.M., began circling the field in his car while sipping his beer.

"Not good, Dave," I said.

"I'm going to score," he replied. The car picked up speed, and Dave steered for the soccer net at the far end of the field. I put my hand in front of my face, as Dave roared through the net at thirty miles an hour, bringing down the wooden posts. The netting covered the car so we could barely see; Dave turned around and headed downfield, picking up speed, and roared through the other net.

With the car almost invisible beneath the soccer netting, Dave drove over the curb and back out onto 16th Street, and turned north again for Military Road. Sipping his Gunther and laughing all the way, he dropped me off on Utah Avenue. It was broad daylight now, and he headed home in his camouflaged car to the magnificent Ambassador's residence across from American University where we had our Saint Paddy's Day parties. I wished him luck. More than almost anybody else I knew, Dave needed it.

He used that old car as an extension of his personality and an instrument of retribution. When Jackson, the belligerent black attendant who dictatorially operated the parking lot behind Peoples, denied him a parking place, Dave got into his battered old car, drove around the block, and, in zero-degree weather, rammed and collapsed the wooden shack that kept Jackson warm in the winter. (Because of diplomatic immunity, nothing could be done to him.)

As the years went by, Pop, not without reason, had come to the conclusion son Pat was the *primum mobile* of Bill's and Hank's troubles. More than for his other sons together, he had been required to visit the juvenile center downtown or Number Eight to collect me. So, when he and Mom took the younger children to Ocean City, after my sophomore year in college, he announced I would be going along and kept under surveillance, while Hank and Bill would be left in charge of the house. Another error in judgment.

When we came home around Labor Day, I noticed my father standing at the fence and conversing animatedly with our neighbor, Mr. Bernstein. When my father got in, he was shaking his head; his divide-and-conquer strategy had not worked. When my brothers got home, I got the story.

The night of the All-Star game at Soldier Field in Chicago, my brothers had thrown a stag party; and half of Chevy Chase had shown up. As we were on eastern time, the game did not end until near midnight. By then, everyone was in high spirits; and the Homers challenged the Benders — the Georgetown Prep alumni who boasted of their drinking prowess — to an All-Star game in our front yard, which was almost the size of a football field.

The game got loud and boisterous and out of hand around the second quarter, because Mr. Bernstein had awakened, gotten into his car, driven around to the front of our house, and yelled to the players on both teams to quit and go home. Then, as Mr. Bernstein told my father, two huge young men who appeared to be identical twins, came out into the street and started rocking his car in an attempt to turn it over — with him inside. Both teams poured off the field to lend a hand.

After Mr. Bernstein escaped in his vehicle, the game resumed. But someone had called the police, whose sirens were audible. So both teams stumbled in the darkness up toward the house — sixty yards from the street. Radio silence was imposed; all lights were extinguished; and the police arrived on a tranquil suburban scene. When two cops came to the door to see if the family at 5501 was aware of any disturbance, Hank appeared in my father's bathrobe and pipe — a portrait in suburban serenity — and asked the officers what exactly was the problem that caused them to awaken him at this ungodly hour of the night.

As the blackout was being maintained, the gang appeared to have pulled it off, and the police, satisfied this house was not the source, were about to depart — when, suddenly, a rug dropped onto the heads of the police officers from the balcony a floor above, where Larry Sullivan had crawled out to watch the proceedings. The game was up — so Hank shut the door, saying that, if they didn't have a warrant, good-night. Later, a valedictory barrage of empty bottles and cans from our front yard had rained down on Neighbor Bernstein's roof.

This was the story related to the Old Man at the fence. For once, I trusted, Pop would begin to see the unfairness of ascribing all his sons' troubles to the black sheep he had taken to the beach.

While our hell-raising in the '50s might appear of a piece with that done by the radicals in the '60s, there was more than a small difference. Some of the '60s young openly despised the government and the "system"; they regularly reviled the cops as "pigs." We weren't in the least unhappy with the "system." We loved the world as we found it. We didn't want to change anything — not even the draft. We did not think the cops were all "pigs"; they were a mixed bag, social referees doing a necessary job; and while we might brazenly dispute their calls, we never denied we needed police.

We wanted to enjoy youth, and postpone adulthood. Our occasional breaches of the peace were no more a manifestation of contempt for the rule of law than our occasional breaches of the Ten Commandments were a manifestation of contempt for traditional morality.

A fight, or a brawl, in those years was simply no big deal (so long as it was not among friends). Whenever we were arrested for fighting or came home bloodied, we were not punished by my parents, so long as we had fought fairly. Pop was usually more interested in how well we had done. When Jack, nine years younger than me, got into a bloody fight with the son of one of JFK's Irish Mafia — a fight that ended with Jack's suspension and his opponent's expulsion from Gonzaga — Pop relished the story of how well his son had done against a truly tough kid.

At my bachelor party in the first week of May of 1971, two dozen of us watched the eleven-o'clock news clips of the D.C. police battling the May Day "demonstrators," the college students who had blocked traffic and trashed Georgetown. My friends from Chevy Chase cheered and laughed loudest every time a cop was shown clubbing one of our out-of-state visitors — even though several of us had been clubbed ourselves little more than a decade before.

If the issue were between a friend and a cop, we sided with our friend; but, if the issue was between police defending the peace, order, and security of our town, and fifteen thousand overprivileged radicals trying to upend it, we were all for the cops. It was as simple as that.

My little brothers, however, must have thought we were professional outlaws. They listened, transfixed, as we would relate the tales of the Friday-night fights and Saturday-night arrests. One afternoon, when Hank took Tom along to get gas at the Esso station and they heard sirens coming up Connecticut Avenue, six-year-old Tom panicked, grabbed Hank's shoulder, and desperately asked, "Should we run? Should we run?"

While I paid more fines than most, my "record" was a subject of humor to friends, if not to my parents. In high school and college, we had to fill out those long forms on our personal history; and I could always count on one of my classmates calling out loud, "Hey, Pat, it's question number thirty-four!"

Looking down, I would see the inevitable "Have you ever been arrested, held, etc? If so, please provide details on a separate sheet of paper." Someone like Chick Leasure would raise his hand, be called upon by the class proctor, and say, "Sir, Mr. Buchanan over here will be needing several separate sheets of paper — to complete question thirty-four."

Something else I learned, long before George Gilder wrote it so well. The girls, the young women of that era, most of them far more mature than the males, were, indeed, the "civilizers" of our adolescence. When one of my friends started "going" with a girl, invariably his behavior improved; and as soon as they married, he was a different man. Now, he had responsibility, which is what we were missing.

The guys with whom I grew up were of another breed than most of those with whom I went to journalism school, worked in politics, and served in the White House. Almost everybody we ran with from Chevy Chase was a good athlete; many were extraordinary athletes. Steve Chase and Millard (Ox) Crouch were all-Prep in football; Donny Klemkiewicz and Mike Loh — Roach as we called him from his appearance when he got off the bus after working all day scrubbing pots and pans in the kitchen of the Sholl's Cafeteria his father managed — were all-Metropolitan. Tommy McCloskey was voted the best basketball player in the Washington area in 1956; Lew Luce was the last high school athlete to make all-Metropolitan in three sports. Dick Drummond was an all–Southern Conference running back at George Washington University, drafted by the Redskins; Mike Sommer played in the same backfield with Unitas, Alan Ameche, and Lenny Moore in the Colt–Giant NFL classic. Hatchet Keaveny and "Squeaks" Wilson fought Golden Gloves; and Dave Flynn was, pound for pound, the toughest guy I ever knew.

They were all tough, competitive, loved athletics, took fights as something that was part of growing up, good for laughs the next night at the Piccolo. They drank, played hard, loved the ladies and the rock-and-roll music of the era. Only a handful of us could be called "students." Growing up with them, you knew where they stood, and where you stood — unlike the two-faced, gossipy, backstabbing types so frequently encountered in politics, government, journalism, the bureaucracy, and, yes, even in a few of the West Wing offices at 1600 Pennsylvania Avenue.

Though most of the awards I won growing up were academic, not athletic, I always felt more at home riding around in a car with these C and D students, than ever I would with most of the deans-list, student-council types with whom I was thrown together — in graduate school, the Washington press, and even the White House. One night I heard Dick Cavett speaking at the White House correspondents dinner, and at the end of his monologue, he dropped this wisecrack: "In order to be truly happy, it is not only necessary to succeed in life; one's friends must also fail."

A penetrating remark; and everyone laughed, because it captured an aspect of this city perfectly.

At the apex of political power, the resentment, the envy, the malice, hidden behind the smiling mask of synthetic bonhomie, are almost a felt presence in the room. In the Washington where I grew up, it wasn't that way.

Yet, as Kipling wrote, "The Gods of the Copy Book Maxims, with fire and sword return."

The laughter died for Dave one Saturday afternoon. He and Shags, another friend, driving home from a Maryland game, struck and killed a black woman in Northeast. The accident made national headlines. All of Dave's prior arrests were now national news, and the editorial writers talked of the gross abuse of diplomatic immunity. Dave's father, the Ambassador, departed for Dublin and the Irish Foreign Ministry, and Dave went home with him. After a year, Dave slipped back into the country from Canada, joined the Marine Corps, and is now an American citizen.

The last word about Shags was that he was finishing up a third term at the Maryland State Prison at Jessup's Run.

Mike Loh left Chevy Chase for the Air Force Academy where he graduated in 1960, winning top honors in physics; he flew in Southeast Asia during Vietnam, and came home to design fighter planes. Roach is a general now.

Around 1968, Richie was arrested for gambling, and half of Chevy Chase had to testify they were laying off bets with him; he was given ten years. Richie came to see his old friend from Blessed Sacrament and Gonzaga, now a thirty-year-old Special Assistant to President Nixon. I had my own "counsel" sit in, a conservative young Indiana attorney I had brought with me into the White House, who would himself gain some national notoriety — twenty-eight-year-old Tom Charles Huston, the author of the Huston Plan. The Ram, as we called him, opened by explaining that ten years in Lewisburg seemed excessive for a first-time gambling offense, especially since he, with no prior arrests or convictions, had less of a police record than I. The point was noted. I memoed the Department of Justice that ten years did indeed seem almost malicious, when bank robbers and rapists were walking away with three and four. Why are we doing this?

Word came from John Mitchell's Department of Justice that the heavy sentence had been imposed because the gambling operation for which Richie had been making book provided income for a criminal syndicate that was into more than taking bets on Redskins' games. Richie came in for a second meeting.

"They want names," I told him.

"Sure, Pat," the Ram said, "I'll give 'em eighty names — and spend the rest of my life living on air force bases."

We both laughed.

Richie did not give up any names; he went to Lewisburg and was paroled after nineteen months; a few years later, he was back again in Lewisburg — caught with a shoebox full of cocaine in the lobby of a downtown hotel at three in the morning.

When he called me to ask for a "reference" before sentencing, I asked Richie if he had tried Father Lyon — of whom Richie had been a great favorite at Blessed Sacrament. "I did Father Lyon the last time, Pat," Richie said. "This time, I want to spread it around."

Dave Flynn's bar at 14th and U went bust; owing thousands, he joined the merchant marine, hauling cargo to Danang, paid off his creditors, and wandered through Laos. Dave came home militantly and obsessively antiwar, and became part of the Quakers' months-long, twenty-four-hour vigil outside Mr. Nixon's White House.

A reporter with whom I lunched one day was startled to see me stop and talk with the shirtless, bearded demonstrator in front of the White House. Some days, with the temperature below freezing, Dave could be found in Lafayette Park; he told me he lived off the berries he found there. Two of Dave's brothers were killed in tragic auto accidents: the youngest, Pat, was run down by a speeding car while innocently horsing around with a friend late at night on the same Ocean Highway along which Billy Barnes and I had run our Graduation Race.

The Kadows went to the University of Omaha on football scholarships. Kevin met his future wife, Mary Kay, there, came home, and joined with Brian, who also married a Nebraska girl, Ellen, to set up their own real estate firm on Wisconsin Avenue in Bethesda. Together, they have run it for twenty years.

Hatchet never liked the big city. (An early environmentalist, he would become enraged when anyone would throw an empty beer can into a creek.) He went to dental school with Crick, then moved with his wife to North Dakota, where he could raise his seven kids in a land where the great cultural event is the Calgary Stampede.

Peter Sommer, Michael's younger brother, with whom I double-dated and whose social conduct earned him the sobriquet Filthy McNasty, served in Paris and Brussels with NATO, and came home in the early 1980s to be hired by his friend from Wilson days, "Buddy" McFarlane, to serve on the European desk at the NSC.

At the American embassy in Tokyo in the spring of 1986, I sat beside the President and McNasty sat, on the opposite side of the table, beside the Secretary of State at the intimate lunch where U.S. strategy on terrorism and trade was being set for the Economic Summit. Peter and I worked together at both the President's Geneva and Reykjavik summits with Mr. Gorbachev; he is now U.S. Ambassador to Malta, and a long way from the Homer-BMF Ball.

And the Mo-Par?

A black attendant at the Amoco Station on Connecticut Avenue at Livingston had it about right. Taking a second look into the back seat of that Plymouth, with all the "dead soldiers" on the floor, the attendant said: "Good Lord, if you guys ever get into a wreck, the glass inside this thing alone will kill ya."

One night, after dropping Carole Fentress off in Georgetown, Brian climbed into the Mo-Par and motored north up New Mexico Avenue. As the car steamed toward American University, Brian fell asleep at the wheel and somehow slumped down onto the accelerator. Driverless, the Mo-Par jumped the sixteen-inch curb, ran across the grounds, and slammed into its final resting place, the south wall of the United Methodist Church. An hour later, police found Brian, bleeding and dazed, wandering in Glen Echo, two miles from the scene. The car did not survive.

Charlie Leasure wrote its epitaph: "The Mo-Par died as it lived, a symbol of defiance against the Church."

8

Georgetown —
On the Five-Year Plan

"What about Saint Cyprian! He practiced black magic!"

To HAVE a sense of purpose and a settled direction in life was the exception among those with whom I grew up.

In our family, only Hank seemed to know what he was going to do — be an accountant like my father. He had applied his half-scholarship from Gonzaga to the Foreign Service School at Georgetown, which then housed the business school. For Bill and me, neither of whom had any idea of what we wanted to do in life, the general notion was to steer toward becoming a "professional" man. For that, a "liberal arts" education at Georgetown College was fine.

What was critical to my father was that we not "go into government." His father and mother had both worked in the Treasury Department; and, to him, "going into government" meant getting "hooked" on the salary and job security, and spending the rest of one's life in predictable, routinized labor that stunted the mind and sapped the spirit. My father would tell us of accountant friends who had passed their C.P.A. exam, then gone to work for the generous starting salaries offered by the IRS. While he was struggling in his mid-twenties, they were bragging about the cash they were taking home. Now, he said, he rarely saw them. Now, they had a defeated look; now, they were taking orders from some bureaucrat, and would be taking orders the rest of their lives.

He admired the disposition to roll the dice and risk everything that his Jewish friends and clients, Benny Ourisman, the Chevrolet dealer, and Harry Viner and his son, Melvin, who had made a fortune with Sunshine Laundry, had exhibited. "They didn't have a damn dime when they started," Pop would tell us, emphatically. "They went to friends, borrowed money, started a business, went broke; went back to their friends, borrowed again, went broke again. Finally, they made it. They built something of their own. Now they work for themselves, and everybody else works for them. Be your own man!" That was the attitude we should adopt.

But, about government, we did not need convincing. Around us in Chevy Chase, the families that were doing well were headed by doctors, lawyers, accountants, dentists, and small businessmen who worked for themselves. The families whose fathers worked for the federal government were not living in the big houses, or spending three weeks at Bethany Beach or Rehobeth. In those families, the kids had to work during the summer.

Even though I was first in my class in the premier Catholic school in the city, the Ivy League was never an option. With nine children, the family could not afford it; and there were no Ivy League recruiters hanging around Gonzaga, no affirmative action scholarships to Harvard and Yale for deserving Catholic boys. Most important to my parents, Ivy League colleges were places where you went and "lost your faith." They would never have permitted me to go; all nine Buchanan children would graduate from Catholic colleges. *The Seven Storey Mountain,* the autobiography of Thomas Merton's hegira from atheism at Columbia to Trappist monk at Gethseme, Kentucky, made a profound impression on the postwar generation of Catholics. "What doth it profit a man if he gain the whole world and suffer the loss of his soul?" was the rhetorical question from Scripture my father most often posed when deriding the Ivy League schools.

Even though Notre Dame was the dream of countless Catholic boys, I was privately relieved my lack of "depth perception" cost me the NROTC scholarship to South Bend. That spared me the necessity of choice; secretly, I didn't want to go to Notre Dame. I had no desire to leave friends, family, or Chevy Chase. Why go away to school? For what? I hadn't the vaguest notion of what I was "going to do," and no particular ambition to be rich or famous. Both my brothers were at Georgetown; it was an excellent college; many of my friends were already there, or on the way.

We had a humorous term of derision in those years; it was "local." You were "local" if you had never been out of the city, if you resisted the idea of going somewhere new, like Fort Lauderdale for spring break, or Ocean City, New Jersey, rather than Ocean City, Maryland. ("Let's face it, Beef, you're 'local'; you are completely lost out beyond Jones Mill Road!") In truth, almost all of us were "local." When the Kadows' parents indicated the family might be moving to Wisconsin, the boys warned that, if the move took place, they would sit on the front porch of their Grafton Street home until they starved to death.

At Georgetown, it was soon clear we had come to a different place. Unlike Gonzaga, where everyone commuted, the student body at Georgetown was divided — into boarders and "dayhops." We had separate cafeterias in separate buildings; boarders ate the hot breakfasts, lunches, and dinners prepared by the kitchen staff; we brown-bagged it. While we took classes together, we dayhops were out of there as soon as classes were over. The boarders lived on campus and were subject to rules about "chapel" and "lights out" — about which they were constantly griping — that were of no concern to us. They drank at Teehan's and the Hilltop on 36th Street; we went back to the Piccolo and Chevy Chase.

While the Jesuits at Georgetown, who lived in the same dormitory complex, got to know the boarders well, we rarely got to know the Jesuits at all — except as teachers in the classrooms. Just as our Chevy Chase crowd had been an elite at Gonzaga, the boarders from New York and Boston set the pace at Georgetown. I did not get along particularly well with the New York–New Jersey–Boston types, many of whom I thought snooty and cocky, with little in the way of athletic or academic attainment to be cocky about.

When I was a freshman in ROTC, some of the senior officers of the cadet corps behaved as though they were young Pattons or MacArthurs. "Bat-tal-ee-onn! Tennnnnnnn — hut!" they would bellow out in the enclosed quadrangle, before we marched down the hill, our heavy M-1 rifles shouldered, past the jeering pre-med students — mocking us and gesturing obscenely in front of the biology lab — to the football field below, for ninety minutes of drill. Many of the seniors carried swagger sticks and wore their hats so low over their forehead they had to tilt their heads back to look you in the eye. "Mr. Buchanan, that brass isn't polished! I want a spit

Pop, in his early thirties, strikes pose as "one tough apple."

Mom and Pop on Whitehaven Parkway, 1942.

Following First Holy Communion, spring, 1946.

Christmas, 1946, on Chestnut Street, with (L to R) Bill, Hank, me, Crick, Kathleen (Coo); famous Hudson engine is in front of Coo.

That is me, preceded by Millard Crouch and Mike Loh, accompanied by George Mattingly, and followed by Jimmy Dolan, as the 1952 May Procession at Blessed Sacrament wends its way up Patterson Street toward Chevy Chase Circle.

Bill, spring, 1950 (with toe plate on right spike).

1A freshman class at Gonzaga (1952–1953): front row, Peter Grau (beedle), me (class president), Mr. Frank Bourbon, S.J., Mike Loh (vice president), Steve Chase (class treasurer). Directly behind Loh in second row is Paul Bayliss, killed in action, Vietnam. In third row, directly above PJB, is Stan Fiore.

That Championship Season. City CYO (sixteen and under) champions return to Union Station, Washington, D.C., following Sunday victory in Middle Atlantic tournament in Philadelphia, March 1954. (L to R): Larry Altemus, me, Tony Carroll, Millard Crouch, Hank, Denny Flynn (with trophy), Mike Loh, Richie, Rabbit Sinclair, Fred Horman, Pop.

Young Elvis, circa '55.

ROTC Military Ball, Georgetown University, December 6, 1957. (Clockwise from left): Connie Roberts, Denny Pekin, me, Miss Beth, Hank, Joan Whelan, Bill, unidentified.

The nine Buchanan children, circa 1959. Top row (L to R): Jack, Crick, Hank, me; first row (L to R): Brian (Buck), Kathleen (Coo), Angela (Bay), and Tom and Bill, "The Bookends" as Mom called her youngest and eldest.

Author, at twenty-three, at the Columbia School of Journalism (Class of '62) preaches undiluted Goldwaterism to skeptical class president Chris Trump. Don Oliver (now with NBC), at desk, has heard it before.

Columbia Journalism School, Class of '62. Top row (L to R): Jon Kapstein, Tom Daffron, me; in second row from the front, directly below Daffron, is Father Miguel D'Escoto, then a Maryknoll priest, now Foreign Minister of Nicaragua, and winner of the 1987 Lenin Peace Prize.

This photo, with Richard Nixon and David Ben-Gurion, was taken by UPI outside Ben-Gurion's home in Jerusalem, in June of 1967 in the immediate aftermath of the Six-Day War, seventeen months before Nixon's election to the presidency.

President Nixon and First Lady sit down to historic first dinner with Chou En-Lai, during Nixon's February 1972 "Opening to China." Author searches for table. (Courtesy, Time magazine)

Wedding Day for Shelley and me at Blessed Sacrament, May 8, 1971. (White House photo)

Last photo of the family together, at Pop and Mom's fiftieth wedding anniversary party at my house in McLean, December 1984. (L to R): Kathleen, Buck, Crick, Jack, me, Tom, Bill, Hank, Bay.

Meeting Gorbachev at Geneva summit, November 1985; Raisa looks on approvingly. (White House photo by Pete Souza)

Author and Leslie Stahl, following "Face the Nation" interview, January 1985 — before return to the White House.

Working under pressure with President Reagan on remarks to be delivered in minutes at Keflavik Air Base, Iceland, following collapse of Reykjavik summit, October 1986. (White House photo by Pete Souza)

Cardinal O'Connor comforts the afflicted, West Wing, White House, 1987. (White House photo by David Valdez)

Presentation of the Shoes. President Reagan confers bronzed running shoes on captain of the White House jogging team in the Nike Capital Challenge, a going-away present following two years in the White House, February 1987. (White House photo by Terry Arthur)

shine on those shoes, so I can look down and see myself in them like a mirror. Understand!''

When most of the boarders came around to Chevy Chase to our parties, we went out of our way to let them know they were unwelcome. I can yet recall walking in front of Copley Hall, on one of my first days of class, when Rabbit Sinclair and I were stopped by a shrimp of a sophomore, a boarder, with a high-pitched voice.

"Just a minute there, freshmen, where are your beanies?''

We both looked at him.

"Freshmen, where are your beanies! You are supposed to wear your beanies walking between classes.'' I laughed and told him we weren't into beanies; but Sinclair, a tough customer who enjoyed fighting as much as Hank, put down his books. The sophomore scurried off to report us.

Among the boarders, I did not make a single permanent friend in five years. I always felt that I "went" to Georgetown; I did not belong there as I did at Gonzaga. And, after I left, I never went back. The same was true of my older brothers. Our friends were the guys with whom we grew up, raised hell on weekends, and played ball. We didn't need any new friends and, candidly, we did not bring to Georgetown any great desire to make them. The boarders and dayhops, by and large, went their separate ways. As I said, we were "local,'' and, in some ways, we still are.

One afternoon, during freshman year, the dean asked my brother Bill and me (as we were not only dayhops but scholarship students and actually lived *in* Washington) if we would represent the college at a soiree in a private home on Foxhall Road, to debate the issue of "home rule.'' Okay, I said. Neither Bill nor I had any idea what he was talking about.

The day of the dinner, we went in early afternoon to the library and got from *Reader's Guide* a listing of all the magazine articles we could find on home rule. "Which side should we take?'' Bill asked me.

"I don't know,'' I said; "maybe they're going to assign us; let's study both sides.'' For hours, we studied, familiarized ourselves with the arguments, pro and con, and prepared for the dinner debate. The most common argument in the magazines in favor of home rule was, "No taxation without representation''; the arguments against seemed to be tradition, the fact that D.C. was the seat of national government and should thus be controlled by neither party, and the remote possibility that, if we had local elections, Washington could conceivably elect a Negro mayor. How would that look to foreign leaders, coming to visit the capital of the United States? the magazines asked rhetorically.

Prepared to teach it round or teach it flat, as they say in Texas, we arrived at the posh residence on Foxhall Road, were offered drinks, and discovered, after dinner, we were not in a debate at all. The issue had been settled. Everybody there was in favor! The discussion was about what ideas each of us "college leaders" had to advance the cause of home rule in Washington, D.C. The hostess was burbling with enthusiasm about having us all dress up in Founding Father costumes, wigs and all, picketing Dwight Eisenhower's White House with placards reading, "No Taxation without Representation!" I had to keep from looking at Buchs, to prevent my breaking out laughing. Bill and I decided the evening was shot; we faked enthusiasm for home rule for two hours and were among the first to leave. I sometimes wonder how happy they are, out there on Foxhall Road, as we enter the second decade of the Periclean Age of Marion Barry.

For years politicians and press kept up a steady drumbeat for home rule for the "people" of D.C. But the beneficiaries of the total politicization of what was once a peaceful, tranquil town appear not to be the "people" at all, but the bickering politicians, the monstrous bureaucracy they created, and the press who now have plenty to write about. When Paul Johnson wrote in *Modern Times* that the politician may be the curse of the age, he had more than a small point. Having spent a professional life in politics, government, and the press, I sometimes wonder if all of us do not create and exacerbate more problems than we resolve, and if Pogo was not right when he said, "We have met the enemy and he is us."

Looking at what Washington is in 1988, and remembering what Washington was in 1958, I am reminded of the Africans' gibe about the European colonizers: "When the missionaries came to us from Europe, they had the Bible and we had the land; and, now *we* have the Bible, and *they* have the land."

In retrospect, Georgetown, in the years I attended (1956–1961), was entering a transition — from a traditionalist Catholic college, which saw its duty as preparing Catholic students for a Christian life in the secular world, to today's elite school, which considers itself a rival of Princeton and Yale, which burns incense at the altar of "academic freedom," which would never dare impose upon its students the regimen it confidently imposed upon us. We were taught that the Church "had" the truth; and that we were there to learn it. Today, one hears the faculty and students at Georgetown are all engaged in a mutual "search" for truth — which suggests they had something in the 1950s they subsequently lost.

To be educators of the Catholic elite was Georgetown's ambition; and we dayhops had "middle class" stamped all over us. Not long after I arrived, the tradition of half-scholarships to Gonzaga students with a B average was discontinued. Georgetown, it was explained, could no longer "afford" such generosity. Perhaps the sentiment was unwarranted, but I came to feel as though the Jesuits at Georgetown looked upon the boarders as the students they wanted to teach, and upon the dayhops as the students they had to teach. We reminded them of where they came from, not where they wanted to go.

At Gonzaga, most of the younger Jesuits were tough, masculine, serious, and even athletic men, some of whom played football and basketball and boxed with the students. The younger Jesuits at Georgetown, though undeniably bright, looked as though they had spent their lives conjugating verbs. They were more boyish, bookish, cerebral than the teachers at Gonzaga (perhaps they had to be, to teach at the college level).

School spirit at Georgetown was nothing like Gonzaga. Football had been abandoned half a decade earlier, and the alumni had been soured, as Georgetown in the prewar years had a national reputation, rivaling that of Boston College in the Charlie O'Rourke era. But, while the sense of family pervasive at Gonzaga was not there (at least for me), the quality of education at Georgetown was undeniably excellent.

Twenty-four course hours of philosophy were required of all college students; and religion was mandatory all four years. From what happened to the Catholic Church and the Society of Jesus in the 1960s, the virus of dissent and rebellion was already present in the bloodstream of the younger Jesuits; but I never detected it. We were out of Georgetown before the epidemic hit.

The freshman curriculum — religion, Latin, math, English, French, history — was a continuation of the "liberal arts" to which we had been introduced at Gonzaga. But gone was the intense competition. Grading was done by letters; the dean's list was simply posted at semester's end; with few exceptions, the teachers seemed more aloof, distant, professional.

What was different from Gonzaga was ROTC. In the '50s, military service was obligatory. Every young man had an eight-year obligation — six months active duty, followed by seven and a half years of active reserve, or two years of active duty, followed by two more in the active reserve and four years in the inactive. A number of friends from Chevy Chase opted to do their six months in the Marines; they went to Parris Island the summer of graduation from high school, and were out in time for the second semester of freshman year. Others entered six-month programs in the Coast Guard or National Guard. My two brothers preceded me in army ROTC at Georgetown.

What is remarkable about those years is how little protest there was about mandatory military service. While there was no martial enthusiasm among friends or classmates, there were no demonstrations either, on campus or off. No one doubted we had a duty to serve our country. When JFK declared in his Inaugural, "Ask not what your country can do for you . . . ask what you can do for your country," he was speaking out of a tradition in which we, too, had been raised.

That America confronted in the Soviet Union the enemy of everything we believed in was not even debated. Pearl Harbor, Corregidor, Kasserine Pass, the Pusan Perimeter had taught Americans the price of unpreparedness; and Korea was fresh in the minds of many students. One of the senior ROTC cadets, a mature ex-soldier in his mid-twenties, had been wounded there, and several of the regular army sergeants and officers who instructed us were decorated combat veterans. During the fall of 1956, while we were drilling haphazardly on the field beside McDonough gym, the slaughter of boys our own age in Budapest, and the British-French-Israeli invasion of Suez — with Khrushchev rattling his rockets at London — brought home the realization that, perhaps, another war was not out of the question.

At Georgetown, Hank and I took up intramural boxing, under the tutelage of Marty Gallagher, a heavyweight of Gene Tunney's generation, who had fought the famous and colorful contender "Two-Ton Tony" Galento. A friendly Irishman, around fifty at the time, with a red face, blue eyes, and white hair, Marty got on well with all the dayhops; and he ran our cafeteria during the day. Some afternoons, I would watch him work out. Sweating, snorting, and pounding that heavy bag, Marty seemed transported back in time to the glory days when he had Two-Ton Tony on the ropes.

Boxing is today considered a barbaric anachronism; but both Marty Gallagher and Eddie LaFond taught the sport and ran their gyms in a way even the pacifist-columnist of the *Washington Post,* Colman McCarthy, might approve. They monitored the sparring closely — to make certain no one was outmatched, humiliated, or badly beaten. When a fighter started losing it, they were in the ring, shutting him down for the afternoon.

Once over at Catholic University, Eddie LaFond invited me to spar with one of his Golden Glovers, a competent fighter but a plodder. When I got into the ring, I went after him, and was doing well. I was the aggressor, took the first round handily, even tried to knock him down, though I had tired at the end; the plodder just kept backing away, jabbing, taking punches, and slipping punches. By the second round, I was arm-weary, and the plodder went methodically to work, moving onto the offensive. By the third round, I was exhausted, and he dropped me onto the canvas. I was less hurt than humiliated, and totally disgusted with myself.

"That's a good lesson for you, Pat," Eddie LaFond said as he took me out of the ring and put in another sparring partner for the plodder, who was just warming up, "learn how to pace yourself." A good lesson for political battles as well. In late 1967 and early 1968, I recall how the national press kept coming into our campaign headquarters in New York telling us how George Romney was barnstorming New Hampshire, taking the state away from us. "Nixon had better get into this thing quick," Nick Thimmesch, the columnist, told me, "or you guys are gonna lose it."

Concerned, I conveyed the message to Nixon. Others were bringing Nixon the same counsel. Nope, Nixon said, let's wait; we've got a good game plan; we've thought it out; let's stay with it. The Old Pro delayed and delayed his entry into New Hampshire, until within hours of the filing deadline on February 1. When we arrived in Manchester, suddenly the state was full of excitement for Richard Nixon; and the press was bored stiff with George Romney, an indefatigable campaigner, who was almost dead of exhaustion. Fresh and energized, Nixon blitzed Romney in three weeks;

and we drove him out of the race. Timing and pacing, in politics, too, can be everything.

There are few better ways for youngsters — especially the tough, friendless, fatherless kids of the inner city — to gain a measure of genuine self-esteem, and there is no better channel for the natural aggressiveness of youth than "putting on the gloves." On a football field or a basketball court you can dog it, and your 80-percent performance may not be noticed. Natural ability can compensate. Climb, out of shape or unprepared, into a boxing ring with your equal for three rounds, however, and you pay a visible price. Human nature is a given, enduring and unchangeable; the better part of wisdom is to accept it, and make safer this unavoidable channel for masculine self-expression.

It was while sparring with Hank in the spring of '58, in a ring badly in need of repair, that I twisted my right leg and fell, tearing the cartilage in my knee, putting me on crutches for the first time since seventh grade. The twisted knee eliminated me from the spring fights; the boxing trophy for which I had been working all spring was gone. Brother Henry, however, brought one home. In the summer of '58, the torn cartilage was removed at Georgetown Hospital.

Other than intramural sports, the one "activity" we pursued was the Washington Club, the dayhops' social club and the largest organization on campus.

Because the Washington Club was authorized to hold parties, on and off campus, to which the most stunning girls in the area were invited, from legal secretaries to Maryland cheerleaders, it was worth controlling. In the spring of 1958, with the election of George Reese, our crowd took control; Hank was installed as treasurer. Nor were we disappointed in the Reese administration. The parties were wilder than ever. As the spring of 1959 approached, we decided to maintain control. I announced my candidacy for president, my running mates being Chick Leasure from Prep and Mike Cavanaugh from Gonzaga, a popular figure in the Foreign Service School. We had all the bases covered. But the Jesuit administration did not wish the election to go uncontested. A fellow graduate of Gonzaga, a pre-med student, announced his candidacy; and it was clear to all on campus who was the administration candidate. The Jesuits were thoroughly disenthralled with the dayhops, with their drinking and the reputation we were helping Georgetown develop as one of the great "party schools" on the East Coast. That was not the direction in which they wished to steer the university. And one of them went out of his way to let me know. When I was driving several elated members of my victorious intramural basketball team through campus (we had won our league championship that night), a priest waved me down. When I opened the car window, he started raging about how fast I had been going, and then blurted out, "Don't you understand? We don't want your kind around here."

"Yes, Father," I said, respectfully; but I had gotten the message; and we reciprocated.

In my junior year, when the annual homecoming queen was chosen — the competition was usually among five girls, one from each of the five Catholic women's colleges in the Washington area — we entered a sixth candidate, a freshman from Marjorie Webster. We wanted to put the administration into a box, and we did. Fortunately, our candidate looked like Grace Kelly in *Rear Window*. As there was a campus-wide controversy over whether a non-Catholic girl, from a non-Catholic school, should even be permitted in the pageant, a vote for her became not only a ballot for a genuinely lovely girl, but a gesture of defiance as well. She won in a landslide. Among many of the Jesuits, to whom "The Web" was a constant occasion of sin Georgetown students ought to avoid, there was deep consternation. While the Catholic women's colleges had midnight curfews, and an occasional "one o'clock," the girls from Marjorie Webster had seventeen "overnights" each semester, which meant they could be brought home at any hour to the Meridian Hill Hotel where they stayed. If Georgetown was considered a coming party school, The Web was notorious. Many of the girls in that two-year college, some of them both wealthy and gorgeous, seemed less interested in academics than having a good time, finding a boyfriend, and getting married. Whenever we decided to throw a party in Chevy Chase on a Friday night, that evening at seven, we could drive over to The Web, march into the lobby, and ask if anybody was game. Half a dozen of the girls would be upstairs, changed, and back down in ten minutes.

There was another reason the administration was unenthusiastic about my candidacy; it dated back to the homecoming dance in McDonough Gymnasium the fall of '58.

My parents were visiting my brother Cricket at Saint Francis of Loretto in Pennsylvania for parents weekend — and they had left me the black-and-white, '56 Oldsmobile, while they had taken our new yellow-and-black "cream puff" Olds to Loretto. This was the weekend Hank was breaking up with the blonde from Chicago he had met in Fort Lauderdale. The relationship was in ruins, as Hank sat silent and morose, brooding throughout the festivities. A junior classmate of mine, a scholarly type, asked me if I thought Hank would mind if he asked Colette to dance, as the two did not seem to be getting on.

I couldn't believe that brilliant student could not size up a potentially explosive situation any better than that. "It's your funeral," I said, "go ahead." The student observed Hank closely for a minute, thought better of the idea, and walked away. A wise decision.

At evening's end, as we headed for the Olds — we were going to throw a follow-up party at the big empty house on Utah Avenue — Hank asked me for the keys. Nope, I said; the car's mine this weekend; I drive. "Give me the keys," he insisted, arguing that I could get a ride home with the Kadows. I handed him the keys.

Henry started the car, and roared off up to the top of the hill, above the parking lot, where I saw the Oldsmobile turning around. He's changed his mind, I thought. Too late, I saw what he was up to. My heart was in my throat as I watched that black-and-white Olds 88 take its long valedictory run, streaking down the hill, accelerating as it passed me, racing across that long parking lot. Head-on, it hit the eighteen-inch curb at the far end. The crash was tremendous. The Olds leaped into the air and pirouetted ninety degrees before its plunge into the earth. By the time I arrived at the scene, a crowd had gathered. Hank was lying on the ground beside the open door on the driver's side. All I could think, once I saw he wasn't hurt, was "I gotta get him outta here."

I started yanking away people hovering over him. The last guy I grabbed was Joseph A. Sellinger, S.J. In the darkness, I had not recognized the dean of students at Georgetown College. Apologizing profusely, I grabbed Hank from behind in a bear hug, and marched him to the Mo-Par, which had moved up alongside as an assist vehicle. Shoving Hank into the back seat, I told the Kadows to get him out of there; I would meet them at the house. I put Beth and Colette in another friend's car, but then noted that Father

Sellinger had trailed me to the Mo-Par. He pulled open the front door to see the two Kadows — and three cases of liberated beer. "Hello, Father, how are you this evening?" they said, smiling.

Then, they drove off with the beer — and Hank in the back seat. Father Sellinger and I stood silently side by side as the Mo-Par eased out of the university parking lot. "See me in my office, Monday," the dean said, and strode off.

The car had been totaled; and on Sunday afternoon, I got a tow truck to remove the hulk from campus. When my parents came home that night, and I related some of what had happened, they were shaken; not only had a wonderful weekend been ruined and the car totaled, this was no longer collegiate fun and games. Monday, in Dean Sellinger's office, he told me I was on unofficial probation, and skating on thin ice at the university. As Hank was in the Foreign Service School, which was not under Father Joe's jurisdiction, he never even got a reprimand.

And, thus, my candidacy for the presidency of the Washington Club was not warmly received in the Healy Building.

My opponent was shameless. He campaigned openly on a Nixonian "Bring us together" platform, saying he would mend the frayed ties between dayhops and faculty. The Washington Club would henceforth be having regular communion breakfasts, and the range of activities would be broadened beyond the "parties" that had given the club so narrow a focus and negative an image.

We didn't back away an inch from our platform; and we ran a single-issue campaign: The Washington Club gives the best parties on campus; under the Buchanan-Leasure-Cavanaugh administration, it will continue to give the best parties on campus. To clarify the issues, one night at home I wrote out in longhand an 800-word satirical attack on my old Gonzaga classmate, had 500 copies printed, and distributed it in the day-hops' cafeteria.

After reading it, only Hank and Paul, the future Trappist, would co-sign.

In what I thought was clever and witty language, the pamphlet savaged my opponent as a consummate faculty fanny-kisser, a poodle of Father Kaifer, Georgetown's apostle to the dayhops, a book-burrowing stiff, whose election would convert the best club on campus into a boring annex of the administration, and whose hidden agenda in running was to have the title "President of the Washington Club" appended to his résumé, so he could get into medical school. The piece ended by drawing a parallel between my old Gonzaga classmate, whose name was Richard, and stuffy Malvolio of Shakespeare's *Twelfth Night.* "Dost thou think, Dicky Boy, that, because thou art virtuous, there shall be no more cakes and ale?"

The pamphlet was a sensation. (Regrettably, I never kept a copy of my first political attack.) The enthusiasm with which it was received convinced me that, in dealing with the smug and the self-righteous, the best defense is not to bother defending anything, just go after them the way Jack Dempsey did, while they are still sitting on their stool taking the applause.

Following its release, our campaign got a tremendous break. One of Richard's running mates, it was unearthed, had applied to move onto campus for his senior year, to be closer to faculty and friends. Some dayhop! We tried to have him thrown off Richard's ticket. While the election was close, we learned belatedly that our strongest supporters, the freshmen and sophomores who loved the parties, had never bothered to pay any dues; they were ineligible to vote. We were down the tubes.

At that point, Hank drew up plans for Operation Circular Flow, a voter registration program of which the Honorable Richard J. Daley would have approved. No one, except the treasurer, knew how much money was in the Washington Club coffers, and no one cared. The money was the surplus from successful parties, and we always used it to hire an even better band or lower the price of admission to the next party. Even then, we were supply-siders. But Hank had more than $400 in cash.

Giving me a wad of five-dollar bills from the treasury in the morning, he would set himself up in the cafeteria at noon — to accept "new memberships." (New members, President Reese decreed, would be eligible to vote, and voter registration was permitted right up to election day.) Cash in hand, I would recruit reliable freshmen and sophomores, "lend" them the five dollars, and tell them there would be no need to repay, if they joined the club. At lunchtime, they would sign up with President Reese, who would turn the five-dollar dues over to his treasurer, who turned the money over to me for further recruitment.

When the first ballot count was complete, Richard had apparently won by only four votes. A recount was demanded; and, *mirabile dictu,* that ended in a dead heat. Father Kaifer wanted to know who had been present when the ballots were recounted. The answer came back: the president of the club — and the treasurer, Henry M. Buchanan.

After the ballots were impounded by the administration, it was discovered that four of them had been suspiciously folded exactly the same way, as though folded together at the same time. On each, only the box for president had been checked; and all were Buchanan ballots. The other side alleged voting fraud, and demanded to be installed — but we demanded a new election. We lost that one, too. Mistakenly, we scheduled the second election the day when Georgetown's air force and army ROTC cadet corps marched in parade. Along with me and Hank, many of my best friends were in ROTC; and numerous Buchanan voters disappeared the minute the parade ended. In a tough campaign, we had gone down to defeat; but that's democracy.

Perhaps as a consequence of that dismal night in high school, the course I found most painful was public speaking. While I had no difficulty answering spontaneously in class, to be required to deliver a "speech" in front of one's friends, for three or four minutes, was Purgatory. Georgetown was wise to force us through a semester of it.

Speech class was not made easier by the way it was conducted. The student would go to the front of the room to deliver his speech; meanwhile, the teacher, Mr. Murphy, would sit in the front row — and take notes on the performance. Behind Murphy, the other thirty students had been issued signs to hold up silently, to alert their classmate as to what he was doing wrong. The signs read, "Slow Down," or "Stop Moving Around," or "Use More Gestures."

Unfortunately, while monitoring the speaker, Murphy did not monitor the class. By the time I had gotten to the front of the room and into my speech, McCloskey and Leasure and Walter Smith would be hoisting a new panoply of signs. "Bomb Shelter This Way," and "No U Turn" were the most printable, with others containing commentaries on Miss Beth, the dean, Murphy, and so on — to force the speaker to lose concentration or stare at the ceiling to maintain composure while speaking. Meanwhile, Murphy would mark me down for losing "eye contact" with the audience.

By the end of the year, I was doing better; but Murphy, who had given me a C on an early speech, refused to use my later A grades — as promised. I went up to Murphy's desk to reason with him.

"Surely, sir, this was the purpose," I told him, that, "I work and improve and be graded on where I ended the semester as a speaker, not where I began."

"Correct, Buchanan, and you have improved, but every time I see you clowning," Murphy said, "that first C gets bigger and bigger and bigger."

As my appeal for an A was being rejected, Charlie Leasure advanced ingratiatingly toward the desk — to appeal his grade on identical grounds. "Forget it, Charlie," I said, "this bastard won't give you anything. You haven't got a prayer."

Unfortunately, Murphy had heard the ancestral reference, and he also observed that Charlie, while stunned by the loudness of my comment, had smiled in seeming concurrence. Charlie should have held off his appeal; instead, he plunged ahead, then and there, lost, and forever blamed me for poisoning the well.

The winner of Georgetown Prep's scholar-athlete award in 1956 (Charlie was quarterback, linebacker on defense, and centered for punts — Prep not then being terribly deep in talent), "Chick" Leasure, who had gone through Blessed Sacrament with me, became a fast friend. On the sophomore football team, which won only one game, Charlie was quarterback, and I was his prime receiver.

A genial, easygoing guy who rarely lost his temper and almost never got in fights, Charlie came in one day during sophomore year to announce he had married his sweetheart, Harriet. He and his bride took an apartment out near Chevy Chase Lake. One night, Miss Beth and I had visited his new pad for dinner, and spent a long and delightful evening talking and arguing, ending on the relative merits (and demerits) of Generals MacArthur and Marshall. We left around two-thirty in the morning. Outside, in the parking lot of the tiny apartment complex, I noted Charlie's neighbor was walking his dog. Knowing Harriet's nervousness at how the newlyweds were being received in their first apartment, early the next week, I penned a letter:

Dear Mr. Leasure:

I had hoped, that, when you moved in, we could become friends. But I don't know now how that will be possible. Late

Friday night (rather Saturday morning), as I was walking my dog — following a loud argument in your apartment that kept me awake — a red-faced, belligerent character emerged from your apartment with his girlfriend, and started shouting at me in the parking lot, about General MacArthur. When I tried to answer him, he verbally abused me, and physically abused my dog. I plan to protest to the building owner, your continued residence here.

    Sincerely,

And I signed the name I had gotten off the apartment door.

When Chick got home, Harriet was near hysteria. But Charlie spotted the phony. When he went to work the following day (this was summer), he noticed some streetcorner solicitors for the American Nazi Party of George Lincoln Rockwell. Acquiring some Swastika-emblazoned stationery, Charlie wrote a letter, thanking me for having enlisted and looking forward to working with me in advancing the Führer's historic objectives. He addressed the letter to me, but sent it to my father's accounting firm. Where I never saw it; apparently, it was forwarded to the FBI.

The last year of the decade, 1959, was not a good one.

I began the New Year with mononucleosis, which cost me three weeks of class; in the spring, I had lost the election; and, in late May, I came down with a debilitating disease, which one doctor diagnosed as Reiter's syndrome, the most crippling and enduring symptom of which was a severe and recurring rheumatoid arthritis, which, with some victims, lasted for decades. Hospitalized for three weeks, I was bedridden much of the summer of '59, unable to walk without crutches, and missed summer camp for the ROTC cadets entering their senior year.

From that agonizing experience, repeated half a dozen times until I was forty, I came to have great empathy for those old folks one sees bent and crippled; I knew precisely the pain they were going through. Even when young, I could sit down beside some old lady with arthritis and compare notes on the best treatments — and their side effects — cortisone tablets, cortisone shots, indocin, buthazoladine, aspirin. Except for the gold treatments, I had tried them all. If I did not tell the old lady I had arthritis myself, she would think I was a doctor. We arthritics come to know our illness as well as those who only treat it.

As fall approached, the event that captured the whole city's attention was the arrival, for the first time in history, of the Secretary of the Communist Party of the Soviet Union, N. S. Khrushchev. Less than three years previous, the Butcher of Budapest had run his tanks over the Freedom Fighters; now he was being feted in the American capital. Some of us wondered why.

With thousands of others, I skipped work in the early afternoon — I was clerking at the Weaver & Glassie law firm on 19th Street that September — went over to Lafayette Park opposite the White House, and waited. I was ready to give K the Bronx cheer. Before Khrushchev rode up Pennsylvania Avenue, however, a lone convertible passed by. The rider held up a sign that read: "Don't clap, don't wave; stand silent in memory of the Hungarians."

That's what we did. When Khrushchev's open car rolled by, just thirty feet away, with him waving and grinning, we just stared back at him; there was only the tiniest smattering of applause. After Ike escorted Khrushchev into Blair House, and started back alone for the White House, however, we gave a thunderous cheer for the old soldier.

Khrushchev could not have missed our manifestation of cool contempt. Later on, he would say that, if the cold shoulder from the American people continued, he might pack up early and go home. Which was fine with us.

As for the Old General, about to enter the final year in his half century of service to his country, we should probably have cheered him louder and longer. From the time I was fourteen until after I turned twenty-two, Ike was my President; and those years — of peace and prosperity, of unity and harmony, when America was at the pinnacle of her power and prestige — were the best years of our lives.

It was in late October of 1959, two weeks before my twenty-first birthday, that my academic career came to a temporary close.

After a Saturday-night date with a tall blonde from Virginia, I was cruising across Georgetown toward Key Bridge, to take her home. It was around midnight, as I drove across O Street, east of Wisconsin, and approached the rear of a patrol wagon tooling along at about twenty miles per hour. I honked the horn, and the wagon simply slowed down. Honking the horn again, I decided to pass. When I crossed Wisconsin, the patrol wagon now behind me signaled me over, and the cop made the customary request for license and registration. To which I complied, without cordiality. Then, he announced he was charging me with speeding.

"Well, [expletive], you'll have a tough time making that one stick," I said, "since my girlfriend here and I watched the speedometer as we passed; and it never went above twenty-seven — and we'll testify to same."

"Well," said the cop, "in that case, suppose we make the charge passing at an intersection." As he wrote out the ticket, I told him, in X-rated language, what I thought of him.

"Out!" he yelled. "Get out of the car!"

Which I did. As I was being walked to the patrol wagon, I told the cop and his partner in graphic terms what I thought of them. While I was not so dumb as to punch a cop and get myself shot, I was not so smart as simply to cooperate; when they ordered me to get into the back of the paddy wagon, I can fairly be said to have been "resisting arrest."

After they finally forced me into the wagon, they decided to work me over. But, as one of them climbed up inside the wagon with me, while I was lying on my back, I put a size ten-and-a-half cordovan where I thought it might do some good — and vaulted him back into the street. His buddy then climbed into the truck and started using his club on my head and face. After some of this, he climbed out and, together they went to work with their sticks on my legs, which were dangling outside the truck. Finally forcing the legs inside, they slammed the truck door. Still, I could hear them. They were breathing heavily, and one of them had lost his hat during the workout and decided to come back in and fetch it. As I heard the door being opened, I sprang out into the street, and we went through the same exercise again.

A Georgetown citizen had decided to give the police a hand, and I indicated what I thought of him and the concept of citizen's arrest. After more pulling and hauling, I was back in the truck. Whereupon, enraged, I hammered with my fist on the thick glass pane separating the back of the truck from the front seat where the two cops were now observing the caged beast they had just apprehended. They radioed ahead for help.

We arrived at Number Seven, to a welcoming party of eight

officers, slapping their clubs in their palms and forming a semicircle at the back of the wagon. They were waiting, praying, for the first move, which I didn't give them. I walked quietly into the station, straightening my tie.

While I was being booked, one of them sidled up alongside. A young tough-looking customer, he declared, in the hearing of everybody in the station, that, had I resisted him, I would now be in Georgetown Hospital where his two fellow officers had been taken. So, standing about two feet away, I listened politely, then suddenly spun, buckled my knees, and threw a left hook at his solar plexis. Only I stopped the punch two inches short of his uniform, stood up straight, and winked at him. He recoiled three feet, without having been touched, and knew instantly — as did the half-dozen cops observing — that had it been a genuine blow to his midsection, he would not have been taking home any trophies that night. Embarrassed and humiliated, he started yelling and threatening me with his billy club — until the cops had to restrain *him*.

It was among the great, dumb, deeds of my life.

Clearly, the cops had been looking for trouble; later, I heard from a friend that one of them had reportedly left the force after allegations of police brutality. But, within a fortnight of my twenty-first birthday, I was not about to take "grief," as we called it, from anyone. We preferred to get beat up. So, instead of letting them get away with the phony ticket, I had to mouth off. The consequences were many and immediate.

By midweek — the story was in the press and on the popular "new WEAM" radio station all day Monday — Father Sellinger told me I was out of Georgetown. (My father, by personal pleading, had the expulsion reduced to a year's "withdrawal," with loss of my scholarship.) The girl who was with me, Bobbie — whom I hoped would be a friendly witness — said, when I called her the next morning, "You oughtta have your mouth washed out with soap!" (The cops had talked with her as they drove her home.) Miss Beth called in sympathy; said she was sorry. But clearly this was the final performance for her. I never saw her again. Charged with assaulting two police officers, a felony, I was released on $2,000 bond. (When I would bring a nice date to the Piccolo, in the months following, the Kadows would tell the young lady, early in the evening, "Miss, you look like a lovely girl; did you know your date was out on a two-thousand-dollar bond?") My left hand was broken and in a cast, whether from the sticks when I was covering my face, or from my hitting the glass pane, I don't know.

Not only was I out of college, I was out of army ROTC and was called up in December of '59 for my physical. At Walter Reed Army Hospital, they found that the success of Dr. Rush's knee surgery in the summer of 1958 had been nullified by the damage done by the rheumatoid arthritis in the summer of '59. I was now 4F, ineligible for military service. Even when I returned to Georgetown, I would not be permitted back in ROTC. The three and a half years I had invested toward a commission as a second lieutenant were now down the tubes.

What to do? My father handed me *General Principles of Accounting*, and told me to study it and learn it. Each day, I completed a chapter, until I mastered the course in several weeks, and Pop put me to work in his firm for the year. By December of 1959, I was working full-time as a bookkeeper-auditor for Councilor, Buchanan, Mitchell & Hayes, a rewarding year's experience that took me to West Virginia, Pennsylvania, and Boston for two summers, where we annually audited the books of the Howe's Leather Company near South Station.

As for the felony charge, I had made one smart move that night at the Seventh Precinct. When a detective asked me who I wanted to call, I responded, "Cliff Alder."

The name brought him up short. Clifford Alder, a family friend, was partner to the "Third Street Cicero," Charlie Ford, one of the most famous criminal lawyers in the city. Alder had regularly defended cops charged with brutality and corruption, and had defended the police captain caught up in the D.C. scandal in the '50s; he was a respected, capable trial attorney to whom the D.C. police were heavily in debt. The detective on whom I dropped the name picked up on it instantly.

"You know Cliff Alder?" he said.

"An old family friend," I assured him.

In early 1960, I walked into D.C. criminal court and pleaded guilty to simple assault, a misdemeanor. The fine was $25, less than Montgomery County charged for a routine disorderly conduct. Charlie Leasure and Walter Smith, who expected to see me packed off to Occoquan for six months with a Virginia road gang, were incredulous; they were heard complaining in the halls of the court house about the injustice of the system.

Clearly, I did get a break; having Cliff Alder as advocate was the reason for it. But, even though some of the younger cops in the Seventh Precinct were said to have been ticked off, the police hierarchy knew their boys were hardly blameless in the episode; and they would not appear all that heroic in court either. For what purpose a trial, when I had already taken three hits, first, being expelled, second, losing a scholarship, and, third, getting a record.

During the 1970 campaign, when I was doing the law-and-order speeches for Spiro T. Agnew, I got a call at the White House from one of Jack Anderson's young assistants; he wanted me to comment on a column they were writing about an episode in Georgetown eleven years previous. What did I have to say for myself? All I could tell Brit Hume was, "Brit, I was ahead on points — until they brought out the sticks."

Some twenty years after that night, Richard Whalen, a friend from the Nixon campaign of 1968, who had built a magnificent town house in Georgetown, invited me over for dinner. He and his wife, Joan, walked Shelley and me through their new home, explaining how the posh town houses on Volta Place had all been constructed out of Washington's old Seventh Precinct; then, he took this syndicated columnist down into his basement to show me where the old cell block had been. I had spent time in Whalen's basement before.

It was in Boston in the summer of 1960 that I recall first picking up a *National Review* from a newsstand. My reaction was not unlike that of John Keats, On First Looking into Chapman's Homer. There was nothing within the pages of Bill Buckley's blue-bordered magazine with which I disagreed. Here was stated, with style and grace, but especially with fire and wit, the political philosophy in which I, too, believed. Central to it, then and now, was a militant but intelligent anti-Communism — the recognition that in Lenin's party, which held the old Russian empire and so much more in its iron grip, the United States faced an implacable and mortal enemy who could not be appeased.

James Burnham, Frank Meyer, Russell Kirk, Whittaker Chambers, John Chamberlain, and Bill Buckley not only believed as I had come to believe, they wrote with passion, insight, and authority. Not content to contradict what passed for the conventional wisdom, they lampooned and ridiculed it. They did not politely disagree with the Liberal Establishment; they lacerated it.

They had no doubt as to what Fidel Castro was, and what he was about. (At Georgetown, many of our Latin students, sons and daughters of the aristocracy, were enthusiastically pro-Castro.) Buckley & Co. went after the *New York Times*'s Herbert Matthews relentlessly, for having sold Castro to Americans as the "Robin Hood of the Sierra Maestre." *National Review* suggested that perhaps Castro's photograph might be used in the new *Times* classified advertising campaign, with a picture of the smiling, bearded Communist dictator alongside the ad campaign's slogan, "I Got My Job Through the New York Times."

When *National Review* wrote that, in the war against the West declared by Communism, our goal should not be containment, but victory, what they said corresponded with everything I knew from history, experience, and instinct. No one wins a fight by simply defending himself until his adversary tires; you have to deliver blows of your own.

"In war there is no substitute for victory," MacArthur had said in his Farewell Address; to us that was not militaristic or provocative, it was a distillation of common sense. Instinctively, I felt Eisenhower and Dulles had blundered in 1956, when they sided with Nasser and the U.N. against the British, French, and Israelis at Suez, and failed to lift a finger to help the Hungarians.

Among the reasons I preferred Nixon to Kennedy in 1960, when most Catholics were behind Kennedy, was that Nixon seemed to me to have a greater understanding of the world and the Communist enemy. He had nailed Alger Hiss cold, when still in his early thirties; he had been the proponent of a tough line at the time of Dien Bien Phu; he had been the particular target of Communist mobs in Caracas, and had stood up well; he had conducted himself competently against the bullying Khrushchev in that Moscow kitchen debate. Nixon, to me, was young and smart and tough, and that was what America needed in dealing with a Soviet Union that now had Sputnik and was building ballistic missiles; and the people in politics and press who were savaging Nixon worst were the ones I liked least.

By 1960, I had pretty much concluded that my ideas and convictions were shoving me toward the Republican party — even though it was much the less interesting of the two. While 80 percent of American Catholics would vote for JFK, I supported Nixon openly and enthusiastically, first against Rockefeller, then against Kennedy. Most of my Catholic friends were all out for JFK. My beliefs and convictions were, by then, more important to me than whether or not Jack Kennedy and I belonged to the same Church, or whether he was going to be our first Catholic President. I was delighted he got the nomination over the liberal Humphrey and LBJ, but when it came to the presidency, his charisma and dash and Catholicism could not compensate for my distrust of the Democrats, as a party, on foreign policy. And foreign policy was not only the political subject that held the greatest interest for me, it was, and remains to this day, the most important issue in any presidential election. Economics may be about who gets what, about prosperity and recession, about good times and bad; but foreign policy, in the second half of the twentieth century, is about life and death, for entire peoples, and whole nations. It is about what makes history.

Whatever they had done for America in the 1930s, the Democrats under Truman had mishandled America's postwar power and position abysmally. So far as I was concerned, they had broken their pick — permanently. While the Marshall Plan was a great achievement, and Truman had stood up to Stalin in Turkey and Greece, his second term had produced one disaster after another. Nor have I changed that assessment, even though Harry Truman is as popular today as he was d⁻   ⸱d in 1952.

When Eisenhower took over, America had already lost — in seven short years — all of Eastern Europe and Mainland China, and hundreds of Americans were dying weekly in a bloody, thirty-one-month stalemate in Korea that Truman could neither win nor end. Eisenhower ended that war, he restored America's dignity and prestige, he understood power, and he knew how to deal with thugs. He had dealt, after all, with the Thousand Year Reich. Dulles, who kept the books of Lenin and Stalin on his bedtable, and Nixon, I felt, understood the enemy. Twice, however, the Democrats had nominated Adlai Stevenson, and, while Elizabeth Nugent, an author and a lovely lady who taught me Renaissance English, was heartbroken Adlai had not been nominated a third time, I privately thought Stevenson too wordy, too weak, and too foppish a figure to run the greatest country in the world.

While my father felt that both Nixon and Kennedy were "fine Americans" giving the country an excellent choice of leaders, I never leaned toward JFK. Sitting in a bar with Whitey Toland, who avidly supported JFK, I was privately disappointed during the first debate. I didn't care how Nixon looked; there was entirely too much of the "I agree with Senator Kennedy" deference. Though the Democratic nominee had been impressive, I still thought Nixon won on points, and that he won the other debates as well.

It is difficult to exaggerate the debt conservatives of my generation owe *National Review* and Bill Buckley. Before I read *NR,* there was virtually nothing I read that supported or reinforced what I was coming to believe. We young conservatives were truly wandering around in a political wilderness, wondering if there was anyone of intelligence and wit, any men of words, who thought and felt and believed as we did. Other than that one magazine, young conservatives had almost nowhere to turn for intellectual and political sustenance. For us, what *National Review* did was take the word *conservatism,* then a synonym for stuffy orthodoxy, Republican stand-pat-ism and economic self-interest, and convert it into the snapping pennant of a fighting faith.

Others might call themselves Robert Taft conservatives; I never did. The Ohio Senator may have been a principled legislator and great man, and I respected him, and my father admired him; but I could never identify with the late Robert A. Taft. What attracted me to Bill Buckley and *National Review* was that these people not only wrote brilliantly, they didn't give a damn who disagreed. I cherished their attitude; they were intellectual battlers looking for a fight. When the sainted (but naïve) Pope John XXIII issued his gauzy encyclical *Mater et Magister* (Mother and Teacher), Buckley headed his dissent, "Mater, Si; Magister No!" That was just the right touch of faithfulness and fire, irreverence and spirit. That was what I felt, too.

That year out of school, working for my father's accounting firm, gave me time to think, long and hard, about what to do with my life. I knew I was going back to Georgetown to finish up in 1961, but what then? I dreaded the idea of law school, which meant three more years as a student, then spending my life at work in which I had no interest. Medicine had never interested me. Several of my friends from the Class of '60 had signed on with major companies, like IBM and A.T.&T., for $120 and $130 a week — excellent starting salaries on which they could get married and start a family in 1960. But those giant companies were, to me, no different from the government, against which my father had warned us; once hooked by that salary, you were locked on a ladder for life.

Unlike my parents' generation, my generation, I felt, could choose its own destiny. We had no excuse for "selling out." Both my parents *had* to work, almost out of high school; family necessity dictated it. The generation after theirs got hit with the Depression and the war; they, too, had to play the hand that fate had dealt them. We had the luck of the draw. We could decide what we wanted to be, and, by the late '50s, almost every profession offered enough of an income to live comfortably, if not luxuriously. We were the fortunate generation, almost the first to have that opportunity; and I wasn't going to blow it.

I decided my first step would be to get a master's degree in journalism.

While I wasn't confident I could write well enough to make a living, the investment of a year's time would be worth it, to determine if I could learn. My ambition was either to write a syndicated column like George Sokolsky and Pegler had done, or become a writer like the best at *National Review*. If I found out after a year I didn't have it, well, at least I would have the credential, the master's degree; from there, I could go on and become a college teacher in English.

Penning that polemic against "Dicky Boy" (during the Washington Club campaign) had been more exhilarating than anyone knew; I was elated when friends howled at my wit, calling it the funniest thing they ever read. Not only might journalism provide a legitimate outlet for my combative proclivities, the life would surely be more exciting, if less financially rewarding, than the lives being laid out by classmates signing away their futures to A.T.&T. "It is required of a man that he should share the passion and action of his time, at peril of being judged not to have lived," Justice Holmes had said; I quoted him often, and approvingly, in those days.

There was only one place to go: The best journalism school in the United States, the famous Graduate School at Columbia University in New York City. I applied there, and also to Missouri and Northwestern; but anything other than Columbia would have been a crushing disappointment.

Looking back, being expelled was among the best things that ever happened to me. Not only did I learn accounting and have a terrific year working, that collision with Authority, that butting of heads with the System, where I had come off a sorry second best, sobered me. It ended adolescence. *Le bon temps* was not over; but, now I was no longer adrift and floating. Now, I, too, had a goal in life, a destination toward which to channel my talent and energy. Like my friends who always knew from second grade what they were "going to be," I, too, now knew what I "wanted to do." I set as my immediate objective straight A's the first semester of my second senior year at Georgetown, a perfect 4.0 QPI, and, on the strength of that transcript, to get myself accepted at Columbia.

Never again would I get arrested, and only once would I get into something that could remotely be called a fight. In that one year, I grew up half a decade; I learned how to take it, how to smile, and how to walk away. That next senior year at Georgetown, I not only stayed out of trouble, I stayed out of sight. Now, I was on thin ice. I went to school early each morning, took classes until noon, studied all afternoon in the library, and took accounting classes in the Business School every night. My friends were graduated and gone. Roger Haley, a buddy from Gonzaga, was pointing toward a Ph.D. in Russian area studies at the Foreign Service School — so I had a squash partner. About ten-thirty, I got home and went to bed.

One innovation that final year surprised me. For the first time since eighth grade, there were females sitting beside me in class. Georgetown had opened its English courses to students at the nursing school; the '60s were closing in.

Choosing an English major proved fortuitous; it was at least something to bring to journalism school. Over thirty-six course hours, we were taken from a summer of Chaucer in Middle English, through a full year of Shakespeare and a year of the British Romantics, from Wordsworth, through Byron, Shelley, and Keats, to Robert Browning. We studied the American writers from Hawthorne and Melville and Poe, to Whitman and Stephen Crane and Mark Twain, through the naturalists, Theodore Dreiser and Jack London, to T. S. Eliot and Ernest Hemingway. Almost every course, almost every writer, I enjoyed.

From these classes came a love of literature, an understanding of the symbols through which great writers communicate, and an awareness of the potential of language, which, as Voznesensky has written, is truly the music of thought.

Hawthorne and Melville and Poe introduced in story an idea of human nature, of Fallen Man — of evil being rooted not in institutions as Rousseau and others taught, but in the human heart itself — that was congenial with what I had come to believe, even though the idea was in conflict with the gauzy optimism then fashionable about the perfectibility of man. T. S. Eliot's "Prufrock" and "Gerontion" and "Hollow Men" and "The Waste Land," which talked of a desiccated, weary, emptied Western civilization, seemed to me more "relevant" to our century than anything "dreamt of" in the bubbly philosophy of Hubert Horatio Humphrey.

Years later, when I was conscripted as a speechwriter by Mr. Nixon (a wholly different style of writing from editorials or column-writing), I discovered that one gift those years of scanning lines and reading verse had left me with was an excellent ear — for rhythm, for cadence, for the way words can march to a melody in the mind. When in mid-1970, I wrote a speech for Vice President Agnew and decided to include a paragraph on the trendiness of the mainline Protestant churches, I deplored organized religion's readiness to "cast morality and theology aside as not 'relevant' and set as its goal on earth the recognition of Red China and the preservation of the Florida alligator." (Garry Wills, the columnist, did not agree with the point, but found the prose "witty"; it is also easy on the ear.)

The great orations that reach down inside and move men — William Jennings Bryan's Cross of Gold speech, MacArthur's Duty, Honor, Country valedictory at West Point, Martin Luther King's I Have a Dream — all have about them that musical quality, as though the words are actually marching in cadence. Which is why the rewriting of the Bible, handed down to us in the poetic English of Shakespeare's time, induces the same sense of rage as would the rewriting of Mark Antony's funeral oration, in *Julius Caesar*, by some literalist who wanted "young people to understand what it was Mark Antony was really trying to say."

My freshman (and senior year) teacher in American literature, Tom Walsh, had decided to come to Georgetown, he once told the class, because "at least at Georgetown, when you discuss Emerson's view of the oversoul, the students will know what a soul is."

More than any other teacher, Tom Walsh introduced us to a new world, of poetry and prose, that we could visit for future vacations, or even in a time of trouble; it was a splendid world, the language and symbols and signs of which he taught us to recognize, a separate world the unfortunate do not even know exists.

Just as I considered Fats Domino's rollicking "I'm Gonna Be a Wheel Someday" my theme song in the mid-1950s, so I identified with Prince Hal, in *Henry IV, Part I*, as soon as I read it. (Brother Hank reminded me no small amount of Hotspur.) The prince, too, had been a rascal and roustabout, the despair of his father, but he had turned out splendidly; and I read and reread his famous soliloquy:

> *I know you all, and will a while uphold*
> *The unyoked humor of your idleness:*
> *Yet herein will I imitate the sun. . . .*

Choosing English over history as a major was a calculated decision. While I knew I would probably spend the rest of my life reading history, if I missed out on the English classics, the opportunity would never come again.

Strong in many areas, however, the "liberal education" I received was deficient in others. I had managed to go through eight years without having taken a single course in government, politics, economics, biology, or chemistry. My views and values had been shaped by immersion in literature, languages, religion, history, and philosophy.

But the most memorable course at Georgetown was ethics.

The year-long emphasis of Father Stephen F. McNamee, a grand Jesuit of the old school, was on natural law as indispensable companion to religious faith and reliable guide to human behavior. A giant of a man, with iron-gray hair, who wore glasses, a black cape, and a three-cornered beretta, and moved slowly, Father McNamee was one of the few teachers at Georgetown with whom I felt a personal bond. "Boys, you need a frame of reference in which to live," he would tell us again and again. Father McNamee, too, lived the lessons he taught.

It was he who made us understand the natural code of morality that a beneficent God had left written on the human heart, even for those who disbelieved in the Christian faith. He introduced us to moral dilemmas, to the principle of double effect, to the reasoned choice of the lesser of two evils; he taught us to differentiate between what was illicit (shredding documents, for example) and what was truly immoral, inherently evil, and always impermissible (the deliberate taking of an innocent human life, as in an abortion). He taught us the morality of an act is determined not only by the deed itself, but by the motivation and circumstances. A man who steals money to provide food for his starving family may be guilty of theft in the legal sense, he taught us, but, in the higher moral realm, he is a just man, doing his moral duty, compared to the man who steals an equal amount of money to support his drinking habit.

As the civil-rights movement was breaking upon the country, Father McNamee taught us when civil disobedience was justified, when it was not, and what the criteria were for deciding when and how to use civil disobedience. I came out of his class understanding what I felt, i.e., that the black students who sat in at the segregated lunch counters may have been disobeying the laws of South Carolina, and may have to be arrested to uphold the idea of law, but they were not morally wrong.

About Prohibition, Father McNamee taught us that it did not conform with human nature, representing an illicit state intrusion on personal behavior; thus, it was not immoral for our parents to have violated Prohibition and taken a drink.

But what kind of society would it be, we asked, if everyone picked and chose which laws to obey? Fair question, he answered; and natural law is not an invitation to anarchy. All he was saying was that when public laws prohibit private acts that are not inherently immoral, a man may follow the dictates of conscience, so long as he is willing to pay the price society imposes for civil disobedience.

We even debated the morality of using lethal force to keep a neighbor out of the family fallout shelter. If the food supply is limited, he said, and family survival depends upon that food, then the neighbor who is forcing his way into that shelter becomes, morally speaking, an enemy, and can be dealt with as an enemy.

While it was always wrong to "lie," Father McNamee taught there were those not entitled to the truth (enemies in wartime, for example; or a criminal breaking into one's home); and there were such things as legitimate "mental reservations."

He taught the Augustinian conditions required for waging a just war. World War II was legitimate; we had been attacked. But, even though the war was just, the means used to prosecute it must also be moral. Hiroshima and Nagasaki and Dresden could not, he believed, be squared with the ethical proscription against the direct killing of noncombatants. As for nuclear weapons, their use should be subject to the same moral conditions. Against enemy soldiers and defense installations, yes, if that is their primary purpose, and collateral damage to civilians is not excessive; against civilian targets, no. If the deterrence strategy of the 1950s (or today) entailed using thermonuclear weapons against Russian cities, Father McNamee would have said that, while it may have been moral to threaten "massive retaliation," it would have been grossly immoral to carry it out. There is never any justification for the direct and deliberate killing of innocent men, women, and children.

"What about an enemy, as in Korea, who uses women and children as a shield behind which to attack?" we asked him. Yes, the old Jesuit said, a soldier can fire on that enemy — because his purpose, his motive, is not to kill those civilians; it is to kill those enemy soldiers, a legitimate act of self-defense. The civilians' deaths are an unintended consequence of a legitimate moral act.

To understand the code he taught us is to understand Ollie North. Ollie never claimed some amoral right to lie, or some cynical right to pick and choose which laws to obey. What he was saying to the congressional committee — and the country — was that he had been confronted with a moral dilemma, a choice of evils. If the nebulous Boland Amendment forbade him to fight America's enemies and help the friends he had sent into battle, whose survival depended upon Ollie North, then, faced with that moral dilemma, he must follow the commands of his heart. Whether or not he did the legal thing, Ollie North, in his heart I believe, did the right thing. And it is because Americans have the same code written upon their own hearts, that they responded as they did.

Our Declaration of Independence refers to "the laws of nature and nature's God," upon which all other laws are to be based. Blackstone, the great legal scholar, himself asserted that "The law of nature . . . dictated by God Himself . . . is binding . . . in all countries and at all times; no human law is of any validity, if contrary to this. . . ."

That is what Father McNamee taught us. There *is* a transcendent order, a higher law to which man-made law *must* correspond to be legitimate. Indeed, men do not need to study to know this; they need to study not to know this. Congress understood this, when it craftily moved to impeach Richard Nixon, not for the massive secret bombing of the Communist sanctuaries in Cambodia, but for the misdemeanor of covering up a third-rate theft, in which nothing was lost. Defending that secret bombing, to save American lives, Nixon, as Commander in Chief, could have appealed to the higher law, *Salus Populi Suprema Lex*; and history would have vindicated him, even if Congress had not.

Admiral Poindexter and Colonel North may be condemned by the pettifoggers, but in the judgment of history my friends will be vindicated — just as the Minutemen who illicitly stocked arms against the British were vindicated, just as the men and women who ran the Underground Railroad in violation of the Fugitive Slave Law were vindicated, just as Lincoln, who asserted dictatorial powers to save the Union, was vindicated, just as Billy Mitchell was vindicated. All were true to the higher law.

Father McNamee taught that while we could not, without Faith, know that Jesus Christ was the Son of God, even an atheist could reason to the existence of God, and could discover, through his or her own reasoning, the natural law, the *Tao*, of which C. S. Lewis wrote in *The Abolition of Man*, a small book that Father McNamee had one day pressed upon me.

He taught us to be Thomists, to appreciate and understand the great achievement of Saint Thomas Aquinas, the discovery that between right reason and true faith there is no conflict, that the former is complement to the latter in teaching us how to live. More than any other teacher I ever knew, that good priest left me with a comforting, consistent, and coherent code of how men, and leaders, ought to behave. We might break the code, but at least we had one.

And the old Jesuit always showed a great personal interest in me. Early my second senior year, he asked me to visit him for a talk in the Healy Building. "Patrick, what is the matter with you?" the old priest asked.

"Nothing," I responded, "I was booted out of here; now, I'm back; I'm staying out of trouble, and I'm doing my work."

"You're doing splendidly," he said. "That is not the problem. The problem is every time I look over in your direction, you look as though you're going to explode. What is the matter with you? Why are you so angry?"

I don't know, I told him. And the truth is I didn't know, then, why we got into so many fights and so damned much trouble.

The hereditary attributes of the southern Scotch-Irish, that Tom Sowell chronicled in *Ethnic America*, had something to do with it. We were always a clannish, parochial people, comfortable with our own, uncomfortable among strangers. While we kept friends for life, we didn't make friends readily. With the possible exception of Cricket, none of us was the fraternity-brother type.

And, until I decided on getting that graduate degree from Columbia, there was no "goal" toward which I was sailing, no clear purpose for which I was working at Georgetown. ("I'm just a rollin' stone, down a lost highway," as one of my favorite songs of the era put it, was not an inapt description.) Unlike Gonzaga, there was no demanding competition, physical or intellectual, no steady pressure, no constant demands, to drain off the excess energy and spirit of youth.

But those are excuses, not reasons.

The truth is the game chickens had reached an age where they were taking on the game rooster, and everyone else. The truth is we loved to party and drink and fight guys we didn't know and didn't like; and, dammit, raising hell at eighteen, nineteen, and twenty can be great, great fun. But I certainly wasn't going to try to sell that bill of goods to the old Jesuit.

While our social behavior left us constantly on the cusp of disciplinary action, neither my older brothers nor I ever dogged it on the books.

Dean's list (second, if not first) was routine, and, after the "sabbatical" at Father Sellinger's request, I racked up that perfect 4.0 the first semester of my return. Third in the class of '61, I was graduated *cum laude,* with honors in both the English and philosophy orals. Admitted to the Gold Key Society (Georgetown did not then belong to Phi Beta Kappa), I also won the Ryan Medal for Rational Philosophy. And, graduation night, it was announced that Mr. Buchanan had received a fellowship to study at the Columbia

Graduate School of Journalism in New York, the following year. I was on my way.

A decade after I was expelled from Georgetown, in the fall of 1969, I climbed aboard *Air Force Two* before dawn, for the flight to Cape Canaveral, to witness the launching of Apollo 12. It was the morning after Vice President Agnew had delivered his now-famous attack on the networks at Des Moines ("a tiny and closed fraternity of privileged men, elected by no one, and enjoying a monopoly sanctioned and licensed by government"), a speech I had written — with the silent benediction and collaboration of the President of the United States.

"Gangbusters!" Agnew said exultantly, as he spotted me in my window seat. (Contrary to published reports, Agnew was elated with the firestorm we had ignited.)

Sipping my coffee at five in the morning, feeling satisfied with myself, who should suddenly appear in the forward cabin of *Air Force Two*, but the president of Baltimore's Loyola College, the good friend of former Governor Agnew of Maryland — Father Joseph A. Sellinger, S.J. The good father was as startled as I.

Ten minutes into the flight, Father Joe came back, sat down beside me, and told me confidentially the FBI had been around. They had wanted more information on Mr. Nixon's thirty-year-old Special Assistant, who had been expelled from Georgetown while he was dean. He had done his best, Father Sellinger said, to throw the least unattractive light possible upon my social behavior. But, clearly, J. Edgar's men were doing their job.

Much had changed in that year of my expulsion. Miss Beth would marry in the summer of 1960 and move away from the area for good. Brother Hank, the summer after the incident in the parking lot, had entered the Jesuit seminary at Wernersville, Pennsylvania.

My father had decided to throw a stag party for Hank, the Sunday before he departed. Starting quietly at three in the afternoon, it was going strong at ten. While it had begun with the guys with whom Hank had grown up, drinking beer on the patio with the parents, I got on the phone around six and started calling some of the girls who might, also, want to wish Hank farewell. Peggy Shaw was invited over; and by ten, the house on Utah Avenue was rocking. It was a great party, and at the height of the revelry, Charlie Leasure walked into the kitchen for another beer and found my father standing there.

"Well, Mr. Buchanan," he said, making conversation, "when you think about it, it is really not all that surprising that Hank would one day go into the seminary. After all, he has always been pretty devout. Now, if it had been Pat!"

The Old Man cut him off in midsentence. For Pop to castigate my social behavior was one thing; for someone outside the family to cast aspersions on the family Black Sheep was quite another. "Just a minute, there," Pop interrupted; "some people forget that Saint Peter denied Christ three times! And he was the greatest of the apostles! What about Saint Augustine; he was a great sinner half his life. And, today, he is one of our greatest saints!"

Taken aback by the vehemence of my father's defense, Charlie started backing out of the kitchen. As he reached the front hall, he heard the final retort: "And what about Saint Cyprian! He practiced black magic!"

The next morning, however, Pop was back to form. "We held a gathering here," he told one of my little brothers, "to send a Christian boy off to the seminary; and Pat and his friends turned it into a pagan orgy."

Which was more than a mild exaggeration.

9

Columbia, Class of '62

"No motive power of his own."

THE Graduate School at Columbia was in 1961 — and remains today — the finest journalism school in America. When I arrived, I was probably the least prepared student in the class of '62.

I had never worked on a newspaper, high school or college; I had never had anything published, not even a letter to the editor; I could not type. Though my straight A's in early senior year, and my "experience" as an auditor had helped to win me the $1,500 Clapp-Poliak fellowship for "economic writing," I had never taken a course in economics. Soma Golden, who had won the $1,000 Clapp-Poliak fellowship (and who now is national editor of the *New York Times*) had been graduated *summa cum laude* in economics from Radcliffe. Twenty-five years later, as I reviewed my personnel file at Columbia, the commentaries of my teachers suggested that they saw me as a rude amateur, dropped in among young professionals. Students like Joe Salzman of U.S.C. and Arnie Abrams of Columbia were award-winning editors of their college papers; others, like Tony Sargent and Don Oliver, both of whom had had years of on-air experience, were already well into their careers.

Everything at Columbia was new to me: how to report, how to write a lead, how to put together a story, how to write a headline, how to edit copy, how to piece together a magazine article. Only crusty George Barrett, the assistant city editor at the *New York Times*, seemed to think this student had promise. And George was a contrarian. The curt and dismissive comment on my midterm report, by copy editor Betsy Wade, was not untypical: "I met this student 12/7 and 12/14 and had to take him by the hand for every single thing that needed doing. He seems not to have any motive power of his own."

The most memorable teacher at Columbia in those years was Professor John Hohenberg, who taught advanced news writing to the class of '62. Hohenberg was an institution at the "J" School; his fine book, *The Professional Journalist,* was scriptural text.

An intense, emotional man, for whom journalism was a calling, not an occupation, and an honored calling at that, Professor Hohenberg began his hours-long morning course with a brief lecture on what this particular writing exercise was all about. Then, we were handed "fact sheets" from which to produce a news story at our desks. "Editors," many of them active newspapermen and women, would start down each aisle, lean over our typewriters, and criticize and correct what we had written.

Years later — after I had penned Vice President Agnew's famous attack on the networks at Des Moines, November 13, 1969, and his follow-up assault on the *Washington Post* and *New York Times* ("The day when . . . the gentlemen of the *New York Times* enjoyed a form of diplomatic immunity from comment and criticism of what they said is over. Yes, gentlemen, that day is past.") — John Oakes, editorial editor of the *Times,* was chatting with me at a party. When I volunteered that *New York Times*'s reporters and editors had taught me at Columbia most of what I knew about news writing, he mused, "That must have been quite painful for you."

The very opposite is true. Whatever their politics, the men and women who worked for the *Times* were thought, by all of us at Columbia, to be the New York Yankees of American journalism. "If the *Times* went on strike in the morning," one of my professors told me, "every afternoon paper in the city would have to shut down," so dependent were they on the Gray Lady of 43rd Street.

We may have rankled beneath their airs of superiority, but, liberal or not, the *Times* was considered the finest newspaper in the world, setting a standard of excellence against which other newspapers should measure themselves. Students taken on as night copy boys were envied; upon graduation, they might be hired as apprentice reporters, and soon have their by-lines in the greatest newspaper in the world. To have the most respected journalists in

America take a personal interest in my miserable copy was what I had come to Columbia for.

The Journalism School was everything I had hoped it would be; and I have always taken a measure of pride that, after nine months at the toughest graduate school in America, I was competitive with young journalists who had started years ahead of me. That liberalism was in vogue, with respectable dissent coming from the fashionable left, made the experience all the more cherished. "Pat, how did you ever survive up there at Columbia?" conservative friends would ask me, years later.

I did not just survive; I had the time of my life.

About the ideological predilections of the best and brightest in the profession I had chosen, I was never in doubt. (Some of my professors, like Penn Kimball, refused to cross a picket line set up by students outside the campus bookstore, even though they were simply passing through the store to get to class. They walked all the way around the building, to come in another entrance, lest they be *perceived* as crossing a picket line!) The chasm that opened wide and deep between the Establishment press and the American people during Vietnam and Watergate came as no shock to me; I was present at the creation.

The first time I got one of those long fact sheets, I read it over carefully and began ruminating silently about my lead. Two minutes had not elapsed, however, before I heard one typewriter start up, then another; then, what sounded like a battery of machine guns was firing in the newsroom. All the cocky young journalists were breezing through this easy calisthenic. As I could barely type, I panicked, tearing page after page out of the big Underwood, until Professor Larry Pinkham came down the aisle and told me to calm down and take some of the aspirin I kept on my desk and ate like jelly beans because of the arthritis.

One of the earliest fact sheets described an elderly philanthropist and art collector, a friend of the publisher, who had taken as his third wife an eighteen-year-old coed. We were asked to write up this delicate item in a style suitable to the Sunday *Times*. My lead ran something like this: "Dr. Harold Ross, noted philanthropist and contributor to New York's Metropolitan Museum, added a new piece to his celebrated collection this afternoon. The objet d'art is Miss Becky Woodham, an eighteen-year-old graduate of the Student Art School; Becky and Dr. Ross were wed, etc. etc."

The *Times* editor working my aisle that day, bug-eyed, ripped the copy out of my typewriter, and ran it up to Hohenberg, who read it to the class, which howled with delight. A gracious man, John Hohenberg declined to divulge the name of the author.

From the day classes opened, I felt I was in over my head; I was nervous and tense in class and had serious doubts as to whether I could catch up with the other students, before the faculty caught up with me. Each afternoon, I would go home and work on my assignments (and typing) until all hours of the night.

My personal best, however, came on election day in November, the night the ethnic dream ticket of Lefkowitz, Fino, and Gilhooley went down to defeat before Mayor Robert Wagner, who had campaigned brilliantly for reelection against the bosses who had put him in office, and whose tool he was said to have become.

The election for Bronx borough president was being held the same evening, and I was assigned to cover the almost certain winner, a protégé of Democratic machine boss Charley Buckley. Sitting in the Democratic headquarters from six until after nine, talking with the pols, I sensed this crowd did not have the feel of a winner. Operating on a hunch, I found out from a telephone operator the address of Joe Periconi's headquarters and took a cab over to assess the mood in the Republican reformer's camp. When I arrived, the returns were bringing in the upset of the night. Flushed with a victory they had not anticipated, Periconi and his people were ebullient, talkative, and quotable. Before the metropolitan press arrived, I had Periconi's quotes phoned in to our "city desk."

Exhausted but quite pleased with myself, I left the Bronx around midnight and headed for the West End bar across from Columbia, arriving back at my room near three in the morning. The next day when I walked into the 9 A.M. class five minutes late, Hohenberg, who was speaking, did not appear angry. He looked over and nodded with a smile, as I walked back to my desk. Don Oliver, who had the desk in front of me and who was now a constant companion, whispered loudly, "Your ears should have been burning."

Hohenberg had related to the class, apparently in gratifying detail, the exploit of the intrepid and savvy young reporter who had had the initiative to drop his given assignment and go get "the story" of the night. Great reporters get their start that way, Hohenberg had explained to the class. The "objet d'art" incident was forgotten; I knew I was going to make it.

During that election campaign, the professors and teachers did little to disguise their political bias. They didn't like the ethnic bosses, the Charley Buckleys and Carmine DeSapios; and they loved the reformers. When Congressman John V. Lindsay, then forty, held a news conference in front of the class, arguing indifferently the case for the mayoral candidacy of Louie Lefkowitz, one professor asked Handsome John, "Why didn't you run yourself?"

The professors and teachers, gathered in the front of our large "newsroom," purred with pleasure. Smiling at the suggestion, Lindsay was coy in his response, but, even though he was chairman of the failing Lefkowitz campaign, he seemed not at all displeased with the question. When Lindsay departed, they spoke of him as a future mayor and even a future President of the United States, a Republican JFK. And, although Lindsay was on the far left of the Republican party, I had to concede they had a point. Compared with some of the Republicans whose golf bags I had carried around the fairways of Burning Tree, the handsome, debonair liberal from Manhattan's "silk-stocking district" did indeed strike me as a man with a future.

The aspect of Columbia I found most puzzling and off-putting was the seriousness, bordering on stuffiness and sanctimony, that pervaded much of the faculty and student body. We were young; we were gifted; we had our whole lives in front of us; but one would have thought many of us had just been condemned to a life of mortification and prayer with the Carthusians. Some students and teachers seemed to carry the weight of the world; a look of barely suppressed pain was forever in their faces. Some were downright grim.

Growing up with my family, with my friends, laughter was a part of life. Even the worst of the troubles into which we had gotten ourselves invariably yielded up a rich harvest of humor and anecdote. Among the reasons I had gone into journalism was because I wanted an enjoyable life; and newspapering was known to be an occupation where *le bon temps* was never far away. To many of my classmates and professors, however, journalism was their religion; and they had adopted the aspect of mournful missionaries, sent out to certain martyrdom, to save a sinful world.

All too often, an overdeveloped social conscience is accompanied, *pari passu,* by an atrophied sense of humor.

Oliver, who was from Montana and studied even harder than I, and I were forever on the lookout for ways to lighten things up. When, in our history of journalism course, each of us was assigned to write about some journalistic institution and the contribution it made to our profession, I chose the *New York Graphic,* the most outrageous daily ever published in the United States.

The delinquent child of millionaire health nut Bernarr Macfadden, the *Graphic* in the Roaring Twenties faked composite photographs ("composographs"); its reporters had the manners and ethics of barnyard animals; and it libeled everybody. In the world of "gutter journalism" the *Graphic* was in a class all by itself. Once, when the tabloid's lead story was about a lunatic who had escaped from an insane asylum and gone on a rape spree, a senior editor had to sprint to the composing room to take down the screaming banner headline his copy desk had sent over: NUT BOLTS AND SCREWS! Macfadden and his editor had once been hauled into court — by the New York Society for the Suppression of Vice.

Even though the daily *Graphic* had perished thirty years before, however, the teacher did not think my paper funny, or me funny, or the subject funny. The *New York Graphic* had been an unpardonable affront to American journalism, a throwback to a dark age, and I had exhibited a juvenile tolerance of the outrage. (Presumably, he wanted yet another essay on the importance of James Gordon Bennett and the *New York Herald.*)

Told to write an editorial imitating the style of a major daily, Oliver and I collaborated on "Ransom for Red Beard," an editorial crafted in the brawling 1962 style of the *New York Daily News* — carving up JFK for his plans to ransom the Cuban patriots he had left stranded at the Bay of Pigs. Some of the students thought it a clever enough imitation of what the *News* would produce to win the editorial writing award; but some of the professors let us know that the *Daily News* editorial style was something we had come to Columbia not to emulate, but to change. We didn't even come close. (Less than a decade and a half after Oliver and I penned "Ransom for Red Beard," the executives of the *Daily News* sounded me out on becoming their editorial editor.)

One of the best decisions I made, on arriving at Columbia, was to go down to the International House for graduate students (built forty years before with Rockefeller money), at 123rd Street and

Riverside Drive, opposite the Riverside Church and Grant's Tomb, and to persist after they told me they had no rooms. When I took out my *Washington Star* clipping, complete with photograph, which reported on my impressive scholarship, the admissions officer was suddenly impressed. Yes, they did, after all, have a tiny single room left on the sixth floor. Some two hundred American and three hundred foreign students lived at "I" House, the men and women in two wings separated by huge, steel fire doors. The foreign students came from Asia, Africa, and Latin America, as well as Europe. The cafeteria and the lounge were lively places; that was a time of newly won independence and brimming self-confidence in the Third World.

The first night there, I bought a beer and sat down with an African graduate student; within ten minutes he was shouting incoherently at me, as I argued that Katanga had a right to secede from the Congo, that Moise Tshombe was a great man, the hope of Black Africa. The spluttering Congolese got up and stomped off.

That discussion over, I got into it with another student, who brought up Joe McCarthy. "That horrible man destroyed a professor of mine," the student said.

"How could that be?" I shot back. "I've never even heard of your professor."

The student explained that his teacher had taken the Fifth Amendment during a state legislative hearing investigating Communism on the campuses of California, and, consequently, had lost his job. "If he wasn't a Communist, why did he take the Fifth Amendment?" I asked.

He had no answer, but was appalled a fellow graduate student at Columbia did not automatically join him in a ritualistic trashing of the anti-Communist crusader from Appleton, Wisconsin.

At 123rd and Riverside Drive, colonialism and McCarthyism were two of many subjects about which even the most tolerant of liberals, I learned, were not all *that* tolerant. Those subjects were simply closed for discussion. And the International House was not dissimilar to the Journalism School. Father Abraham had an easier time finding "just men" in the twin cities of Sodom and Gomorrah than I did finding fellow conservatives at Columbia or "I" House.

But good friends were made in both places. Within a few days of my arrival, I gathered up Kusum Lal, a pretty Indian classmate, and took her out to Yankee Stadium to watch Roger Maris break

Babe Ruth's record of sixty home runs in a single season. A Brahmin lady decked out in a magnificent sari, Kusum did not have the least idea why all these Americans were standing and roaring. At our twenty-fifth reunion, she fondly recalled our afternoon. (Several years older than Oliver and me, Kusum Lal was a good sport. Once, when she was arguing passionately with us about some matter of great importance to India, Oliver told her, "Kusum, if you don't calm down, Buchanan and I are going to walk you up to the head of the class, nail one end of that sari to the wall there, and spin you out until it unwraps." She laughed more loudly than we.)

The two subjects in which I was given a C− that first semester at Columbia were "copy editing, typography, and newspaper makeup" — about which I knew nothing — and "basic issues in the news." The grade is understandable. My views on such questions as the U.N., a revered institution at Columbia, must have been considered neolithic (I was not that far removed from the John Birch bumper-sticker position of "Get the U.S. out of the U.N. and the U.N. out of the U.S."); and my thoughts about "urban problems" were nonexistent. (Growing up in D.C., with no home rule, my friends and I were probably the principal "urban problem" in Northwest.)

Hohenberg gave me a C+ in "advanced news writing," which was more than fair. While no longer writing about comely "objets d'art" being added to the collections of philanthropists, I often missed the "lead" completely in the stories I wrote. Handed, for example, FCC Chairman Newton Minnow's famous philippic against network television as a "fact sheet," I left his now-anthologized phrase, "vast wasteland," out of my first two paragraphs. My "news judgment" was not what it ought to be. In economics and libel law, academic subjects and more familiar turf, I got A's; and was given an A− in mechanics of expression and magazine writing. A couple of teachers (with professors, instructors, deans, and so on, there must have been a score of them who graded us) felt I had some native ability to communicate. All the other grades were B.

It was in that magazine writing course that I first came to feel I could actually "write." Far into the morning hours at the "I" House, one night, I wrote a long piece about the 1920s I can remember to this day, all about the "confident young men who had roared into the nineteen twenties in their Stutz Bearcats and raccoon coats, and departed via the upper floors of Wall Street skyscrapers."

For ten minutes, the teacher read long passages to the class, and he read it well; to me, it rolled beautifully. The class listened in silence. When he was done, Glenn Mitchell, the young black from Shaw College with the lilting Caribbean accent, said, "We have a writer in the class!" Some of the other students, including Anna Kisselgorf, now dance editor at the *New York Times,* and the late Judy Klemesrud, a friend from Iowa (who would also spend most of her career at the *Times*), agreed that it was beautifully written.

"What exactly is the point?" the magazine editor blurted impatiently. "This may be nice writing," but what he had assigned us to do was go to the library, plagiarize the best "anecdotes" from other magazine articles, and string them together in our own. That was the way professional writers produced and sold magazine stories. And that's what this course was supposed to train us to do. Even though he seemed frustrated by my failure to follow the course he had recommended, I was not at all displeased; fellow students, whose judgment I respected and whose approval I relished, were saying Buchanan was a "writer." The old self-confidence was coming back.

Looking back on that year, that tightly organized program at Columbia was immensely productive. Instead of hanging around Columbia for two academic years working toward a master's degree, the course work was intensified and completed in nine months. There were only eighty students in the school — sixty-five Americans and fifteen foreign students from countries like Japan, Indonesia, Pakistan, Aden, Germany, Holland, Canada, and Nicaragua. (India, with three students, had the largest foreign contingent.) There were three blacks and eighteen women; and Jewish students were probably the largest ethnic contingent. While there were no black teachers, women taught in virtually every area.

Almost every day, we went to school from nine in the morning until five in the afternoon, shifting from one course to another; and we studied and wrote far into the night. It was baptism by immersion; we were introduced to every form of journalism: radio and television broadcasting, news reporting and writing, copy editing, movie and book reviews, editorial writing, photography, newspaper management and production. We were taught the theory and history of communications in America, and were solidly grounded in libel law. As my scholarship was for economic writing, that was where I had to specialize, not foreign affairs, which is where I had wanted to be. While the economic writing seminar was meeting under the guidance of Dean Richard T. Baker, and we discussed and wrote about the theories of David Riccardo and Karl Marx and Thorsten Veblen, Penn Kimball's class on national issues was shooting the bull with Theodore H. (Teddy) White, who had just completed *The Making of the President, 1960,* and who regaled students with stories of the Nixon–Kennedy campaign. But because I arrived with so much less skill and knowledge than the other students, I took away much more from Columbia. The assignments they found boring and redundant, I found fresh, interesting, and challenging.

When I arrived at Columbia, in September 1961, my knees were in miserable shape. In late August, I had driven home from Boston, straight through in the kind of long overnight drive I loved, smoking two packs of cigarettes along the way. For someone with arthritis, however, it was unpardonably stupid. When I got out of the car on Utah Avenue, after ten hours on the road, my knees were locked in place; I could barely make it into the house. Not until the day I flew to New York to register did I get off the crutches, for the fourth time in two years.

At International House, I had to get up at six each morning, to get the knees working adequately to walk the eight blocks to school. The agony of that long walk would begin to ease only after I reached Columbia. Swollen to the size of grapefruits, both knees had "water" on them, and I had to make an appointment at Columbia University Medical Center on 169th Street to have them drained. After the knees were punctured and the fluid removed, cortisone was shot directly into the joints. The relief was immediate and total. While I could barely walk into that hospital, by the time the doctors worked their magic with the needles and the cortisone, I could almost run out. When I heard people wondering in those years about the occasional puffiness in Jack Kennedy's face, I knew the answer: he and I were taking the same drug; the cortisone was doing it.

As the knees improved, I took to shooting hoops with Oliver at International House, and running in the early mornings along the Hudson River with classmate Howie Cohn. Eventually, it worked. By late fall, I was full of energy, in fighting trim; the arthritis seemed to belong again to a distant past.

Then, once again, I almost blew it.

When Father McNamee had recommended me to Columbia, he had been asked to "handicap the applicant." The truthful old Jesuit priest put down a single word: "Irascibility."

Under "additional comments," he explained: "This applicant has only one drawback — the temper of the Irish! Yet it is this very intensity of spirit that gives him his drive and ambition. He wants to be a journalist because of his recognition and ready acceptance of the challenge of the work. He could move into a comfortable position in his father's firm. I think he will be a success at journalism."

Irascibility, the old priest had said; and he was dangerously close to the truth.

At the Christmas party, before our departure home for the holidays, Oliver, a "streetcorner conservative" like me who would have meshed nicely with the Homers, told me he had had about enough of Kim Willenson, a superior student who would seek out occasions to demonstrate that superiority. As a member of the "entertainment committee" for the party, Oliver had suggested the class sing some old cowboy songs he recalled from Montana days, such as "I Ride an Old Paint." Willenson had mocked the idea in front of the other students, and thus, Oliver said, had mocked him. As we went to buy more beer for the class midway through the party, Oliver informed me he was going to take Willenson out.

While I had nothing against Willenson, I had nothing going for him either. However, Oliver was my best friend at school and I now recalled darkly that, when Willenson had been "slot man" on our copy desk, he had flipped back a headline he had assigned me to write, with a contemptuous remark about its stupidity. This was something I would have accepted from a *Times*man, but not from a contemporary. *"Nemo me lacessit impune!"* (no one wounds me with impunity!), is, after all, the motto of the Scot.

So, I associated myself with Oliver's grievance. With you all the way, I told him. Then, I forgot about it. Later that night, as we partied in the World Room and the library, I tried out the Christman Game on a female student, in whom I had taken no prior interest. Lo and behold, who should amble up and begin exhibiting an interest of his own, but Kim Willenson. When I commented caustically on his behavior, he sent a short burst of obscene invective in my direction. Which was all I needed.

Willenson never cleared the holster. After I sucker-punched him, Willenson was on the library floor at the feet of Dean Baker, who was staring quizzically at me, wondering what in God's name he had let into his Graduate School. The whole class stormed in.

While I was relaxed about the episode, Willenson was enraged and had to be restrained. So, Oliver and I decided to call it a night. As we departed, however, I paused, turned back toward Willenson, who was still being held by a couple of students and glaring angrily at me, and said in a sweet voice, "Good night, Kim." It worked. Willenson wrestled himself free of his retainers and charged. I was waiting for him; and, now, he was on the deck a second time, with half the faculty staring incredulously and Oliver standing over him, yelling that if he tried to attack me again, he, Oliver, would "beat the shit" out of him. Which, at that point, would have been redundant.

Oliver and I laughed all the way down Broadway to Fred Appel's apartment (and after-party party) on 110th Street.

On Monday, Willenson showed up in class with a large black patch covering his eye, which, I was told, had been severely damaged. I started getting nervous; and by late afternoon, a dozen students, including several of the girls, escalated the affair by wearing black eye patches in a show of solidarity — with me.

Came word from the fifth floor that Dean Barrett wanted to see me in his office, immediately; and I could feel the old volleyball return to the abdomen. There was no doubt who had thrown the first punch; indeed, I was unsure Willenson had thrown any. The thought occurred that Dean Barrett was inviting me up to inform me he did not want me back for the second semester. Willenson, after all, was at or near the top of the class, and, as a journalist, I was, at best, expendable. I did not know how I would handle a second expulsion.

But, when I got there, the dean, who had already consulted with class president Chris Trump, was anguished only about the "destruction of class unity." Class unity was something important and vital for our future, Dean Barrett said; and he had worked tirelessly to build it. Whatever the cause, the Buchanan–Willenson fight had exposed and deepened divisions that he felt already existed within the class. Now, these eye patches, mocking Willenson, showed the class was choosing up sides. All this was deeply disheartening.

"Pat, what can we do about it?" he said.

My relief was total: "Whatever I can do to restore class unity," I said, "Dean Barrett, you've got it."

"Excellent, Pat," he said. With that, I raced downstairs, walked over to Willenson, shook hands, and implored my buddies to drop the eye patches. Which they did.

For a dozen years, after we left school, I never saw Kim Willenson. Then, in 1974, I was coming down the steps of a hotel in Yalta, during President Nixon's final summit, and there was Kim Willenson in the lobby. He had spent much of the preceding decade in Southeast Asia, and was now a respected, veteran correspondent for UPI. We had a couple of beers together in the hotel bar.

As early as May of 1961, I had made a profession of political faith. The great Jesuit scholar and teacher, John Courtney Murray, had come to Georgetown to speak in Dahlgren Chapel at the close of ceremonies inducting graduating seniors into the Gold Key Society. At a small reception for Father Murray, I was asked by a fellow senior whom I preferred for President in 1964. (JFK had been in office only four months, but long enough for the Bay of Pigs.)

"Barry Goldwater," I replied.

"Me, too," he volunteered. We looked around, laughing, to be certain no one was listening.

If Bill Buckley was spiritual guide in our wilderness years in American politics, Barry Goldwater was our political idol and champion. At the Republican convention that nominated Nixon and Lodge, Barry had stood up to wild applause and declared, "Let's grow up, conservatives. We can take over this party."

Then, Barry had campaigned loyally for the Republican ticket, while Nelson Rockefeller had played dog in the manger. After imposing his wretched Pact of Fifth Avenue on Nixon ("The

Munich of the Republican Party," Barry had called the secret meeting at Rocky's New York apartment, where Nixon had acceded to the Governor's demands for changes in the GOP platform), Rockefeller had selfishly refused the vice presidential nomination, and gone into the tank during the fall campaign.

Already, the 1964 Republican nomination was beginning to take shape as a titanic struggle between Rockefeller, paragon of the rich, powerful "Eastern Establishment" that had dictated to the party for decades, and Barry Goldwater, the Man from the West, who personified the militant conservative "movement" for which *The National Review* was beacon, and we were the mujahedeen. "Let the bloodbath begin," would have nicely summarized the anticipation we all felt.

In my application to Columbia, I had given Goldwater's *Conscience of a Conservative* as a book of "paramount importance" that I had read outside class. Not only does this book reflect "a strong undercurrent of national thought," I said, it was "written by a man who I feel has a bright and integral future in American and international affairs." (The "only television program I watch with consistency," I added, was Walter Cronkite's "Twentieth Century.")

What attracted me about Goldwater was his principled militancy. When people called us "the radical right," they had a point. *Radix* is the Latin word for "root," and Barry Goldwater wanted to restore America by returning to her "root" ideas of constitutionalism and limited government. His book called for dismantling the welfare state, removing the federal government from education and agriculture, and restoring states' rights; and Barry did not flinch from letting the great Dwight Eisenhower himself have it with both barrels for bringing into our beloved country the Butcher of Budapest: "A craven fear of death is entering the American consciousness; so much so that many recently felt that honoring the chief despot himself was the price we had to pay to avoid nuclear destruction."

We are on the "brink of possible disaster," Goldwater warned, because, "our enemies have understood the nature of the conflict and we have not. They are determined to win the conflict, and we are not."

Like the civil-rights movement, then in full flower, the conservative movement in 1961 had the unmistakable attributes of a "rising" cause: fervor and intensity, a willingness on the part of the faithful to sacrifice, the conviction that the cause was right and just — and must not, above all, be compromised. Those attributes, however, that enabled us to tear the Republican party away from the ancient but weary grip of the Establishment, also, however, frightened away millions. Unlike genial Ronald Reagan, with his soothing conservatism of the early '80s, we crew-cut militants of the Goldwater era, twenty years before, were unsuited to the television age. In the sixty-second bites offered up to Middle America by the emergent network news, the young conservatives seemed to fit the stereotype being drawn of them in those endless documentaries about Thunder on the Right. At the '64 convention, when the defeated Rocky stood at the podium, smiling and taunting the Right, the conservatives in the balconies played into his hands, howling, jeering, and booing for five minutes at the Governor of New York — on national television. To the intelligentsia, which had laughed off the conservatism in the '50s as country-club boorishness, the sight of these militant youth was unsettling; and they spread the alarm.

Many younger conservatives today — when a mature movement has captured the Republican party and triumphed in a series of national elections — do not, I think, appreciate what it was like then. As national voices, Buckley and Goldwater were virtually all we had; they were indispensable. And I have never been able to associate myself with their young conservative critics, who, after all, were not there "upon Saint Crispin's Day."

As soon as I knew I was going to make it in journalism school, I decided to volunteer part of my time to the cause. But, when I showed up at the national headquarters of Young Americans for Freedom, they treated me like a Rockefeller plant. (Perhaps it was because I told them I was a graduate student at Columbia, not exactly a hotbed of Goldwaterism.) Repeatedly, I volunteered to write, free of charge, their press releases, to help with publicity for the upcoming rally in Madison Square Garden, featuring Goldwater himself. But some character who called himself "Shafto," and who told me several times he had gone to Princeton, impatiently explained that my services were unneeded. He left me with the impression I was consuming valuable corporate time. Apparently, this Shafto had been sent out to run me off by the YAF executive director, one Richard Viguerie, who, I later learned, was in the back room. Denied the chance to make my case directly to Viguerie, I was thanked and pointed toward the outer door.

Later, I applied to *National Review* — with similar results. But this turndown was not unanticipated. I had no impressive file of by-lined articles to send Priscilla Buckley, Bill's sister and the managing editor, and my writing did not remotely meet the standards being set in the wittiest, liveliest, and most irreverent journal In America. *National Review* was a vade mecum for young conservatives; it was our Iskra, "the Spark" of the revolution; it maintained our morale and spirit, kept us in communion with our leaders, our philosophy, our cause. We waited for *National Review* in those years; and then we quoted it back at our critics and tormentors. In applying to *NR,* I felt I had fulfilled a duty.

Elected to the student affairs committee the second semester, I went to the dean's office and asked that, among the fifty or so speakers and panelists to be brought to the Journalism School at year's end, conservative journalists also be included.

"Excellent idea, Pat," Dean Barrett said, "why don't you go work me up a list?" I thought and thought — and went to him with only two names: William F. Buckley, Jr., and George Sokolsky, whom I had heard debate Senators Ken Keating and Harrison Williams on campus. (Afterwards, I had gone up and introduced myself to Sokolsky, who had been my father's journalistic hero after Pegler. Though Sokolsky had a thundering voice, he seemed old and frail and his grip was feeble when I shook hands with him. Still, to me, he was a historic figure who had actually been inside Russia only a few years after the revolution; and had personally known Stalin, Trotsky, Bukharin, Zinoviev, Kamenev, and all the old Bolsheviks who had launched the Ten Days That Shook the World.)

The dean nodded at my two names, said both were acceptable, and then said, "Fine, Pat, now which of the two would you like us to invite?" He was not joking and he was not being hostile; that was the attitude at the school. We conservatives were Hare Krishnas. Of course, we had a right to our strange beliefs, and we must not be discriminated against. But we were not taken seriously, as representing other than some aberrant strain of thought that had resurfaced somehow in the Eisenhower years and that was difficult to accord any great respect.

Students who wrote tough articles about the John Birch Society were praised; they were "out there — on the cutting edge of social change," as one professor repeatedly put it.

Once, when I covered a Ban-the-Bomb demonstration, I decided to follow the participants into a bar. (They thought I was sympathetic.) There, the demonstrators confided, while I listened and took notes, how indispensable it was, to euchre good publicity, to bring along a baby in a baby carriage as a prop — even if they had to borrow someone else's baby. The press would always photograph a woman pushing a baby carriage, they said; this tactic always got them into the paper. "Was this papoose a ringer?" I asked. No, they said; but we've used one before. So, I wrote up both what they had demonstrated about, and how they manipulated the press. I was led to understand I was letting my opinion get in the way of the real story.

But while I had different beliefs and heroes, the professors and teachers graded me as fairly as I had a right to expect. Penn Kimball, an unapologetic liberal (who later discovered some of his liberal colleagues had blacklisted him for a government job, by falsely suggesting he was a security risk, and who wrote a book about it called *The File*), gave me an A in his course. Virtually all my other grades the second semester were B and B+; I was improving by the week, and George Barrett even thought they should consider me for one of three traveling fellowships given the top students in the class. And the dean at Columbia, Edward Barrett (no relation to George), who had served as Assistant Secretary of Defense in the Eisenhower Administration, was always gracious.

When I went to Columbia, I had determined to sever all ties of economic dependency, and make it on my own. So, I wrote the school that I could expect no financial help from my parents. The $1,500 Clapp-Poliak scholarship I had won covered the $1,400 tuition; the money I had earned as an auditor, plus a $1,000 student loan, covered room and board at International House. But, as the spring of 1962 approached, I was tapped out. So, I went home one weekend and retrieved my sole asset, my DKW, and brought it to New Jersey for my cousin, Bucky Boy, to unload. (A pretty little German car, the color of a lemon, the DKW — the initials were Bavarian for "remarkable little wonder" — had been sold to me for $1,700 by the manager of Capitol Cadillac, Howard Jobe, when I had gone there to buy a Renault. That DKW was no end of trouble. It sounded like a washing machine that had thrown its bearings; and the tires were the size of Soap Box Derby wheels. Once, the air-cooled engine had overheated on the way home from Somers

Point, New Jersey. With Peter Sommer and Hatchet in the car, the DKW exploded on the Baltimore–Washington Parkway, splitting the engine block. For two years, the little lemon had eaten up my savings, but it had become my trademark. You could spot it a mile away maneuvering beautifully in traffic. In one humorous incident, Cricket and I had taken it back, for the umpteenth time, to Capitol Cadillac for repairs, and while I was walking toward the show-room, I saw the salesmen looking out at me with apprehension in their faces. Absentmindedly, I had brought along my squash rac-ket, which I was swinging energetically back and forth. The sales-men thought I was coming to settle accounts with Howard Jobe, for having sold me the little lemon.)

After running ads for several weeks, dropping the price every few days, Bucky Boy finally dumped my DKW for $300 on "Smil-ing Sam" Rosenberg, "the Fairview Cowboy," a used-car dealer and the only man I ever knew who had his picture on his checks. When I showed the check to the dean, with "Smiling Sam's" pho-tograph on it, in a cowboy hat with a cigar, he said, "I'd cash that right away."

Still, I was short. So, I went back to the dean, and told him my situation.

"We have a special scholarship fund for students who have shown great improvement," he said; "I think you qualify." He made out a check for $100 to me to finish the year. It was an act of generosity and graciousness, for which I am permanently grateful.

In yet another sense, Columbia in the early '60s was more a challenge to me than to the other students. Where conservative clichés were ridiculed, by faculty and students alike, liberal clichés were accepted as recitals of the catechism in which all educated men and women supposedly believed. The total disparagement with which Columbia viewed my heavily Catholic education is something I inadvertently discovered, going through my records twenty-five years later. On my Georgetown transcript, sent to the admissions committee, a line had been drawn through all my theol-ogy and philosophy grades from college, crossing out some forty hours of course work. As though these grades were for basket-weaving, they were not even factored into Columbia's assessment of my true grades from Georgetown. A knowledge of Catholic theology and Christian philosophy was apparently irrelevant to the making of a modern journalist.

That liberals were unprepared for the radical onslaught of the '60s, and for our conservative counterreformation in the '70s, came as no surprise. They had it too easy. They rarely had to defend their beliefs in the colleges and universities they attended. Liberal opinions were received as revealed truth, while I was ideologically embattled night and day in the newsroom, at the West End Bar, at classmate Fred Appel's TGIF parties, at the International House — with everybody and about everything.

When Khrushchev detonated his fifty-eight-megaton superbomb over Novaya Zemla, the greatest man-made explosion in history, and laughed about how his scientists had miscalculated the force of the explosion, some of the professors almost "freaked out," in the parlance of the time. I can recall Larry Pinkham expostulating about what would happen to Manhattan if that bomb were dropped on us.

But, to me, Khrushchev was a blusterer; this superbomb was set off for propaganda effect; and, from Pinkham's reaction, it was working. From my reading of history, the Soviet Union had never attacked a prepared and powerful nation; they had cut a devil's bargain with the Third Reich; they had preyed upon weak and defenseless countries like prostrate Poland, Finland, the tiny Baltic Republics, Romania, and Iran; and they had only attacked Imperial Japan after the United States had broken Japan completely. We had nothing to fear from the Soviet arsenal — so long as we kept our own nuclear gun pointed at their head and were prepared to retaliate if they dared to attack. Materialist to the core, they wanted to die even less than we did.

Another day Larry Pinkham told us how shaken he had been, when, working in daily journalism, he saw a fourteen-year-old Puerto Rican kid, who had been charged with murder, described by all the tabloids as "the Umbrella Man"; and he spoke in anguish of how such terrible journalism precluded a fair trial. But where were his priorities? Tabloid labeling seemed to me less of a problem than rising crime, when Columbia girls were being warned to stay out of Morningside Heights for fear of being raped by some of the little Umbrella Men below, whose adverse publicity so exercised the sensitive social conscience of Professor Larry Pinkham.

When India sent its army into the centuries-old Portuguese enclave of Goa, and annexed the tiny colony, rather than negotiate its future, I had a field day at International House. For years, Nehru and Krishna Menon had been lecturing the United States on the Gandhian principles of nonviolence. Now, the pair of pious hypocrites had invaded tiny Goa, and all India was caught up in a full-throated nationalistic roar of approval for the unprovoked attack.

Early one morning at breakfast I sidled up to one of the Sikhs I knew at the International House. "How are your nonviolent tanks doing this morning?" I asked him.

"About as well, Mr. Buchanan, as your 'clean' atomic bombs," the Sikh shot back in his clipped British accent. Just as I would have, the Sikh defended his country. Secretly, I liked the Sikhs, with their beards and turbans (though I argued with them constantly); they seemed to me a patriotic, proud, and fearless people.

Today, it is fashionable to deride as amoral Stephen Decatur's famous toast at Norfolk in 1816, "Our country . . . may she always be in the right; but our country, right or wrong." But, like those Sikhs, that is what I believed — and what most men still believe. In the hierarchy of values, the claims of one's country must take precedence over the claims of "international law." When America has committed herself to a military course of action, even if ill-considered or unwise, she deserves the service and support of her people. Was not that the lesson of the life of Robert E. Lee? Offered command of the Union armies, Colonel Lee declined the honor, surrendered his commission, rode across the Long Bridge, and volunteered to fight against his oldest friends in the U.S. Army, on behalf of his people and state, Virginia, that he believed were in the wrong, both on secession and slavery. Confronted with one of the great moral dilemmas of American history, Robert E. Lee chose to go down to defeat alongside his own misguided countrymen. That is patriotism; that is nobility; and that is why even military foes respected and admired Robert E. Lee.

A decade after leaving Columbia, when I read of American journalists declaring themselves "neutral" in a war in Vietnam in which our own brothers were fighting, and when some openly made clear their preference for the other side, I was appalled. In attitude, I felt closer to some of the Third World students at International House than to the Americans. Like those students from the emerging nations, I, too, was an ardent nationalist. And when the country music song of the early '70s came out, "When You're Running Down My Country, You're Walking on the Wrong Side of

Me," that was a simplistic summary of how I felt. While I could understand Africans and Asians, in the spirit and militancy of their newly won independence, trashing Europeans and Westerners as colonialists, I could not understand Americans and Europeans eagerly agreeing with them.

The ancient indictment against men of the Right is that, deep down inside, we are antiintellectual; we distrust men of thought; we are more at home in the world of legend and myth and faith than in the cooler realms of reason. While understandable, the charge is itself simplistic and false. What we believe, rather, is that faith precedes reason, that affection precedes understanding; that before we come to know, we first believe. Growing up, we did not have to have it explained to us that we should stand by brothers and sisters and family and friends. That came naturally. To us, the right and honorable duty of men of words and men of thought is not simply to seek and record abstract truth, but to deploy our talents, the arguments of the mind, to defend the treasures of the heart: family, faith, and country. When a man of thought uses the weapons of the mind to attack his own — family, faith, or country — this, to us, is truly the *trahison des clercs,* the treason of the intellectuals.

In his book, *Behind the Front Page,* David Broder, a critic from the *Washington Post,* suggests that, in answering a plea from Ronald Reagan's men — and my former political comrades — to come down to his hideaway at Wexford, Virginia, and grill candidate Reagan in preparation for his debate with Jimmy Carter (while I was still a columnist), I behaved unethically. "Pat Buchanan . . . has always put his ideology ahead of anything else," Mr. Broder wrote. But that decision, to step out, for an afternoon, from the role of journalist and into that of partisan, was neither easy nor unthinking. I crossed over the line because some of my best friends were invoking the claims of friendship, because I had personally urged Ronald Reagan in print to get into the race, and, because he now wanted and needed my help for an afternoon, ten days before the presidential election. Finally, I believed that the country's future depended on this man's defeating Jimmy Carter.

The only "ideological" statement my run to Wexford with fellow columnist George Will made that Saturday afternoon is that the claims of friendship and country and cause sometimes clash with, and may even supersede, those of career. I am a Catholic, a conservative, and an American, *before* I am a columnist. Nor was I ever able to sit with my colleagues in harsh judgment of those older journalists, who, in the early years of the Cold War, cooperated with their own CIA. To me, these men and women were motivated by a spirit of patriotism and a love of country. How condemn that? If that be professional treason, make the most of it.

About the best friend I made at Columbia, Don Oliver sat directly in front of me. Taller and heavier than I, athletic, with brownish-blond hair, he was several years older, had a beautiful wife named Sharon back in Montana and a little girl, and he worked as though — which was true — he had been given, with his $3,500 NBC scholarship, the greatest break of his life; and he wasn't going to blow it. Graduated from a state college, he studied even harder than I at Columbia and was a great fellow to spend time with.

Tom Daffron, whose father was an editor at the *Times,* Karen Brady, a Catholic, a confidante and friend at I House, and Jon Kapstein from Brown, whose grandfather was a famous rabbi, were among the friends I made. (Kapstein was so militant about his Jewishness, we nicknamed him Dov Landau, after the hero of the Warsaw ghetto in Leon Uris's *Exodus.*) Yet another buddy was Dick Oliver (known as "Loud Oliver," both to describe him accurately and contrast him to "Big Oliver"). Dick's lifelong ambition had been to write for the *New York Daily News,* where he worked as a copy boy at night. As Dick lived in Astoria, only blocks from Diane, a girl from Queens College I met around Christmas, I took to spending weekends in Archie Bunker's America. The neighborhood bar at which Dick's parents hung out, the Avenmore, reminded me of the Piccolo. Except for the strange accents, I was right at home in Queens.

Another friend was Miguel D'Escoto, a Nicaraguan Maryknoller and one of two priests in the class, the other being a Dutchman. As one of several fellow Catholics, Miguel and I were friendly, but never close. The only time I saw him truly animated was when five veterans of the Bay of Pigs — lately released from Castro's jails — were put on display in the World Room.

To me, the Bay of Pigs disaster had shown a hesitancy, a timidity, and a confusion on the part of President Kennedy, in the use of military power, that were ominous. Strike hard, or not at all, was among the oldest of military maxims. That is the way Americans had fought and won World War II. Yet, the young President had put ashore at the Bay of Pigs a force not much larger than a thousand men to invade an island of seven million, which then boasted an armed force one hundred times that size. I recall driving to Georgetown that April morning in 1961 listening to the radio reporting Castro's exultant statement, "We are exterminating them on the beaches," and was sick about the loss of the brave Cubans and the humiliation of the United States.

The patriots of Brigade 2506, before us in the World Room, wore bright yellow T-shirts, which Castro had given them as marks of cowardice, but which they now wore proudly as reminders of their sacrifice for their country's freedom. Some of them were years younger than I. But Father D'Escoto, who came from a family of Nicaraguan aristocrats, was contemptuous in his questions, challenging the morality, as well as U.S. sponsorship, of the invasion.

Several years later, Father Miguel was put in charge of the publications at the Maryknoll Order, a position he thoroughly politicized. The decline of that magnificent missionary order, whose business it once was to win souls to Christ in the forgotten lands of the earth, is among the countless tragedies of late twentieth-century Catholicism. That my old friend, Miguel D'Escoto, was a Communist at Columbia, I do not believe; that he became one, as Daniel Ortega's Foreign Minister and front man, I do not doubt. Either that, or he is a crass opportunist whose hatred of the United States has blinded him to his own betrayal of everything to which he dedicated his life when he took the vows of a Maryknoll priest. Today, a defrocked Miguel D'Escoto shills for a bogus and heretical little rump sect called the "Popular Church" of Nicaragua that is the creation of the Communist regime he has served for almost a decade.

At President Reagan's reception for foreign heads of state at the United Nations in 1986, I walked over and introduced myself to Nicaraguan junta leader Daniel Ortega; and mentioned that I had gone to school with his Foreign Minister. A short, sleek, bearded man in a magnificently tailored gray suit standing near Ortega turned, on hearing my voice, and said, "Hello Pa-treek." It had been a quarter-century since I had seen my old friend; Father D'Escoto interpreted for us. In Moscow in June of 1987, Miguel D'Escoto was awarded the Lenin Peace Prize, a rare first for the Maryknoll Order.

The Ortega brothers, D'Escoto, and Tomas Borge are winning in Nicaragua, as they won at the Bay of Pigs, for the simplest of reasons. Because, as Barry Goldwater wrote almost thirty years ago, "Our enemies have understood the nature of the conflict and we have not. They are determined to win the conflict, and we are not."

At Columbia, I spied the harbingers of the changing season in the Catholic Church. At Corpus Christi, near International House, which Catholic students at Columbia attended, I heard a priest declaiming on the need for new civil-rights legislation. That a priest would use Sunday mass to stump for a political reform was astonishing to me. I had never heard politics from the pulpit before.

Sermons on the Good Samaritan, wherein the priest would remind us that today's Samaritans were the Negroes of our inner cities, were common; but, calling for specific legislation seemed to be the Church telling the State not only the requirements of Christian charity, but precisely how, legislatively, they were to be realized. The Catholic clergy were dipping a toe into the political waters in a worthy cause; finding it bracing, some would never get out. From saving souls, they would move on to civil rights, to "giving peace a chance" in Southeast Asia, to boycotting grapes and lettuce for Cesar Chavez, to advancing gay and lesbian rights, to ridding the world of nuclear weapons, to saving the Sandinistas, forgetting in their hegira from the sacred to the secular what Christ had said to his disciples: "My kingdom is not of this world."

"Don't let them immanentize the eschaton!" was a Buckleyite witticism and lapel button of the sixties. A loose translation might be: Do not believe Paradise can be found here on earth; do not make your deepest commitment the creation of some secular utopia. Yet, that is the heresy to which a significant slice of Catholicism, clerical and lay, has lately succumbed.

The current condition of the American Catholic Church is testament to how effectively the Good News has been distorted and debased by some of those whose calling it presumably was to preach the Gospel.

Field Observation Week was among the major events at Columbia, a week during which students were assigned to news bureaus around the country, to observe the professionals in action. The largest contingent headed for Washington, and we arrived at a splendid time, the week John Glenn became the first American to fly in space, inside the tiny capsule called Mercury VII.

While I was assigned to the Associated Press — "a deadline every minute" — others went to UPI, the *Washington Post,* the *Daily News,* the *Star,* and so on. Don Oliver went to NBC where he would make his career.

One student, however, a progressive and correct Southerner named Jim, was assigned to the Washington bureau of the *New York Times,* then under the guiding hand of the great James "Scotty" Reston, next to Walter Lippmann the most prestigious name in American journalism. It is no exaggeration to say that Jim worshipped at Reston's shrine. When the *Times* columnist accepted an invitation to lecture at Columbia, Jim was uncontrollable. "Scotty Reston's coming to Columbia!" he told us half a dozen times. "Did you hear? Scotty's going to be here next week!"

The remorseless adulation of Reston and the *Times* became insufferable. So, having come by some of the dean's stationery and envelopes, we forged a note to Jim, and put it in his pigeonhole, the box in the newsroom where each of us got our graded papers, notes from professors, and so forth. The note read something like this:

Dear Jim:

> *I regret to inform you that the Washington bureau of the* New York Times, *because of the press of a number of national stories next week, will be unable to take you on for Field Observation Week, as they had hoped. "Scotty" Reston has said himself it will not be possible. Knowing, however, of your desire to observe news gathering in the nation's capital, we have arranged to have you spend the week at the Washington offices of* The Afro-American. *The gentleman to contact on Monday is Mr. Washington Jones, the editor; the news offices of* The Afro-American *are located at 512 Ninth Street, N.W.*
>
> > *Good luck,*
> > *Edward Barrett*
> > *Dean*

Oliver and I were sipping coffee at our desks, when Jim came in, walked over to his pigeonhole, and pulled out his letter from the dean. He opened it, read it, and — before we could tell him it was a joke — he was out the door of the newsroom, taking the steps two at a time to the dean's office on the fifth floor. He burst in, yelling that *The Afro-American* was a racist newspaper, that this was an outrage, that he wasn't going to Washington. When the startled dean calmed him down, and looked at the letter, the dean said simply, "Boy, you've been had."

Not five minutes elapsed before the dean's secretary sauntered into the newsroom and walked directly over to where Oliver and I were standing. The secretary said simply, "Dean Barrett says he will consider this incident closed — on one condition; you turn over to me, now, all blank copies of his stationery and all envelopes." The dean was not in doubt as to who could have done such a thing.

Every vacation break I got at Columbia — Thanksgiving, Christmas, Easter — I went home. The parents were elated at the progress I reported, with Pop picking up on my success election night and elaborating on the story to my younger brothers and sisters until you would have thought I was a candidate for that year's Pulitzer Prize. When I asked the parents if I might bring home to the house on Utah Avenue, during Field Observation Week no fewer than four of my classmates, they were delighted, and we made room. Don and Dick Oliver, John Fialka (now with the *Wall Street Journal*), and Dave McLean stayed that week at the family homestead.

There was beer in the icebox, and Mom had food ready whenever they came in at night; and the younger Buchanans were excited to meet my friends from parts of the country they had only read about. Under questioning about his home state, Don took my thirteen-year-old sister, Bay, into his confidence. There were no Catholics in distant Montana, he said, because they had taken out the only two they could find and hanged them.

On the first Sunday there, I took the four on a tour of downtown Washington in my father's newest Oldsmobile; they were astonished at my ignorance.

"What's that building there?" Don Oliver would ask.

"How should I know?" I answered, again and again.

"It's the Interior Department," I hastily said at one point.

"Yeah, I can read that, too," he said.

They assumed anyone raised in Washington was conversant with the government; but other than the major monuments, the Pentagon, the White House, the Library of Congress, and the Capitol, I hadn't the least notion where the departments and agencies were located. Not until I was in the Nixon White House did I learn the House chamber was on the south side of the Capitol. Most Washingtonians, who were born and raised in the capital, were apolitical in those years. Even in 1962, no Washingtonian had ever voted in a municipal, state, or federal election. We were spectators to the business of governing ourselves — except for those Washingtonians who worked in the bureaucracy. In college, I had never taken a course in government or politics; in high school, we did not study "civics"; and neither my parochial school nor Gonzaga was into "field trips."

The bureau chief at the AP in 1962 was Marvin Arrowsmith, whose daughter had gone to Blessed Sacrament and Georgetown Visitation with my sister Kathleen. The AP had just moved into new offices on Connecticut Avenue, and Arrowsmith explained that when the building superintendent handed him the keys, he handed them back. "The AP offices never close," Arrowsmith had said; "we operate around the clock; we don't need keys." I was impressed.

On consecutive days, the AP correspondents at State, the White House, the Pentagon, and the Hill took us along on their "beat." They were more than generous with their time. The White House, however, was initially a shock and a disappointment. When the AP correspondent brought me into the West Wing lobby, I was astonished to see some of the reporters had been drinking on the job; one was snoring on a couch, and a card game was going on. White House correspondents are "the waterboys of American journalism," one of my professors had warned me; now I knew what he meant.

Presently, the British Foreign Minister, Hugh Gaitskell, emerged from the Oval Office and held a press conference in the Fish Room. I shouldered my way in. The press performance seemed mediocre, and I departed determined not to pursue a career path that would lead me into this cul-de-sac. The White House press room was obviously the end of the line. (Seven years later, President Nixon would sweep the correspondents out of the West Wing, rebuild the lobby, and install my future wife, Shelley, as receptionist for the

White House. Now, the place had a touch of class. Looking back, no one did more than H. R. Haldeman to beautify the West Wing, where the Oval Office is located and where the President's top aides work. At the behest of Richard Nixon, Haldeman had the reception area totally remodeled: FDR's Fish Room became the Roosevelt Room; a new briefing room and press center was built where JFK's and LBJ's swimming pool had been; and, to the White House mess in the basement was added a paneled Executive Dining Room. There is no more intoxicating place in the world to work — and Messrs. Nixon and Haldeman created the surroundings to fit the honor.)

For us, the event of the week was President Kennedy's press conference in the auditorium of the Department of State. With Press Secretary Pierre Salinger seated beside him as he stood at the podium, JFK was in high spirits and fine form. What made JFK's press conferences memorable was not the information imparted, but his demeanor, his carriage, his humor. Scotty Reston had been right in his Columbia lecture: "This guy can charm the birds out of the trees."

Asked, by a reporter from the *Washington Daily News,* if he would consider that newspaper's recommendation of a holiday in D.C. and suburban schools when John Glenn came to town, the President responded, to laughter: "We always follow the *Washington Daily News.*"

When the conference started to slow, Kennedy turned to May Craig, with her famous hats. At the end of the half hour, Kennedy preemptively announced, "Thank you, Mr. President," and walked off, while everyone laughed and Arrowsmith and Merriman Smith, the senior UPI correspondent, ran for the phones. I was right behind them. As Smith dictated into the telephone, I eavesdropped. For fifteen minutes Merriman Smith talked, flipping the pages of his notebook back and forth. What he was saying was going out, almost verbatim, onto the wires and into the newsrooms of a thousand newspapers, where it would go on page one. The moment that press conference ended, the story had begun writing itself — lead, second paragraph, and so on — in the trained and professional mind of the famous UPI correspondent. Oblivious to the noise around him, Merriman Smith was focused on getting the story straight, clear, and first. It was a truly impressive performance; my estimation of White House correspondents began to rise.

260 ◆ RIGHT FROM THE BEGINNING

Twenty-one months later, Merriman Smith would win the Pulitzer Prize for his Dallas coverage of the assassination of President Kennedy, and, eight years later, when I went into the White House with Mr. Nixon, I came to know him. By then, however, with the three networks having gone to a nightly half hour of news, the White House "beat" had become a coveted assignment; and the White House press corps had changed character. It was now younger, brighter, more aggressive, more ideological, more adversarial.

During the final months at Columbia, I was becoming more and more outspoken in my opinions — and more and more identified with them. As I came into class one morning, in a black raincoat and rain hat, Professor Robert Shipman introduced me as "Patrick Buchanan, S.J." At the International House, the Paks had seen me arguing with the Indians at the dinner table over Goa; and they recruited me for the Political Science Club as "moderator" for their debates. During the debates, I had the Paks cheering at the questions I put to the Brahmins about their caste system, and their "untouchables."

When I went downtown one evening with classmates, I got caught up in a streetcorner debate. The older man on the soapbox was either a Communist or a sympathizer, because, amazing to me, he was openly defending on the streets of New York the invasion of Hungary and the Berlin Wall as legitimate acts of self-defense. As I listened, the crowd of East Europeans listening to him seemed enraged, but incapable of rebutting. So, from the back of the crowd, I started heckling the speaker: "Was it self-defense to run down Hungarian students with tanks; was it self-defense to throw Masaryk out of that window in Prague in 1948? Why is the mighty Soviet Union afraid of schoolboys?"

The East Europeans turned, delighted, and started shuffling me closer and closer to the soapbox, urging me to mix it up with the speaker, until, finally, I was right underneath him; then they started yelling for me to get up alongside him, which I did. The speaker got down, and, for five minutes I trashed everything he had said, to the cheers of the little crowd, while my classmates walked off toward the subway shaking their heads.

When the socialist Michael Harrington spoke to a small crowd outside Low Library on how, together, we had to build a socialist

America, I made so many caustic comments ("How's socialism doing in Britain these days, Mike?") that, after Harrington was finished, a man pulled me aside. Introducing himself as a New York detective, he asked me who I was; when I told him I was in Journalism School, he asked if I would be interested in filing occasional reports with the New York City police, on "left-wing activity" on campus.

"Just keep us up to date," he said.

"No can do," I said; "I don't have the time." What "left-wing activity" the detective had in mind, other than these orators outside Low Library, I didn't know.

To some of my classmates, however, I was becoming a caricature of myself. A final, satirical edition of the school "paper" had a montage of photographs; each class member was given an identifying word beneath his or her picture. Recalling the Christmas party, the editor had put beneath mine the single word: "Violence!"

Looking back, while I was indeed an oddity at that elite school — a right-wing student in a citadel of liberalism, a Goldwaterite studying to become a journalist, an educational product of nuns and Jesuits who accepted as true what Columbia regarded as mystical nonsense — it was they who were falling out of touch with America.

Repeatedly, students would come up to me and say, "Now, tell me, Pat, why did you hit Willenson?" When I told them the abusive language he had thrown into my face, it was clear that they felt this could not be the *real* reason. "It was political, wasn't it?" they would press.

But, my brothers and the friends I grew up with would have understood in a second. They would have reacted the same way; a thirty-second fistfight was no big deal. Indeed, their question to my classmates who accepted that kind of abusive language would have been, "Why the hell didn't you hit him?" To us, someone who threw that kind of language in your direction was insulting you and looking for a fight; and, if you took that without responding, something was wrong with you, not him. The only reason America sits still for the kind of abuse vomited upon us routinely at the U.N. is because, too often, we have had the wrong kind of Americans sitting there.

Philosophically and politically, the young-journalist and student-editor types at Columbia may have been compatible with the professors, but they and the professors were living in another country, as far as Middle America was concerned. The politicians they admired — Stevenson Democrats and Lindsay-Rockefeller Republicans — were on the way out. Both would become irrelevant, as the years went by; as would many of the causes in which they devoutly believed, like the U.N.

Half a century ago, the newsmen who wrote for major papers, as often as not, were high-school graduates or dropouts, tough men from working-class families who had never cut their roots, and who respected the values they had learned in neighborhood and home and church. In Washington, today, the journalists all come from somewhere else; but most consider themselves at home here. Part of our permanent governing elite now, they are never going back whence they came. But their views on social, political, and foreign policy issues are further and further removed from the convictions of the heartland. The gulf between the American people and their national press is not closing; it is widening; and the distance is breeding a distrust "out there" deeper than anything dreamed of in 1962.

With the spring of '62, student concerns turned to their future jobs. The *Washington Post* came around for interviews, and I signed up — only to get sidetracked into a foolish argument with the *Post* editor over their biased coverage of everybody from Joe McCarthy to Richard Nixon. (That "intensity of spirit" that Father McNamee had discerned was, once again, asserting itself.) The interview wasn't half finished, before I was all through. I would not be going home to D.C. The dean's prediction was coming true: "Pat, you have no experience; you will probably have to go out into the provinces."

Of the newspapers that came to Columbia to interview, only the *Charlotte Observer* seemed genuinely interested in me. Sometime in the spring, the class had been given an IQ test. While we weren't given our scores, I knew I had done well. There were fifty questions to be completed in twelve minutes, and while no one was expected to finish, I was on the last one, a complex accounting question, when time was called. I might have difficulty reading copy off a teleprompter or making up a front page, but IQ tests had always been a piece of cake. Then, the folks from the *Charlotte Observer* came to town; and when I asked to be interviewed, they were delighted. My "economic writing" background was exactly what they were looking for. Pete McKnight, the editor, and an associate invited me to a midtown hotel, to talk about my future and the *Charlotte Observer*.

When I arrived, they handed me a surprise test, to take in twelve minutes. When the clock started and I looked down, it was the same test I had taken only weeks before. I polished it off in nine minutes, walked out, and asked them what I should do when I finished their test. They looked at each other in amazement. Soon, there came a firm offer: If I would come down to Charlotte and work a full year on their business page, they could almost guarantee me I would be business editor of the *Charlotte Observer* by June of 1963. Pete McKnight's offer was gracious and tempting; but by the time it came, my employment search had been under way for weeks and was bearing fruit.

Studying *Editor and Publisher Yearbook,* I had carefully selected seventeen newspapers, from Oakland to Miami, which met four criteria: (A) The editor would be impressed that a Columbia graduate was writing, and thus would not automatically round-file the letter of application. (B) The paper was not so rich in talent that I would have to spend months doing obituaries or years reporting from the county court house. Thus, "second papers" in major cities were targeted. (C) The paper was large enough so that, if I wrote well, editors of the nation's top papers would see my work. (D) The paper should be at least moderately conservative. My résumé was pared down to less than two pages and fewer than 500 words (sound advice, kids), but it was carefully laid out, and the academic credentials and awards were all painted up. The accompanying letter, five terse paragraphs on a single page, left the impression that, from afar, I had developed a consuming interest in this community and in working for *this* paper. Night after night, I carefully and flawlessly typed those individual letters, attached two photographs that showed my face wouldn't frighten off sources, and sent out the package.

The strategy worked brilliantly. In a tight job market, four offers came back, which (in addition to Charlotte) I pruned to the *Albuquerque Journal* and the *St. Louis Globe-Democrat*. Warren Burkett, my second-semester adviser and an ex–AP correspondent from Texas, recommended Albuquerque. "Those Indians throw some wild parties," he said. But wild parties were not what I was interested in. When St. Louis told me they would like to interview me right away, and sent an airline ticket, I was deeply impressed. I had never been west of Pittsburgh.

Arriving at the Sheraton-Jefferson Hotel on Twelfth Street for the interview-lunch, I encountered a fortuitous coincidence. Not only were both interviewers Catholics, the executive editor of the *Globe-Democrat* was Charlie Pierson, a diminutive Irishman, one of whose sons had been sent away to a Jesuit-run high school in the distant suburbs of Washington. Was I familiar with a high school named Georgetown Prep, and the wild "Latinos" and diplomats' sons who went there? We were trading stories and laughing within fifteen minutes.

From that lunch till the day he died, Charlie Pierson and I were friends. While the business manager and later publisher, G. Duncan Bauman, seemed to think I was heavier on conservative philosophy than journalistic aptitude, he, too, felt they should hire me. In the class of '62, I was among the first to land a reporting job in daily journalism. Even the Columbia faculty seemed impressed. Judy Klemesrud and other classmates came by my desk and asked me how I had done it. When I told them of my research-and-targeting program, they asked for help with their own applications.

Though they might resent the comparison, the professors and teachers at Columbia inculcated the values of their "religion" into the students as determinedly as had the Jesuits.

Journalism was our vocation, we were taught; P.R. was "selling out." No courses in public relations were given at the school, and professors would have looked upon a student going directly into P.R. with the same sense of loss and waste the Jesuits would have viewed a Georgetown student who announced on graduation he had become an atheist. The teachers at the Journalism School had attitudes about income and wealth not dissimilar to those of the nuns and scholastics and priests who had taught me for the previous sixteen years. Money and material rewards were not the important things in life. If you believed they were, what were you doing at Columbia? (The students, however, talked privately of how Dave Jayne, the most successful '61 graduate, was already making $300 a week — on the air for ABC! This was an extraordinary salary for a journalist still in his early twenties. Years later, Dave Jayne and I became good friends; he was a bon vivant, a splendid fellow to spend an evening with; he was killed when the Lear jet carrying him, and his ABC footage, crashed during takeoff in the Middle East.)

Most of the teachers at Columbia had a bias toward the printed word. Electronic journalism was considered beneath the higher calling of the daily press. And if our graduate school was the novitiate of the higher journalism, the College of Cardinals was cloistered in the editorial offices off Times Square.

Among the final pieces of advice Dean Barrett gave us was to build, as soon as we arrived at our new place of employment, a "Go-to-Hell Fund." That some of us would have to resign on principle, he did not doubt. The fund would enable the idealistic graduate to march in and tell the editor or publisher where to go — when the principles learned at Columbia had been trampled upon. A word of caution, the dean added: Be certain, before you quit one job, the next job is already lined up. A publisher told where he could go is not a useful reference.

The final weeks at Columbia, the pressure abated and then disappeared, and I spent more time with Diane, who was graduating from Queens College with her degree in math. As we approached our final days at Columbia, with parturition near, even the somberest of the professors seemed to unload, temporarily, the weight of the world from their shoulders, and seemed to be more open, friendly, engaging, and even nostalgic. The class of '62 was a "great class," they now agreed; we all had "great promise." We should stick together. At least one of them became weepy.

Before taking the train home to Washington on graduation day, I checked out of the International House and spent the morning celebrating with Dick Oliver at the West End. In the afternoon in the World Room, some of the students, for the first time, brought their wives, and even children, from far away, to see their graduation and meet the professors and classmates with whom they had spent one of the most important years of their lives. But I left early; I was anxious to get home — and get on with my life.

Riding by train those five hours down the East Coast from Pennsylvania Station in New York to Union Station in Washington, I reflected on the nine months that had just ended. Choosing Columbia had been among the wisest decisions of my life. Not only had I made good friends there, friends for life, more important, having started far, far down the track, I had ended competitive with the best and brightest of the coming generation in American journalism. I had a master's degree from the most prestigious journalism school in America, a degree that could open doors the rest of my life. Most important, however, I had learned I could write; I could say what I believed and felt as well as any of my peers at Columbia, and better perhaps than most. In nine months of intense and hard work, I had more than made up the ground lost in my year's expulsion from Georgetown. That was now history. Full of self-confidence, I was now looking forward to St. Louis, to living in a part of America I had never seen, to a new experience.

Soon enough, they will know my name, I thought to myself. Ruminating on my future, as the slow train rumbled down that decrepit roadbed to Washington, I felt certain that all I needed now was one break, one big break, and I would be a syndicated columnist within ten years, with all America hearing and reacting to what I had to say. It was only a matter of time; there would be no stopping Prince Hal now.

10

St. Louis, 1962–1965

S T. LOUIS, in the early '60s, was both similar to and different from Washington.

Both were way stations for the black folk migrating from the rural South to the Northern cities during the Depression and World War II. Both had been segregated; and their populations were almost identical in size and racial composition. Both were river cities, where the summers were humid and hot and the winters bitter and cold, though in St. Louis the extremes were somewhat greater.

St. Louis had a larger concentration of poor, both black and white; its inner city was decaying, while Washington's was coming alive under JFK. Between the war's end in 1945 and 1962, not a single major new office building had been constructed in downtown St. Louis. At lunch hour, the area around 12th and Delmar, where the *Globe-Democrat* was located, seemed almost deserted, while Washington's downtown was bustling. In metropolitan St. Louis, the building boom was then taking place in "the county" (St. Louis County), which wrapped around the city and touched the Mississippi River north and south of the city. The affluent young were moving there, to Clayton and University City; and the rich had already moved out to townships like Ladue.

Where St. Louis in 1950 had been among the top ten U.S. cities in population size (ranked eighth), by 1980 it was not even in the top twenty-five. Also, St. Louis still had ethnic enclaves in 1962 — like the Germans in the south city and south county, and the Italians who lived on the Hill, or "Dago Hill," as it was called when Yogi Berra and Joe Garagiola grew up there.

Even though D.C. played host to the federal government, Washington was an apolitical town in 1962 compared to St. Louis, which was awash in politics — city, county, and state. Washington University, self-proclaimed "Harvard of the Midwest," was the area's academic center, more dominant than any university in the D.C. area, while Jesuit-run St. Louis University (like Georgetown in D.C.) was alma mater to the Catholic elite.

When I arrived in early June of 1962, knowing no one, with a salary of $93 a week ($73 a week take-home), the housing options were limited. The one place that paycheck could rent an acceptable apartment was south St. Louis, across the tracks from downtown. The want ads listed scores of apartments for $12 or $15 a week, or $60 a month. For several weeks, I moved from one to another, finally settling at 1624A Compton Street, across from a playground where I could run at night, and down the street from Frank & Em's, a neighborhood tavern where the student nurses from the south St. Louis hospitals came to relax.

At the *Globe-Democrat*, the job went well from the first day. Writing obits on Monday and Tuesday of my first week, by Wednesday I was covering speeches and competing with reporters for the *St. Louis Post-Dispatch*. When my first week was up, Charlie Pierson, the executive editor, came around to my desk and asked me to put in a few weeks on the business page. (The junior member of the two-man staff was taking all the vacation and overtime he had stored up.) Delighted, I said.

The business editor was Jim Cockrell, a bachelor and an intensely moody man in his mid-thirties, who had gone to the Medill School of Journalism at Northwestern. Jim loved trade talk and shop talk, but seemed to care about nothing much else; he gave me immense leeway. Each day, around 5 P.M., after we had produced the three business pages, I would walk the two blocks to the *St. Louis Post-Dispatch*, which housed the presses on which both newspapers were printed, and work directly with the printers. Nine months before, I hadn't known what a "lead" was, or what "typography" meant; now I was helping the printers make up a small slice of one of America's largest newspapers. It was challenging and exhilarating. Before 5 P.M., all of our copy had been written and edited, and sent by vacuum tube underground the two blocks to the linotype operators and the printers in the basement of the

Post. For the next hour, we could make late changes. Then we "locked up" the business pages for the bulldog edition (or "first country" as we called it), which hit the street about quarter after seven.

During the mornings, I would interview corporate executives and local financial leaders for feature articles; and during the afternoons, Jim and I would edit the wire copy and P.R. releases. Within two weeks, I had converted a short-items column into a personal by-lined column, to which I was routinely adding light editorial comment. The business and executive editors were pleased, and the publisher himself was said to be delighted with the new sprightliness of his business pages — and the city editor, George Killenberg, wandered over and asked when I would be returning to the news side.

As my "major paper" at Columbia (our substitute for a master's thesis) had been on expanding Canadian-Cuban trade — the commerce had tripled in 1961, the first year of the Kennedy embargo — I sold Cockrell on the idea of my rewriting the paper for the business page. "Get it down to twelve hundred words," Cockrell said, "and we'll run it."

Each day after work, I edited and retyped the paper, reshaping it for publication. After three evenings, one of the night copy editors came over.

"What are you working on — at this time of night?" he said.

I told him.

"You're charging overtime, I trust?" he said.

"You got to be kidding," I said; "Cockrell's doing me a favor publishing this thing." If you're not charging overtime, he told me caustically, you're in violation of guild rules. This was my first introduction to unionism; that "rim man" on the copy desk was shop steward for the *Globe-Democrat.* While he would later come to be one of my best friends, at that point he was a pain in the posterior, and I let him know it.

On the weekend of July 21–22, five weeks after arrival, my "exposé" led the business section under the eight-column banner, "Canada Sells to Red Cuba — and Prospers," with the overline, "Flouts U.S. Embargo." Fidel Castro had stolen $1 billion in American property, I wrote; yet, Canada's Trade Minister George Rees had sycophantically described these Communist thieves as "wonderful customers." "You can't do business with better businessmen anywhere," Rees had said.

Republican Senators John Tower of Texas, Prescott Bush of Connecticut (George's father), and Ken Keating of New York were quoted, as was the *Globe-Democrat*'s favorite Congressman, Tom Curtis of Webster Grove, Missouri. The piece closed with this bouquet to our northern neighbors: "Canada appears bent on . . . making herself the richest nation Khrushchev or his followers have to bury in the Western graveyard."

When I came to work the following Monday, the publisher, Richard H. Amberg, suddenly appeared at my desk. "That was a terrific piece you did on those Canadian bastards," he said; "we're delighted to have you here." Richard H. Amberg was well to the right of me.

Suddenly, the temperamental Cockrell seemed almost jealous. A loner with few friends and almost no interests other than his job, Cockrell had a mercurial personality. One minute, he was praising me to the skies and talking about going out to dinner together and discussing Hemingway, the next he would explode and demand I stop reading the newspaper at my desk whenever Charlie Pierson walked by.

"Jim," I said, "the only reason I'm reading the paper is that I've done all my work. If you've got some more editing or rewrite, give it to me."

And so he did. He piled on me every press release that came into the *Globe*; and I dutifully edited and rewrote every one, and sent the copy over to be set in type as "filler" — until, one day, Frank, our veteran printer, called up: "Pat, Frank here! Have you gone nuts over there? We couldn't cram all this crap into the paper in a month."

Cockrell stopped giving me copy to rewrite; I went back to reading the paper; and he sat there, fuming. At times, we were barely talking. I had just about made up my mind that if he hassled me once more (we sat only three feet from each other), I was going to show him what a sucker punch was. But Ray Vodicka from the copy desk, who could sense the tension in our tiny shop, came by and told me to cool it, that Cockrell's temperament was the reason the number-two job on the business page was almost always open.

Then, in late July, word went through the paper that John Costello, one of only two editorial writers, was quitting, leaving immediately for Washington and the USIA. Half his labor force suddenly gone, the editorial editor, Hamilton Thornton, was about to start running ads for a replacement in *Editor and Publisher*.

To Dick Amberg, a power in Missouri politics, who sometimes

dictated the lead editorial to his secretary, the page was of immense importance. Not only was it the voice of the *Globe-Democrat*; it was the voice of Richard H. Amberg, speaking *ex cathedra, urbi et orbi*. He used his newspaper, and its editorial page, to promote the causes and candidates he believed in, and to bedevil and defeat those he opposed. And it was a powerful and respected voice, in the state and the nation. Ten years earlier, Louis La Coss, the editorial editor of that day, had won a Pulitzer Prize for his philippic on American ethics in the wake of the cheating scandal at West Point.

Six weeks on the job, and, suddenly, here was the break I had dreamed of. I strolled back to the editorial editor's office, introduced myself, and asked to compete for the vacant position. "We're looking outside the paper," Hamilton Thornton told me, "for someone with experience, who can fill in as editorial editor when I go on vacations, and who can replace me when I retire." They had in mind a much older man, a veteran editorial writer, not some twenty-three-year-old fresh from college — that was the message he left me with. Fine, I said, would you mind, sir, if I volunteered some editorials, written "in my spare time"?

A bald-headed, soft-spoken, pipe-smoking, slow-talking "Missourah" gentleman near sixty, the publisher's exact opposite in demeanor and temperament, Hamilton Thornton was among the most gracious men on the paper. "Certainly, I'll take a look at them, Pat," he said. That was all the opening I needed.

As soon as noon came, I would hustle across the street to a diner, wolf down a sandwich, and write out short editorials in longhand. Returning early, I would type them up and take them back to Hamilton Thornton. He began running them regularly. After ten days of moonlighting at noon, Ham Thornton came by my desk, and invited me to come back and write editorials full-time — until the new man was hired. Eight weeks after getting off that train in St. Louis, I was ensconced in one of the five offices on the north wall of the fifth floor, between the publisher and editorial editor on one side and the executive editor on the other. I decided it wasn't me who was going back to the newsroom.

Every day, I arrived earlier than the senior writer, produced more copy, and left later. The pressure was on. Occasionally, now, my editorials were leading the paper; and the publisher and his conservative and corporate friends were sitting up and taking notice of the enhanced muzzle velocity of the *St. Louis Globe-Democrat*.

When a thousand telegraphers at the Chicago & North Western Railroad went on strike, suddenly imperiling the economy of the Middle West, I asked Mr. Thornton to let me write the lead editorial. "The publisher will probably want to write that one, Pat," he said, but "he hasn't called; so, give it a try."

In a 600-word lead editorial titled "The Public Be Damned," I followed the wise counsel Westbrook Pegler had once given a young journalist who asked what was the proper posture a newsman should take toward a politician. "Stand flat on your feet," Pegler had responded, "and swing for the belly!"

That's what I did. "In a selfish cold-blooded strike, George Leighty's union is destroying this railroad for not acceding to its outrageous ultimatum. . . . Many telegraphers do nothing in useless offices while their old tasks are done by machines." (Leighty's men had been offered sixteen and a half months of severance pay, moving expenses, travel costs to search for new jobs, and preference in new hiring and retraining programs. Their strike demand: guaranteed jobs for life.)

Calling the strike "Big Labor's answer to . . . technological change," I coldly detailed the injury being done to hundreds of thousands of people by the thousand strikers: ". . . today, 35,000 Chicago commuters travel clogged freeways, two-thirds of Wisconsin's pulp and paper industry shuts down, timber in Michigan piles up beside the tracks, lumberjacks await layoffs, grain elevators are idle in Nebraska and Minnesota and the Midwestern economy grinds to a sluggish halt. . . ." Then, I rolled into my peroration: " 'To hell with America, with the Midwest, with the President's board and the President, with Mr. Goldberg and Mr. Wirtz, with the problems of thousands of people, with everybody,' Mr. Leighty is saying. . . . 'My friends and I demand insured income for life.' "

"I see where the publisher cut loose this morning," one of the female reporters said to me, laughing, the next morning when she came back to our office.

"No," I said, "he wasn't here yesterday; that was my contribution."

She was startled; and the crowd at the city desk was astonished at the right-wing vehemence of the youthful graduate of the ultraliberal Columbia School of Journalism. Into the *Globe* switchboard, however, and on into the publisher's office, the calls were pouring, in praise of us having given Leighty's union the hell it deserved. (Even in retrospect, it was an outrageous strike.) And the publisher dropped by to compliment me.

Soon, however, the ads in *Editor and Publisher* paid off; Mike Bradshaw, former editorial editor of the *Toledo Blade*, a man of Hamilton Thornton's generation and graciousness, arrived and was immediately named deputy editorial editor. Now, there were three editorial writers crammed into that office barely large enough for two; and we were churning out, along with the publisher and Mr. Thornton, more copy than the editorial page could possibly publish. With Mike Bradshaw permanently hired, the pressure was now on me — and the senior man. One of us was redundant.

At the editorial meetings each morning at eleven, I was junior man, which meant that before my turn came to speak, every juicy topic had been discussed and assigned — to someone else. Weeks of feverish competition ensued, ending one Monday morning in September, when I came into the office and found the senior writer's desk had disappeared. He had been "sent back to rewrite."

Three months out of journalism school, at twenty-three, I was the youngest editorial writer on a major paper in the United States; and I was intoxicated with my success. Six months before, Betsy Wade, the *Times* copy editor, had written about me, "He seems to have no motive power of his own." Proud of what I had accomplished — but with no one in St. Louis to share the triumph — I decided to drop Dean Barrett a note. "I clear about $73 a week," I wrote him, "put $15 into the Go-to-Hell Fund, $15 in a car fund, $15 for rent, leaving $28 for eating, drinking, and being merry." About the new job, my exultation came through: "Some of my ideas would and did bring cries of 'fascist' from the more liberal-minded group I left at school, but here, they just get the editorial nod of approval. I am ideologically at home . . . this is one of the few papers left where I can swallow the editorials along with my lunch. . . . Mr. Thornton says to hit as hard as I like, which is like a license to kill."

After I sent a package of editorials home and phoned, my mother was elated at the elevation, and Pop paid me his highest journalistic compliment: "Some of them are as good as Pegler."

Editorial freedom at the *Globe-Democrat* was extraordinary. Each of us wrote in his own style on what we cared deeply about; and, now, everything we wrote went into the paper.

Decades before the term was invented, I was an ardent supply-sider. In November of 1962, in a lead editorial, I urged President Kennedy to forgo his social spending plans and, instead, "to revise the tax system and let the unchained economy pull itself to its feet and government revenues along with it. . . .

"The corporate [income tax] rate of 52 per cent and the personal rates which run from 20 per cent to a confiscatory maximum of 91 per cent should obviously be cut as soon as possible, not as a temporary shot in the arm of a sluggish economy, but as a permanent necessity if America's growth is to keep abreast of the world." (Which was the course Kennedy eventually followed, as did Ronald Reagan, twenty years later, producing the two greatest booms of the postwar era.)

We never even bothered to ask the publisher whether he favored cutting taxes — in the teeth of a deficit. Driving down the Daniel Boone Highway, six months later, I recall thinking, 'What an incredible country — where, at twenty-four, I can criticize the mayor of St. Louis and the Governor of Missouri, and admonish the President of the United States, before an audience of 300,000; and no one, but the publisher and the marketplace, can shut me up."

The only formal advice I ever received about my writing, and sound advice it was, came from Mr. Thornton. "Pat, I notice you keep using the phrases 'the American people will not tolerate' and 'the American people will never support,' " he said. "Why don't you drop them? You see, I think the American people are not only going to 'tolerate' a lot of these Democratic programs; they're going to enjoy them. Now, you can speak for yourself; you can speak for the *Globe-Democrat*; but, neither you nor I speak for the American people."

Wise counsel for editorial writers of all ages.

Reading back over my file of clips, from a quarter-century ago (they are not remotely the equal of Westbrook Pegler either in quality of the writing or the savagery of the commentary), a stark difference stands out from the editorial commentary of today. Even though we were among the most conservative papers in America, there is a deference and respect routinely accorded the President, whether JFK or LBJ, that has since disappeared from American political discourse.

Liberal and leftist assaults upon Ronald Reagan today (and conservative counterattacks upon Congress) are much more cutting and derogatory than anything we ever wrote about Presidents Kennedy and Johnson. (We had heard stories from our Washington bureau that LBJ was "drinking a quart a day," but nothing like that — or about JFK's romances — was ever even alluded to.) We live in a cruder, coarser age than the Eisenhower-Kennedy-Johnson era from 1953 to 1965.

Part of the reason for the brutality of modern political warfare is, I believe, the metamorphosis of politics into something like religious faith. For thousands of journalists, intellectuals, ideologues, and office-holders in Washington, who set America's political style in the national capital, politics has become central to their lives. They live it, breathe it, and some almost die when expelled from its innermost concentric circles.

Another reason is that we Americans no longer agree on much of anything — on a common code of morality, or a common idea of patriotism, or a common view of the world. And less and less do we like one another. In national politics, it is no longer enough that one's adversaries be defeated; now, they must be disgraced, humiliated, impeached, imprisoned. Our political quarrels — more and more defined as "moral issues" — have taken on a savagery once associated with religious wars.

Reading back over those conservative editorials, I also see a clear philosophical line from there to here, a consistency I do not believe could be found comparing, say, the editorials of the *New York Times* in 1962 and the *Times* editorials of 1988. There is nothing I wrote then I could not easily defend now. It is liberalism that has changed its meaning.

In the summer of 1962, JFK was perhaps the world's leading anti-Communist, a hawk on defense who was building a new strategic deterrent that included a thousand land-based missiles and a thousand B-52s. He was for cutting taxes in the teeth of a deficit, and was sending thousands of military advisers into South Vietnam to prop up the anti-Communist Diem regime. He was the presidential patron of the Green Berets; and, though we did not know it, he was secretly plotting the elimination of Fidel Castro. On the day of his death, JFK was about to deliver a speech calling this generation of Americans the "watchmen on the walls of freedom." Compare that record, and that rhetoric, with the 1988-style liberalism of his younger brother, Edward M. Kennedy.

(There is one editorial I may yet have some trouble with, however. One fall, I wrote an endorsement for an unknown young Democratic reformer running for the Illinois legislature. Even though liberal, the bespectacled young man had the nerve to come in and ask for the endorsement of the Midwest bastion of conservatism, and to make a persuasive case. The former state representative is now U.S. Senator Paul Simon, candidate for his party's nomination for President of the United States.)

After establishing permanent residence on the editorial page, I decided to introduce myself to the *Globe*'s rising star on the "news side," Denny J. Walsh. Walsh, who had just won the St. Louis Press Club award as the outstanding young journalist in the city, was already a formidable character in the newsroom. In his middle twenties, an inch or two shorter than I, Walsh was about fifty pounds heavier and was rarely seen without a cigar clenched between his teeth. A former Marine and Los Angeles cab driver, who treasured his Teamster's card, Walsh had the tenacity of a pit bull and seemed to be developing some of the facial features of the breed. Already a feared figure in the city, Walsh could not unfairly have been described by the phrase "a hardhat with a degree." His laugh was loud and uncontrolled and bordered on the malicious, and he had reached what Murray Kemptom once described as "that point in life when one's greatest pleasures lie in the misfortunes of others." When Walsh sank his teeth into a politician, he usually did serious damage, and he was always reluctant to let go.

The excuse I used to introduce myself was to congratulate Walsh on his award. He nodded pleasantly, flicked his cigar on the city room floor, and said: "I'm impressed. Three months here — and already you've got permanent quarters north of the john." Then he nodded over in the direction of the ex–editorial writer I had displaced, and said, "They pumped twenty pounds of brains into his head, told him he was an editorial writer, and it didn't take."

Walsh and I hit it off immediately.

With the exception, however, of a mutual fondness for colorful writing, we were utterly different in our journalistic interests. I was interested in the world of ideas, issues, philosophy, and foreign policy, and didn't care in the least about scandals; but Walsh loved them. He was a reporter, first, last, and always, a genuinely nonideological journalist; he viewed politics the way he viewed sports: he loved the foibles and follies, the stories and anecdotes, and he was as fond of the old-style Democratic pols and their shenanigans as the Columbia professors were of the reformers. A born investigative reporter, Walsh would have made a great detective, in real life or on the screen.

Bob Jackson, a *Globe* reporter and contemporary (now with the *Los Angeles Times*'s Washington bureau), relished how — with an incriminating letter in hand — Walsh would phone the politician who had written it, and sandbag him. "Senator, there's a nasty report around that you wrote a letter recommending a friend for a state contract, without competitive bidding. Nothing to that, is there, Senator? Just checking."

The Senator would assure Walsh this was malicious gossip.

Commiserating, Walsh might ask who could have started such a rotten rumor?

His confidence growing, the politician might volunteer, "off the record," the name of some enemy.

Walsh would then pause, clear his throat loud enough to alert the entire city room that he was about to spring his trap, and then say loudly, "Senator, I am holding a letter purportedly signed by you; I wonder if I might read it to you, and get your reaction."

After the embarrassed politician got off the line, Walsh's laughter would fill the city room. Within half a decade, he would win the Pulitzer Prize for ferreting out corruption in the north county steamfitters' union, and join *Life* magazine's celebrated and controversial team of investigative reporters. In 1971, when Walsh was an usher in my wedding, I noted that he was then being sued for libel by the Governor of Ohio for $6 million and by the mayor of St. Louis for $12 million.

"Walsh, I don't recall you having that kind of money when we roomed together in St. Louis," I said to him.

"Oh, Pat, you can make it," Walsh said, "if you just put a little bit away every payday." Walsh collected a dozen libel suits, and never lost one.

By September of '62, I was producing more copy than anyone on the page; and my editorials were routinely leading the paper. So, I went to Charlie Pierson for a raise. While $93 a week gross was a living wage, I said, it hardly seemed appropriate for someone setting editorial policy for the paper. Charlied jumped me to $118 a week, the third-year guild scale. As soon as he delivered the good news, I went out and bought something I had always dreamed of owning — a new, fire-engine red, British TR-3 roadster convertible. With the $1,000 I still owed on the student loan, and the $3,000 I owed on the Triumph, I could probably have been classified as near-poor; but I cannot recall being happier.

My friend, former Harvard professor Edward Banfield, author of *The Unheavenly City*, was right. To view poverty simply as an economic condition, to be measured by statistics, is simplistic, misleading, and false; poverty is a state of mind, a matter of horizons. My income may have been meager, but my horizons were now limitless — unlike those of the black folks being left behind in St. Louis's central city, and the "Hoosiers" who lived all around me.

I had never heard the term before.

To St. Louisans, Hoosier did not mean someone from Indiana; it meant rural people, ex-farmers and ex-farmhands, displaced by the mechanization of American agriculture, who had come into the city, like the black folks, from southern Illinois and southeast Missouri, the famous "Bootheel." They were the lost souls of the big city. The white-collar crowd at Frank & Em's laughed at the blue-collar Hoosiers, who never came into that middle-class, white-collar bar, but they respected their toughness. "We're safe down here in south St. Louis in case of a race riot," the regulars used to joke, "because, before the niggers ever reach us, they'll have to run over the Hoosiers, and the Hoosiers are tougher."

And they were a tough and hardy people. As I had no friends those first two months except Rich Koster, the young sportswriter who was first to stop by my desk and introduce himself, I took to visiting, on foot, the bars down closer to the river, where the Hoosiers did their drinking and dancing and courting. In the "Hoosier bars," they played only country and hillbilly music; and fights were constantly breaking out, almost always over their women.

On some Friday and Saturday nights, before I bought the Triumph, I would pile into one of their cars and we would drive over to Collinsville Avenue in East St. Louis, Illinois, where there were honky-tonks on every block, and live music was played until all hours of the morning. One Friday night, Walsh and I went over to Collinsville Avenue and, at the 400 Club, while the Hoosiers were dancing early into the morning, one of them threw up all over the floor. His lady friend waited until he had stopped retching, then they went back to dancing again. After the song was over, somebody brought out a mop. As we left, there was another mess out on the front step, and Walsh observed as we gingerly stepped around it, "That fella who came out of here ahead of us, Pat; he just went and came apart right in front of me." This was a long way from Chevy Chase.

On Sunday evenings (Missouri was dry on Sundays; across the river in Illinois, however, it was wet), I used to walk down to Jefferson Avenue and Lafayette, and peer into the storefront churches; there, you could see them, men and women together on stage, singing their hearts out to Jesus in repeated refrains and asking forgiveness for all they had done the night before. It was a moving and memorable scene. I had never been in these storefront Protestant churches before, and it is hard to remember those folks, whom the world had passed by and left together in their loneliness, without recalling the passage from Steinbeck's *Grapes of Wrath*: "And because they were lonely and perplexed, because they had all come from a place of sadness and worry and defeat, and because they were all going to a new mysterious place, they huddled together; they talked together; they shared their lives, their food, and the things they hoped for in the new country."

Unlike the Okies, though, the Hoosiers weren't going to any "new country"; for them, south St. Louis was the end of the line. As though it were yesterday, I recall glancing into the bar mirror of the Ohio Grill at the face of a huge man of almost fifty, who sat, drinking for hours on end, tears welling up in his eyes and running down his face, the jukebox blaring away some sad country songs.

After I bought my TR-3 and started dating dark-haired Marie from Maryville, whom Rich Koster and his future wife, Pat, had introduced me to, I changed my "life-style." Marie had grown up in Bethesda, gone to Visitation, knew Crick and had met Hank, and had heard reports on me, not all of them positive, from girlfriends back home; she was intrigued. A senior at Maryville in 1962–63, she laughed easily and loved a good time. Now, it was tennis in the park, double-dating with Koster on Gaslight Square, and float trips with Marie on the Current River in the Ozarks — no more nights listening to Ferlin Husky and Webb Pierce in the Hoosier bars of south St. Louis.

During those first six months in St. Louis, I had a second collision with the Newspaper Guild. The *Globe-Democrat* was not a "closed shop," but it was a "union shop." We did not have to belong to the Newspaper Guild to be hired, but we were forced to join as soon as we came to work. I had never believed in compulsory unionism; nevertheless, I accepted the rules. They had, after all, been set before I arrived.

But, in December of 1962, New York Printers Union boss Bertram A. Powers struck all nine newspapers in the big city, and the New York Newspaper Guild voted to honor the picket lines. Anyone who knew the economic crisis the business was then in, nationwide, knew that indefinite shutdown of nine newspapers meant a permanent loss in circulation, and probable death for one or more of the weaker sisters. In editorial after editorial, I berated Powers and his printers for the selfishness and stupidity of the strike, and the New York Newspaper Guild for honoring the picket lines and thus threatening the survival of the newspapers for which they worked.

The St. Louis guild voted to assess all local members to support our idle brothers in New York. When the shop steward came around to collect — for our retroactive assessments — I refused to pay. The total was six dollars, but they weren't going to get ten cents, voluntarily. If the assessments were mandated by my contract, fine; but I wasn't ponying up to support the most destructive strike in the history of American journalism. My resistance was not rooted in simple obduracy. We had been taught at Columbia that the death of any paper was a death in the family, a tragedy, which destroyed forever the jobs of our fellow journalists and stilled forever an independent voice the people had a right to hear.

The angry guild representatives went to the publisher, who told me that, if I didn't make the contribution, they could kick me out of the union. If they did, the publisher said, he would be forced, under the contract, to fire me. I pondered that — and decided to hold out. Either the publisher paid on my behalf or the guild felt the six dollars wasn't worth the aggravation; because, from then until I left the paper, my union card was stamped "Not in Good Standing."

Ultimately, in matters like this, it comes down to where one's *primary* loyalty lies. The guild had not gotten me my job; I had gotten my own job. The union, I felt, had no legitimate claims upon me, other than the contractual ones. In withholding that piddling sum, I felt I was standing with my principles and being more loyal to my profession and to its best interests than were they. I wasn't going to subordinate my beliefs — to their majority vote.

The longer I remained in St. Louis, however, the better I came to know the guild militants; they were some of the best men and women on the paper. They had a sense of community and solidarity, they shared the same values I did, and they were romantic about the old battles and heroes who had sustained the guild for three decades. But we had different priorities. I wasn't interested in maximizing my income; I wanted the opportunity to write. They seemed wedded to an us-versus-them militancy more suited to the 1930s, when the fight was about whether a man could feed his family, while working for a newspaper. Had I been there in the '30s, I would have been with them. But these were the '60s; and newspapers were dying with dismal regularity. Any man with open eyes could see that. With television gobbling up our ad dollars, with suburban papers biting into our circulation, with salary costs soaring, we faced a necessary choice: Either we could all sink together, or we could save our newspapers by modernizing and by reducing our labor force. When I went over at five in the afternoon to make up the business pages, in the noisy press room of the *Post-Dispatch*, dozens of linotype operators and printers were smoking and joking. They had nothing at all to do. Others were making up ad pages, then throwing the type away — because the advertisers had already sent over pre-prepared rubber mats.

In the months following that devastating 114-day New York newspaper strike, the *Journal-American* went under, with 400,000 subscribers aboard, to be followed by the *New York Mirror* and the *New York Herald-Tribune* and the *New York World Telegram & Sun*. And there we were in St. Louis, assisting our bullheaded brethren in New York in bringing off that disaster.

For the three and a half years I spent in St. Louis, the great domestic issue was civil rights.

The glory days of the Montgomery bus boycott and the freedom rides were over; and illegal demonstrations were now routine in St. Louis. The position of the *Globe-Democrat* was unequivocal: We were against illegal demonstrations. There was none of this "on the one hand, on the other"; we unloaded. When young Bill Clay (now a Congressman) and his coterie from the Committee on Racial

Equality (CORE) sat in at the Jefferson Bank — in violation of a court order — we urged stiff jail sentences for the lot of them; and that's what they got.

At the inner-city rallies, Clay & Co. used to denounce the *Globe-Democrat* — Amberg, Walsh, and Buchanan by name — as they sang chorus after chorus of "We Shall Not Be Moved." When I ran into Clay at the Bismarck Cafe on 12th Street one evening, he called out from his booth, "How's it going, Poison Pen?" One afternoon, his sympathizers showed up outside the *Globe*, chained our doors, and burned our newspapers in wire trash cans on the sidewalk. A manifestation of their regard.

On the civil rights bill of 1964, we were not far from the Goldwater position. Segregation was wrong; we didn't believe in it; we didn't practice it at the *Globe* and people who did ought to put a stop to it; but in his choice of customers and friends, a local proprietor had a constitutional right to be wrong. Freedom meant the freedom to choose, even if one chose to be a bigot.

To me, the most powerful arguments Roy Wilkins and the civil-rights community mustered for federal legislation were two: First, when the exercise of individual freedom by *millions* of whites, not just a bigoted handful, results in denial to a whole class of Americans of their freedom to travel and associate, the federal government had a duty to step in. Second, as many of America's new hotels and motels were booming because of a *federal* highway system to which the tax dollars of minority Americans had also contributed, the federal government had a right to step in.

On the question of Ollie's Barbecue and the corner tavern, I thought Goldwater was right. Even if the local proprietor was wrong in what he was doing, i.e., discriminating, he was beyond the reach of the federal government; just as the Muslim restaurants in central St. Louis, which kept out whites, were beyond its reach.

But the national civil-rights movement — even given the questionable tactics the local free-lancers employed — had the moral high ground. They were victorious, ultimately, because America is a good country; and because they deserved to win. They were asking that federal law reflect the New Testament teaching about how a man should treat his brother; and Edmund Burke was no match for that.

On civil rights and race relations, the publisher, from another generation, was a much harder man than I. When I wrote an editorial telling Judiciary Chairman Jim Eastland to cut the hijinks and get on with the nomination of Thurgood Marshall to the Federal Appellate Court, the publisher came by to let me know I had made a mistake; there were good reasons to block the Marshall nomination.

A great admirer of J. Edgar Hoover, the publisher was in regular contact with the FBI, and we were among Hoover's conduits to the American people. Through Amberg, the FBI channeled us constant information on local Communists, radicals, and even national civil-rights leaders. The bureau's penetration of the local Communist party and the extreme Left in St. Louis was something to behold. We knew their schedules as well as they did. Truly, speaking of the Far Left, J. Edgar Hoover could say, with near biblical certitude in those years, that "Where two or three are gathered together, there I am amongst you."

One day, the publisher handed me seven pages of single-spaced reportage on the travels and associations, with leftist and Communist-front groups, of the Reverend Martin Luther King, Jr., and told me to write a lead editorial based on the information. There was no attribution. Reading it over, I told him some of the material was close to libelous; we could be sued if it wasn't true. I needed time to double-check. "We need documentation, sir, other than seven sheets of unsourced paper."

"You write the editorial," Amberg said. "I'll take the responsibility."

I had not the least doubt that the bureau was our source.

None of the material, however, dealt with King's sexual escapades, although the publisher let Walsh and me know what he thought of King ("the morals of a tomcat"), based on what his friends at the bureau had told him. (What we did not know out in St. Louis was that, with the knowledge of Attorney General Robert Kennedy, and on the orders of President Johnson, Dr. King's phones were being tapped and his rooms bugged; the salacious personal material thus scooped up was being disseminated by LBJ's top aides in the White House to key members of his administration and the national press. And much of Washington knew it. It was not liberalism's finest hour. It was a genuinely nasty piece of business, bordering on official blackmail. Long before he got to Memphis, Martin Luther King had been the target of an assassination attempt — ordered by, approved of, and fully known to men who would later take great public pride in the contributions they made during the struggle for civil rights.)

At the *Globe-Democrat*, we supported and defended the police and the FBI; and they, in turn, depended on us and fed us. They had a friend in the *Globe-Democrat*, and they knew it. Once, when I was stopped late at night, while driving carefully, but suspiciously, home to my apartment, I handed my *Globe-Democrat* press card to the officer, along with my driver's license. He straightened up: "Mr. Buchanan, can you make it home; or do you want one of us to drive you?"

"Thanks, officer, I'm fine," I said.

He saluted and drove off. That month, we had battled editorially for a pay raise for the county police.

Partly as a consequence of Barry Goldwater's vote against the landmark Civil Rights Act of 1964, the Republican party's share of the black vote fell to less than 10 percent in 1964. In the five elections since — three of them Republican landslides — the GOP share of the black vote has never risen. Today, the gulf between black America and the conservative movement is greater than ever. To much of the black leadership, this is explained by "racism," the supposedly ingrained hostility of conservatives toward black people — because they are black.

But that does not make sense. The conservatives who oppose Ben Hooks of the NAACP on his entire political and social agenda are also the foremost champions of Jonas Savimbi, the most charismatic black warrior-leader on the continent of Africa. The root of the quarrel can be found, rather, in our conflicting "visions" of America.

Back in 1964, in a blunt essay titled "The Negro Revolution," longshoreman-philosopher Eric Hoffer, writing about his fellow dockhands, said, "The voice of the Negro revolution grates on us and fills us with scorn. . . . The simple fact is that the people I have lived and worked with all my life and who make up about 60 percent of the population outside the South, have not the least feeling of guilt about the Negro. . . . Our hands are more gnarled and workbroken than his, and our faces are more lined and worn. . . ."

Here, I believe, we approach the heart of the matter.

Most of the white working and middle class has an altogether different sense of shame, a different sense of guilt, and a different sense of remorse than liberal America, to which Mr. Hooks and Senator Kennedy and Mario Cuomo belong.

To us, sin is personal, not collective; it is a matter for personal confession, personal contrition, personal reconciliation with God. Our sense of shame and sense of guilt are about what we have done ourselves, our own transgressions against our own moral code. We have no sense of guilt about Wounded Knee; because we weren't *at* Wounded Knee. If we suffer from what the Jesuits used to call a "scrupulous conscience," it is not about "colonialism, neo-colonialism, imperialism, racism," and all the collective sins for which the United States is routinely condemned at the United Nations. Collective guilt is an affliction from which liberals suffer acutely; we do not.

Asked about the town-house rendezvous between Donna Rice and Gary Hart, Jesse Jackson replied huffily that the crucial moral question was not adultery, but where one stood on apartheid. Conservatives howled with laughter — not because Jesse Jackson was black, but because that is a quintessentially liberal response.

Again and again in politics, I have seen this fundamental difference, over this matter of guilt, manifest itself. One night, in 1967, watching on television the riveting footage of the riots tearing apart Newark, New Jersey, my anguished colleagues from the Nixon office were saying, "We've got to get some money in there." My reaction was, "We'd better get some troops in there."

Their feeling was that the only conceivable explanation (and justification) of this collective rampage had to be some collective injustice — of which *we* were surely guilty, and which *we* had a moral obligation to redress. My feeling was that the root cause of the riots in the 1960s was the rioters in the '60s. The burning and looting of Newark no more created some moral obligation upon me to meet the looters' "demands," than did the student rampage at Columbia, the "Days of Rage" in Chicago, or the May Day hell-raising in Washington, D.C.

Here, I think, is the source of much of the rage, resentment, and misunderstanding between conservatives and the civil-rights community. They argue, with anger and passion and conviction, that America has been an unjust country and remains a racist society; that because we are white, we have a moral obligation to hear them out, to redress their grievances, to accept their demands, to use the power of government to make us all equal in result. We do not agree. For us — despite the sins in America's past, whether slavery or segregation, mistreatment of the Irish immigrants or Native Americans — America is among God's great gifts to mankind. She is a good country — for all of us — and deserves to be defended, by all of us. Here, 28 million black people have achieved a measure of material prosperity and human freedom they have found nowhere else on earth. While Mr. Hooks's stance toward America is accusatory and condemnatory; ours is reverential. That is why the collisions have come, and will continue to come. Our disagreement is far more fundamental than race; it is about America.

The decision to go to the *Globe-Democrat* was one I never regretted; my research at Columbia had proven flawless. While the *Post-Dispatch* had a larger circulation (350,000 to our 320,000 daily), we had the morning position; we had a core staff of young journalists like Walsh and Jackson and Al Delugach and Jack Flach in Jefferson City, the state capital, and Dennis McCarthy in the county, that was superior to theirs; and, while we were outmanned (they had eleven correspondents in Washington to our one, six editorial writers to our two), they were outhustled, and everybody in St. Louis knew it.

The *Globe* was a great place to work. All our copy was produced on one floor of that big old building at 12th and Delmar, and reporters were constantly coming back with anecdotes and jokes, which moved through the staff every day. There was a delightful democratic cast to the news operation; sixty-year-old copy editors and fifty-year-old rewrite men laughed and joked as equals with twenty-five- and thirty-five-year-old reporters. Everyone, except the senior editors, was on a first-name basis; there was camaraderie and spirit; we were number two, but we were closing. (While there were no black reporters or writers while I was there, there were women reporters, writers, editors in almost every department, except the sports page.)

Since its purchase by S. I. Newhouse several years before, the newspaper had been recast in the image of its publisher, Richard H. Amberg. "The difference between a thermometer and a thermostat," the publisher used to tell me, "is that a thermometer tells you what the temperature is; and a thermostat does something about it. The *Globe-Democrat* is a thermostat!"

It was also the personal megaphone of the publisher, a bull of a man in his early fifties, with white hair, a florid countenance, and a big voice, a conservative of strong opinions and stronger rhetoric. (It was Mr. Amberg's blast at the Nobel Prize–winning Dr. Linus Pauling, not mine, that cost us some cold cash in a libel suit.) When Richard H. Amberg demanded a million-dollar median strip on Lindbergh Boulevard — a dangerous stretch of highway in the county that he regularly rode to the airport and on which a friend had been killed — he got the median strip.

Amberg had come to St. Louis from Syracuse, was highly regarded in the Newhouse organization (which had saved the *Globe* several years before, after a strike), and was a tremendous booster of the city. A friend of Herbert Hoover and General MacArthur, whom he idolized (we endlessly campaigned to have the five-star General given a sixth star that no other American military figure had ever received), Amberg was close to the business community, and dedicated to reversing the city's economic decline.

When he had a cause that needed advancing, or a poltroon who needed attacking, he assigned Walsh to get the story and me to write the editorial. One morning, he walked into my office, threw down a copy of the *Post-Dispatch*, wherein some liberal had misstepped, and roared, "Pat, I want you to cut this bastard from rectum to belly button."

"I'm already working on him, sir," I answered.

On idle days, we would pick fights with the *Post-Dispatch*, attacking one of their editorials or news stories. The rivalry was intense, robust, and healthy. At the Press Club in the McKinley Hotel, acerbic old Ernie Kirsten, senior editorial writer at the *Post-Dispatch* and author (*Catfish and Crystal*), would wait for us to show up at 6:30, and make insulting comments — and we would reciprocate in kind.

It was the time of the Cassius Clay–Sonny Liston fights, and Kirsten said one night, "Boxing is a barbaric sport! It ought to be abolished. Your editorial defense of it is outrageous and disgusting."

"You say that Ernie, first, because you never had to put on the gloves; and, second, because it's not your door of opportunity that's gonna be slammed shut, when you abolish the sport." (Looking today at Muhammed Ali, I think Ernie at least had an argument.)

Ernie often turned personal, and once, having heard enough, I responded: "Ernie, I'm not going to sit here arguing with a man who has me by fifty years and five martinis." Walsh and I walked out.

The competition between the two papers was sometimes bitter, but almost always beneficial to the city. The *Globe* was, in those years, the most conservative paper in America, with the possible exception of Bill Loeb's *Manchester* (N.H.) *Union-Leader*, which used to reprint my editorials; and the *Post-Dispatch* was to the left of the *Washington Post*, outlandishly liberal for Middle America. (Years later, it was revealed there had existed, all this time, a secret deal between the Pulitzer family, which owned the *Post*, and the Newhouse organization, to split the profits. The secret arrangement was apparently legal under a federal law that permitted endangered newspapers to collaborate to survive. We knew nothing about the deal; everyone I knew at the *Globe* was shocked when the news broke after I left. Unwittingly, we had all been working our hearts out to win a great struggle, the outcome of which — a perpetual draw — had already been fixed in advance.)

To my knowledge, S. I. Newhouse, Sr., who was not much over five feet high and who used to visit the *Globe* with his son and namesake (we called them "upper case" and "lower case"), never tampered with editorial policy — except once. And that intervention had to do with the most important position the *Globe* took in my years there — the presidential endorsement of 1964.

If the civil-rights movement was the place for liberals to be in the early '60s, for young conservatives, it was the grass-roots movement to capture the Republican nomination for Barry Goldwater.

Not six months after Nixon's defeat, I was already openly championing the cause of the junior Senator from Arizona. Goldwater's appeal, before November 22, 1963, was immense; and it is easy to recollect.

The Democratic party had been captured by Jack Kennedy, wealthy, Eastern, pragmatically liberal — *beau ideal* of a new breed of politician and a new generation. In Washington, his coterie, the Best and the Brightest, ruled the roost. But JFK's hesitancy and incompetence at the Bay of Pigs, his weak performance at the Vienna summit, his acquiescence in the Berlin Wall, told us, nine months into his term, this was not the man to lead the West. Parodying his Pulitzer Prize–winning *Profiles in Courage*, the same placard was rising at every Kennedy rally: "Less Profile, More Courage."

In the Republican party, Eisenhower was a revered figure and Nixon a respected figure, but we conservatives now felt it time to move on. While Eisenhower had been an excellent President, who had presided over a marvelous time of peace and prosperity in America — an era the like of which we had not seen since the '20s — a twenty-two-year-old in 1960 could not "identify" with this septuagenarian father figure from a previous era. Ike's penchant for obfuscating issues, his Big Business cronies, his disinclination to confront the Democrats, his aversion to ideas, his golfing holidays, his passive presidency, were not what we were looking for.

In a sense, JFK, with his youth, his energy, his dash, and his disparagement of the '50s as a dowdy, unimaginative time, was responsible for downgrading Ike and his era; and the young President unsettled us more than he imagined. His campaign of 1960 was all about the politics of dissatisfaction and the politics of promise. "Good-bye to all that!" JFK was saying, "We're off to the New Frontier." He raised hopes no politics or policies could satisfy. Black and white, Left and Right, he stirred us all up.

"If they can take over their party, we can take over ours," was the attitude among young conservatives. Barry Goldwater joined in disparaging the days gone by. When Milton Eisenhower had been suggested as compromise candidate in 1960, Barry had reportedly scoffed, "One Eisenhower in a generation is enough."

Eight years later, in November of 1969, when I was in a White House surrounded by 500,000 demonstrators howling to "Get U.S. Out" of a Vietnam war into which JFK's Best and Brightest had marched the United States, I did not realize that, in a way, John F. Kennedy had sent them there. The '60s generation had discovered where the "pay any price, bear any burden" rhetoric was taking us, and now they wanted out. JFK was the Pied Piper of our generation, who never lived to see the dashing of the hopes he had raised.

As for Vice President Nixon, he was, I felt in 1961, the most experienced, capable leader in the party, but he had had his chance. The Republican party lost in 1960, we believed, because of its kowtowing to Nelson Rockefeller and its me-tooing of the Democrats. We were young, self-confident, looking to fight it out, intellectually and politically, for what we believed — not only with the new Democratic Establishment that JFK epitomized, but with the old Republican Establishment that had imposed its candidates upon our party since before we were born. And in Nelson Aldrich Rockefeller, the business elite was not only again claiming the Republican nomination for one of its chosen, like Willkie or Dewey or Ike, but for one of its very own. No one could rattle the cages of the Right like Nelson Aldrich Rockefeller.

Barry Goldwater, out of Arizona, with his square jaw, chiseled profile, horn-rimmed glasses, principled conservatism, and uncompromising rhetoric, was our peerless leader.

And we had nothing to lose.

Often, I recalled those pleasant, middle-aged Republicans whose golf bags I had carried around Burning Tree. Their idea of political struggle was to put some ghostwritten conservative boiler-plate into the House hopper, be recorded as a "no" vote on the pending legislation, and get out to the first tee in time to get in eighteen holes before martini time. Meanwhile, the Soviets had Sputnik; they had Castro and Cuba; they were reaching for Laos and South Vietnam. And young, handsome, articulate JFK, who had promised to hurl back the Communist challenge, was floundering.

If there was a single issue that drove the New Conservatism, and the Goldwater campaign, it was this: The United States was in a mortal struggle with the Soviet empire; the tide was going the other way; we needed leadership that understood the nature of the war we were in, leadership as dedicated to the advance of freedom as our enemies were to the spread of their ideology. Containment was not enough.

While James Reston of the *New York Times* might be writing that Rockefeller had about as much chance of losing the Republican nomination "as he does of going broke," we knew better. Down deep, I sensed the Republican Establishment was all hat and no cattle, that we could not only beat Rockefeller with a grass-roots rebellion, but that maybe, just maybe, we could bring down the vaunted Kennedy machine and JFK.

When Barry Goldwater defeated Nelson Rockefeller in the Illinois primary — and, again, in critical California — I wrote the exuberant lead editorial chortling about how "the lamps are burning late tonight in the chancellories of the American Left."

Barry was on his way to triumph at the Cow Palace. At long last, we were capturing and converting the Republican party into the political instrument of our conservative movement. While embarrassed over Barry's campaign blunders, including the offhand suggestion that we "defoliate" the jungles of Vietnam with atomic weapons, we at the *Globe-Democrat* remained squarely behind the Arizona Senator.

Then, in the late fall of 1964, came the day to endorse. Everyone expected the Goldwater endorsement, because no politician in America more exemplified our values and views. The publisher penned the endorsement; and, when I read it, I could not believe it.

The fighting *Globe-Democrat* was taking a dive, going into the tank, refusing to endorse either candidate. Even with Barry's blunders, this seemed craven and cowardly; and I went back to the publisher's corner office to protest. "Let's criticize Barry's blunders, admit our disappointment with the campaign, but, dammit, sir, let's endorse him," I pleaded.

Amberg seemed more subdued than angry with me, and from what he said, I came away with the clear impression LBJ had phoned Sam Newhouse, and Sam Newhouse had phoned Richard Amberg and told him that, whatever he chose to do, he could not endorse the Republican nominee. Richard H. Amberg, too, was a man under authority.

After the publisher finished his editorial, he left for Chicago. As Mr. Thornton was on vacation, I was acting editorial editor — the man to whom all phone calls were transferred. By the score, state legislators, businessmen, conservative leaders, and common folk telephoned all day long, to tell me we were a pack of gutless cowards. The men were choking with rage; some of the women were crying. All day long I took the abuse. For the first time, I was genuinely ashamed of the *St. Louis Globe-Democrat*.

The night Barry Goldwater went down to his humiliating defeat, I drove out to commiserate at his campaign headquarters. They threw me out. A couple of red hots looked as though they were anxious to do more than that to the apparent turncoat from the *Globe-Democrat* who had deserted them in the final moments of the campaign; and I really couldn't blame them.

Following our Pontius Pilate performance, the publisher reprinted hundreds of letters, many questioning his morality, courage, and manhood. For a man as proud as Richard H. Amberg, it was a painful thing to do. But that did not diminish the sense of betrayal of people who swore by the *Globe-Democrat* in those years. Rarely have I felt so rotten as that week when we took a walk on a candidate everyone knew could not win.

When JFK, the Democratic champion, was assassinated in Dallas, Lee Harvey Oswald had killed his challenger as well. Because Dallas was a conservative city, because conservatives had been JFK's most visible adversaries, some of the national rage and disgust at what had been done was directed at us — even though Oswald was an itinerant Marxist, a Castroite, a man of the anti-American Left.

With the assumption of power by LBJ, a Texan and a Vietnam hawk, we no longer had the clarity of the Kennedy–Goldwater, Eastern liberal versus Western conservative match-up. By the time November 1964 rolled around, LBJ had been in office less than a year; he was working miracles on the Hill; he was bombing the Communists in Southeast Asia. The American people, still sickened by what had happened in Dallas, did not want a third President in thirteen months.

And the national press — in one of the most malevolent media campaigns in modern history — painted one of the most decent and principled men in American politics as a bomb-thrower, a racist, and maybe even a fascist. Speaking in West Berlin, Martin Luther King himself claimed to have detected the "danger signs of Hitlerism" in a candidacy that was as American as Ronald Reagan.

Even columnist Walter Lippmann, thought then to be the quintessence of intelligence and reason, joined in, calling the Goldwater campaign, the "rallying point of the White resistance." "It is quite evident," Lippmann said authoritatively, "that Senator Goldwater is relying heavily on attracting Democrats from the White backlash. . . . He appears to be gambling recklessly on racism and jingoism." And again: "This new Republican Party is to be a White man's party and not conservative at all, but radically reactionary. In Barry Goldwater we have a demagogue who dreams of arousing the rich against the poor." This was the great "moderate" voice of the era.

Among conservatives, that election left a permanent reservoir of bitterness and distrust toward the national press. We knew we were going to lose; we didn't know the referees would help the other side run up the score. After what the national press did to

Barry Goldwater, millions would never again believe in its professed neutrality, objectivity, or fairness.

Friends tell me Barry Goldwater never recovered from what was done to him. He felt betrayed, they said; he was never the same man again. The scars were deep, and the wounds permanent. And the journalists who did it to Barry Goldwater cost our profession a goodly slice of its reputation. Ironically, many who had done the most to brutalize Barry Goldwater would turn with equal ferocity upon the President, Lyndon Johnson, on whose behalf they had done their work on the 1964 Republican nominee.

When America responded, with its roar of approval, to Spiro Agnew's attacks on the media in 1969, some of the resentment of the press that came pouring forth in that spontaneous national reaction could be traced back to the fall of 1964.

11

Movin' on Up

"Don't worry, Crawford, we'll be in touch."

BEING an editorial writer at twenty-three was a heady experience, but there were drawbacks. There were no by-lines; nobody knew my name; and there was no action. I spent the entire workday at the office, as though I was in city government. The politicians who ridiculed their "ivory tower" critics had a point.

Several times, I requested assignments outside St. Louis, the first being the gathering storm in Oxford, Mississippi, which I told Mr. Thornton I could reach in a night of driving. But the *Globe* was tight with its cash; it could use inexpensive wire copy for faraway stories; and it saw its opportunity for beating the *Post* in the city, in the county, and in southern Illinois, where the circulation battle would eventually be won.

At nights, I took to covering stories with Walsh, like the visit to south St. Louis of J. B. Stoner, the racist chairman of the National States Rights party. While we did not know it then, Stoner had been involved in the bombing of a black church. Short, curly-haired, chubby, walking with a pronounced limp and looking not a little like a miniature Rodney Dangerfield, Stoner ambled back and forth in front of that audience of eighty people, spewing out his hatred of the "niggers" and the Jews.

The people of south St. Louis to whom he spoke, though, seemed to fear blacks more than they hated them. The women in that hall, especially, seemed more frightened than militant. Their world was turning upside down, and they wanted to create a "line of demarcation" through the middle of St. Louis, they said, which blacks and whites would both respect and never cross.

While Stoner later attacked the *Globe-Democrat* editorial (we covered a follow-up meeting months later) for ridiculing him and his speech, he praised the fairness of the news story. Which made me feel good, as I had written both.

Another issue that was front burner at the *Globe* in the early '60s was extremism — of the Left.

A front group of the American Communist party, the W. E. B. Du Bois Club, had formed a chapter in St. Louis; and a number of avowed Communists, trying to piggyback on the publicity of the civil-rights movement, regularly picketed and demonstrated alongside the black organizations. Our friends at the bureau alerted us to what was up.

Then, we got an excellent tip. Dr. Herbert Aptheker, the Mikhail Suslov of the American Communist party, its leading theoretician, was about to make a secret visit to St. Louis. Six months previous, Aptheker had been in Red Square, alongside Mrs. Khrushchev, hauling the remains of American Communist leader Elizabeth Gurley Flynn toward their final resting place in the Kremlin Wall.

We had Dr. Aptheker's flight number, and Walsh and I staked him out. As Walsh was a familiar figure, I waited at the gate and confronted Aptheker as he came off the plane. "Hello, Dr. Aptheker, can you tell us the purpose of your visit to our city?" I asked him as he came through the gate.

Aptheker recoiled, as though I had just pulled a gun on him. "How did you know I was coming?"

"We got some advance notice, Dr. Aptheker," I said; "we're mighty interested in what you have to say." Then our photographers nailed him cold. The middle-aged gentleman who had met Aptheker hustled him away, and I rejoined Walsh, in his big new Ford; we put a tail on Aptheker and his unknown friend. As we followed them south through the county toward University City, Walsh read their license plate over his car radio to the city desk. Within minutes, the desk was back with the registrant, a "Theodor Rosebury of University City."

Walsh directed the desk to make a run through the "morgue," to see if we had anything on Theodor Rosebury. Back over the radio came word that we had done a feature story on a Dr. Theodor

Rosebury of Washington University Dental School. He had been assigned to Fort Detrick during the war, was an expert in germ warfare, and carried the informal title of "Mr. Biological Warfare."

We were on page one.

The next morning, a Sunday, our reporters staking out Rosebury's home trailed Aptheker to the Mound City Medical Center, in the black area of central St. Louis; and, there, the story got better. As we watched from across the street, some forty Communists, leftists, and radicals — all the usual suspects we had been writing about — gathered together under the auspices of the W. E. B. Du Bois Club, to hear Communist party theoretician Herbert Aptheker. (Because the bureau had tipped us this might be the site of the conclave, we had a young reporter, a graduate student at Washington University, planted inside.)

When we called the black superintendent at the Mound City Medical Center and confronted him, asking why he had rented his rathskeller to "a Communist front like the Du Bois Club," he was incredulous. "Communists! My God, they told me it was a meeting of the Boys Club!"

Monday morning, Walsh and I had a dual by-line on the copyrighted stories — with pictures of Aptheker and Rosebury, and Aptheker and Mrs. Khrushchev marching across Red Square, on page one, and, inside, pictures of Aptheker entering the Mound City meeting, attendees at which included James Peake, ousted leader of the East Side NAACP, and Robert Curtis, formerly of CORE and the Jefferson bank sit-in. For the forty-eight hours Aptheker was in St. Louis, we had a full-court zone press on him, a box-and-one; he didn't move outside Rosebury's house without a *Globe-Democrat* escort. Not before or since have the Marxists of eastern Missouri gotten so much publicity. By the time I left St. Louis six months later, they were still digging out from under. The FBI tip had paid off; the publisher was elated; there were bonuses all around.

Another issue on which Walsh and I collaborated was reform of the Missouri Penitentiary. From the halfway house of Father Dismas Clark, the famous Hoodlum Priest of the movie of the same name, several convicts had come to visit me at the *Globe* to describe the appalling conditions at the state pen — five and six black inmates crammed in a single cell, routine homosexual rape, and a callous administration, headed by Warden E. V. Nash, which permitted the toughest of the inmates to run the prison.

I had come to know Nash in 1963, during the death penalty debate between the *Globe-Democrat* and the *Post-Dispatch*. Missouri Attorney General Tom Eagleton, a rising star in the Democratic party, had written a piece denouncing the death penalty for the *Post*; and the publisher directed me to answer Eagleton in the *Globe*. After the published debate, Tom Eagleton, an engaging and popular politician, and I got to know each other; he was already being talked about as a future Senator, and perhaps more. But, in my defense of the death penalty, a number of critics threw up the caustic gibe "Have you ever seen anyone executed?"

I decided to shut down that line of argument. With the intercession of Jack Flach, our Jeff City correspondent, Walsh and I got "invited" by Warden Nash to witness the execution of Sammy Aire Tucker, who had been sentenced to death for complicity in killing a Missouri patrolman during a cross-country crime spree.

We arrived in Jeff City, about 110 miles from St. Louis, around eight-thirty, ate a late dinner at the hotel where the state legislators gathered, fortified ourselves until around eleven, when we were to meet in the warden's office to be escorted through the prison yard for the execution.

From their cells, the convicts did not curse or yell, but they did provide background music for our crossing of the yard by scraping their tin cups on the bars. It was eerie, the only sound in that yard, except for our shoes scuffing on the gravel. Nobody said anything as, huddled together, we followed the warden. The "death house" was deep inside the prison, and divided within by a retaining wall. Once inside, Warden Nash went to the right, to the holding cell where Tucker was waiting with a clergyman, while Walsh and I, and the brother of the cop Tucker and his friends had shot to death, walked to the left.

We took up positions at the windows of the little hexagonal chamber, into which Tucker was led by two guards. There were two chairs inside the chamber, and the guards quickly strapped Tucker to one of them. He was about my age, with wavy black hair, and his eyes were covered by a black blindfold. Heavyset, he wore only black boxer shorts. From what we could see of his face, he was terrified. He was jerking his head around as if trying to look at us, though he could see nothing through the blindfold.

Once he was strapped in, a guard walked into the chamber and put cyanide crystals into a little container attached to the rear of Tucker's chair; the bucket with the acid solution was brought in and placed beneath the container. The guard hurried out; and Warden Nash paused beside the large lever and waited for the door to be sealed. When Nash threw the big lever, the box tipped over and the cyanide crystals were dumped into the acid solution. A small cloud of gas suddenly filled the chamber with a tiny muffled explosion; almost as suddenly, the cloud seemed to disappear.

Tucker's head snapped back, as though he had been hit on the chin; then, his head came forward slowly and fell on his chest; drool began to come out of his mouth. Eerily, his feet began rapidly and rhythmically tapping on the floor of his death chamber. Then, suddenly, his head would fly back again; and, then, again, slowly come forward. After several minutes of this macabre dance of death, his head slumped forward on his chest, and feet and body ceased to move. I glanced over at the dead cop's brother; he had been impassive throughout.

Before they opened the gas chamber, we were led out of the death house into the night. (The gas chamber had to be aired out before the doctor could examine Tucker and pronounce him dead; they didn't want us in the vicinity when the gas was vented.) On the walk back across the yard, the penitentiary was silent, except for the sound of our footsteps. Walsh and I were back in St. Louis by 3 A.M.

Six months later, I returned to Jeff City, alone. I wondered if I could have pulled that lever and put a fellow human being to death. If I was supportive of the death penalty, would I have been willing to carry it out? When Nash moved to the right this time — it was the execution of Ronald Lee Wolfe, who had escaped from prison, lured a little girl away from a picnic, and viciously assaulted her — I went in with Nash, strode past Wolfe's open cell, and stationed myself at the entrance to the gas chamber. They brought Wolfe right by me. When Nash asked me what I was doing there, I told him I had been assigned to stand next to him as he pulled the lever. He looked puzzled, but didn't make a fuss. Wolfe seemed even more terrified than Tucker. Nash threw the big lever; the crystals fell from the back of Wolfe's chair into the solution; and the same little dance of death began anew. I said a few prayers for the soul of Ronald Lee Wolfe on the long drive back to St. Louis.

Watching a man's life taken away from him is not pleasant, but I yet believe in the morality and necessity of capital punishment.

Some crimes are so odious only the death penalty is fit punishment and retribution; and the suffering the criminal endures is not in the execution itself — that is over in a split second — it is in the knowledge he has been judged unfit to live by his fellow men, in the knowledge his life is coming to an end, by a date certain and a date soon.

A modern society that outlaws the death penalty does not send a message of reverence for life, but a message of moral confusion. When we outlaw the death penalty, we tell the murderer, the rapist, the cutthroat that, no matter what he may do to innocent people in our custody and care, women, children, old people, his most treasured possession, his life, is secure. We guarantee it — in advance. Just as a nation that declares that nothing will make it go to war finds itself at the mercy of warlike regimes, so a society that will not put the worst of its criminals to death will find itself at the mercy of criminals who have no qualms about putting innocent people to death.

We Americans are forever declaring some new "war against crime" and "war against drugs," but almost all the fatalities, thousands annually, are on one side, the side of the innocent. That is not war, that is slaughter, a not inaccurate description of what is taking place in America today.

By late 1964, repeated stabbings and bloody racial brawls were calling national attention to the 128-year-old institution in Jeff City. The publisher sent Walsh to investigate; and I wrote editorial after editorial, attacking the prison administration, trying to make prison reform an issue in the gubernatorial campaign. After I interviewed Carey MacWilliams, editor of *The Nation,* on local television, he invited me to write an article on the penitentiary. On November 16, 1964, it appeared in his magazine. "In one twenty-eight-month period ending a year ago," I wrote, "145 inmates of this warren were stabbed and seven died of their wounds. Nothing radical has been done to improve the odds for survival because convicts hire no lobbyists, and cadres of graduate volunteers do not patrol legislative halls buttonholing representatives for reform."

Not only was the brutalization barbaric, I wrote (we were, after all, punishing these people, not torturing them), nineteen of twenty of these inmates would one day be returning, many to St. Louis. As W. H. Auden had reminded us in "September 1, 1939":

Those to whom evil is done
Do evil in return.

With the election as Governor of Warren Hearnes, who had promised to look into the horrors, action seemed at hand. Nevertheless, we kept the pressure up, with a final blast in the weekend edition of the *Globe,* on December 15, titled "New Broom for the Prison." In the editorial, I took Warden Nash apart — and demanded his dismissal. The paper and editorial hit the streets at 7 P.M. Friday, and ran the entire weekend. (Our Friday-night weekend edition competed both with the Saturday and Sunday *Post-Dispatch*.) Saturday afternoon, when Walsh and I returned from Christmas shopping, we found outside our apartment the Saturday-morning *Post-Dispatch*. The banner headline read, "Warden Nash Kills Self."

"Congratulations, boys, you've killed your first one," Charlie Pierson said as we came into the staff Christmas party that night. To Charlie Pierson, who disliked the term "journalist" intensely and called himself a "newspaperman," suicides went with the territory. As nothing else, however, that campaign to clean up the Missouri Penitentiary — taken for good motives and with legitimate cause — brought home to me the awesome power of the press.

The steady hammering of stories and editorials upon Warden E. V. Nash, an uneducated man who had risen from prison guard, was worse for him than any physical beating could have been. We destroyed his professional reputation; and, then, we destroyed his self-esteem. Later, friends would tell me Nash had unknown and grave family problems that troubled him deeply; but it was that same Friday night that we leveled a final volley at him, that he had come home from a Christmas party with his wife, pulled out his revolver, and shot himself to death.

When I drove home for Christmas a few days later, I arrived late, and when I got in after twenty-two hours on the road, I ran into my father in the kitchen. He knew I was coming; he had read all my prison editorials; and he was waiting. "Pat, I know what's on your mind," he said when he saw me, "I read about that man killing himself, but you can't blame yourself. Only God Himself knows why men do that." It was some consolation to know someone else knew how I felt.

But preaching, and passing judgments from the pulpit of that editorial page was not all we did in St. Louis. One afternoon, Brad O'Leary, a local ad and publicity man, came to visit me at the paper; he had had a brainstorm. He and I, Brad said, should organize a new social club in St. Louis, the purpose of which would be to introduce us, at one fell swoop, to two dozen of the most beautiful women in the metropolitan area. His idea was to invite to join our new club one prominent, successful bachelor from each of two dozen professions — law, journalism, public relations, advertising, TV, government, politics, education, restaurateuring, and so on — and each of us would invite one gorgeous young woman to our social function, who could not be one's steady girl. Thus, we would meet twenty-four of the loveliest women in St. Louis, all of whom would be unattached.

The idea had intrinsic merit, I told him, but, to pull it off, the club needed cachet. One Saturday, I went down to the *Globe-Democrat,* rummaged through the history of the paper, and, borrowing a few facts from the ancient files, fabricated a hundred-year history of the semisecret Prince of Wales Society. The society, I wrote in our brochure, had been formed, at the request of Queen Victoria's eldest son, when he had visited St. Louis (that part was true). Ever since, the bachelors of the city, to keep the memory of that famous visit alive, hosted a secret annual party to commemorate the occasion.

Until it fell apart, after two parties, I was the historian of the Prince of Wales Society. When the curious young women in St. Louis wanted to know who belonged to this secret social set, how it had been formed, how they might get invitations to its famous parties, Brad referred the calls to me.

With the "ivory tower" problem on my mind, I decided to schedule my vacations — all of which eventually ended up at home — to see something of what was going on in America, in the early '60s. When I heard that the great March on Washington for jobs and civil rights was to take place in August of 1963, I built my vacation around it. Driving home on Route 40, I picked up Buchs, and we got down to the Monument grounds around ten in the morning.

While the crowd was building, it was nowhere near the 250,000 who would eventually be at the Lincoln Memorial. Our first "assignment" was to find George Lincoln Rockwell, the ex–naval officer and articulate Nazi, who had set up headquarters in Arlington, and whom I had never met. We wanted to know if there was going to be trouble, which many had predicted. As we wandered through the Monument grounds asking people where Rockwell was, someone on the platform shouted, "Ninety thousand! The police tell us there are ninety thousand of us here already!"

"Ninety thousand baboons!" came the echo from across 15th Street. We had a fix on Rockwell.

The little troop of Nazis and sympathizers Rockwell had mustered could not have numbered more than a hundred. We went across the street and talked with them; and it was clear there would be no violence, no collisions. They were irrelevant to the story. The demonstrators pouring onto the Monument grounds ignored them; and even before the march to the Lincoln Memorial began, Rockwell and his storm troopers had packed up and headed back across the 14th Street Bridge to their Arlington *Führerbunker*.

As the march began, the spirit and mood were festive and friendly; there was none of the air of confrontation that marked the demonstrations in St. Louis. There was a felt sense that something historic was happening; and as Martin Luther King and Walter Reuther and A. Philip Randolph and even the militant John Lewis walked up Constitution Avenue toward the Lincoln Memorial, it was all smiles and joshing and laughter.

At the Memorial, at least an hour elapsed before the speeches began; and, inside the Memorial, where my press credentials got us admitted, Peter, Paul, and Mary started singing spontaneously below the statue of the Great Emancipator. A great fuss was made at James Baldwin's arrival; *The Fire Next Time* was a best-seller. And Lena Horne caused a minor sensation. As the speeches started, I spent an hour chatting with the Reverend Fred Shuttlesworth, who had been the civil-rights leader in Birmingham when the Sixteenth Street Baptist Church had been bombed. When Lena came through, however, Shuttlesworth broke off the conversation in midsentence and went chasing after her, calling "Lena, Lena."

Lewis, apparently at the behest of Cardinal O'Boyle, who had spoken out publicly against his divisive rhetoric, proved less militant than predicted. Then, Dr. King rose to speak, and as he talked, he went into rolling cadences about his "dream," that "one day,

303 ◆ MOVIN' ON UP

this nation will rise up and live out the meaning of its creed," that "one day, on the red hills of Georgia the sons of former slaves and the sons of former slaveowners will be able to sit down together at the table of brotherhood. . . . I have a dream today!"

"Let Freedom ring," he rolled on, from every mountaintop in America. "When we allow freedom to ring . . . we will be able to speed up that day when all of God's children — black men and white men, Jews and Gentiles, Protestants and Catholics — will be able to join hands and sing in the words of the old Negro spiritual, 'Free at last, free at last; thank God Almighty, we are free at last.' "

No one there was unmoved. I knew I had just heard from a few feet away one of the memorable addresses in American history. What made King's oration so powerful and affecting was that it was a passionate appeal to the best in America, delivered without rancor or malice or warning of retribution for past wrongs. King had evoked pictures of an America everyone knew and loved. His cry came in a Gospel rhetoric, in the resonating cadences that Southern and rural people, black and white, so well understood.

The next summer, I went home to Washington by way of Philadelphia, Mississippi. Michael Schwerner, James Earl Chaney, and Andrew Goodman, three civil-rights workers, had disappeared near Philadelphia, in Neshoba County; but their bodies had not been discovered, when, on July 2 (the day of the signing ceremony for the Civil Rights Act of 1964), I drove south to Memphis for the night, and the next morning into Mississippi.

They did not like outsiders in those years; particularly, they did not like the civil-rights militants from the Northern campuses, and the journalists who came south to romanticize them. After I had driven through Oxford, looking for Faulkner's house, and was well down the back road to Philadelphia, I stopped at a roadside diner for a late breakfast. As I was sitting and eating, several country boys came in and stared over at me coldly. The flashy TR-3 convertible and my Missouri license plate were a problem; and I knew it.

The St. Louis Board of Aldermen, on the disappearance of the civil-rights workers, had voted to boycott all products produced in Mississippi. It was big news in the Magnolia State; and my fellow diners would not know I had written an editorial denouncing the aldermen for punishing a sister state for a crime probably committed by a handful. I said nothing, just sat and ate my food.

An elderly black man came up to the diner and started throwing pebbles against the window, signaling me. I couldn't make out what he was saying, so I got up and started for the door to go outside and hear him out. But the country boys had seen him, too, and I didn't make it to the door. Brushing past me, one of them, about thirty-five years old, went to the door, opened it, and yelled, "Nigger, get your black ass outta heah!"

The old man tried to say something, but the country boy yelled at him again, "Did you hear me, nigger! I said, 'Move!' " The old man in overalls broke into a pathetic shuffle, and didn't stop running until he had crossed the highway and reached the steps of a filling station a hundred yards away. I sat back down and finished my breakfast, and didn't say a word. After I paid the bill, I drove over to the gas station, where the old man was sitting, sweating and mopping his brow. "What did you want?" I asked him.

He had wanted me to mail a letter for him, he said; the mailbox was inside the diner, and he wasn't permitted to go in. Still shook and mopping his brow, he smiled toothlessly and added, "They shoah ran my ass off, didn't they?"

"Well, I'm sorry," I said. But he just laughed it off as though this were not the first time. It was going to take more than a federal law to change the heart of Mississippi.

Around noon, I drove into Philadelphia and went to the motel where the Eastern press had been staying; they had pulled out that morning. For an hour, I drove around the little town, and got myself invited for lemonade by a white lady and her husband on the porch of their home. They were portraits in Southern graciousness. When I asked their thoughts about the missing civil-rights workers, they laughed and assured me. "Mr. Buchanan, those boys are pulling a stunt," the lady said. "They're probably up there in New York, right now, laughing at us."

Not two miles away, the three were entombed in an earthen dam, victims of the worst atrocity of the civil-rights era, with the possible exception of the girls dynamited to death that Sunday morning in that Birmingham church.

Late that night I made Meridian, and the next day, drove around town. Around noon (it was July 4), I came through the town square, where the American flag, the Stars and Stripes, was flying upside down, at half staff. It was the day the Civil Rights Act of 1964 took effect.

"What in the hell is going on here?" I asked a hitchhiker I had picked up.

"Oh, that! That's an accident!" he said, chuckling. "Somebody there has made a little mistake." As we drove by some blacks at a bus stop, the hitchhiker hung half out of my TR-3 swinging wildly at them; then he started yelling lewd remarks at some girls. He was playing redneck — for my benefit.

From Meridian, I drove over to Birmingham to visit the black church where the four children had died in the bombing; and, from there, over to the Anniston bus terminal, where the Freedom Riders had been beaten up and had their bus burned. I was surprised. A black soldier and a white soldier were talking and eating together in the diner of that Anniston bus terminal, being served by a white waitress; and no one was paying them the least attention. That was the last time I drove through the Deep South, until more than a dozen years later, when I learned my father's family roots were planted deep in the soil of that same northwest quadrant of Mississippi through which I had driven down to Neshoba County and Philadelphia.

Like many Americans in those years, my feelings about the civil-rights movement were ambivalent. While the Montgomery bus boycott of 1956 had bravery and beauty about it — a people standing up for their own dignity in peaceful protest — the endless, illegal demonstrations in St. Louis were, many of them, arrogant, pointless, belligerent publicity stunts by local politicians, black and white. One day, a group who planned yet another illegal sit-in at the Jefferson Bank called KMOX to give the news team the time of their arrival. When the station said it had no crew on hand, the demonstrators asked if there might be "a crew available tomorrow, if we postpone the sit-in till then."

While the Northern editorial writers and moralists always seemed to me insufferably self-righteous in their lectures to the South, the behavior of the Southern white trash, who beat up non-violent black kids sitting at lunch counters, was cowardly and contemptible.

In retrospect, the civil-rights movement was liberalism's finest hour. The liberals paid a heavy price for having championed civil rights in the '50s and early '60s, for preaching and advancing the ideal of equality and justice under law. If they have stumbled and blundered terribly since, they knew what they were doing then, and what they were doing was right. Segregation in the '50s was truly the biggest thing wrong with a country about which so very, very much was right. When Vietnam came, the black soldiers denied the opportunity to fight alongside their countrymen in World War II and Korea fought and died bravely. As my brother Cricket told me when he came home in 1969, "One of every two of those dead troopers into whose mouth I had to put a dog tag was black; that settles the civil-rights issue for me."

And it should for the rest of us.

From Alabama, I drove on through Washington to Stone Harbor, New Jersey, where the parents were now spending a good part of the summer. "The second family" was growing up. I had seen little of my younger brothers and sisters for three years; and they were elated to see me, though they were caught up in their baseball teams. The game chicken and the game rooster could now walk the beach together, without argument. And Mom and Pop were in high spirits. Buchs had finally found himself; he had left home to become a Maryknoll priest, and was now in the seminary at Ossining, New York. Pop, who had had running arguments with Buchs since he came home from the military, was now singing his praises.

Leaving Stone Harbor early one morning, I drove up the Garden State Parkway to visit Bill. When I reached Ossining, for what I thought would be two hours of conversation with a cloistered seminarian, I was astonished. Buchs wanted to "check out the World's Fair." He got out his civilian clothes and we drove down to Queens, and for hours wandered the pavilions, then drove over to Yorkville, where he told me the reason he had gone in, in words I will always remember. "For twenty-five years," he said, "God has been good to our family; and I felt it was time to give something back."

I returned to Stone Harbor to watch Barry Goldwater deliver his acceptance speech. As soon as Barry got through his line, "Extremism in the defense of liberty is no vice," my father got up and walked out into the kitchen saying, "He's finished." Pop was right. As much as fifty points behind in some polls against LBJ, Barry

Goldwater not only would need every conceivable break to win; he could make no more mistakes; and now he had made a beaut.

What Goldwater *meant* by those words — that a man should fight if necessary to defend his country's freedom — was fine. What the country *heard* in those words — i.e., political extremists are welcome in my campaign — played right into the hands of Barry's enemies. Rockefeller had tagged the Goldwater movement with the "extremism" label; and Barry seemed to be saying, well, yes, we are extremists. The liberal Republicans now had the excuse they were looking for to take a walk on the Republican nominee, and Barry had just dealt the ace of trumps to a Democratic campaign that already had a fistful of trumps to play. From that day forward, we knew the only open question on election night in November would be the extent of the Republican casualties. And they were enormous.

En route back to St. Louis on my 3,000-mile drive, I decided to visit my mother's home in Charleroi, Pennsylvania. While only a mile or two off the new interstate now, Charleroi was as impoverished a town as I had remembered it from fifteen years before. There was the same low, flat Monongahela River, and on the hills across it, mountains of some ugly, coallike substance my Uncle Jim had called slag. Unlike Chestnut Street and Utah Avenue, which had an open, suburban air about them, Charleroi seemed like a tiny slice of old Pittsburgh, transplanted thirty miles to the south. And the world seemed to have passed Charleroi by.

Grandfather Crum, "Bid Ed," was eighty-six. He suffered from diabetes, had just had a leg amputated, and was bedridden.

"You're Catherine's boy, aren't you?" he said. "The one who became a newspaperman."

"Yes, sir," I said.

As he talked, he would spit the tobacco he constantly chewed down the side of the bed. Loyal to his own, he listened to the Pittsburgh Pirates every day, and supported William Scranton, the Governor of Pennsylvania, because of all the wonderful things the Scranton family had done for the people of Pennsylvania.

"I don't think your friend, Goldwater, is going to win this thing," Grandfather said. Neither did I.

An even-tempered, mature woman like her daughter, Grandmother Crum had raised her own six boys and sent four off to war.

When I was nine years old in 1948 and visiting Charleroi, and had a loose tooth, she had explained to me that, with her own sons twenty years before, she used to tie one end of a string to the loosening tooth and the other end to the doorknob, and then slam the door — to remove it painlessly. Would I like to try it? I nervously volunteered; after Grandmother had tied the string to my tooth, and I was waiting apprehensively for her to tie the other end to the doorknob, she gave the string a yank. Out the tooth came, and she broke out laughing. "Surprise," she said. "It's gone."

As though I were still a nine-year-old, Grandmother Crum fixed me two huge ham sandwiches with homemade bread, insisted I drink two glasses of milk, and then handed me two dollars as I was going out the door.

"It's for you, just in case you have an emergency."

It was the last time I saw Big Ed or Anna Blanche Crum, except to go back to Charleroi for their funerals. In material blessings, fame, and fortune, they began in Ohio with nothing and ended with little. But they had each other. After they married and moved to Charleroi, they never left the tiny town. There, they raised eight children; from there they sent them out into the world; and, there, they passed away — givers all their lives, not takers.

Not long after I got back to St. Louis, I turned in the TR-3. Beautiful as it was, that little convertible was almost the death of me and Josette Daniels, a girlfriend.

One evening, following a masquerade party at the home of Jim Allman, our friend (and source) in the St. Louis police department — where I had come in a burnoose as an Arab sheikh, and Josette was a sensation as a harem girl — we drove off in that Triumph and came to the end of a street, entering onto Delmar. What I failed to see, and what was not clear at night, was a chain stretched low across the road — to prevent daytime commuters from using it as a cross street. Unlike the imaginary wire my brothers and I used to stretch across Utah Avenue, this chain was real.

While it would have stopped a normal car, or snapped, the Triumph was so low to the ground that the taut chain scraped along the top of the hood, rode up the windshield, and tore part of the snap-on canvas roof off the car. Two more feet, and it would have decapitated both of us. Had I been speeding, it would have been all over. A sobering experience.

After eight months in south St. Louis, I had decided to move out to University City, answering an ad in the paper from two bachelors, Dave McKinstry and Dick Saunders, both salesmen several years older, who spent many of their days on the road. From the fall of 1962, I had been attending classes at Washington University at night, studying Russian (in anticipation of one day being a Moscow correspondent); and 8333 Delmar was closer to school, and the young social set, than south St. Louis.

Soon, after I moved in, the FBI came around asking the neighbors about the new resident who was apparently one of the only people in St. Louis County who was a daily subscriber to *Pravda.*

After another week-long hospital stay with arthritis early in '63, I joined the downtown YMCA, and started running nightly.

This time, the doctor had put me on Indocin; it was working, and I could sense I might have the arthritis contained, if not defeated. The jogging was my idea; it was my sense that tension, stress, and overwork triggered the arthritis, and that someone in first-rate physical condition was more likely to "keep the wolf away from the door," as I used to put it. Within six months, I was running easy six-minute miles.

Walsh, whose first marriage was already heading for rough weather, partly because of the time, day and night, he devoted to reporting, was becoming the best friend I had in St. Louis. When Jimmy Masucci, the city's most famous restaurateur, who had started Gaslight Square, opened a new tavern on the waterfront, Cafe Louis, Walsh and I, along with Bill Feustal, assistant city editor at the *Globe,* and Jim Allman, became fixtures. The Four Musketeers. Nightly, after I had run my three miles, skipped rope, hit the bag at the Y and lifted some weights, I would show up at the Cafe Louis, where Walsh was already standing at his stool.

We would have Masucci fix us a couple of sub sandwiches for dinner, then get on Walsh's car radio, and invite Feustal to quit the city desk ("Slow news night, Bill") and join us as we headed across the Mississippi for the Hoosier bars on Collinsville Avenue and the black nightclubs farther east. While we held the liquor well, we drank too much; some summer nights, we would drive back across the Mississippi River with the sun rising at our back.

Friday and Saturday were "amateur nights" at Cafe Louis because the married folks, who were home all week, went out to dinner those evenings. "My carriage trade," Masucci called them; but we kept him in business. At the time, "Masuch" was rapidly going blind, developing the stomach cancer that would kill him. His blindness was a source of some humor, with him and us. One night, Charlie Pierson ambled in with his wife after a night on the town, and Jimmy sat down in the booth with them. They talked and laughed for fifteen minutes, before Jimmy inquired cautiously, "By the way, Charlie, how's your wife these days?"

"For cripes sake, Jimmy; she's sitting right across from you!" Charlie howled.

Masuch had thought Charlie was stepping out; he hadn't recognized the lady's voice.

It was in 1964 that Walsh and his wife separated, and he came out to Delmar to share the apartment I had rented. McKinstry and Saunders had both gotten married and moved out. Driven, intense, a workaholic like me, Walsh had a ferocious temper. But it did not manifest itself so much in explosive Irish outbursts; it burned deep, rather like a fire in a mine.

One Saturday morning, while Walsh was still driving his beat-up old Ford, I suggested we go down to the *Globe,* to get in a couple of hours' work before going out for the afternoon. We piled into Walsh's big '59 Ford and started the seventy-block drive. As we drove through University City, I was silently sipping my coffee. Walsh, who was in a foul mood that morning, began growling at a Volkswagen bus that was honking its horn and trying to pass. "He's crowding me," Walsh grumbled; but the bus kept honking and nearly cut Walsh off.

"Forget him, Walsh," I said.

"Two can play this game," Walsh muttered; he moved up alongside the Volkswagen and started crowding the bus over the line in the middle of the street. As the bus was resisting, Walsh suddenly swung the wheel of his big Ford to the left and crashed the vehicle, almost driving the Volkswagen into on-coming traffic. There was a horrible scraping sound as the two vehicles banged into one another, rolling toward the city. Clearly, the Volkswagen was not backing off.

"Walsh, are you insane?" I said.

Jaw set, teeth clenched, Walsh pulled ahead of the little bus, which fell back; but then the gutsy Volkswagen thought better of it, and raced to catch up and pull us over for the damage Walsh had wreaked. As soon as the battered Volkswagen bus pulled alongside, with the driver yelling at us out his window, Walsh looked over to him and yelled, "You want some more, eh?"

And, a second time, he slammed the big Ford into the side of the vehicle. This time, the impact of the crash against the Volkswagen almost tore its fender off. You could hear the noise two blocks away.

"Walsh, are you crazy?" I repeated.

Ignoring my protests, Walsh crashed the vehicle again and again, until the Volkswagen broke it off, and dropped behind us. The Volkswagen was game, but it did not have Walsh's perseverance. It's driver had had enough; Walsh was triumphant.

Then, as I looked desperately into the rearview mirror, I saw my career going up in smoke. The battered Volkswagen had stopped beside a police patrol car; and the driver and the cops were conferring about the two lunatics in the battered Ford that was pulling away.

"It's all over, Walsh," I said.

"No problem," Walsh said, "you see, that's a University City patrol car back there; and we just crossed over into St. Louis. They have no jurisdiction here. They'll just have to work it out together."

With that, Walsh's malevolent laugh took over and accompanied me all the way downtown to the *Globe*. The coffee was all over my lap.

On Monday, I expected a visit at the office from the police. It never came. A week earlier, Walsh had told me nonchalantly that on the way to work that morning he had been forced to run a cab off the road and into a fire hydrant, as the cab had been crowding him in traffic. I had not totally believed Walsh then. Now, I did.

Walsh did not always evade accountability, however. Covering stories all over the state, he collected a file of speeding tickets, which apparently he considered to be advisory. He ignored them, especially the tickets he picked up out of state.

I had been with Walsh when he had acquired one of them. Spending the weekend in Springfield, on the other side of the state at a GOP convention, Walsh and I had started home late. As Walsh pumped his big new Ford up into three digits — I had a date in Illinois that night with society editor Judy Jones and did not want to miss it — we came over a rise in the road. There, before us, laid out beautifully, was the perfect radar trap. Walsh flashed by the first parked car, which was clocking us, in an eyelash, and then by the second car, a quarter-mile beyond, which was supposed to flag us down. Eyes riveted on the road along which he had been rolling at a hundred miles per hour, Walsh nervously asked me to look back and see what was up. I didn't have to. But I turned around, turned back, and said simply: "Walsh, it looks like a Le Mans start."

The startled Missouri troopers were all running for their cars to give chase. Another half-mile down the road, Walsh pulled over, and we waited. As best I recollect, the ticket said 94 mph. Either the cops were being generous that Sunday, or Walsh had managed to brake it somehow, as he was airborne coming over the rise. I felt badly about it; because Walsh had been speeding solely for my benefit.

One morning, after we had rented a new apartment in Jennings, just across the city line in the north county, Walsh told me he was going out to get something he had left in his car. A puzzling hour passed before the phone rang. It was Walsh.

"Where the devil are you?" I asked him.

"I'm in jail," Walsh said. "Oberts [the Jennings police chief] got me; he's locked me up." For once Walsh sounded despondent.

"How did Oberts get you?" I asked; "I thought you were just going out to the car."

Walsh explained. When he had gotten to his car, he found that someone had jacked it up and stolen one of the wheels. Using his radio, he had contacted the Jennings police to report the theft. When he gave them his driver's license number, the Jennings police had routinely sent it on to Highway Patrol, who called back, ecstatic, to say they had a warrant for Walsh's arrest. Would Jennings please pick him up, while Highway Patrol dispatched a car to bring Walsh down to central Missouri, for failure to appear in court?

Incredulous at their luck, the Jennings department sent an officer around, who arrested Walsh and took him down to the station house run by Chief Oberts, who had no love for the *Globe-*

Democrat and was delighted to have the famous reporter in his cell block. Walsh was making his one call, to me, before they carried him off to central Missouri.

This was above my pay grade; so I called the *Globe* editors, who went to bat for Walsh, and got him released. For months thereafter, the *Globe*'s premier reporter was driven around by a chauffeur.

I had a lot of laughs with Denny Walsh, and not a few at his expense. But, my brothers and sisters alone excepted, I never had a better friend.

In the early 1960s, the *Globe-Democrat* strongly supported the Vietnam war, though we argued for bombing, blockading, and mining the harbors of the North. We had parted company on the 1962 Laotian agreement, worked out by Ambassador Averell Harriman, which left the Ho Chi Minh Trail in enemy hands. As long as this military situation obtains, I wrote as early as 1962, the war in the South could not be won. When the Administration sent Cy Vance, then Deputy Secretary of Defense, to brief the *Globe* editorial board at the Sheraton Jefferson Hotel, I asked him pointedly, "Mr. Vance, how can we ever win the war, if the enemy supply lines have been made permanently secure by Harriman's treaty?"

Vance's answer was evasive. Again and again, even in the postmortem piece I did on the Goldwater defeat, we made the point: "This is the Administration," I wrote, "that with premeditation sold out Laos and thus left South Vietnam and the Americans there hopelessly out-flanked to fight an enervating and seemingly endless war which will now likely culminate in the loss of all Asia. . . ." That was 1964.

Outraged at the overthrow and murder of Diem, we suspected an Administration hand in the coup; but, in the battle between LBJ and the antiwar movement, we were all the way with LBJ.

Then came the "teach-ins." Conducted at Washington University, these were less debates than hours-long antiwar rallies, where the opponents of American involvement had their arguments applauded, and defenders were heckled and mocked.

Well known by now in political circles in St. Louis, I was repeatedly invited to defend Administration policy; there was not a lot of competition for the honor. A mediocre speaker, who did not enjoy it, I did not look forward to these appearances. I drafted my speeches at work at night, and read them to the audience. They sounded less like the persuasive arguments of a trial lawyer than extended editorials, which is pretty much what they were.

There is a world of difference between writing for the eye and writing for the ear; at twenty-six, I had not yet discovered it. And my voice was unsuited to the podium; when excited, it has a tendency to rise so high that only the dogs can understand me. But, at these mock debates, I did develop one talent: handling Q&A. Once the speech was done, the butterflies that dated to my disastrous debating experience at Gonzaga disappeared. My answers were quick, pointed, factual, and barbed. I was good at this; and I soon came to understand it. When one student noted that it was South Vietnam and the United States who had resisted Vietnamese elections after the 1954 Geneva Agreements, I retorted: "If Uncle Ho believes in elections, why hasn't he held a free election in North Vietnam in the ten years he has ruled there? Why has no Communist regime, anywhere or ever, held a truly free election?"

When another yelled a personal insult, I retorted, "Well, I always thought that insult was the last recourse of an exhausted mind; I'm just a little surprised your mind is exhausted — this early in the afternoon."

Silence.

During one Saturday teach-in at Washington University, the whole auditorium booed as I entered. My speech was mocked, but when the time came for Q&A, the moderator asked "all of those who want to question Mr. Buchanan" to get in one line, and "any who want to question the other panelists" to get in the other. Thirty people lined up to have at me; only one or two went into the other line. As the villain of the piece, I was a good drawing card; and I gave as good as I got.

They didn't much like me, and they detested the *Globe*; and I reciprocated warmly; but at least one liberal moderator got up at the end and paid me a gracious tribute. "If I were on Mr. Buchanan's side, I don't know if I would have had the courage to come here today," he said. "Let's give him a round of applause." The applause was tepid.

What the antiwar students of 1964 and 1965 had, however, that most of us in the late '50s did not, was, first and foremost, intellectual self-confidence and social nerve. We *were* the Silent Generation. In college, I would have preferred a gang beating to standing up in a crowd of students and confronting some national politician. When Hubert Humphrey came to Georgetown in 1959, I went over to hear him, but when he was done, like everyone else in the audience, Republican or Democrat, I applauded politely.

Some of the student participants at those teach-ins knew as much or more of the history of Vietnam, and the details of French and American involvement as I did. And I read constantly and was paid to know. Though many exuded an almost snotty moral arrogance, they were not stupid; they were not speaking from ignorance; and they were not being adequately answered by their inarticulate government in Washington.

Confronted by these True Believers, the Establishment proved as incapable of defending itself intellectually, as it did in winning the war militarily. The central problem was that LBJ's Washington wanted negotiations and "peace," not victory; and Uncle Ho wanted South Vietnam.

In 1969, the American Establishment itself finally broke and ran and joined the demonstrators, denouncing as "Nixon's War" a bloody conflict into which, for five years, they had marched my generation. Nothing in politics, not even Watergate, embittered me more than to read and hear President Nixon's Vietnam policy derided as corrupt and immoral in 1969, 1970, and beyond by some of the same liberal icons whose hawkish cleverness I used to quote at those teach-ins in 1964 and 1965.

By the time Mr. Nixon went into the White House, the students and demonstrators at places I went to speak, like Kent State in Ohio, were a different breed; they seemed to me boorish ignoramuses. Students for a Democratic Society in the early '60s had a foothold on the Washington University campus; but these SDS students were different from the mob that tried to pull off the Days of Rage in Chicago, years later. The early SDSers seemed cerebral, socialist, pacifist, and polite; they called me "Mr. Buchanan" (I was twenty-six), and reminded me of the kids who had skipped high school in Washington and gone directly from the eighth grade into Saint Charles Seminary.

One Saturday afternoon, when I saw them picketing outside an empty federal building, I stopped and talked for an hour. They desperately wanted to "communicate," and there was nothing in the least threatening about them. Where they needed answers, their successors, whom I saw up close in Grant Park during the

1968 convention in Chicago — spitting out their contempt for the "pigs," chanting "F—— you! Da-ley!" and "Dump the Hump," night after night, for hours on end — got exactly what they deserved.

Candidate Nixon had sent me from Mission Bay to "observe" the Chicago convention up close and report to him almost hourly down at Key Biscayne. From the nineteenth floor of the "Comrade Hilton" Hotel, along with Norman Mailer and the boxer José Torres, who had come by our suite, I watched the Chicago police settle accounts with the "kids" in Grant Park. Mailer and Torres were on the side of the kids; I had spent part of two nights down there in that park, with them, listening to their abuse; and I was for the cops.

The American military did not lose that war in Southeast Asia; the American soldiers fighting there never lost a major military engagement in seven years. When President Nixon approved the Paris Peace Accords in 1973, every single provincial capital was in South Vietnamese hands. No, the Vietnam War was not lost in the Mekong Delta, it was lost in Washington, D.C., in the corridors of our capital city, because the Establishment that had marched this country into Southeast Asia in the early and middle '60s lacked the mental stamina and moral courage to see that war through to victory. Vietnam was liberalism's last great adventure, and greatest debacle.

And America has not yet fully recovered from it.

After two years in St. Louis, I began to feel as though I had achieved all I was going to achieve. I was assistant editorial editor, but the idea of succeeding to the editorship, in five or ten years, did not have great appeal. Five years was an eternity then. While I was writing what I wanted, the way I wanted, there was no by-line. *Human Events* and other conservative publications might be reprinting my editorials, but nobody knew who had written them. Nobody knew my name. St. Louis was not where the action was, and the Goldwater disaster and the *Globe*'s refusal to endorse him were deeply dispiriting.

Bob Poos of the AP, a friend, had asked for reassignment to Vietnam, had gotten it, and had gotten himself wounded by the ARVN forces during one of the Buddhist riots. Journalists not much older than I were winning Pulitzer Prizes covering Vietnam.

In early 1965, I told the publisher I wanted to apply for a Nieman Fellowship at Harvard. While he did not oppose it, he was not for it either; whenever St. Louis journalists went to Harvard for Niemans, they rarely came back to St. Louis. Nonetheless, I applied; and within months, I was in the finals, invited to Chicago for an interview. My major drawback — given my academic credentials and thirty months as an editorial writer — appeared to be my youth. Niemans usually went to journalists with more years in the profession. Nonetheless I flew to Chicago, full of anticipation, for my interview with the Nieman board, which included the dean of Harvard, John U. Monro.

The interview did not go badly; it went disastrously. As questioning was about the begin, I gazed down and saw that I had on one black sock and one brown one. Getting dressed in that dark room at the Drake Hotel, I had mixed them up.

Somehow, the subject of the death penalty came up early, and, instead of steering around this emotional issue, I drove right into it. One of the emotional liberals on the panel started arguing, and I made one riposte after another, eating up my time alienating him, and persuading at least a blocking minority that this was not the type of young journalist who ought to be advanced. Midway through, I sensed I had blown it. When I got up to leave, one of the interviewers said soothingly, while looking over at a fellow interviewer, "Don't worry, Crawford, we'll be in touch."

"Irascibility," the old Jesuit had warned the professors at Columbia; this student has a certain "intensity of spirit." In those years, I had not yet developed the ability to separate myself, clinically, from my opinions, to sit back quietly and watch someone butcher an argument I had just advanced, without rushing passionately to its defense. This capacity — to sit calmly and coolly, carefully framing your riposte, while an adversary is trying to beat your argument to death in front of you — is, I have found, an invaluable asset, whether on national television or sitting across the Cabinet table from the President of the United States. Twenty-six years old in the spring of 1965, I didn't have it, not remotely.

After that session, I went home to St. Louis and began thinking. Clearly, my conservative convictions were going to prove lifelong impediments in my profession. When the telegram arrived in Jennings, telling me I had not been accepted for the Nieman program, I was disconsolate, but unsurprised. (Years later, pressed by a reporter on some conservative outrage I had perpetrated in the White House, I was able to respond, "None of this would have happened — if they had let me into Harvard.")

Now, I had to find a way out of St. Louis, and another way up in my profession. That fall, 1965, the publisher gave me the stimulus I needed.

The Aptheker-Rosebury controversy that Walsh and I had stirred up was still boiling on the Washington University campus that fall. Alumni were bitter that a tenured professor, whom they were supporting financially, would be hobnobbing with an avowed Communist party leader. Most of the faculty and student activists supported Dr. Rosebury's freedom of association.

Invited to debate "academic freedom" with Barry Commoner, the famed ecologist at Washington University, I decided to puncture the biggest balloon on campus, Chancellor Thomas Eliot, who was standing forthrightly behind Professor Rosebury. After Chancellor Eliot's name was invoked during the debate, I told the audience that it was fine to be a great advocate of academic freedom by day, but what did they think about Tom Eliot visiting Richard H. Amberg, "like Nicodemus by night" — to plead with us not to exercise our press freedom to endorse an alumni boycott of the Washington University fund-raising campaign? (Eliot was panicky that the *Globe* might urge alumni not to contribute until he fired Rosebury.) That Eliot had been in secret communion with Richard Amberg, publisher of the loathed *Globe-Democrat,* stunned the audience; I had scored a direct hit.

Informed almost immediately, Eliot fired back; he phoned the publisher. When I came to work the next morning, an enraged Richard Amberg told me I would never participate in another teach-in at Washington University, or I would be fired. Charlie Pierson, who had hired me three summers before and given me all my pay raises (I was now at top of the scale, $180 a week), came over to the Press Club to commiserate and calm me down. He knew I was smoldering over the chastisement. "I knew something was up when the publisher called to tell me to meet him this morning in his office at eleven o'clock," Charlie said. "At eleven o'clock in the morning, I can't even spit. Now, Pat, don't let it bother you; the publisher'll get over it; it'll pass."

I didn't think so, and I sensed it was time to go. Within several weeks, an idea had formed.

Raised in Washington, which had no elective officeholders, I knew I could never be a Congressman or Senator; but in the early Kennedy years, I had followed the tremendous press coverage JFK's Special Assistants — men like Ted Sorenson and Kenny O'Donnell — regularly received. To me, they had the most glamorous job in national politics I could ever aspire to.

Now, here in front of me, was a clipping that said that the former Vice President of the United States, Richard M. Nixon — my candidate for 1968 — would be filling in for Senator Everett Dirksen at a Republican dinner in Belleville, Illinois, just fifteen miles from St. Louis. The date was December 9.

It was almost too good to be true.

Out of Goldwater's defeat, Nixon had emerged as a class act. He had campaigned harder for Barry than Barry had campaigned for himself; Nixon could unify our bitterly divided party; he knew foreign policy; he was the most qualified man in America to be president; and, besides, I had always liked Nixon, even before that afternoon at Burning Tree.

Don Hesse, the *Globe* cartoonist and my good friend, who also liked and admired Nixon, had volunteered to host a cocktail party for the former Vice President, following his Belleville speech. I went to Don; and he agreed to arrange a face-to-face meeting where I could make a pitch to join up with him in 1968 — or hopefully sooner.

While Nixon spoke at Augustine's restaurant in Belleville, I waited at a tavern across the street with Josette, the attractive and spirited girl I often dated, who had volunteered to come along and play her part. Then, I fortified myself with a couple of scotches. (What was it Sam Rayburn had said to his Board of Education: "Why should we all be cowardly and stupid when, with two of these, we can all be clever and brave?")

Trailing Nixon's motorcade at a distance, I arrived at Hesse's house minutes later; and Don quickly introduced me to the familiar face in his kitchen. Telling Nixon of my admiration for what he had done for Senator Goldwater, and my hope he would run again in 1968, I blurted out, "Sir, I'd like to get aboard early."

"Before we get to 1968," Nixon said, "the Republicans will have to win in 1966, or the nomination won't be worth anything. That's what I will be working on this coming year." Then, he quickly asked me what I did.

"Assistant editorial editor," I said, foolishly emphasizing the title.

"But, do you write?" he demanded.

"Three or four editorials a day, Mr. Vice President, on local, national, and foreign issues," I answered.

Nixon quizzed me further, then added, "I need someone to help handle my correspondence; it's getting to be too much for me alone, and also to help me write a monthly column I've signed to do. I may be in touch."

It had gone extraordinarily well; Josette looked terrific, and Nixon thought so, too. After five minutes, I broke it off, to let him talk to the other guests. I hoped I had made a permanent impression. The next morning, I debriefed Hesse, who had driven Nixon to Lambert–St. Louis airport. During the forty-five-minute ride from Belleville, the former Vice President had quizzed him at length about the young editorial writer who had approached him the night before.

After ten days, when I thought my offer to join the former Vice President had been forgotten, I picked up the phone to hear that familiar deep voice. Richard Nixon was calling direct. Could I come to New York for a day to chat, he wanted to know.

Certainly, I told him; but a day's absence here would not go unnoticed. Why not call the publisher, and go through him?

Amberg walked into my office, a look of puzzlement on his face. Former Vice President Nixon had just called from New York, he said, and wanted to meet with me.

"What do you think I should do, sir?" I asked the publisher. Obviously, you should go, he said.

Arriving at 20 Broad Street, I saw a petite, redhaired lady sitting behind a mountain of mail in the tiny office next to Mr. Nixon's. Rose Mary Woods introduced herself, and handed me a swatch of mail to review. After a half-hour, I was ushered into the former Vice President's corner office for an interview that lasted, off and on, more than three hours.

Of the distinctive features of the two Presidents I have known best, the most striking is in the eyes. Ronald Reagan's eyes twinkle and shine like those of a man whom nature has favored, and upon whom the world has showered all its blessings. When I would catch President Reagan's eye at a White House meeting, he would automatically nod and wink, and his eyes would smile, as if to say, "We're doing okay, aren't we, old friend?" Mr. Nixon's eyes, however, are bright, savvy, experienced, cautious, weary, and wounded, and they say with Breaker Morant, "Thanks, but I've seen the world."

To anyone who has gone through it, a conversation with Richard Nixon (then fifty-three) can be an exhilarating and exhausting experience.

Unlike the Nieman interviewers, some of whom — not unlike me — could not hear their ideology contradicted without storming to its defense, Nixon, the least ideological statesman I ever encountered, was cool and calm, a first-rate interviewer, thoroughly interested in where I came from, what I knew, and where I stood — on everything.

When I said something that contradicted his position, he curiously wanted to know why. He was not bothered by contrary opinions; and he was a vacuum cleaner for information. What did I think of Romney, of Rockefeller? ("While the conservatives do not want Romney, sir, they will not accept Rockefeller.") What did I think of Goldwater? ("He'll never run again, sir, but the Goldwater conservatives are the key to the nomination.") What did I think would be the issues in 1966? If I worked with him on a syndicated column, what should we write about? How did I stand on a surtax, on civil rights, on Vietnam? What should be done there?

I told Nixon that, on Vietnam, I felt LBJ's incessant "searches for peace" were ridiculous, that we ought to use the full brunt of American military power against North Vietnam, mining the harbors and bombing, until they ceased supporting the Viet Cong, that the on-again, off-again pressure of the President sent the enemy a signal that America was irresolute and uncertain.

Nixon led me to believe he was much more hawkish than the President, that he would act much more decisively to bring the war to a successful end. He felt LBJ was confusing the enemy, sending conflicting signals, bombing at one moment, halting, and begging for peace the next. Occasionally, Richard Nixon will telegraph the answer he expects by making a strong assertive statement, and then ending it with "or am I wrong?"

After hours of talk, he had listened closely to my opinions, knew I was more conservative than he, and he suddenly asked, "You're not as conservative as Bill Buckley, are you — or am I wrong?"

Clearly, he was expecting me to say, "No, sir, not quite that far right."

But the truth was Bill Buckley was then the most respected voice in our movement; he was writing the best column in America; and I had written the *Globe*'s long-distance endorsement of his mayoral candidacy in the race against John V. Lindsay that had ended only a month before. Even though Nixon had recently called the "Buckleyites" more "dangerous than the Birchites" (which I did not know then), I agreed with Buckley on virtually everything. So, while I didn't contradict Nixon, I didn't back off either. "I have a tremendous admiration for Bill Buckley," I said. Nixon picked up what I meant, nodded, and quickly moved on.

At one point, his buzzer sounded, and he was called to the phone. "Hello, John," he said, and, as I got up to leave, he motioned me to sit back down. From his conversation, it was clear he was advising Senator John Williams of Delaware on how the Republicans in the Senate should handle any LBJ tax request. Then another call came, from Ray Bliss, chairman of the Republican National Committee. Nixon wasn't practicing law at all; he was senior adviser and political guide to the national Republican party.

"From this office, Nixon is running the GOP," I thought to myself; "the things I am writing about in St. Louis, he is helping decide right here in New York." This is excellent. This interview seemed to have gone even better than the first one in Don Hesse's kitchen; Nixon and I were talking as though we had known each other for some time.

I felt certain an offer would come to work for the former Vice President, and I was prepared to roll the dice and take it, whatever it was. Not only was he my first choice for the '68 nomination, he was a formidable political talent, a figure in history, the most controversial politician of his generation, potentially a great man. I could learn from him, and I thoroughly subscribed to his view that it was in the world arena, not on domestic issues, that the action and passion of our time would be engaged. About foreign policy being the central issue of our age, Nixon and I always agreed.

At his elbow, I could advance the conservative cause while contributing to the Republican recapture of the White House, and maybe, just maybe, go into the White House myself — as Sorenson and O'Donnell had done — as a thirty-year-old Special Assistant to the President of the United States. Having spent more than three years writing and refining my conservative views for the 320,000 readers of the *Globe-Democrat,* I now saw the opportunity to present those views to the nation — through the unique voice of the leader, past, present, and future, of the Republican party.

In my heart, I knew our movement was not dead; that, indeed, we were now the body, as well as the soul, of the GOP.

In my valedictory to the Goldwater campaign, written two days after his defeat, I had said, "The new conservatism antedated Goldwater, made him a national figure to rival Presidents and will postdate him. For that conservatism depends primarily for its momentum upon one fact: The abject failure of the ideology of Western liberalism to either halt or reverse the advance of totalitarian Communism. . . . [Conservatism] has lost a battle, not the war."

At the end of our conversation, the former Vice President was ready to hire me, for one year. I agreed instantly, but suggested the way to handle the situation would be for him to phone Mr. Amberg, then and there, and cut the deal for a year's leave of absence, before I got back to St. Louis.

Nixon phoned Amberg, and there was no other answer the publisher could give the former Vice President of the United States and probable future nominee of the Republican party: "Certainly, I will give Pat a year's leave of absence."

Returning to St. Louis, I gave all my furniture to Josette, who was moving out of her parents' home into her own apartment, said good-bye to D. J. Walsh, who helped me move out, filled up my new Buick Wildcat convertible with the pots and pans and papers and clothes accumulated over three and a half years, and headed east toward home, traversing Route 40 through Terra Haute, Indianapolis, Columbus, and Wheeling, West Virginia, for the last time, to tell my parents my journalistic career had just taken a detour — directly into the outer office of the former Vice President of the United States, Richard M. Nixon.

I, too, was "movin' on up."

12

A Death in the Family

"The third 'I' stands for illegitimate."

F OR almost nine years, from January of 1966 until August of 1974, when he resigned the presidency to go into political exile in San Clemente, I worked for Richard M. Nixon. They were memorable years.

During that first year, 1966, when the former Vice President's permanent staff consisted of Rose Mary Woods and me, Richard Nixon and I wrote together the column he had talked about that night in Belleville; and we traveled the country together on behalf of the Republican party, visiting thirty-five states and four-score congressional districts in the most exhausting, and successful, GOP off-year election since 1946.

Within months of that political triumph for the party, and personal triumph for Richard Nixon, we began preparing the ground for the coming presidential campaign, and, during his six-month political "moratorium" in 1967, Richard Nixon and I traveled to Europe, Africa, and the Middle East, arriving in Morocco the morning that Israeli planes destroyed the Egyptian Air Force on the ground, in the decisive battle of the Six-Day War.

We stayed in Rabat that night and the following day as the King rode up from Marrakesh, to review, marching through the streets of his capital, the Moroccan troops he was sending off to join the Arab cause on the Suez front; the units did not even make it to their ships before the war was over. Within several days, Mr. Nixon and I were in Jerusalem, sitting in David Ben-Gurion's living room, as the old man explained that Nasser *must* survive his debacle, because Nasser alone could make peace with Israel and make it stick with the Arab world — and America, he told the future President of the United States, must come to terms with China.

In February of 1968, with the tiny staff he had assembled, Mr. Nixon launched his campaign in the snows of New Hampshire; it was one of the great comeback stories in American history, and it unfolded during the most divisive year of the twentieth century. As we flew at night in a private plane to Boston's Logan Airport, the Tet offensive was being launched in South Vietnam; within days George Romney would drop out of the race, leaving us a clear field in the Republican primaries. A fortnight after Romney's disavowal of candidacy, Lyndon Johnson stunned the political world, announcing he would not run again. Less than a week following that political bombshell, Martin Luther King was assassinated in Memphis, and a hundred American cities were burning in the worst racial violence in our history. Two months after Dr. King's murder, Robert Kennedy was assassinated in a Los Angeles hotel kitchen; and the Democratic convention, virtually dissolved in bitterness and chaos one August night in the streets of Chicago, as I watched from that nineteenth-floor window of the Conrad Hilton Hotel.

With our narrow triumph over Hubert Humphrey, I became a Special Assistant to the President, and helped to write several of the more controversial speeches of the Nixon era — the President's Great Silent Majority speech in November of 1969, Vice President Agnew's follow-up attack on the networks at Des Moines, and the President's announcement of the U.S. incursion into Cambodia, which was followed by widespread student disorders and the killings at Kent State University.

I was part of the fifteen-member official delegation on the President's historic opening to China, and was with him at the final summit in Yalta, Moscow, and Minsk, a month before President Nixon resigned. In late September of 1973, I had spent five and a half memorable hours in televised testimony before the Ervin Committee investigating the Watergate scandal.

After President Nixon departed for San Clemente, I stayed on with President Ford for several months, then left the White House, after six years, to write *Conservative Votes, Liberal Victories* (since remaindered) about how conservatives should proceed with the recapture of the Republican party. Then, I realized the ambition I had taken to journalism school, becoming a syndicated columnist, television commentator, and co-host, along with Tom Braden, of the new Cable News Network show "Crossfire."

In January of 1976, after a New Year's interview with President Ford, in which he said that Justice John Paul Stevens, who had won Senate confirmation virtually without dissent, represented the kind of appointments he would make, if elected in his own right, I publicly endorsed Ronald Reagan's challenge against President Ford in the primaries. Putting noncontroversial moderates on the United States Supreme Court was not why I had joined up with Richard Nixon.

While that 1976 presidential effort fell short, Ronald Reagan succeeded in 1980, by telling America it was time to face the truth about the nature of our Communist enemy, time to turn away from government and back to the people, time to restore to their natural position of primacy in our society those selfsame family values I had learned in my formative years. The Conservative Hour in American politics seemed, at long last, to have arrived, as Ronald Reagan defeated Jimmy Carter and then Walter Mondale in two of the great landslides in modern history, capturing the Senate in 1980 from a Democratic party that had held it for a quarter-century.

In 1985, after ten years writing, broadcasting, and lecturing, I returned, at the invitation of Donald T. Regan, to become President Reagan's Director of Communications. When Don Regan made his gracious offer, I didn't even think twice.

But, the story of those two decades "close to the Western summit" — from the day I joined up with former Vice President Nixon in January of 1966 until I left President Reagan's White House in March of 1987 — is for the next book, not this one.

In those same two decades, in which my hometown of Washington, and the country, changed so dramatically, the Buchanan family, too, was changing.

Brother Tom, the ninth and youngest and among my mother's favorites, went from Gonzaga to St. Louis University, then to Georgetown Law School, worked for sister Bay as "bourser" on the Reagan campaign plane in 1980; and became, for three years, Assistant U.S. Attorney for the Eastern District of Virginia. Married to Theresa Carroll, herself a lawyer, he is now a partner in the Washington firm of Heron, Burchette, Ruckert & Rothwell.

Brian, "Buck," the second youngest, went to Xavier in Ohio

during the Nixon years, then to St. Louis University Medical School; he did his internship and residency at Charity Hospital in New Orleans's inner city. An internist in private practice, he lives with his wife, Phyllis, and four children in Bedford, Virginia, in the Shenandoah Valley where he always wanted to settle.

Angela Marie "Bay" Buchanan-Jackson, the beneficiary of all those prayers and novenas at age ten, graduated from Georgetown Visitation, and Rosemont College in 1971; and studied mathematics in graduate school at McGill. When she came home from Montreal in 1972, she went to work for CREEP, the Committee to Re-Elect the President. Disillusioned by Watergate, Bay moved to Australia, converted to Mormonism, and came back home two years later, to work as treasurer of the Reagan campaigns of 1976 and 1980. In 1981, Bay was sworn in, at thirty-two, as the youngest-ever Treasurer of the United States. Every dollar bill printed between late 1981 and late 1983 bears her signature. Married to a lawyer, Bill Jackson, she has three children, lives in Orange County, California, and was, for a time, manager of the exploratory presidential campaign of former Senator Paul Laxalt, who, last August, chose not to run.

Like all seven brothers, Jack graduated from Blessed Sacrament and Gonzaga, went to Saint Benedict's in Kansas, earned his CPA, worked for my father for a decade, and became comptroller of Capitol Cadillac in Greenbelt, Maryland. In 1987, he acquired his own Pontiac dealership, Buchanan Motors, in Easton, Maryland. For fifteen years, Jack coached the CYO intermediate basketball team for Blessed Sacrament; he has two daughters. Known to his brothers as "The Dragon," Jack is working on a black belt in karate.

Kathleen Theresa, or Coo, went to Visitation and Notre Dame in Baltimore, came home to marry John Connolly of Boston (and Boston College), who served as a naval officer during Vietnam, and who is a lobbyist in Washington with Hecht, Spencer and Oglesby, Inc., whose board chairman is presidential confidant Stu Spencer. Coo has four children, two with severe disabilities, and works in the White House correspondence division under Anne Higgins. She received her master's in English literature at George Mason University in 1986.

Crick graduated from Saint Francis of Loretto, Pennsylvania, where he was president of his fraternity, delivered mail for a year, then entered Georgetown Dental School, getting his degree in June of 1967. In December, after breaking his ankle in his first jump with the 101st Airborne ("Pat, I left my claw marks all over the side of that plane"), he joined his comrades in South Vietnam, where he served thirteen months, coming home in time for Richard Nixon's Inaugural. Mustered out a year later, Crick established his dental practice both in Chevy Chase (one block south of the circle) and in Poolesville, Maryland. In 1972, he married Carole Betterley of Springfield, Massachusetts, who worked in the Nixon Administration; they have six children, the eldest of whom, Michael, is at Gonzaga.

After coming home from the Jesuits, Hank served his six months active in the army artillery at Fort Sill, Oklahoma, and married my father's receptionist, Micheline Curran, who was born in London. He worked for my father for a decade before setting up his own accounting firm. A daily communicant, Hank has for years taught religion at night to Catholic kids in Protestant schools; he is convinced of the authenticity of the apparitions of the Blessed Virgin at Medjugorje, Yugoslavia, having made three visits to the shrine.

During Watergate, Hank was falsely charged by CBS News with operating a "laundry" for dirty money in Bethesda; had he persevered in the libel suit, CBS would have educated all five children. His oldest daughter, Rachel, is at the Columbia School of Journalism; his second daughter, Stephanie, is finishing up at the University of Virginia after a year at Cambridge. His only boy, my godson Bill, graduates this year from Gonzaga. The antithesis, in deportment and demeanor, of what his father and uncles once were, Bill has his heart set on the Naval Academy at Annapolis.

Mom and Pop still live in the big white house at 5501 Utah Avenue, and regularly host the annual family get-togethers on Christmas and Easter. Having sent his oldest son to Holy Trinity in 1941, the year the Japs bombed Pearl Harbor, Pop sent off his last tuition check — for brother Tom at the Georgetown Law School — in 1979.

While I was still living in south St. Louis, my oldest brother, Bill, whom we always called Buchs, came driving through; he was on his way to "become a dealer" in a Las Vegas casino, he said.

His whole life, brother Bill could not settle on what it was he wanted to be. After graduating from Georgetown in 1958, he had gone to law school, quit after six months, and gone on active duty in military intelligence at Fort Holabird in Baltimore, doing "photo interpretation" for two years on what turned out to be the pictures brought back by the U-2s Ike had flying over the Soviet Union. When he got out of the service in 1961, Bill went into real estate — the coming thing in D.C.'s bedroom suburb of Montgomery County. For weeks, he "sat" on a house, and finally sold it to a young Brazilian diplomat. Feeling good about his big sale and coming commission, Bill returned to work and was told by one of his superiors, "Congratulations, you unloaded a real dog."

Sick at having been party to cheating the Brazilian family out of the kind of home the man thought he had bought, Bill penned his famous "Three I" letter of resignation.

"The Roman numeral 'III' after your name is altogether deserved," Bill wrote the senior and name partner of the prestigious real estate firm. "The first 'I' stands for ignorant, because you are devoid of knowledge about basic ethics; the second 'I' stands for indolent, because you spend your time on a golf course, not knowing what's going on in your own company, while the rest of us do your work; and the third 'I' stands for illegitimate — because you're a real bastard." Bill knew how to slam the door on the way out.

At twenty-seven, he joined the Maryknoll Order to become a missionary in South America; but, after two years, he left the seminary, convinced he did not have a vocation. He came home and went to Maryland University, where he earned his master's in history, and taught freshmen. Quitting Maryland in 1968 to help manage the Nixon campaign in Prince Georges County, he joined OEO as a fraud investigator, chasing the militants of the American Indian Movement around Mount Rushmore, and worked with the famous "Wrecking Crew" of Howard Phillips to dismantle the agency. Under Gerald Ford, Buchs got a lateral transfer to AID.

When Jimmy Carter was elected, I told Buchs he was a goner. "Start looking for a job," I warned him. But Buchs insisted that even though "Buchanan" might be a recognizable and not popular name inside the Carter Administration for a political holdover from the Nixon years, he would probably be kept on — so effective had his work been. "I've done a great job here, why would they want to fire me?"

Six weeks into the new administration, he got the pink slip.

Buchs decided to become a stockbroker and went to work first for Merrill-Lynch, then for Paine-Webber, after he was fired for having routinely signed the names of clients — at their request — so they wouldn't have to drive out to Tyson's Corner every time paper had to be processed.

The bitter winter night he lost his job with Merrill-Lynch, Bill arrived at my front door at five in the morning. He had had a date in Leesburg, and on the way home, got caught in an ice storm. Moving at ten miles an hour, his car had gone off the road countless times, but he finally made it to McLean and down the narrow lane to my house. "I guess I've sort of screwed up my life," he told me in exhaustion, before going to bed.

Buchs was among the most distracted people I have ever encountered. Often, you could be talking directly to him; and see clearly you had been tuned out. His mind was focused totally on what *he* was going to say.

It was a routine of my mother's to mix a huge cooking pot of lemonade for the entire household, before transferring some of it to a pitcher; and she often left the lemonade sitting in the big pot. We would come home on a hot summer day and pour the lemonade directly from the huge pot into a tall ice-filled glass.

One day, however, my mother was soaking that same cooking pot with a Lestoil solution, and she left the Lestoil-contaminated water in the pot on the sink. Sweating from several sets of tennis, Bill walked in, poured himself a glass of Lestoil, and downed it in a gulp, as he gazed out the picture window in the kitchen, musing. He was starting with his second glass before he realized something was amiss.

When my mother found him gagging all over the kitchen, she got on the phone to Doc Keegan, the family physician who lives across the street. "Charlie," Mom said, "Bill just drank a glass of Lestoil; what do I do?"

"First, Catherine," said Charlie Keegan, who had known Buchs for thirty years, "tell me why Bill drank the Lestoil."

"My crutchin' taste buds were destroyed for a week!" Buchs complained. (In the Maryknolls, they had been taught to use the word "crutchin'" in place of any vulgarisms the novice may have used in his previous life; "crutchin'" was Bill's trademark.)

A lifelong romantic, Buchs had half a dozen loves, but never married. He was looking for a Miss America with a 180 IQ, who would idolize him alone, his friends used to say. ("Buchs, we can understand why you're looking for this mythical creature," we used to needle him, "but assuming she exists, why, exactly, would she be interested in you?")

For almost thirty years, he had a routine of going to our house on Utah Avenue, to enjoy my mother's home cooking and company every night, and to do verbal battle with the Old Man. After dinner, he would drive to the American University library, read and study the history and biography he loved, then, around midnight, repair downtown, refreshed, and meet his friends, who gathered at F. Scott's, the Sign of the Whale, and the Desiree.

One year, Bill came by my house once a month, borrowed a new volume of Will Durant's eleven-volume series on civilization on each visit; and returned them all — completely underlined. An exhausting conversationalist, he would sit in my kitchen from noon to three — taking the afternoon off — and relate the most humorous of the anecdotes of history's great men.

"If you're tired of London, you're tired of life," Dr. Johnson had said; and that was Bill's view of this city he loved — and left only when he went into the Maryknolls.

It was Friday, September 20, 1985, just before a noon lunch in the White House Mess with Senator Phil Gramm, who wanted to persuade me of the merits of his new budget-reduction plan. The call came from Hank's wife, Micheline. Normally effervescent, this time the voice with the British accent was full of pain and grief. "It's Bill," she said. "He's got cancer. Hank's terribly upset; he came home crying."

"I'm going home," I said.

"No, stay there, your mother will be calling you about the CAT scan."

During lunch, I tried to focus on the idea about which Gramm was so enthusiastic. But all I could think of was Buchs. How could this be? Then, my mind flashed back several weeks. Bill had complained of a pain in his right side, thinking he had strained some muscles while weight-lifting. And, just last Sunday, Shelley had received an abrupt telephone call from him. "Hey, Shelley, do you have a Jacuzzi?"

No, my wife replied; we have a steam bath and a sauna — and you're welcome to come over and use them.

"Thanks, but I need a Jacuzzi; I have to get rid of this back pain!"

The Filipino attendant placed the telephone on the table. It was my mother, with confirmation.

On Monday, Bill had come to the house from his apartment, running a high temperature. Around 5 P.M., he said he had to get some exercise and was going next door to run the Saint John's track. Early today, she said, Hank and Crick took him to Sibley Hospital for a CAT scan. Bill, who detested hospitals and distrusted doctors, insisted on returning home as soon as it was done.

At 11:30 A.M., my brothers got the devastating report. The scan showed that Bill's liver was shot through with holes, and the doctor wanted him to return to the hospital. To spare him the truth, Hank and Crick told him the CAT scan "didn't take," because he was so anemic, and he would have to go back.

"I can't talk anymore," my mother said.

The White House car drove me through Rock Creek Park to the big white house where my eight brothers and sisters and I had been raised. After Shelley arrived and we got more details from my mother, we went over to Sibley, and up to the seventh floor. Bill was covered with a single sheet that his legs kept kicking away. He searched my eyes for some reprieve from the death sentence his heart told him had been passed against him.

He was only "run down," we assured him; he had probably not been eating right; possibly he had hepatitis; the doctors were going to keep him a while to build him up.

"What did the CAT scan say?" he asked over and over.

"The CAT scan shows an enlarged liver," we lied. The doctors want to take more tests in the morning. Don't worry.

We called Bay in California.

"I'll catch the next plane," she said.

"Bay," I said, "if you fly back here and show up in Bill's hospital room, he will know you aren't coming all that distance because of hepatitis."

"I want to see my brother before he dies," she said in tears. "I'm coming home."

We stayed with Bill until 6 o'clock, and then returned to my parents' house. My father, who had spent most of the summer in

Sibley with complications following hip surgery, was on the patio. He was staring straight ahead into his rose garden, toward the statue of Saint Francis beyond.

"Bill's eyes," I said, "looked at me like the eyes of some hunted animal, begging me not to take its life. And I couldn't do anything, anything at all, to help my brother."

Silent for a moment, Pop answered: "Eye has not seen, nor ear heard what things God has prepared for those who love Him," he said. "Saint Paul has taught us that."

Then he added, "Bill's been a good boy, always faithful to the Church."

That evening the whole family returned to Sibley; Bay arrived at midnight; Shelley and I went home at one, and Jack and Buck kept the vigil through the night.

On Saturday morning, the doctors injected a needle into a lump "the size of a baseball" they had found under Bill's arm; they said the results of the biopsy would not be back until 5 P.M.

By early afternoon, my parents, and all of our family, were on the seventh floor of Sibley Hospital. We took over the waiting room, breaking into shifts of two or three at a time, going in and out of Bill's room. Bill, who loved the Maryland "Terps," insisted on watching the football game on television, but at each commercial break, he asked the same question: "Has the report come back?"

It won't be back until five, we told him.

"Is this the end of Rico?" my younger brother, Buck, the doctor, heard Bill say at one point. What did he mean, Buck asked? Was that some name by which Bill had been known when he was growing up? No, I said, "Is this the end of Rico?" was a line from a movie we had seen as chidren; and in the '50s it had meant "the end."

At 5:10 P.M., the elevator doors opened and Bill's doctor, accompanied by an oncologist, stepped out. Their faces were grave. As the family gathered around, they gave us the details.

Bill had cancer inside the lump, cancer in the adrenal glands, cancer in the liver, "cancer all through his body."

"How long does he have?" Hank asked.

"I give him no more than twenty-four hours," the doctor replied.

The shock was immense. Bill had walked into the hospital yesterday. The doctor then asked if we wanted any special efforts made to keep my brother alive. We said no. We told Bill the biopsy was positive, that he would have to start chemotherapy Monday. At the same time, we called Father Dooley at Gonzaga; he arrived within an hour. Using a coffee table as his altar, Father Dooley said mass, and gave communion to the family; then he went alone into Bill's room.

In Vietnam, Crick had doubled as a "medical officer," putting dog tags between the lips of dead eighteen-year-old troopers before sending them home. Nevertheless, he got up and left, saying, "I can't take this one — not Buchs." Around 9 P.M., Shelley and I left as well. Bay drove our parents home.

At ten, Jack called to say Bill was dying. The agonal breathing that is prelude to death had begun. Shelley and I were five minutes late. Jack had closed his eyes. I held Bill's wrist, and tried to close his slackened jaw; it would not stay closed, but fell open, again and again, leaving the mouth forming the *O* of death. As I came out of his room, the dam burst and the tears came freely.

Within minutes, we had all left the hospital to drive back home to Utah Avenue; and there, again, the tears came freely, from a family not much given to tears.

Sunday morning, I went down to my basement and drafted the obituary of William B. Buchanan, Jr., my oldest brother, and Shelley and I delivered it ourselves to the *Washington Post*.

The three days that followed brought to the house on Utah Avenue, and to Gawler's Funeral Home on Wisconsin, not only the friends of Bill's manhood, but the friends of our childhood. Among the first to arrive at the house were the Kadow twins, Brian and Kevin, with all the liquor and beer that would be needed at the wake.

The shock and the anguish of that thirty-hour ordeal, coming, like the thief in the night of which the New Testament speaks, to a family that had been spared tragedy, I shall never forget. Watching my oldest brother dying in front of me, seeing him in agony on his deathbed and then in his coffin, was the most searing experience of my life. For months afterwards, I could see his desperate eyes looking back up at me, pleading with me, his younger brother, for help I could not provide. And I could not speak about him, or look at a picture of the family — with Bill in it — without coming close to breaking down again.

Bill's death was, in a sense, a beginning, a beginning of the end of the family as we all knew it and loved it, parents and children, growing up, getting on. The family would never again be whole or together, on this earth.

And that death, as nothing else, reimpressed upon my soul the ultimate inconsequentiality of all the things of this world — the fame, the fortune, the titles, the money — and the centrality of friendship, family, and faith.

"You will learn there are only two important things in this life," an old priest once told me, "to live well, and to die well." The old priest did not mean to die full of honors, surrounded by admirers, but to die bravely, and in the Faith; and he did not mean to live successfully and comfortably, but to live truthfully and honorably and with courage.

My oldest brother lives now, "where, beyond these voices, there is peace," but that is what he is telling the family he loved, which will also, soon, cross over.

13

Democracy Is Not Enough

As political philosophy derives its sanction from ethics, and ethics
from the truth of religion, it is only by returning to the eternal
source of truth that we can hope for any social organization which
will not, to its ultimate destruction, ignore some essential aspect of
reality. The term 'democracy,' as I have said again and again, does
not contain enough positive content to stand alone against the forces
you dislike — it can be easily transformed by them. If you will not
have God (and He is a jealous God), you should pay your respects
to Hitler and Stalin.

— *T. S. Eliot,* 1939

WHILE my late brother was an idealist all his life, and an
incurable romantic, Bill believed in candor; he believed
in the truth, in telling it and in living it. That quality
sometimes made Buchs an uncomfortable companion to have beside you on the next bar stool, but Bill would have endorsed heartily the sentiment of the late Arthur Koestler: "One should either
write ruthlessly what one believes to be the truth, or shut up."

That is what I have sought to do in these concluding chapters, to
write what I believe to be the truth about what today imperils the
body, but, more importantly, afflicts the soul of the American Republic, and about what, I believe, is required of us to meet the
biblical injunction "Physician, heal thyself."

In many ways, a nation may be compared with a family not
unlike our own family. Its health, spiritual as well as physical, is
always more important than its wealth. The things that truly count,
the character of its people and the bonds of its unity, cannot begin
to be measured by reference to any number on a balance sheet.
And the threats that can exist to a family's security and survival

have their direct counterparts in the threats to the fabric of a society, a country, a nation.

Though a wealthier people than our forefathers could ever have dreamed of our becoming, we Americans are today as divided as we have been in our modern history; and the divisions are far deeper and more profound than those that separated us, say, in the 1950s. We no longer share the same religious faith, the same code of morality, the same public philosophy. It is not simply about the role and responsibility of government that we disagree; today, our ideas of freedom and virtue and patriotism collide. As the conflict between the Communists in Managua and the *contras* in the hills reveals, we Americans no longer even agree on who our enemies are. And because our disagreements go far beyond the old political question of how we divide the pie, of "who gets what," our politics have taken on a new aspect. Our political and social quarrels now partake of the savagery of religious wars because, at bottom, *they are religious wars*. The most divisive issues in American politics are now about our warring concepts of right and wrong, of good and evil. In a way the Kerner Commission never predicted, we have indeed become "two nations."

What I offer, then, in these final chapters, is an agenda on which Americans must necessarily disagree, not only about the means proposed, but about the ends. It is an agenda, then, only for those who wish to see Judeo-Christian values ascendant again in American society and undergirding American law, for those who believe that in economic matters, modern government is, more often than not, the impediment of genuine progress, for those who yet understand there can never be true detente, and no true peace, until the Soviet Union, the sole cause of the East-West conflict, is, in author George Weigel's word, "de-Leninized."

JUDEO-CHRISTIAN VALUES

Half a century ago, during a depression in which a third of America's wealth would be wiped out and a fourth of her labor force left idle, Franklin Roosevelt said our difficulties, thank God, "concern . . . only material things." That time is gone. No matter the *Les Misérables* rhetoric of Mario Cuomo, America's crisis in 1988 is a crisis of prosperity, not poverty.

Materially, we have never been better off; the United States is the most vibrant, energetic society on earth. If our political system is gridlocked, our economic system has been unleashed. Over the past five years, the U.S. economy has undergone the longest peacetime expansion in a century. Fourteen million new jobs have been created; 61 percent of adult Americans are employed, the highest figure in history; $2 trillion has been added to the value of a stock market where the Dow-Jones industrial average (even after Black Monday) has almost tripled since 1982. While Western Europe's labor force has remained frozen in size since 1960, the United States has added 45 million jobs. The per capita income of minority Americans is at an all-time high, having risen 15 percent in four years. While not all Americans have shared equally in the prosperity, most Americans will likely look back upon the middle 1980s as "the good old days."

Yet, beneath the glittering prosperity of a $4 trillion economy, there is a deepening social crisis in America. Between 1960 and 1985 funds for income support in the United States rose from $20 billion to almost $400 billion, from 4 percent of the Gross National Product to 10 percent. Yet, this spectacular explosion of the Welfare State was accompanied, writes Dr. Roger Freeman of the Hoover Institution, by an equally "spectacular rise in all forms of crime, family abandonment, child neglect, widespread adoption of ruinous lifestyles and destructive behavior, and an exponential growth of drug and alcohol use."

In 1948, one in eight black children was born out of wedlock; in our major cities, today, it is closer to five in eight. The black family that survived segregation, depression, and war collapsed under the Great Society. The greatest cost of the Welfare State is not to be measured in dollars; and it has not been paid by taxpayers. Begun with good intentions, the Great Society ended with the worst of results. While hundreds of billions have been piled upon the national debt, we have created in America's great cities a permanent, sullen, resentful underclass, utterly dependent upon federal charity for food, shelter, and medical care with little hope of escape.

But America's social crisis is not confined to the inner city, nor can all responsibility be laid at the feet of the federal government.

Since the 1973 Supreme Court decision *Roe v. Wade,* some eighteen million unborn children have been aborted in the United States; the equivalent of the population of Australia has been sliced up in the womb and sucked out, in a country that endlessly lectures the world on human rights. While the Supreme Court may have given its *nihil obstat* to the slaughter of the innocents, the federal government did not mandate those eighteen million deaths. We, the people, did. For those who believe in the sanctity of all human life, the abortuaries of the West are the Free World terminals for the trains that left earlier this century for destinations like Vorkuta and Kolyma, Treblinka and Auschwitz, killing fields founded on the Orwellian principle that while all human beings are equal, some are more equal than others.

Since Rachel Carson wrote *Silent Spring* a quarter-century ago, Americans have shown a robust determination to preserve our natural environment, to clear lakes, rivers, and streams of the raw sewage of the industrial society. No commensurate concern, however, has been manifest over the raw sewage that, simultaneously, began to flow through America's culture, courtesy of the Supreme court. In the Secular City, what enters the mind seems of less concern than what enters the stomach.

Then, there is AIDS. Has ever there been a more telling example of the mental confusion and moral cowardice of our time than the timidity of our Lords Temporal and Lords Spiritual in refusing to condemn the perpetrators of this epidemic that will kill more Americans than Korea and Vietnam?

Compassion for the victims of this dread disease does not relieve us of the obligation to speak the truth: Promiscuous sodomy — unnatural, unsanitary sexual relations between males, which every great religion teaches is immoral — is the cause of AIDS. Anal sex between consenting adults is spreading the virus from one homosexual to another, thence into the needles of addicts and the blood supply of hemophiliacs.

Five years ago, when I wrote that New York City, on the eve of that celebration of sodomy known as "Gay Pride Week," should shut down the squalid little "love" nests called bathhouses, the incubators of the disease, I was denounced as a "homophobe" by the Governor and Mayor of New York. Because these men were morally confused, men and boys continued infecting one another in the bathhouses, and continued killing one another. And, today, nine-year-olds are being educated in the use of condoms. But, it is not nine-year-olds who are buggering one another with abandon, spreading this deadly virus; it is not nine-year-olds who threaten doctors, dentists, health workers, hemophiliacs, and the rest of society by their refusal to curb their lascivious appetites. By the way in which they define themselves, the militant homosexuals are killing themselves. What, precisely, is "gay" about that?

To destroy a country, Solzhenitsyn wrote, you must first cut its roots. If America's roots are in Judeo-Christian values and traditions, they have, in large measure, been severed.

To some Americans, the rise of the Religious Right, a decade ago, was an ominous development; to others of us, however, it was the natural, healthy reaction of a once-Christian country that has been force-fed the poisons of paganism. As Bernanos wrote of another time, to be a reactionary today may simply mean to be alive, because only a corpse does not react any more — against the maggots teeming upon it.

Religion is at the root of morality; and morality is the basis of law. Many decades ago, America's intellectual elite privately uttered its *non serviam* to the God of Christianity. America, meanwhile, continued to live off the inherited capital of the old faith. Now, the dissent from, and disbelief in, traditional Hebrew and Christian values and proscriptions is widespread. The routine deference once accorded the traditional churches is no longer proffered. In books and plays and films, priests and pastors and rabbis are mocked for the amusement of modernity. The Secular City is brimming with self-confidence.

And, here, we come close to the heart of America's social crisis. The United States is divided not only between Left and Right. What is social progress to secular America is advancing decadence to traditionalist America.

While some of us look back, nostalgically and fondly, on American history, the liberal and radical now look back and see more that is sinister: slavery and segregation, the despoliation of the environment, the maltreatment of the Native American, the repression of women, the exploitation of labor.

Washington, D.C., the only electoral precinct to vote for both McGovern and Mondale, is Vatican City to secular America. Here, abortion is a matter of choice; sex and morality are separate realms; the use of "recreational drugs" is rarely prosecuted; and the great sin is "discrimination." Aeroflot may fly in to Dulles Airport; South African Airways is banned. You do not violate the Second Commandment here by taking the Lord's name in vain, but by ridiculing affirmative action and telling ethnic jokes. When they violated this commandment, Cabinet secretaries James Watt and Earl Butz were driven from our Garden of Eden with the flaming sword of hostile publicity. Like all militant faiths, secularism has its own methods for punishing heretics and policing orthodoxy. Poor Gary Hart. Caught *in flagrante* violating the traditional moral code, he appealed to the higher morality of this capital city, plaintively asserting he had faithfully refused to take PAC money for his presidential campaign.

The hard truth with which conservatives must come to terms is that the resolution of America's social crisis may be beyond the realm of politics and government, in a democratic society. If men have come to believe homosexuality is a "legitimate" and even commendable "life-style," that abortion is a matter of personal choice, that "pornography" exists only in the eye of the beholder, no federal law will dissuade them. If a woman has come to believe that divorce is the answer to every difficult marriage, that career comes before children, that the day-care center is the proper place for infants and toddlers and the boarding school for the younger children, no democratic government can impose another set of values upon her. If half of America has given up "the old-time religion," no political party and no national administration can reconvert that half of a country. If our traditional pastors and priests and rabbis and preachers have lost their congregations, even the most brilliant of political communicators or leaders will not retrieve the lost sheep. Politics alone cannot change the human heart. Much of what ails America, then, is not a "problem" that can be "solved" by political action; it is a predicament with which we must learn to live.

But this necessity — that we understand and accept the limits of politics in a democratic society — is not an argument for quietism. Traditionalists and conservatives have as much right as secularists to see our values written into law, to have our beliefs serve as the basis of federal legislation.

"Why are you trying to impose your values on the rest of us?"

Among too many raised in the Judeo-Christian tradition, that taunt has engendered a moral disarmament and political paralysis. But the underlying premise is that a democratic society may be constructed upon values and beliefs found in the books of Rachel Carson, Ralph Nader, Betty Friedan, and Alfred Kinsey, but not upon values and beliefs found in the Pentateuch and the New Testament. To accept that argument is to permit ourselves to be driven permanently from the public square.

Someone's values are going to prevail. Why not ours? Whose country is it, anyway? Whose moral code says we may interfere with a man's right to be a practicing bigot, but must respect and protect his right to be a practicing sodomite? Why should the moral code of modern secularism prevail? Simply because the militant homosexuals have come marching out of their closets is no reason for the saints to go marching in.

The Old and New Testaments are not only infallible guides to personal salvation; they contain the prescriptions for just laws and the good society — for building a city set upon a hill.

Again, religion is at the root of morality; and morality is the basis of law. The only questions are whose religion, and whose morality, shall we consult. Environmentalism, feminism, humanism, consumerism, secularism, and socialism have all taken on the aspect of religious faiths in our time, but these "isms" have no greater preemptive claim to serve as the basis of law than the tenets of Judaism, Catholicism, Mormonism, or Protestant Fundamentalism.

The only option the traditionalist and the conservative have, then, is never to cease struggling — until we have re-created a government and an America that conforms, as close as possible, to our image of the Good Society, if you will, a Godly country. That struggle will be endless; and it will define us, test us, and likely provide us the only temporal reward we shall know.

"THAT EMINENT TRIBUNAL"

For the past three decades, the true "rogue elephant" of the American government has not been the CIA; it has been the U.S. Supreme Court. *No conservative reformation of American society can succeed, without its recapture — for constitutionalism.* Since the mid-1950s, using its power to "interpret" the Constitution, the Supreme Court has literally remade the face of America. The Left has never had so powerful or effective an ally.

Under the rubric of the First Amendment, the court has unleashed a flood of pornography; and told us we are powerless to staunch it. All fifty states have been forced to redesign their legislatures according to a one-man, one-vote dictate the Founding Fathers rejected for the Congress.

The City of Boston — the Cradle of Liberty whose leaders, two centuries ago, dumped His Majesty's tea into the harbor to protest a penny tax — sat supinely by while a federal judge rearranged its classrooms on a racial grid, destroying its public schools. George III would never have dared to do to the American colonists what the federal justices routinely do to us.

In 1973, seven of them discovered in the "penumbra" of the Constitution the right to an abortion neither the Framers nor any previous court knew was there.

In a series of decisions, dating to *Miranda* in 1966, the Court has reinterpreted the Bill of Rights to tie the hands of police and prosecutors, and has manifested its contempt for our system of trial by jury. Jurors have been denied the right to know about confessions, denied the right to see captured evidence, denied the right to hear of the suffering imposed upon the families of murder victims, before imposing punishment. Such knowledge might "inflame" them.

In a nation whose Declaration of Independence presupposes the existence of a Supreme Being, God, the Bible, and the Ten Commandments have been ordered out of the public schools. And for thirty years, one cowardly Congress after another has refused to slap down our legislating justices; and no President has dared stand up to them.

How does one break the power of an Imperial Judiciary? How do conservatives, who revere the Constitution, rein in a renegade Court?

When Mr. Justice Brennan writes his personal revulsion of the death penalty into a Constitution that implicitly provides for a death penalty, what do we do? When Mr. Justice Marshall stands the civil-rights laws of the '60s on their head, asserting, "You guys have been practicing discrimination for years; now it is our turn,'' how does one restrain Thurgood Marshall?

When his National Recovery Act was struck down by the "nine old men," FDR ridiculed this "horse-and-buggy construction of the commerce clause," and proceeded to try to pack the Court. When Thomas Jefferson was ordered to turn his presidential papers over and appear in a Richmond court, he simply refused. Andrew Jackson declared contemptuously of the great Chief Justice, "John Marshall has made his decision; now let him enforce it." And Abraham Lincoln, responding to *Dred Scott,* powerfully challenged any claim of the Taney Court to judicial supremacy: ". . . if the policy of the Government upon vital questions affecting the whole people is to be irrevocably fixed by the decisions of the Supreme Court . . . the people will have ceased to be their own rulers, having to that extent practically resigned their Government into the hands of that eminent tribunal."

For thirty years now, the United States Supreme Court has been on a rampage over the laws and customs and Constitution and mores of the American people. Ideologues carrying the title "Mr. Justice" have abused their power to impose upon a supposedly self-governing people their own idea of the Good Society. Yet, Messrs. Blackman, Brennan, Douglas, and Marshall can hardly be blamed for doing what willful ideologues have always done. The fault lies with our elected leaders, and those of us who put them in office.

A self-governing people should not be waiting for Mondays in October to learn from Olympus what kind of state legislatures we may have, whether the death penalty shall be permissible, whether abortion is a constitutional right, whether racial quotas are to be a permanent feature of America's future. Nor were we left defenseless by the Founding Fathers against a renegade court.

There is, first, the appointment power of the President. Given the advanced age of the liberal justices now sitting, the first term of the next President will likely provide an opportunity to reshape the Supreme Court into the next century. Not only the character, but the philosophy, of the new Supreme Court Justices should be made, by the Republican party, a central issue in the campaign of 1988. Given the malice and ferocity of the assault upon Robert Bork, any traditionalist and constitutionalist should know what to expect. The Left will not surrender control of this institution without the bloodiest of political battles, but the next President should nominate one strict constructionist after another, until he or she is confirmed. If we are to remain a self-governing people, the Supreme Court must cease to be a Super Legislature for the nation.

While the appointment power of the President is an invaluable shaping tool that President Reagan used to excellent effect, it is, however, not the only instrument to contain this usurpatious court.

By the Constitution itself, Congress is empowered to restrict the "appellate jurisdiction" of the federal courts, including the U.S. Supreme Court. For reasons we can now appreciate, the Founding Fathers gave that right to our elected representatives. A strong and self-confident President should, when the next decision of dubious constitutionality is handed down, send Congress legislation carefully restricting the Court's right to decide such matters.

Should the Court attempt to strike down that restriction as itself unconstitutional, we will have set up an overdue confrontation — between the elected branches of government, and the least democratic branch, whose members are subject to impeachment. If the President and Congress will stand up for their own constitutional rights, the outcome of such a confrontation is not in doubt.

And, then, there is the Bully Pulpit, provided for Presidents to comment publicly on the wisdom, or the folly and unconstitutionality, of Supreme Court decisions; that pulpit ought to be used. Felix Frankfurter wrote pointedly to President Roosevelt in 1937, "People have been taught to believe that when the Supreme Court speaks it is not they [the Justices] who speak but the Constitution, whereas, of course, in so many vital cases, it is *they* who speak and *not* the Constitution. And I verily believe that that is what the country needs most to understand." Bringing about that understanding is a necessary duty of the next President.

Why, indeed, are modern Presidents so reverential of Court decisions whose intrinsic lack of merit is manifest to the American people?

In the Nixon era, the Supreme Court, by a single vote, gave the President permission to test a nuclear device at an underground site in Alaska. Environmentalists had gone into federal court to have the test blocked. Had the Supreme Court refused that "permission," President Nixon once told me privately, he would have, as Commander in Chief responsible for the national security, fired off that nuclear weapon — right in the teeth of their prohibition.

And it is past time for some selective civil disobedience. *Lex mala, lex nulla* — an evil law is no law — Thomas Aquinas taught us. A National Day of Prayer, conducted *inside* the classrooms of America's public schools, by Christian teachers, in open defiance of Supreme Court edicts, would send a message of political strength the Secular City could not ignore. The movement to restore religion to a central role in the education of American children is a cause that is just. It is time that cause found its own Rosa Parks.

ECONOMIC POLICY

Wherever it has been imposed upon a people, Marxism has diminished the human condition and degraded the human spirit. Indeed, Karl Marx has been the indispensable textbook for virtually every squalid and failed enterprise of the second half of the twentieth century, from Mao's China to Jaruzeski's Poland, from Castro's Cuba to Gorbachev's Soviet Union. Where democratic capitalism has been tried, however, whether in the United States or Japan, in Western Europe or on Asia's Pacific Rim, prosperity has resulted, and freedom has taken root. The nexus between economic freedom and political freedom has been established.

The principal economic task, then, of the federal government should be to protect and preserve our free system of democratic capitalism, to guarantee a stable currency, and to get the hell out of the way.

In the past two decades, the primary contributions of political interventionists in the American economy have been negative. The $2 trillion debt, the $200 billion deficit, the socialist bias of the tax code that Mr. Reagan has done so much to correct, the ruination of the currency through inflation, the energy "crisis," all have been the contributions of incompetent, meddling politicians. As a breed, the politician is a predator to be watched, not a figure to be consulted. "It would take a genius to screw up the American economy," Richard Nixon was once quoted; but we know from the Carter years, "genius" is not a requisite.

A conservative fiscal policy for the United States would include these elements:

(A) A sustained campaign to reduce the top marginal tax rates — moving toward the ideal of a flat tax, which comports with the principle of equal justice under law. Just as with Social Security, so, too with the national defense: even the poor should pay *something* — not because America needs their contributions, but because for their own self-respect, they need to be contributors. No man or woman should be a freeloader when it involves the national defense.

(B) The current bias against savings and investment in the tax code should be removed. Japan and Taiwan do not tax capital gains; for the United States government to tax the return on investment at 28 percent is a socialist folly that leaves America at a competitive disadvantage with dynamic free Asia. While interest expenses are deductible here, interest income is taxable. Why this bias in the tax code, if it is our purpose to encourage saving and discourage debt?

(C) No new federal taxes should be imposed. The nearly 20 percent of GNP the federal government collects in revenue is enough government. Nor should future tax cuts be ruled out by the foolish prescription that future tax "reforms" must be "revenue neutral."

The political appeal of tax cuts that expand the wealth of people ought not to be surrendered by Republicans, when Democrats would never surrender the political appeal of spending hikes that increase the power of government.

(D) While media interest is forever focused on the size of America's deficit, it is the size of government — i.e., aggregate government spending (federal, state, local) that now consumes nearly 40 percent of America's GNP — that retards America's economy. That load is too immense for the producers' sector to carry, whether that 40 percent is acquired by taxing away the public's income, or "borrowing" away the public savings.

The only realistic hope for halting the inexorable growth of government is a strong, articulate, conservative President able to present his case to the country — over the heads of Congress and the national press. Whatever reform enhances the power of the President, such as the line-item veto, should be promoted.

(E) The congressional budget process should be abandoned; it is a demonstrable failure. Repeatedly, President Reagan proposed the elimination of dozens of programs only to see his own party "compromise" away his political courage, to reach "consensus" with a Democratic House that has not balanced a budget since Lyndon Johnson left office. The reason much of America now holds Ronald Reagan responsible for adding a trillion dollars to America's debt is because, too often, the President followed the counsel of Republican moderates and "compromised" with Congress, instead of using his veto pen and shutting down part or all of the federal government, if necessary, to win his budget cuts.

Budgets are about priorities. As the two parties are in fundamental disagreement over national priorities, resolution should be sought in healthy political conflict.

On the spending issue, both parties have eaten of the forbidden fruit; both have voted to override presidential vetoes; both have partaken fully of the politics of pork. Neither is blameless for the growth of government; and neither can be fully trusted. With the Republicans, the spirit is willing, but the flesh is weak; with the Democrats there is no spirit.

(F) In the fight to maintain open markets, worldwide, a strong President, again, is indispensable. Congress, composed of 535 moving parts, is incapable of resisting the concerted pressures of American corporations and unions.

Among the great American achievements of the twentieth century is free Asia, democratic and capitalist, which arose out of the ashes of World War II and Korea. Hundreds of millions of the most capable and energetic people in the world are prospering, on the side of freedom, because of the bravery of American soldiers, sailors, Marines, and airmen, and the magnanimity and statesmanship of the postwar leadership of the United States and General MacArthur. To squander that in an absurd "trade war" because we cannot compete with Korean cars or Japanese computer chips would be an act of almost terminal stupidity for the West.

(G) While the conservative is first cousin to the libertarian on economic deregulation, on social deregulation we part company. Requiring used-car dealers to be federally regulated lest they rip off teenagers may be a Naderite fantasy; requiring shatterproof glass in new cars is not.

While radio and television stations should be free to form networks and introduce new technologies, there is no constitutional "right" to befoul the airwaves any more than there is a constitutional right to pollute our rivers. The airwaves, after all, belong to the people. Nor is there any First Amendment right of broadcasters to deny legitimate dissenting voices a hearing on matters of public policy. The "fairness doctrine" should be reinstated.

The arrogant claim of the intelligentsia — "Everyone's market must be regulated, except my own" — traditionalists ought not to accept. Polluted ideas have caused greater injury to mankind than polluted water, and the marketplace of ideas is in greater need of watching than the marketplace of goods.

Ideas have consequences; and all ideas are not equal.

The Republican party should stand for traditional values, even when that means standing against laissez-faire; we should set our sights on something higher than the bottom line on a balance sheet. The greatness of a country and the goodness of its people are not to be measured by its GNP.

THE COLOR-BLIND SOCIETY

During the campaign of 1964, with the assistance of Dr. Martin Luther King, the label "racist" was appended to the national Republican party. The proximate cause was Barry Goldwater's principled opposition to the Civil Rights Act of 1964. While the allegation is a lie, the Left has perpetuated that lie, successfully; and in the black community it is now widely accepted as truth.

Only among black Americans did Richard Nixon, who had as strong a civil-rights record in Congress as Kennedy or Johnson, fail to gain between the 43 percent victory of 1968 and his 61 percent landslide in 1972; only among black Americans did Ronald Reagan fail to gain between 1980 and the forty-nine-state landslide in 1984.

Almost every issue today that affects black America — from sanctions against South Africa, to quotas in employment, to add-ons to the Welfare State — is force-framed by politicians and the press into a "moral" question; and resistance by the Right is invariably written off as rooted in racism.

Like all coins, however, this one, too, has a reverse side.

While black America has been persuaded to distrust the conservative, white America has come to believe the Democratic party lacks the moral courage ever to say no to the NAACP or the Black Caucus.

Considering that the Republican party has won four of the last five presidential elections, three in history-making landslides, it is the Democratic party that has the relevant racial problem. The decisive swing vote in presidential politics is *not* a minority vote. The pragmatic, as well as the principled, course for the Republican party, then, is to change neither ritual nor liturgy to accommodate those who disbelieve, but to leave the church door open and keep the welcome mat out. Most of the converts are coming our way; and there is nothing wrong with the philosophy we espouse.

Racial and ethnic quotas are wrong, whether used against black or white, Gentile or Jew; coercive busing is wrong, whether used to take black children out of their home neighborhood solely because of their race, or white children. "Minority set-asides" are scandalous — not only in practice, but in principle as well.

For a quarter-century now, Jesse Jackson & Co. have played Pinocchio to the Foul Fellow and Gideon of paternalistic liberalism, and millions of black people have paid a terrible price for having let themselves be led to the Pleasure Island of the Welfare State — that wholly owned and operated subsidary of liberalism — that has destroyed the moral fiber of America's black poor.

Welfare "is a narcotic, a subtle destroyer of the human spirit," FDR warned half a century ago, "we must and shall get out of this business." Unfortunately, we did not.

If we believe in creating a "color-blind society," where men are judged "not by the color of their skin, but by the content of their character," let us get on with it.

The conservative movement and black America are on many matters natural allies; the values in which we believe are not different from the traditional values black pastors and preachers taught their people through the years of segregation. We both believe in law and order, in the war against narcotics and crime, in excellence in education, a first requisite of which is discipline in the classroom. And as President Reagan has demonstrated, the party of democratic capitalism produces real jobs, not CETA jobs. More black Americans are at work today than ever before in American history; and black income exceeds the per capita income of British and French.

But if black America has come to believe that quotas are the path to progress, that equality of result should be mandated, that the American majority needs to make permanent reparations for segregation, that the federal government will lead us to the Promised Land, then black America should continue to vote as it has voted. Because that is what the party of Mondale and McGovern and Carter and Kennedy also believes.

"Seek ye first the political kingdom, and all others will be added unto it," was the counsel Kwame Nkrumah gave to black Africa. Now, Nkrumah is dead, and Africa is dying — because it followed his foolish counsel.

In America, the Chinese and Japanese, victims of savage racial discrimination, progressed when they abjured the political kingdom and sought, first, the economic kingdom.

"There is no heaven on earth and no promised land . . . around the corner," Eric Hoffer wrote, "only the rights and burdens and the humdrum life of the run-of-the-mill American."

So long as a people, any people, blames the real injustices in its past for all its present misfortunes, it forfeits its future. So long as a people, any people, seeks its salvation through politics, it will seek in vain. Only when the Irish buried their resentment and hatred of the British in the soil of their new country, America, did they get on with building their dreams.

WHOSE SCHOOLS ARE THEY ANYWAY?

When the Baltimore Conference of Catholic Bishops of 1884 mandated the parochial school system, the hierarchy did not walk away because the public schools were anti-Christian. To the contrary, they viewed those schools as militantly Christian; but a Protestant Christianity pervaded, and the Catholic bishops wanted Catholic children brought up in their own faith.

In the intervening century, the curricula of these public schools have been systematically drained of all Christian content; they have lost all trace of their original character. Neither Catholic nor Protestant today, they have become, in the late Will Herberg's description, "secularist and even militantly so."

"Children in public schools are under an influence with which the churches cannot compete and which they cannot counteract," writes Charles Clayton Moore of *Christian Century*. "The public school presents the church with a generation of youth whose minds have been cast in a secular mold."

While the biblical story of Creation is no longer permitted even as fiction, Darwin's theory of evolution is taught as fact. Having explained to generations of American young that they are the descendants of monkeys, we manifest surprise when they emulate their forebears. "In a sort of ghastly simplicity," C. S. Lewis wrote, "we remove the organ and demand the function. We make men without chests and expect of them virtue and enterprise. We laugh at honour and are shocked to find traitors in our midst."

Having captured America's public schools and converted them into the parish schools of secular humanism, the new religion that "dare not speak its name" will not readily surrender these unrivaled pulpits for the propagation of the faith. And the secularists make no secret of their intent. The "battle for humankind's future must be waged and won in the public school classroom by teachers who correctly perceive their role as the proselytizers of a new faith" was the militant message of the award-winning essay of the American Humanist Association in 1983.

Allied with the secularists, the media, the academic community, the state and federal education bureaucracies stand shoulder to shoulder, while the federal courts shelter their monopoly control. But that coalition is not invincible. Secularism remains a minority faith; and more and more Americans are aware that the expulsion of traditional religion and ethical instruction from the public schools has gone hand in hand with a decline in public education and a collapse in public morality. Nor is that collapse difficult to understand. Those who have captured the heights of modern education have no conclusive, convincing answer to the age-old question of youth: "Why not?" Why not casual sex? Why not smoke marijuana? Why not use drugs? Why not steal a pair of Adidas? Why not cheat in class?

Even by utilitarian and pragmatic standards, secularism does not work.

If secularist ideology continues to mandate the permanent expulsion of traditional religious teaching from the public schools, we should probably get on with the building of new prisons. For external force is the only line of defense left, when the internal constraints of an informed conscience and religious belief no longer bind.

Someone's values, someone's beliefs, someone's concept of morality, will be transmitted during the education of the child. The only question is whose? T. S. Eliot's insight, cited at the head of the chapter, is apposite. While democratic rule is in the bones of every American, democracy is not enough. Democracy is an empty vessel into which a corrupt and decadent society may be fitted quite as well as a just and good one.

Today, many Christians, emulating the Catholics of a century ago, are walking away from the public schools, creating their own Christian schools. While these efforts merit sustenance and support — through vouchers and tuition tax credits — there is no reason to raise the white flag and forever surrender the public schools; they can be recaptured.

Why should a secularist minority, rather than a believing majority, see its values dominant? Whose schools are they, anyway?

If there is to be an honorable truce in the religious war over public education, the first necessity is to dismantle the monopoly, to decentralize the system, to terminate federal dictation, judicial and bureaucratic. America is indeed a diverse and pluralistic society; and *any* judicial decree in the modern era — about what textbooks must go in, and which prayers must go out — will trample upon someone's convictions and beliefs.

If tolerance is a necessary virtue in our democratic society, there must be tolerance for the views of the majority. The village atheist has the right to be heard; he has no right to be heeded. While he has a right not to have his own children indoctrinated in what he believes are false and foolish teachings, he has no right to dictate what other children shall and shall not be taught.

The way to bring permanent peace to the war over public education is to replace autocratic, with democratic, decisionmaking. Parents and teachers, not judges and bureaucrats, should decide what the schools shall and shall not teach. Let the character of each public school reflect the character of the neighborhood and the community in which it is located; and let the schools compete with one another for the allegiance, the tax dollars, and the vouchers of parents and taxpayers.

There is no more important battle shaping up in America than for the hearts and minds of the next generation. Whether that generation will be traditionalist and Christian, or agnostic and atheist, whether its code of morality and ethics will be based on Judeo-Christian beliefs or in the secular nostrums of the moment, will be largely determined by America's public schools. And Christianity, too, has the right to compete.

And if the Supreme Court declares that secularism's triumph is irreversible, that secularism's monopoly is permanent, the answer, again, is not to change those beliefs; it is to change the Court.

Modern education appears to be another arena, where modern man has had to study, and study hard — to learn how not to succeed. In the 1950s, there was no "crisis" in American education. There were private schools and parochial schools, ghetto schools and public schools, most of which succeeded, on a fraction of the dollars we spend today.

America, in 1988, invests $300 billion annually in education, more per capita than any nation in the world. Yet, in community after community, the education offered and the education received is abysmal. The answer is surely not another income transfer from taxpayers to an industry that has failed. Rather, it lies in the recognition that monopolies always breed mediocrity, that the calcified education industry is in as great a need of competition as was the American auto industry two decades ago. As parents and teachers are the two groups most interested in, and responsible for, the education of children, surely, the way to improve education is to enhance the classroom authority, the prestige, and the pay of the best of the teachers, and to provide greater freedom of choice for all the parents.

Teacher testing, to identify the best and brightest and to eliminate the incompetents, seems a *sine qua non* of educational progress. The best of the teachers, once identified, need the authority both to impose discipline in the classroom and to remove troublemakers from the school. Parents need to be provided — through educational vouchers — a greater range of choices as to where and how to spend their education dollars. The introduction of competition for the educational dollar is surely among the better, and fairer, ways to improve the educational product. Finally, tuition tax credits, which would strengthen the private, Christian, and parochial school systems, would maintain a competitive system, the continued health of which is vital to the health of a public school system that still educates 90 percent of American children.

In Washington's inner city, black Protestant and agnostic parents have been voting with their children for years — against the free public school system and in favor of parochial schools where Catholic religious instruction remains mandatory. Apparently, exposure to religious instruction is less traumatic to these parents and their children than the federal courts would have us believe. Through vouchers and tuition tax credits, poor and working-class parents can begin to exercise, on behalf of their children, some of the same freedom of choice that wealth has always provided to the rich.

A SECOND CONSTITUTIONAL CONVENTION

The Episcopal Church, a wag once observed, is the Republican party at prayer; and, of all the political notions that have alarmed our high church Tory party, the idea of a second constitutional convention has always stood near the top.

A "runaway convention" would undo in days all the wonderful work of the Founding Fathers, it is argued. But this is absurd. Any amendment adopted at a constitutional convention would still require the approval of three-fourths of the states. As the failure of the Equal Rights Amendment demonstrates, ratification is neither simple nor easy. *No flawed or foolish amendment adopted by a constitutional convention would survive.*

And, as our third century of constitutional government begins, there are crises that need addressing, and deformities in the balance of political power that need correcting.

In 1787, the central government was too weak; and the state legislatures too strong. Today the President has been weakened;

and the Supreme Court has arrogated to itself the power to remake society without the consent of the governed. The least democratic of the branches of government needs to be brought back within the confines intended by the Framers.

Coincidental with a call for a second constitutional convention, a conservative President should propose amendments to both Houses of Congress. Here are ten amendments whose submission to Congress, even if none survived a floor vote, would engender an overdue national debate — and create election-year issues — about where we are going as a people:

1. For purposes of this Constitution, the unborn child shall be considered a "person" whose right to life shall not be abrogated without due process of law.

2. Nothing in this Constitution prohibits the states from imposing capital punishment upon conviction for heinous crimes, or for habitual criminal offenders.

3. English is the official language of the United States, and Congress may legislate to this end.

4. All federal judges and Justices of the Supreme Court shall be subject to reconfirmation by the Congress every eight years.

5. Decisions of the Supreme Court may be set aside by a two-thirds vote of both houses of Congress, with the approval of the President.

6. The Twenty-Second Amendment to the Constitution (restricting Presidents to two full terms) is hereby repealed.

7. The President shall propose and Congress shall adopt, for each fiscal year, a budget balanced between projected revenues and expenditures.

8. Nothing in this Constitution prohibits the free and voluntary expression of religious faith, or religious instruction and association, within the public institutions, or public schools, of the United States.

9. Discrimination on the basis of race, either in favor of or against any citizen, is prohibited by this Constitution, as is the use of racial criteria in the involuntary assignment of children to public schools.

10. Coterminous with each presidential election, the American people may, through popular initiative and referendum, invalidate, or make, laws for the United States.

All the above are populist amendments, designed to broaden the scope of human rights and restore the power of the people to shape their own society and destiny. They would diminish the power of unelected judges and enhance that of elected officials. While the language of each amendment is certainly subject to lawyerly review, the point is: Conservatives have nothing to fear from a constitutional convention and much to gain by focusing national debate on the issues that divide the Republic.

A call for a constitutional convention would reveal which of the two parties is populist, and which elitist, which trusts and which fears the people.

The first of these amendments would not only overturn *Roe v. Wade*; it would broaden the concept of human rights to include the most vulnerable. Restoration of the death penalty as an instrument of retribution and deterrence is the purpose of the second. When we outlaw capital punishment, we send a statement of moral timidity to the criminal elements among us: You may rape our women, sell narcotics to our children, butcher and maim our innocent — but nothing you do will convince us to take away your life. No matter the savagery of the crimes you commit, your life is secure. That is not the kind of message our lawless society can afford to send.

American politicians jabber constantly about the "war against crime," but almost all the dead are among the innocent. Only one in fifty felonies results in conviction and incarceration; only one in a thousand murderers pays with his life. If some celebrated king of organized crime, who made his millions pumping heroin into the veins of children, were once photographed entering the gas chamber, on the way to his eternal reward, the war against drugs would begin to be taken seriously by those against whom it is supposedly waged.

The amendments dealing with the judiciary would redress the balance of government power. There is no reason an excellent President should not serve for more than eight years; nor any reason an incompetent judge or Justice should burden us with his presence any longer than that.

The English-language amendment has already been appended to the California Constitution; if we are to remain one nation and one people, we need a common language. And the right of initiative and referendum is enjoyed by voters in numerous states.

The central problems attendant to a balanced budget amendment are (A) to make it efficacious (as Congress is already annually violating a balanced budget law, what is to be the sanction for violating such an amendment?), and (B) to prevent its being used to force an annual increase in taxes.

The antidiscrimination amendment, a reaffirmation of the spirit and letter of the Civil Rights Acts of 1964, is meant to ring down the curtain on the Second Reconstruction.

Finally, the amendment dealing with prayer and religious instruction would impose a truce in the Supreme Court's thirty years' war against Christianity and restore the intent of the Framers: that the government remain neutral among the various denominations, not hostile to the very idea of religion. The reason the First Amendment prohibited the "establishment" of a national church, after all, was to *permit* the robust "free exercise" of religion in the United States, not to *prevent* it. The "free exercise" of religion is what the First Amendment is all about.

Again, though, what needs to be appreciated, especially by conservatives who preach limited government, is the limits of government.

Americans, from the illegal immigrants to the Silicon Valley Yuppies, are a vibrant, energetic people, capable of working hard and building a prosperity no nation has ever known. But the same free people who built Silicon Valley also built West 42nd Street, built the abortuaries of America, and financed with their ad and subscription dollars the booming new industries in X-rated films, television, magazines, and books. It is we the people, not the government, who created the world's largest market for illicit drugs. While the Welfare State may have contributed mightily to the destruction of the inner-city black family and bears a measure of responsibility for the disasters that followed, government did not destroy the suburban family. The "private sector" did that. What we have found these past thirty years is that while governments can build mighty warships and magnificent superhighways, government cannot build strong families. If these are disintegrating, the best a wise government policy can do is to slow the process; it cannot halt it.

Like a modern hospital, with all the technological advances of the modern age, good government can help restore to health a nation taken ill; it cannot give meaning in life to a people who have lost their faith; it cannot forever restrain a generation that wishes to "live fast, die young, and leave a good-looking corpse." Democracy really has no answer to decadence. Churchill, after all, could halt neither the decline of Great Britain nor the dissolution of an empire whose time had come; and Marcus Aurelius could not save Rome.

Unlike the crisis of "material things" FDR confronted in 1933, our crisis of the spirit in 1988 may be beyond the ken of politics, and beyond government solution. The duty of the political conservative, then, is to do our best to make ourselves, and our government, the allies of our Judeo-Christian values, to make government again the protector and friend of the permanent things, to do the best we can in the times in which we live. And to put our trust and faith, ultimately, not in ourselves alone.

14
Containment Is Not Enough

While capitalism and socialism exist side by side, they cannot live in peace. One or the other will triumph — a funeral dirge will be sung over the Soviet Republic or over world capitalism.

— *Lenin,* On Peaceful Coexistence, 1920

IN THE summer of 1974, at Richard Nixon's last summit, as I disembarked with a party of Russians and Americans from a bibulous boating party on the Black Sea, I was startled to see stumbling toward me the General Secretary of the Communist party of the Soviet Union. Czar Brezhnev gregariously slapped our backs and shook our hands, then he passed on along the boardwalk in the direction of his magnificent power cruiser, repairing to his dacha to sleep it off.

Yet, between that afternoon in Yalta and his death eight years later, this seemingly unexceptional man, who relished fancy cars and fast women, added to the Soviet empire nations, peoples, and territories to rival the imperial acquisitions of Josef Stalin and Peter the Great. Leonid Brezhnev was not a good Communist; he was a great Communist.

Under his nearly two decades of dictatorial rule, the Soviet Union emerged from the humiliation of the Cuban missile crisis to become the first military power on earth. During his final decade in power, Brezhnev appended to the Soviet empire all of French Indochina, Afghanistan, Ethiopia, Portuguese Africa, Grenada, and Nicaragua, millions of square miles of territory and tens of millions of people. While Russian advisers were expelled from Egypt, more important, from Moscow's vantage point, American influence and power were expelled from Iran, on Moscow's southern frontier, the dominant power position on the Persian Gulf.

Historically, great empires have required countless wars and many decades to realize gains of this magnitude. The military cost of Moscow's emergence as a global power was a couple of regiments lost in the Afghan Anschluss. Meanwhile, the West provided $80 billion in bank credits, to pay for the machinery, technology, and grain we pressed upon Mr. Brezhnev to ease Moscow's transition from continental power to global empire.

How did this apparatchik, who presided over a huge, heterogeneous, and, in many ways, backward country with but a fifth of the West's capacity, build the modern Soviet empire?

Brezhnev succeeded, first, by the ruthless, purposeful exploitation of all the human and material resources at his command. (The Soviet Strategic Rocket Forces are estimated to have cost half a trillion dollars, the sweat of a generation.) By Western standards, Brezhnev may have been a stolid and unimaginative leader; but he knew what he wanted: imperial power; and he gave the West the illusion of what it wanted: peace.

"Detente," Brezhnev wrote in the halcyon days of that era, "in no way replaces, nor can it replace, the laws of class struggle. . . . Detente, in fact, creates favorable conditions for struggle between the two systems and for altering the correlation of forces in favor of socialism." And, so, it did.

Second, Brezhnev cheated upon every agreement he ever signed with the United States — SALT I, SALT II, the ABM Treaty, the Code of Detente, and the Helsinki Agreement on human rights. The Yom Kippur War in 1973, the invasion of South Vietnam by the Soviet-supplied armies of the North in 1975, the incorporation of Angola into the Soviet empire in 1976, the invasion of Afghanistan, all took place during the detente decade of the 1970s.

Now that the U.S. Senate is considering yet another arms control agreement, and moving toward a second detente, this time with Mikhail Gorbachev, the history is worth remembering.

Mikhail Gorbachev, who has given our giddy world a new word, *glasnost,* has lately declared it to be Moscow's intent to "open up" the Soviet Union, to democratize, to rid the world of nuclear weapons; and much of Western Europe, exhilarated by the prospect, cannot understand why the Americans have not taken this bold new leader at his word.

In fairness to Mr. Gorbachev, he is not "lying." In his own

mind, he is no more a dishonorable man than was General Eisenhower, who used false messages and phony maneuvers to deceive Hitler into believing the Allies would invade at the Pas de Calais. In the war with the West that is the *raison d'être* of Lenin's party, strategic deception is not immoral, it is mandated. "Telling the truth is a bourgeois prejudice," Lenin wrote. "Deception on the other hand is often justified by the goal." What will perplex future historians is not why Brezhnev and Gorbachev deceived us, but why we believed them.

What is it in the composition and character of twentieth-century Western man that causes him to believe in the efficacy of pieces of paper co-signed by men who have, again and again, manifested their contempt for treaties?

Dedicated to "the pursuit of happiness," secular, hedonistic Western man apparently cannot accept that there are men and regimes dedicated to the proposition that history has passed a death sentence against the West, and their mission is to carry it out. We cannot accept that the Kremlin has in mind for us what it had in mind for Nicholas Romanov, for the Polish officers at Katyn, for Masaryk and Imre Nagy.

Surely, we tell ourselves, they cannot intend *that*.

"Mankind cannot stand too much reality," T. S. Eliot once said; there is great truth in the observation. High among the reasons Western man will not face up to the painful truth is that to accept this truth — that ceaseless conflict is our lot in life — would require sacrifices and risks were are unwilling to bear. Better not to know what is in the medical report.

Naïveté is not our problem; the West's problem is willful self-delusion. The reason we do not learn from history is that we do not wish to learn from history. The truth is: There is no agreement with the Soviets that will make us more secure, because Western security is not the purpose of Soviet policy. There is no big deal that can be brokered to bring us "peace" — because "peace" is not what Moscow has in mind for the West.

When Churchill described Stalin's Russia as "a riddle wrapped in a mystery inside an enigma," he was more accurately describing the West. It is, after all, Western man, not Soviet man, who has, from the turn of the century, invested his hopes in disarmament conferences, naval agreements, Kellogg-Briand pacts, nonaggression treaties, "confidence-building measures," East-West summits, SALT agreements, Helsinki accords — only to see all that parchment, like Christmas wrapping, turned into trash, as nation after nation has paid with its life or its freedom for our relentless folly. It is Western man, not Communist man, who belongs on the psychiatrist's couch. In the quarter-century since the late James Burnham called liberalism the "ideology" of Western suicide, the validity of his insight has come home again and again.

To say that we must "trust" the Soviets rather than distrust them, that we should seek security in SALT agreements and summit meetings rather than superior military power, these are *ideological* assertions, contradicted not only by history but by common sense. It is not natural for men to believe nonsense like that; this is something that has to be taught and learned and held — against the evidence of experience and the evidence of the eyes.

Among the reasons that conservatism remains the hope of the West is that true conservatism, in the aphorism of H. Stuart Hughes, "is the negation of ideology."

As Russell Kirk has written, true conservatism has rejected all the secular ideologies that have arisen since the Enlightenment: Jacobinism, socialism, communism, anarchism, syndicalism, fascism, Naziism, and, yes, liberalism. Only by sweeping aside the nostrums and dictums of ideology can we see the world, and our enemies, clear and whole — and act to save this last best hope of mankind, the United States.

The *raison d'être* of any realistic (i.e., nonideological) American foreign policy must be the preservation of the Republic. Other goals (e.g., the advancement of human rights, the alleviation of poverty and hunger, the spread of democracy) are secondary and subordinate.

If this is true, then, for the indefinite future, the central concern of American foreign policy must be the USSR. With between nine and ten thousand nuclear warheads targeted on the United States, the Soviet Union alone has the military capacity to bring an end to the United States.

Since FDR first met Stalin in Tehran in 1943, every American President has met with the rulers of the Soviet Union, and each has sought some relationship other than permanent conflict. FDR sought postwar peace through wartime collaboration and appeasement; Truman adopted a policy of containment, manifest in the

Marshall Plan and the Korean War; Eisenhower pursued a Cold War strategy of "peace through strength." JFK and LBJ sought coexistence, while Nixon and Kissinger went further, to "detente," in the hope they might "build a generation of peace." President Carter naïvely tried to will the East-West conflict out of existence, telling the world in 1977 that we Americans "have gotten over our inordinate fear of Communism." Carter was awakened from his dogmatic slumber by the sound of the Soviet army rolling southward into Kabul.

Nine American Presidents then, including Mr. Reagan, have sought an end to the conflict between the United States and the Soviet Union. None has succeeded, for a simple reason: None has addressed the root cause of the Cold War.

The reason the permanent conflict between East and West, the Cold War, cannot be negotiated out of existence by any American President is because the origin of that conflict lies in the character and nature of the Soviet regime itself. Lenin's party, which rules the Soviet Union, is a war party; the very reason for its existence is to wage war against the West.

The sole justification for its monopoly of economic and political power, for the massive police state machinery of the KGB, for the enormous military establishment, for the press censorship, for the control of the arts, is that the Soviet Union is in a climactic struggle for survival, and control of the destiny of mankind, against the West. Should the Cold War end in true peace, the Communist party would no longer have any reason to exist.

As Lenin's party exists to advance Lenin's revolution, negotiating true peace with the West would be tantamount to suicide. Like the great white shark, the Communist party of the Soviet Union must swim constantly and feed constantly upon new prey, or it will sink to the bottom and die.

The converse is also true.

When Mr. Reagan tells Mr. Gorbachev the United States does not "threaten" the Soviet Union, Mr. Gorbachev knows better. *We do threaten the Soviet Union.*

The very existence of a free, prosperous, powerful democratic Republic halfway around the world is not only the last obstacle to Soviet global hegemony, it is a vast mirror in which mankind can see the immense depth of Communist duplicity, deceit, and failure.

The United States is mankind's most eloquent statement that Marxism and Leninism are squalid, self-serving lies.

Because the Communist party is, at its core, a war party, every "peace" agreement signed with it is a fraud on their part, and an act of self-delusion on ours.

Peace, to an American, means the peace with justice that exists within a free society, where individual freedom and human rights are guaranteed. Peace, to the Soviets, means an end to all resistance to the dictatorial power of the Communist party, within the Soviet Union and, ultimately, in the world. Americans would fight rather than accept that kind of peace for the United States; and the Communist party of the Soviet Union has struggled for seven decades to impose a Communist peace upon its captive nations, and, ultimately, mankind.

The inescapable conclusion is that the only way to bring an end to the East-West struggle, the only way to bring true peace to mankind, is to eliminate the root cause of the century's struggle, the Communist party of the Soviet Union. Containment is not enough.

True peace requires the de-Leninization of the Soviet Union, the replacement of Lenin's party in Moscow by a regime, military or civilian, responsive not to the Leninist ideology of endless war, but to the legitimate aspirations of the captive peoples within the Soviet Union.

Between the Russian *nation* and the American *nation,* there are no quarrels — historic, territorial, or economic — that could remotely justify war. Indeed, both the Russian and American people share the same enemy, the Communist party of the Sovet Union.

In his fine new book, *Tranquillitas Ordinis,* George Weigel chides Ronald Reagan for saying that we Americans should "let the Soviets have their rotten system." As Weigel correctly comments, " 'Their rotten system' is a principal obstacle to the pursuit of peace, security, and freedom in the world. Changing it is essential."

The day Western man accepts that the struggle is irreconcilable, that it is Lenin's party that must end up on the "ash heap of history," the Communist tide will begin to recede.

The Soviets are not ten feet tall, and the men who occupy the Kremlin have greater reason than we to fear the outcome of their permanent conflict with a spirited, resolute, determined United States.

Vision, moral courage, and leadership are all that are lacking in the West, not material resources. Together, the West and free Asia dispose of five times the economic power, and many times the military potential, of the Soviet empire.

The Communist vision and creed no longer inspires men; too many men and women have followed Lincoln Steffens "over into the future"; they have seen Moscow's Brave New World; and they know it does not "work." Where the '30s generation of leftists turned to the Soviet Union, in the naïve hope of a better world, the modern American who sells out his country's secrets to the Soviet Union invariably does so for drugs or money or sex.

Communism is a death faith, a "shameful ruin" in the phrase of Milovan Djilas. From Ethiopia to Vietnam, from Poland to China, a "Marxist economy" has become a synonym for economic shambles, and Leninism a synonym for state terror.

Mother Russia is a country where alcoholism is rampant, where the average woman has six abortions, where the life expectancy is falling, where the Moslem and Asian populations are exploding while European Russians are barely maintaining zero population growth. It is a nation where the labor force is sullen and nonproductive by Western standards, where the magnets of hedonism and fundamentalism (Christian and Islamic) are pulling youth away from the party. The state religion of the Soviet Union — Marxism-Leninism — has no hold upon the popular imagination. Indeed, the hidden purpose of *glasnost* is to modify the excesses and follies of Marxist economics — to save the Leninist dictatorship.

Everywhere today, the Soviet empire is threatened by men's desire to be free, to worship God, to determine for themselves their national destiny. The empire is overextended, vulnerable at its extremities, in Africa, Afghanistan, and Central America.

Nor does Communism manifest its old self-confidence.

When President Reagan ordered the liberation of Grenada by American airborne troops and Marines, the panic in Havana and Managua was visible. One or two regional reversals of the Brezhnev doctrine, through insurgency or Western intervention, and, worldwide, the message will go forth that the Soviet empire is no more invincible or inevitable than the Western empires it succeeded. The sudden collapse of just one Communist regime — in Nicaragua, Angola, Afghanistan, even a popular upheaval in Yugoslavia — could produce a chain reaction throughout the Soviet empire that would strain its resources to the limit.

If permanent conflict is the hand history has dealt us, and if our necessary aim is the displacement of Lenin's party and the interment of its ideology, we need, first, to understand the new realities of 1988. Nostalgia for the 1950s will not bring them back. An opportunity was lost then that cannot be recaptured.

Neither in real nor relative terms is the United States the dominant power we were from 1945 to 1965; and the world knows it. Similarly, neither Britain nor France is what it was in 1956, before Suez.

With five million men under arms, with at least 2,500 strategic launch vehicles and 10,000 warheads, with 50,000 tanks and a navy twice the size of the combined American fleets, with an air force that dwarfs NATO, the Soviet empire is the greatest military power in history. Upon the Soviet empire today, the sun never sets.

Major regional powers also exist — North and South Korea, Vietnam, India, Pakistan, Iran, Iraq, Syria, Israel, South Africa, Cuba, Nicaragua — that were marginal powers three decades ago.

President Reagan's intervention, with fewer than 2,000 Marines, in tiny, disintegrating Lebanon, where warring factions of thousands are armed to the teeth, proved a bloody lesson that U.S. policy cannot be based upon nostalgia for a world that no longer exists. In 1958, the United States could dictate a political situation in Lebanon with the mere landing of 10,000 Marines; a quarter of a century later, dictating a political solution in Lebanon required the will, and the forces in place, to disarm the murderous militias and to deal with the Syria of President Assad; and the United States came ashore in 1982 with neither.

Second, forces have been unleashed in the modern world — fundamentalism, nationalism, and racism — against which conventional armed forces are as impotent as Conrad's warship firing its tiny cannon into the Heart of Darkness. These forces, especially nationalism and fundamentalism, may ultimately prove to be America's strongest allies in dismantling the Communist empire.

Third, not again in our lifetime will the American people permit

368 ♦ RIGHT FROM THE BEGINNING

the nation to enter a war in which America's vital interests are not clear — and clearly stated — and where there is not a strategy and timetable for victory. Vietnam tore part of the intestines out of the United States; and we ought not pretend we have fully recovered.

Finally, we are a disunited nation and people.

To the American Left, the Soviet Union is not the "evil empire" of President Reagan's depiction, and the United States is not a "shining city on a hill." To the Left, the preferred enemies are not Mikhail Gorbachev or Daniel Ortega, but President Botha and General Pinochet. Dominant in Congress, the mainline Christian churches, the national press, the academic establishment, and the permanent government, the Left does not wish to see the Sandinistas overthrown; it wishes to see the *contras* disarmed and defeated.

This deep and abiding division among Americans, not only over the means but the ends of policy, makes restoration of the foreign policy "consensus" of the 1950s a utopian, unattainable ideal. The hard truth is that in Congress, the Democratic party is becoming an American version of the British Labour party of Neil Kinnock. That our liberal countrymen are today overrepresented in the Congress, the permanent bureaucracy, and the national press presents a hellish predicament, with which any conservative President is simply going to have to live.

Militarily and economically, the United States is a superpower. Diplomatically and politically, however, our President has nothing approaching the flexibility and freedom of action of Gorbachev and his comrades. In some ways, America, post-Vietnam, has become the "pitiful, helpless giant" of Richard Nixon's prophecy.

The only successful approach, then, for a conservative President is dictated by these new realities: Forge a Center-Right coalition with moderate Democrats in Congress, and wage a permanent campaign from the Bully Pulpit against the American Left. Tell the American people the truth, as we believe it, and force the American people to choose again and again — them or us — in national elections, until liberalism is repudiated at the ballot box, and the critical levers of power in Congress have passed into the hands of the Center-Right.

The unvarying recommendation of the moderate Republican — to seek out bipartisan consensus with a Congress dominated by Democrats who agree with us on next to nothing — is a reactionary proposition, rooted in nostalgia for a day that is gone, and a blueprint for permanent policy paralysis.

PEACE THROUGH VICTORY

Like the Russian empire, the successor Soviet empire is truly a "prison house of nations." In seven decades, Moscow has colonized one independent country after another, while the Communist party has sought to extirpate their national self-identity, to replace their institutions with ersatz Communist inventions.

As the hatred and resentment of Communism are greatest *within* the Soviet bloc, populism, nationalism, and fundamentalism are all natural allies of the West. The Catholic Church in Central Europe, the Orthodox faith in Russia and the Ukraine, the Protestant denominations east of the Elbe, and the Moslem believers in Soviet Central Asia are natural adversaries of the Soviet empire.

Instead of constantly seeking to "ease tensions" — i.e., cease resisting politically and diplomatically, and pretend that the philosophical struggle does not exist — the United States should engage the Soviet Union all along the ideological front.

The first requisite of an energetic new policy, however, is an attic-to-cellar housecleaning at the Department of State. While the department contains some of the most able men in American government, the philosophical fault line running through the country runs through Foggy Bottom as well. The career diplomats, by and large, do not share a conservative view of the world; they disbelieve deeply in the politics of confrontation. They are diplomats trained and skilled in diplomacy — when what America must wage on behalf of the West is what one foreign policy scholar, Aaron Wildavsky, has called "a war of ideas to counter a [Soviet] war of violence."

As Moscow beats the drums at Turtle Bay for "independence" for Puerto Rico, let the United States speak up for the independence of Lithuania, Latvia, and Estonia, for an end to colonialism in the Ukraine and Central Asia, as well as Central Europe. As America has returned Okinawa to Japan, we should table in every international forum the demand that the Soviets disgorge the

Kurile Islands, seized from defeated Japan at the close of World War II. As someone once observed, the twentieth century has not brought an end to empires, only the empires of the West. The same powerful rhetoric of nationalism and anticolonialism that was employed against British, Dutch, French, Belgians, and Portuguese should be deployed against the Russians.

And why is the United States not leading the campaign for the peaceful reunification of Germany? The hunger of the German people to have their country restored is a legitimate national aspiration.

To the "national liberation" preached by Moscow, that has produced such horrors in Ethiopia, Cambodia, and Vietnam, the United States needs to preach its own idea of "liberation." The devil need not have all the best tunes.

Young men willing to stand up for their nation's right to be free — whether in the Third World or Central Europe — should have the moral and material support of the United States.

Just as the Soviets have trained Leninists and terrorists and sent them home to rip their countries out of the Western orbit, the United States should establish in Washington a Resistance International, to train patriots, from Communist and Third World countries, on the ways and means to liberate their lands from the great scourge of the twentieth century. The trumpet of freedom may have blown an uncertain sound in our century, but the peoples of the world yet yearn to hear it.

A fundamental element of Western strategy must be to maintain, always, the distinction between the regime and those who are ruled, between the party and the people.

We have no quarrel with any of the peoples held captive inside the Soviet empire, nor they with us. We did not smash their churches, destroy their free unions, murder their poets and priests, strip away their right to speak freely, to travel, to assemble, to vote, to work at a job of their own choice, and to raise their children in their own faith. All these things have been done to the peoples within the Soviet empire by the Communist parties of the Soviet empire.

Indeed, freedom has more steadfast friends inside the Soviet bloc than in many of the chanceries and parliaments of the West.

For decades, Soviet strategic planners have pursued a "strategy of denial" against the West, driving for control of the energy storehouse of the Persian Gulf and the mineral storehouse of southern Africa. With Soviet domination of both, Japan and NATO Europe would be at the mercy of Moscow.

While blocking Moscow's strategy, the United States needs its own strategy of denial — i.e., no more American bank credits, World Bank credits, or Western bank credits to the Soviet bloc.

While we cannot impose our view upon the Europeans and Japanese, we can force our "allies" to choose — between looser ties with us, and closer ties with Moscow. Had Mr. Reagan seized the opportunity when Solidarity was crushed in 1981, and put Poland in default, he could have engendered a credit crisis in the East bloc from which the Soviet empire would have taken a decade to recover.

In early 1985, when I returned to the White House, among my first invitations was to lunch with the late William J. Casey, Director of Central Intelligence. The first thing my friend Bill Casey showed me in his office in Langley was a document detailing the number of Soviet, Cuban, and East bloc spies operating at the United Nations in New York. It was astonishing.

That the United States should, in 1986, be acquiescing in the U.N.'s having become the greatest spy nest in history, operating on American soil, is a mark of the moral confusion that afflicts much of our national leadership. Not a single U.N. agency is tolerated on Communist soil; yet, on New York's East Side, Soviet and East bloc spies, both accredited to and employed by the U.N., spend their days relentlessly looting the industrial and military secrets of the United States. One-fourth of the paycheck of every Communist bloc spy employed by the U.N. is covered by the tax dollars of the American people. From what Bill Casey showed me, the West is the prime subsidizer of the Free World operations of the KGB.

For more than a quarter-century, now, the General Assembly has been the world's foremost forum for the airing of global resentment, bitterness, and hatred of the United States, our allies, and our friends. For our own self-respect, the United States should set a deadline for removal of the U.N., and all associated agencies, from the United States and North America. Any utility the U.N. may have for the U.S. can be realized in New Delhi as well as in New York.

Less than a dozen years before the turn of the century, U.S. foreign policy remains cluttered with the detritus of a postwar era that expired decades ago; cluttered up with ideas and institutions rooted in an internationalism that no longer accords with reality, if ever it did.

Not only the U.N., but foreign aid, the World Bank, the International Development Association, the International Monetary Fund, the Organization of American States, the Inter-American Development Bank, the African Development Bank, all need to be reassessed — and measured against a simple yardstick: Do they any longer advance the national security interests of the United States?

As the U.N. daily reminds us, today's world is a different place from 1960. The United States no longer has any compelling interest in the survival of scores of the 150-plus regimes represented there. In those countries and regions of the world where tyranny abounds, the proper place for an American to stand is, once again, on the side of revolution.

In countless cases, it is time to pull the plug and let nature take its course — to permit these Marxist, socialist, and tyrannical regimes of the Second and Third World to sink in the consequences of their own rancid ideology. What is the sense, for example, of sending a billion dollars to bail out the bankrupt Yugoslav government, or of paying off General Jaruzeski's debts to his American creditors?

Why does the United States continue to send, through the World Bank subsidiary, IDA, more than a billion dollars, free of interest, to the People's Republic of China?

While the Sino-Soviet split is of strategic benefit to the United States, we did nothing to bring it about; and, should the rulers of the two Communist regimes decide again to collaborate, we could do nothing to prevent it.

The United States and China may have a mutually beneficial relationship, but they are no more our "friends" and "allies" than was Stalin's regime during World War II.

While we might applaud the economic "pragmatism" of Deng Tsaio-ping, his Peking regime has upon its hands the blood of tens of millions; it is engaged in cultural genocide in Tibet; its barbaric "one family, one child" policy has resulted in coerced abortions being performed on millions of Chinese women, even into the ninth month of pregnancy. What persecution does Moscow practice that is not endorsed by the People's Republic of China? Our true ally on the mainland of China is not the Chinese government, but the persecuted and oppressed Chinese people.

And what is the sense of this endless flow of foreign aid into the subcontinent of India? What are we getting for it? True, India is a "democracy." So is Sweden, but what has that done for the United States lately that we should pay for it?

To the peoples of Latin America, the government of the United States should say we are not the bill collector for America's big banks; we will no longer collaborate with the IMF in imposing austerity upon their people, to insure they pay their debts. Our national security interest dictates that the peoples to our south be good friends of the American people and good customers of the United States, whether or not their governments are good creditors of Citicorp or the Chase-Manhattan Bank.

As Britain's Lord Bauer has written, "Foreign aid is the source of the so-called North-South conflict, not its solution. It is foreign aid which has brought into existence the Third World as a collectivity." The International Development Agency, the "soft-loan window" of the World Bank, lends Western currencies at zero percent interest to some of the most corrupt, backward, and anti-Western regimes on earth, propping those regimes up, relieving them of the burden of paying politically for their own blunders. What, exactly, is the argument for this kind of international welfare? Why is the government of Tanzania to be preferred to the State of Arkansas, or the State of Mississippi or the State of West Virginia?

We have a "moral obligation" to help "the poorest of the poor" is how the argument runs. But the prime reason the people in these impoverished countries suffer is because of the corrupt, incompetent, and tyrannical regimes with which they are saddled — and to which we are sending this money.

There is no persuasive argument for multilateral aid. If the United States wishes to help a friend in need, or a military ally, America should transfer the funds directly; and Americans, not international civil servants, should reap the benefits and receive the credit.

If the United States is truly serious about "waging war against terrorism," then nations that train terrorists, as well as those that provide sanctuary (Iran, Libya, Cuba, Nicaragua, South Yemen, Bulgaria, Czechoslovakia), should be made to pay a price.

While ambassadorial contact with the Soviet Union remains essential — even given Moscow's appalling record — there is no need for representation in the United States for their malodorous puppet regimes. When Communist and terrorist regimes are using diplomatic pouches to transport bombs, weapons, and drugs into the West, it is an absurdity to treat their "diplomats" as though we were dealing with the Swiss or British or French. What would be lost by shutting down the Bulgarian embassy?

Finally, to demonstrate that an assertive new nationalism is informing U.S. foreign policy, the U.S. should expel the Soviet diplomatic contingent from Mount Alto, the hilltop embassy from which the KGB intercepts messages sent all over Washington, D.C.; second, we should carry out the daylight dynamiting of that eight-story broadcast facility the KGB built for us, at our expense, in Moscow. That the Soviets bugged our Moscow embassy building so massively that we cannot even use it was an act of manifest contempt for the United States; and blowing the place up (it belongs to us, after all) would be the sort of response the Soviets would appreciate and understand.

SOUTHERN AFRICA

Western and American policy toward the Republic of South Africa represents the triumph of moralism over strategic self-interest.

In an Africa beset by corruption, starvation, tribalism, and tyranny, South Africa is arguably the only successful country on the continent. Yet, the West has joined an international cartel to cripple that economy and bring down that government. Apparently, it is necessary to destroy South Africa in order to save it.

As leader of the West, America's place should be at South Africa's side, sheltering this tormented country from her enemies, as South Africa makes the necessary transition from apartheid to a more just society. Instead, Congress has cast our lot with those attempting to kick South Africa to death for a sin of segregation of which America herself was guilty for decades.

Grounded in hypocrisy, economic sanctions are utterly self-destructive. Black Africans are today going without work, their families without income, so that self-righteous Americans can sleep better at night, having struck a blow against apartheid.

The goal of U.S. policy in southern Africa should be a subcontinent oriented toward the West, a subcontinent from which our enemies have been expelled. How does destroying South Africa, a Western as well as an African nation, conceivably contribute to that objective?

In the war between East and West for control of southern Africa, the Communists dominate Angola, wield decisive influence in Mozambique and Zimbabwe, and have placed their wagers upon the terrorist cadres of the African National Congress. The assets of the West are South Africa, democratic Namibia, the UNITA resistance forces of Jonas Savimibi in Angola, and the RENAMO rebels of Mozambique.

Any policy designed to protect vital Western interests — in the minerals, geography, sea lanes, and people of southern Africa — will build upon, not destroy, those assets. And a strategy for Western success, building upon those assets, suggests itself.

If the Mozambican regime refuses to expel East bloc police and military, the United States should shift support to RENAMO. A victory by the RENAMO rebels, overthrowing the Marxist regime in Maputo, would end Soviet influence in Mozambique and leave Prime Minister Robert ("Comrade Bob") Mugabe in Zimbabwe with no friendly outlet to the sea.

Expulsion of the East bloc personnel from Zimbabwe could be made a nonnegotiable demand; and the same squeeze could be applied to landlocked Zambia. From there, Angola could surely be persuaded that the tide of history is running with the West, and that survival for the MPLA in Luanda requires expulsion of the Cubans and a negotiated peace with Jonas Savimibi.

CENTRAL AMERICA

What U.S. policy in Central America has lacked, even under the Reagan Administration, is clarity. What, exactly, do we seek?

If our enemy is the Soviet empire, the answer should be clear:

376 ◆ RIGHT FROM THE BEGINNING

the removal of the Soviet, East European, and Cuban military presence, and displacement of the Communist regime that hijacked the Nicaraguan revolution. America's stated goal in Central America should be the triumph of the Monroe doctrine over the Brezhnev doctrine.

In aligning itself with the Soviet empire, in bringing in Cuban advisers, in fomenting subversion among its neighbors, the Sandinista regime has made itself the enemy of the United States; and the Sandinistas should be treated as enemies.

Unlike their sympathizers in Congress, the Ortega brothers and Tomas Borge are serious men. Having risked their lives to seize power, they will not be talked out of power by Central American diplomats, or bought off by American bribes. Like Fidel Castro, they are dedicated enemies; and seeking their political ruin, not their political conversion, should be our policy objective. (While JFK's CIA, with its exploding cigars and chemicals to make Castro's beard fall out, was off into the absurd, the Kennedy brothers were dead right in their assessment that, in Fidel Castro, they had a permanent enemy whose removal was in the national interest of the United States.)

Both the Guatemala Plan and the Reagan-Wright Peace Plan are rooted in self-delusions. There is simply no "peace" agreement that can be reached that will persuade the Sandinistas to get out of the business of exporting revolution and into the business of exporting bananas. Because the Sandinistas are not businessmen; they are Communists. Either they will be overthrown, and Central America will be free, or they will overthrow their neighbors, and Central America will one day belong to the Warsaw Pact.

With Nixon's hands tied by Congress, and our Vietnamese allies defunded, the Soviet empire prevailed in Southeast Asia.

With Ford's hands tied by the Clark Amendment, the Soviet empire prevailed in Angola.

With Mr. Reagan's hands tied by the Boland Amendments, the Soviet empire has prevailed in Nicaragua.

Off and on for six years, now, Congress has cast a protective arm around an anti-American police state that is laying the foundations for a permanent Soviet beachhead on North America. If the Democratic majority on Capitol Hill ditches the *contras,* Congress should be openly attacked for what it has become: the indispensable partner of the Soviet empire in the communization of Central

America. To Dean Rusk's question, "Whose side are you on?" Central America should yield us the definitive answer.

THE MIDDLE EAST

In June of 1967, in the immediate aftermath of the Six-Day War, Richard Nixon and I flew together into Jerusalem, from the east, in a tiny Israeli observation plane, with a one-armed veteran of the '56 campaign. "This is the first time," the colonel exulted, "an Israeli plane has flown into David's city — from this direction." Beneath us on the road up from Jericho was the burnt-out remnant of Glubb Pasha's Arab Legion: trucks and tanks, sent up by the brave king to relieve his embattled troops in the Old City.

In the two decades since that Six-Day War, East Jerusalem and the West Bank have been integrated into the Jewish State; and here is the insoluble conundrum of the Middle East: No Arab government can acquiesce in permanent Israeli control of the Holy City and Judea and Samaria, and no Israeli government could survive permanent amputation of East Jerusalem and the West Bank.

It takes effort to be sanguine about that region of the world where only the fittest survive. Every year, the number of Palestinians under Israeli rule grows, and the ratio of Arab-to-Jew approaches closer to one-to-one. Every three years, Egypt adds to its impoverished demographic base of fifty million as many infants and children as there are Israelis in the Middle East.

Looking over the sweep of modern history, neither Western democracy nor pro-Western monarchy appears to be a growth stock in the region. Egypt, Iraq, Libya, Ethiopia, and Iran have all seen pro-Western monarchs tumbled in revolution since Eisenhower's time. Syria resides within the Soviet orbit; Tunisia is shaky; uneasy sits the crown upon the head of the King of Morocco, the King of Jordan, and the King of Saudi Arabia. Kuwait and the sheikhdoms waver in the balance; and pro-Western Lebanon no longer exists.

From my two visits to Jerusalem since that June of 1967, it is clear that Lebanon was Israel's Vietnam. The military superiority of the IDF over its neighbors may be greater than ever, but the national spirit within Israel is nothing today like it was in 1967.

The United States' commitments in the region — to keep Israel alive and free, to keep the gulf oil flowing, to keep the friendship of the moderate Arabs, to keep Soviet power out — are among the few foreign policy goals upon which Americans still seem broadly to agree. But America's capacity to maintain these interests has not grown with anything like the accretion of power of those who threaten them.

By the law of unintended consequences, the Islamic revolution, which wiped out the immense American investment in Persia, may yet do greater damage to the Soviet Union, with its fifty million Moslems, than ever it did to the United States. The awakening of the docile Moslem populations inside the USSR, the emergence of a spirit of nationalism in the central Asian "republics" ruled today like colonies from Moscow, could present the Soviet Union with the sort of challenge to its very existence with which it has never heretofore had to cope.

But hope is a virtue, not a policy, and one day, the United States must come to terms with the Iranian revolution. Post-Khomeini, we will have to reach some modus vivendi. For Iran, with her fifty million people and her geographical position, is going to be the permanent power in the Persian Gulf, whether ruled by an Ayatolleh, a General, or a Shah. And, eventually, Iran, even revolutionary Iran, must come to see that the permanent threat to her security and integrity does not come from the superpower on the other side of the world, but from the avaricious superpower with which she shares hundreds of miles of frontier.

Until the day comes, however, when the United States can reestablish with Iran a relationship other than implacable hostility, America's national interest, as well as the vital interests of our friends in the Middle East, dictate a policy of containment of Iran, coupled with a sober awareness that ideas, even terribly misguided ideas, cannot always be contained.

SHALL AMERICA BE DEFENDED?

For two decades, American Presidents have been investing their hopes for security and peace in "the arms control process." To have opposed that process, to have been skeptical about the value and worth of "arms control," is to have placed oneself *extra ecclessiam*. Yet, the results of two decades are worth reviewing.

In 1972, Moscow deceived Henry Kissinger on SALT I, and added to their inventory 2,000 nuclear warheads, aboard 360 new heavy missiles, the SS-19, as a direct consequence of that deception. From the day it was signed, Moscow has cheated on the ABM Treaty, testing surface-to-air missiles at heights and speeds no plane can fly, and building the missile defense radar at Krasnoyarsk.

The chemical and biological weapons agreements have been broken on the battlefields of Afghanistan and Cambodia and in the anthrax laboratory of Sverdlovsk.

By building two new missiles, the rail-mobile SS-24 (ten warheads) and the road-mobile SS-25, the Soviets violated the terms of SALT II; and they have exhibited only contempt for their commitments under the Helsinki Pact. As for the Code of Detente, signed in 1972, which was to govern the behavior of the superpowers when the vital interests of either nation was at stake, Moscow made a mockery of it, within eighteen months of its signing, by collaborating with Egypt and Syria in the Yom Kippur War, and by threatening military intervention to prevent an Israeli victory.

When the "arms control process" began under President Nixon in 1969, the United States was the leading military power on earth; and the Soviet Union had 300 crude missile warheads that could strike the American homeland. Today, the Soviet Union is the first military power on earth; and Moscow has 10,000 nuclear warheads that can strike the United States in thirty minutes; and the United States is forbidden by the ABM Treaty, and, hence, by U.S. law, from defending the American homeland against the only weapons that could destroy it. This is the fruit of the arms control process.

Why, then, does the entire leadership of the Democratic party, and much of the leadership of the Republican party, place such faith in arms control?

The answer again, I believe, lies in "ideology," a system of belief that is impervious to contradiction.

To the comman man, the concept behind the ABM Treaty, i.e., that the more naked we are to atomic attack, the more secure we are, sounds like the very essence of lunacy. To the arms control community, however, mutual nakedness to nuclear attack (Mutual Assured Destruction) is defined dogma, an article of faith. Among arms controllers, the hostility to strategic defense, SDI, which might shield us from nuclear weapons, is as virulent as in Moscow. We must not provoke the Russians by defending ourselves; both nations must remain totally vulnerable, say the arms controllers, for both nations to remain secure.

Nor is this idea — that the more vulnerable we are, the more secure we are — without honorable antecedents.

The Carthaginians destroyed their warships and surrendered their children to Rome as an earnest of good faith that they sought only peace; and modern Americans signed naval agreements with Imperial Japan that required us to destroy battleships and leave our Pacific possessions unfortified and undefended. Eventually, Carthage was razed by Rome; and the Washington and London Naval Agreements led directly to Pearl Harbor. But, to the True Believer, the lessons of history and the record of relentless Soviet cheating cannot invalidate the true faith. Where, one wonders, will this generation pay the price for having burned our incense at ABM and SALT?

It is in the major premise of the "arms control" syllogism that there lies a logical fallacy, the pathetic fallacy, the belief that evil inheres in things, e.g., atomic weapons, not in people. We are threatened, it is said, not by the men in the Kremlin and their awesome military machine, but by the nuclear arsenals on *both* sides; it is the "arms race" that threatens mankind. As we get rid of the weapons, we reduce the danger of war.

But the absurdity of the proposition is self-evident. Canada is more secure, not less, because her neighbor, America, has a mighty nuclear arsenal and a powerful navy; Britain is more secure, not less, now that her ancient antagonist, France, has a nuclear deterrent. What threatens the peace and security of mankind today is not the MX or the Pershing or the Trident or the *force de frappe* (indeed, they have helped mightily to keep the peace), it is the possession of the world's largest nuclear and conventional arsenal by a regime of the character, history, and ambitions of the Soviet Union.

Nuclear weapons are the *ultima ratio* of Western civilization, the last argument against our annihilation. That we are seeking security in their abolition is a manifestation either of religious faith, or mental disorder.

When men cease to believe in God, Chesterton wrote, they do not believe in nothing, they believe in anything. Arms control is the Golden Calf of a West that has lost faith in itself; it is the laetrile of secular man who does not want to believe he is under a sentence of death, or to hear what is required of him to survive. To see Ronald

Reagan speak romantically of a "world without nuclear weapons" is saddening.

That Secretary Shultz, in pursuit of State's obsession with negotiation and treaties with Moscow, has rejected "linkage" is, however, understandable.

For, if we reflect upon the horrors Mr. Gorbachev is perpetrating in Afghanistan, who can take seriously his devotion to "peace"? If we ruminate upon Soviet motives for the transshipment of guns, tanks, helicopter gunships, and Cuban military advisers into Nicaragua, who can believe Mr. Gorbachev seeks true coexistence with the United States? Better to concentrate upon what the Soviets are saying in Moscow and Geneva than upon what they are doing in Central America and the Hindu Kush.

Arms control has become the altarpiece of Western diplomacy, an icon in which it is impermissible to disbelieve. High among the reasons Western statesmen refuse to yield up that belief — despite massive evidence of Soviet treaty violations — is that their own historic reputations are now fully vested, in the "process." Indeed, if arms control one day leads to nuclear blackmail, or, worse, to nuclear war and strategic disaster, Western man will prove to have been the greatest fool history ever produced. And, surely, that cannot be.

Unfortunately, from the East, one hears only the sound of building, building, building.

In a realistic defense policy, America's strategic needs are quite simple — enough weapons, offensive and defensive, to ride out a Soviet first strike, and destroy, with the U.S. retaliatory blow, every major target of military value in the Soviet empire. Under those conditions, the hard-headed men in Moscow would never strike, and the West would be invulnerable to blackmail.

A realistic American defense posture would thus entail replacement of the Titan and Minuteman II missiles (and, eventually, the Minuteman III) with the MX, full deployment of the Trident submarine force with the D-5 missile, and the beginning of an embryonic SDI system, to defend, first, America's deterrent, and, subsequently, America, herself, and her allies. (The Midgetman, a single-warhead, road-mobile missile that may be vulnerable to Soviet SDI, is a $50 billion waste of tax money that should be spent on a deterrent that deters.)

While a recent national survey found that half the American

people believed the United States had a "good" or an "excellent" defense against Soviet missiles, the truth is, we have *no* defense. We are forbidden by the ABM Treaty of 1972 from defending ourselves from rocket attack; and, even if we had the legal right, the United States today lacks the military capacity to stop a single one of the 10,000 atomic warheads Moscow has targeted upon the United States. Given America's near abandonment of its air defense system decades ago, the U.S. Air Force would have a hellish time stopping an all-out attack by Aeroflot. Should, God forbid, deterrence fail, the United States will be, literally, at the mercy of Moscow.

Strategic Defense, SDI, is one of the great ideas of President Reagan, one of the great ideas of our age — a futuristic defense of America based not on the duplicitous signature of some Soviet Party Chairman, but on the technological superiority of the United States. Using space-based, and land-based, antimissile weapons (laser-beam, charged-particle-beam, kinetic-energy weapons), SDI, fully deployed, would be capable of so "degrading" a Soviet first strike against the United States that no sane Soviet commander would even contemplate launching one — and inviting a retaliatory attack upon the Soviet Union.

No treaty Moscow will offer us is worth giving up SDI.

With the advances already made in defensive technologies, with the 150 billion rubles the Soviets have sunk into missile defense, SDI is going to be a reality. The only question left is whether America, or the Soviet Union, will be the nation defended.

As this is being written, the United States is preparing to ratify yet another arms control agreement with the Soviet Union, and to launch a second detente. In such an environment, what is written above will be briskly dismissed as "Cold War rhetoric," utterly unsuited to the warm new era of *glasnost*.

Nonetheless, this arms control agreement will — like its predecessors — leave the West weaker, and Moscow stronger. Early on, the Soviets will ignore the "spirit" of the agreement; later on, we will discover they have ignored the letter. Why? Because they are Communists, and strategic deception in the war against the West is mandated. "In our society," Brehznev reminded the Twenty-fifth Party Congress, "everything which builds up Communism is moral." And, then, one day, this detente, like the Lenin-Stalin "detente" of the 1920s, the wartime "alliance" built around Lend-Lease, and the "detente" of the '70s buttressed by Western credits, will end, as they all end, in disillusionment and despair. Because the root cause of the war against the West — the character of Lenin's party that rules the empire to wage the war — will remain unaddressed. And when this period of "coexistence" passes, perhaps another message will receive a hearing.

This, then, as I said at the outset of this book, is "what we believe and how it is we came to believe it."

While the ideas, thoughts, and sentiments above would have been uncontroversial three decades ago, they are deeply controversial today — because America has changed.

Somewhere, we lost that sense of national alertness and apprehension the Cold War gave to all of us — even though we confront a global empire today more powerful, resourceful, and dangerous than President Eisenhower ever confronted in the time of Khrushchev. Too many of us have forgotten the lessons Washington taught, that "to be prepared for war is the best means of preserving peace," that MacArthur taught, long before Vietnam, that in war there is no substitute for victory.

While we appear to have discovered the Philosopher's Stone, which turns base metal into gold, when it comes to creating prosperity, our $4 trillion economy enriches a society our enemies regard as decadent, and even our friends regard as not entirely well.

Over the past quarter-century, we have sought to substitute ersatz new values for enduring old ones; and the experiment has tragically, transparently failed. The national epidemics of divorce, abortion, desertion, child abuse, drug abuse, wife abuse, teenage pregnancy, suicide, murder, and mayhem testify that something is fundamentally wrong with America.

After a quarter-century in politics, journalism, and government, "close to the Western summit," I am persuaded that while we knew much less about science and technology and economics in the '40s and '50s than we do now, we knew and understood more then about human nature. The old lessons of home and church and school have stood the test of time, while the new theories expounded endlessly on the talk shows are truly the "higher humbug."

In that year of seeming anarchy, 1968, the late Will Herberg put his finger upon the "moral crisis" of our time. "[T]he really serious threat to morality," he wrote, . . . consists not in the multiplying violations of an accepted moral code, but in the fact that the very notion of morality or moral code seems to be itself losing its meaning for increasing numbers of men and women in our society. It is here that we find a breakdown of morality in a radical sense, in a sense almost without precedent in our Western history. To violate moral standards while at the same time acknowledging their authority is one thing; to lose all sense of the moral claim, to repudiate all moral authority and every moral standard as such, is something far more serious. It is this loss of the moral sense, I would suggest to you, that constitutes the real challenge to morality in our times.''

Will Herberg pointed us twenty years ago to the source of the social conflict that is so embittering us and dividing us, a conflict reflected again in the brutal nomination battle of Judge Robert Bork. Part of America believes that if we are to become again a good country, society must conform more closely to concepts found in the Old and New Testaments. Another part of America believes progress is to be measured by how far we get away from such stifling and repressive nonsense.

If we Americans no longer share the same religious creed, the same code of morality, and manifestly we do not, the day is not far off when we will no longer share the same idea of virtue or freedom or patriotism, because, ultimately, these, too, are rooted in one's deepest beliefs, one's "religious" beliefs.

The crisis of America, then, is really not over "material things," and it is not a "problem" that lends itself to a political "solution." It is a terrible predicament with which we Americans are going to have to learn how to live, while protecting and preserving this last best hope of earth.

For one man, however, half a century of life has only persuaded me of the truth of what I was taught, even before I knew how to think. Country, family, and faith, these are the things worth dying for; these are the things worth fighting for; these are the things worth living for.

Index

Nash, E. V., 297, 298, 300
National Review, 218–221, 245, 246
National States Rights party, 294
Newhouse, S. I., 286, 288, 291
Newman, Paul, 159
Newspaper Guild, 269, 280–281
Newsweek, 8
New York Graphic, 237
New York Herald-Tribune, 281
New York Mirror, 281
New York Newspaper Guild, 280
New York Printers Union, 280
New York Times, 233, 275
New York World Telegram & Sun, 281
Nixon, Richard, 4, 9, 16, 27, 40, 48,
   81, 88, 95, 148, 162–163, 186–187,
   205, 219–221, 228, 244–245, 258–
   259, 285, 289, 315, 316, 319–323,
   324–326, 345–346, 347, 349, 364,
   376, 377
Nkrumah, Kwame, 351
Nocturnal Adoration Society, 74–75
Nofziger, Lyn, 108
Nolan, Tommy, 121
North, Colonel Oliver, 227, 228
Nugent, Elizabeth, 220

Oakes, John, 233
O'Boyle, Cardinal Patrick A., 64, 115–
   116, 131, 302
O'Brien, Dr. John, 76, 77
O'Connor, Cardinal, 71
O'Donnell, Dougie, 119
O'Leary, Brad, 301
O'Leary, Jerry, 58
Oliver, Dick, 253
Oliver, Don, 232, 235, 237, 242–243,
   253, 256, 257
Olympics, 84–85
O'Neill, "Bear," 142–143
Ortega, Daniel, 254
Oshisky, David, 91, 96
O'Sullivan Rule, 28
Oswald, Lee Harvey, 292
Ourisman, Benny, 198–199
Owens, Jesse, 85

Pacelli, Eugenio. *See* Pius XII, Pope
Paul VI, Pope, 78
Peake, James, 296
Pegler, Westbrook, 30–32, 272

Percy, Walker, 20–21
Periconi, Joe, 235
Peyton, Father Patrick, 74
Phillips, Howard, 3, 8, 329
Pierson, Charlie, 264, 268, 277, 300,
   310, 318
Pinkham, Larry, 234, 250
Pitts, Milton, 160–161
Pius XII, Pope, 63, 78
Poindexter, Admiral John, 228
Poos, Bob, 316
Powers, Bertram A., 280
Prince of Wales Society, 301
Professional Journalist, The, 233
Profiles in Courage, 288–289
Puller, Colonel Lewis B. ("Chesty"),
   87

racial discrimination, 356
racism, 51, 130–131
Randolph, A. Philip, 302
Reader's Digest, 8
Reagan, Ronald, 3–4, 6, 11, 12, 16,
   126, 252, 274–275, 320–321, 326,
   345, 346, 349, 350, 364, 366, 367,
   371, 380–381, 382
Reese, George, 206, 269
Regan, Donald, 9, 11, 97, 326
Rehnquist, Chief Justice William, 11
religious Right, 14, 340
Remington, William W., 92
RENAMO, 375
Reston, James, 290
Reuther, Walter, 302
Richwine, Dr., 173
Ritter, Dave, 100
Rivers, Caryl, 81–82
Robertson, Pat, 3, 7
Rockefeller, Nelson, 244–245, 289–
   290
Rockwell, George Lincoln, 302
Roe v. Wade, 14, 339, 357
Rollins, Ed, 5
Romney, George, 205, 325
Roosevelt, Eleanor, 30, 31–32
Roosevelt, Franklin D., 30–31, 92,
   337, 344, 363
Rosebury, Theodor, 295–296, 318
Rosenberg, Ethel, 93
Rosenberg, Julius, 93
Rosenberg, "Smiling Sam," 249